The Internet FOR DUMMIES®

9TH EDITION

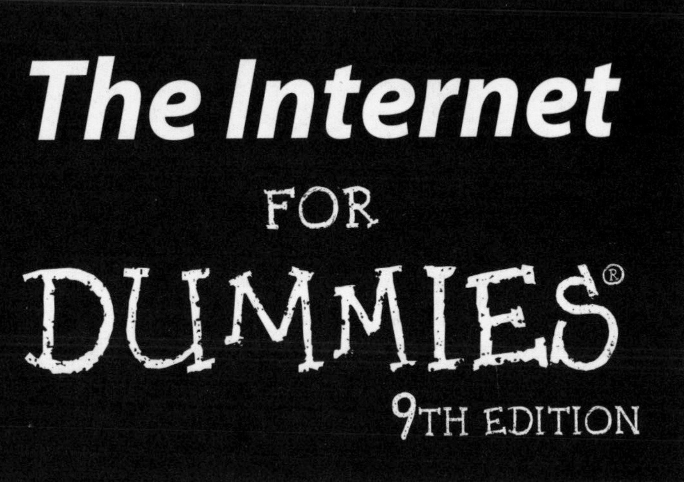

by John Levine
Margaret Levine Young
Carol Baroudi

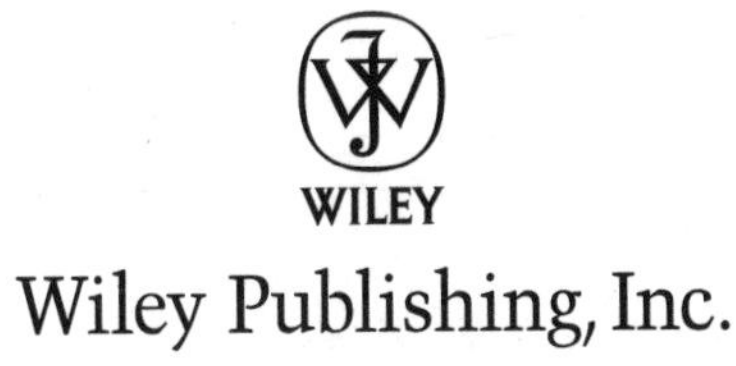

Wiley Publishing, Inc.

The Internet For Dummies®, 9th edition

Published by
Wiley Publishing, Inc.
111 River Street
Hoboken, NJ 07030-5774
www.wiley.com

Published by Wiley Publishing, Inc., Indianapolis, Indiana

Published simultaneously in Canada

For general information on our other products and services or to obtain technical support, please contact our Customer Care Department within the U.S. at 800-762-2974, outside the U.S. at 317-572-3993, or fax 317-572-4002.

Wiley also publishes its books in a variety of electronic formats. Some content that appears in print may not be available in electronic books.

Library of Congress Control Number: 2003105859

ISBN: 0-7645-4173-0

Manufactured in the United States of America

10 9 8 7 6 5 4 3 2 1

9B/RV/QZ/QT/IN

About the Author

John R. Levine was a member of a computer club in high school — before high school students, or even high schools, had computers — where he met Theodor H. Nelson, the author of *Computer Lib/Dream Machines* and the inventor of hypertext, who reminded us that computers should not be taken seriously and that everyone can and should understand and use computers.

John wrote his first program in 1967 on an IBM 1130 (a computer somewhat less powerful than your typical modern digital wristwatch, only more difficult to use). He became an official system administrator of a networked computer at Yale in 1975. He began working part-time (for a computer company, of course) in 1977 and has been in and out of the computer and network biz ever since. He got his company on Usenet (the Internet's worldwide bulletin-board system) early enough that it appears in a 1982 *Byte* magazine article on a map of Usenet, which then was so small that the map fit on half a page.

Although John used to spend most of his time writing software, now he mostly writes books (including *UNIX For Dummies* and *Internet Secrets,* both published by Wiley Publishing, Inc.) because it's more fun and he can do so at home in the tiny village of Trumansburg, New York, where he is the sewer commissioner (Guided tours! Free samples!) and can play with his small daughter when he's supposed to be writing. John also does a fair amount of public speaking. (Go to `www.johnlevine.com`, to see where he'll be.) He holds a B.A. and a Ph.D. in computer science from Yale University, but please don't hold that against him.

Carol Baroudi first began playing with computers in 1971 at Colgate University, where two things were new: the PDP-10 and women. She was lucky to have unlimited access to the state-of-the-art PDP-10, on which she learned to program, operate the machine, and talk to Eliza. She taught ALGOL and helped to design the curricula for computer science and women's studies. She majored in Spanish and studied French, which, thanks to the Internet, she can now use every day.

In 1975 Carol took a job doing compiler support and development, a perfect use for her background in languages. For six years she developed software and managed software development. For a while she had a small business doing high-tech recruiting (she was a headhunter). When she got tired of writing resumes, she went back to writing about software. Now she's an industry analyst consulting to emerging technology companies. (Check out her home page at `www.baroudi.com` to see what she's up to.)

The mother of a fantastic thirteen-year-old, Carol loves acting and singing and will fly to Europe on any excuse. She believes that we are living in a very interesting time when technology is changing faster than people can imagine. Carol hopes that as we learn to use the new technologies, we don't lose sight of our humanity. She feels that computers can be useful and fun, but are no substitute for real life.

In high school, **Margaret Levine Young** was in the same computer club as her big brother, John. She stayed in the field throughout college against her better judgment and despite John's presence as a graduate student in the computer science department. Margy graduated from Yale and went on to become one of the first PC managers in the early 1980s at Columbia Pictures, where she rode the elevator with big stars whose names she wouldn't dream of dropping here.

Since then, Margy has co-authored more than 25 computer books about the topics of the Internet, UNIX, WordPerfect, Microsoft Access, and (stab from the past) PC-File and Javelin, including *Dummies 101: The Internet For Windows 98*, *UNIX For Dummies*, and *WordPerfect For Linux For Dummies* (all published by Wiley Publishing, Inc.) and *Windows XP: The Complete Reference* and *Internet: The Complete Reference* (published by Osborne/McGraw-Hill). She met her future husband, Jordan, in the R.E.S.I.S.T.O.R.S. (that computer club we mentioned). Her other passion is her children, along with music, Unitarian Universalism (`www.uua.org`), reading, and anything to do with eating. She lives in Vermont (see `www.gurus.com/margy` for some scenery).

Dedication

John dedicates his part of the book (the particularly lame jokes) to Sarah Willow, who surprises and delights him every day, and to Tonia, now and always.

Carol dedicates her part of the book to Joshua and Patrick, with all her love, and to her friends, who remind her that there's more to life than writing books — or business, for that matter.

Margy dedicates this book to Jordan, Meg, and Zac, who make life worth living, and to Susan, the world's best cousin.

Authors' Acknowledgments

Linda Morris hustled us through the editorial process while (no doubt at great personal cost) making us look like better writers than we are. Thanks also to the rest of the gang at Wiley Publishing, especially those listed on the Publisher's Acknowledgement page.

For childcare, Margy thanks Jordan and the Cornwall Elementary School. John likewise thanks the Trumansburg Elementary School, where the kids hug the principal and the superintendent when they walk down the hall, whose faculty and staff provided vital and high-quality education and care to the aforementioned surprising person. Carol thanks Patrick, Arnold, the fine folks at Kesher, and her family and friends for their unending help and support. We all thank Matt Wagner at Waterside Productions for encouragement. The entire contents of this book were edited and submitted to the publisher using the Web — practicing what we preach. We thank our Internet providers: Finger Lakes Technologies Group (Trumansburg, N.Y. Hi, Paul!), Lightlink (Ithaca, N.Y. Hi, Homer!), and Shoreham.net (Shoreham, Vermont. Hi, Don and Jim!).

Finally, thanks to all the smarties (we wouldn't say wise-acres) who sent us comments on the previous editions and helped make this one better. If you have ideas, comments, or complaints, about the book, whisk them to us at `internet9@gurus.com`.

Visit our Web site at `net.gurus.com` for updates and more information about the topics in this book.

Publisher's Acknowledgments

We're proud of this book; please send us your comments through our online registration form located at www.dummies.com/register/.

Some of the people who helped bring this book to market include the following:

Acquisitions, Editorial, and Media Development

Project Editor: Linda Morris

(Previous Edition: Christine Berman)

Senior Acquisitions Editor: Steven Hayes

Copy Editor: Andrea Boucher

Technical Editor: Kerwin McKenzie

Editorial Manager: Leah Cameron

Permissions Editor: Carmen Krikorian

Editorial Assistant: Amanda Foxworth

Cartoons: Rich Tennant, www.the5thwave.com

Production

Project Coordinator: Kristie Rees

Layout and Graphics: Carrie Foster, Joyce Haughey, Michael Kruzil, Lindsey Osborn, Mary Gillot Virgin

Proofreaders: TECHBOOKS Production Services, Brian H. Walls

Indexer: TECHBOOKS Production Services

Special Help

Rebekah Mancilla, Teresa Artman, Heather Ryan

Publishing and Editorial for Technology Dummies

Richard Swadley, Vice President and Executive Group Publisher

Andy Cummings, Vice President and Publisher

Mary C. Corder, Editorial Director

Publishing for Consumer Dummies

Diane Graves Steele, Vice President and Publisher

Joyce Pepple, Acquisitions Director

Composition Services

Gerry Fahey, Vice President of Production Services

Debbie Stailey, Director of Composition Services

Contents at a Glance

Table of Contents

Introduction

Welcome to *The Internet For Dummies,* 9th Edition. Although lots of books are available about the Internet, most of them assume that you have a degree in computer science, would love to know about every strange and useless wart of the Internet, and enjoy memorizing unpronounceable commands and options. We hope that this book is different.

Instead, this book describes what you actually do to become an *Internaut* (someone who navigates the Internet with skill) — how to get started, what you really need to know, and where to go for help. And we describe it in plain old English.

For this ninth edition, we've made improvements, we hope, throughout the book. When we first wrote *The Internet For Dummies* ten years ago (yikes!), a typical Internet user was a student who connected from college or a technical worker who had access through work. The World Wide Web was so new that it had only a few hundred pages. Now, a decade later, the Net has grown like crazy to include several hundred million (dare we say it?) normal people, connecting on their own nickel from computers at home, along with students ranging from elementary school to adult education. We now focus on the parts of the Net that are of the most interest to typical users — the World Wide Web and how to find things there, including how to use Netscape and Internet Explorer (the most popular and/or useful Web programs), how to send and receive electronic mail (e-mail) for person-to-person communications, and how to shop online, chat online, and download interesting things from the Net.

About This Book

We don't flatter ourselves that you are interested enough in the Internet to sit down and read the entire book (although it should be a fine book for the bathroom). When you run into a problem using the Internet ("Hmm, I *thought* that I knew how to find somebody on the Net, but I don't seem to remember. . . ."), just dip in to the book long enough to solve your problem.

Pertinent sections include

- Understanding what the Internet is
- Knowing how to get connected to the Net
- Climbing around the World Wide Web
- Finding people, places, and things
- Communicating by e-mail (electronic mail)
- Hanging out with friends using instant messaging
- Getting stuff from the Net

How to Use This Book

To begin, please read the first three chapters. They give you an overview of the Internet and some important tips and terminology. Besides, we think that they're interesting. When you're ready to get yourself on the Internet, turn to Part II and pick the option that best suits you and your circumstances. Parts III through VI egg you on and provide extra support — they describe the Web, e-mail, and other stuff you can do on the Internet.

Although we try hard not to introduce a technical term without defining it, sometimes we slip. Sometimes, too, you may read a section out of order and find a term we defined a few chapters before that. To fill in the gaps, we include a glossary at the end of the book.

Because the Internet is ever changing, we have expanded our book to include an online area to help keep it up-to-date. Whenever you see our special Whoosh icon, it means that we have more up-to-the-minute information available on our Web site, at

```
net.gurus.com
```

When you have to follow a complicated procedure, we spell it out step by step wherever possible. We then tell you what happens in response and what your options are. When you have to type something, it appears in the book in **boldface**. Type it just as it appears. Use the same capitalization we do — a few systems care deeply about CAPITAL and small letters. Then press the Enter key. The book tells you what should happen when you give each command and what your options are.

When you have to choose commands from menus, we write File⇨Exit when we want you to choose the File command from the menu bar and then choose the Exit command from the menu that appears.

Who Are You?

In writing the book, we assumed that:

- You have or would like to have access to the Internet.
- You want to get some work done with it. (We consider the term "work" to include the concept "play.")
- You are not interested in becoming the world's next great Internet expert, at least not this week.

How This Book Is Organized

This book has five parts. The parts stand on their own — although you can begin reading wherever you like, you should at least skim Parts I and II first to get acquainted with some unavoidable Internet jargon and find out how to get your computer on the Net.

Here are the parts of the book and what they contain:

In Part I, "Welcome to the Internet," you find out what the Internet is and why it's interesting (at least why we think it's interesting). Also, this part has stuff about vital Internet terminology and concepts that help you as you read through the later parts of the book. Part I discusses how you get on the Internet and gives some thoughts about children's use of the Net.

For the nuts and bolts of getting on the Net, read Part II, "Internet, Here I Come!" For most users, by far the most difficult part of using the Net is getting to that first connection, with software loaded, configuration configured, and modem modeming. After that, it's (relatively) smooth sailing.

Part III, "Web Mania," dives into the World Wide Web, the part of the Internet that has powered the Net's leap from obscurity to fame. We discuss how to get around on the Web, how to find stuff (which is not as easy as it should be), how to shop online on the Web, and how to add your own home page to the Web.

Part IV, "E-mail, Chat, and Other Ways to Hang Out Online," looks at the important Net communication services: sending and receiving electronic mail, instant messages, and chatting. You find out how to exchange electronic mail with people down the hall or on other continents, how to use electronic mailing lists to keep in touch with people of similar interests, and how to use instant messaging programs to chat with your online pals. A new chapter tells you how to take best advantage of fast broadband connections.

Part V, " Other Internet Essentials," covers two important topics that don't fit in Parts I through IV: how to download things from the Net, and how to use the Net from AOL, the popular (to put it mildly) online service that offers Net access.

Part VI, "The Part of Tens," comprises a compendium of ready references and useful facts (which, we suppose, suggests that the rest of the book is full of useless facts).

Icons Used in This Book

Lets you know that some particularly nerdy, technoid information is coming up so that you can skip it if you want. (On the other hand, you may want to read it.)

Indicates that a nifty little shortcut or time saver is explained.

Gaack! We found out about this the hard way! Don't let it happen to you!

Points out a resource on the World Wide Web that you can use with Netscape, Internet Explorer, or other Web software.

Points you to more up-to-the-minute information on our very own Web site. Hey, this book is *alive.*

Indicates something to file away in your memory archives.

What Now?

That's all you need to know to get started. Whenever you hit a snag using the Internet, just look up the problem in the table of contents or index in this book. You'll either have the problem solved in a flash or know where you need to go to find some expert help.

Because the Internet has been evolving for over 30 years, largely under the influence of some extremely nerdy people, it was not designed to be particularly easy for normal people to use. Don't feel bad if you have to look up a number of topics before you feel comfortable using the Internet. Until recently, most computer users never had to face anything as complex as the Internet.

Feedback, Please

We love to hear from our readers. If you want to contact us, please feel free to do so, in care of:

Dummies Press
10475 Crosspoint Blvd.
Indianapolis, IN 46256

Better yet, send us Internet electronic mail at `internet9@gurus.com` (our friendly robot will answer immediately; the human authors read all the mail and answer as much as we can), or visit this book's Web home page, at `net.gurus.com`. These electronic addresses put you in contact with the authors of this book; to contact the publisher or authors of other *For Dummies* books, visit the publisher's Web site, at `www.dummies.com`, or send paper mail to the address just listed.

Part I

Welcome to the Internet

"As a web site designer I never thought I'd say this, but I don't think your site has enough bells and whistles."

In this part . . .

The Internet is an amazing place. But because it's full of computers, everything's more complicated than it should be. We start with a look at what the Internet is and how it got that way. We tell you what's happening, what people are doing, and why you should care. We give special attention to family concerns and resources and particularly the knotty question of what's the best way for kids to work with the Internet.

Chapter 1

What Is the Internet? What Is the Web?

In This Chapter

- What, really, is the Internet?
- For that matter, what is a network?
- What is the Internet good for?
- Is the Internet a safe place?
- Where did the Internet come from?

What is the Internet? What is the Web? Are they the same thing? The answer (one you'll see more often in this book than you may expect) is, "It depends." The Internet, the Web, and the technologies that make them work are changing so fast that no one can keep track. This chapter begins with the basics and tells you what the Internet and the Web are and, just as important, what has changed during the past couple of years so that you can begin to have an understanding of what it's all about.

If you're new to the Internet, and especially if you don't have much computer experience, *be patient with yourself.* Many of the ideas here are completely new. Allow yourself some time to read and reread. It's a brand-new world with its own language, and it takes some getting used to. Many people find it helpful to quickly read through the entire book once in order to get a broader perspective of what we're talking about. Others plow through one page at a time. Whatever your style, remember that it's *new* stuff — you're not *supposed* to understand it already. Even for many experienced Internet users, it's a new world.

Even if you're an experienced computer user, you may find the Internet to be unlike anything you've ever tackled. The Internet is not a software package and doesn't easily lend itself to the kind of step-by-step instruction that we can provide for a single, fixed program. This book is as step by step as we can make it, but the Internet more resembles a living organism mutating at an astonishing rate than it resembles Microsoft Word or Excel, which sit quietly on your computer and mind their own business. After you get set up and get a little practice, using the Internet seems like second nature; in the beginning, however, it can be daunting.

Okay, So What Is the Internet?

The Internet — also known as the *Net* — is the world's largest computer network. "What is a network?" you may ask. Even if you already know, you may want to read the next couple of paragraphs to make sure that we're speaking the same language.

A computer *network* is a bunch of computers hooked together to communicate somehow. In concept, it's sort of like a radio or TV network that connects a bunch of radio or TV stations so that they can share the latest episode of *The Simpsons.*

Don't take the analogy too far. TV networks send the same information to all the stations at the same time (it's called *broadcast* networking); in computer networks, each particular message is usually routed to a particular computer, so different computers can display different things. Unlike TV networks, computer networks are invariably two way: When computer A sends a message to computer B, B can send a reply back to A.

Some computer networks consist of a central computer and a bunch of remote stations that report to it (a central airline reservation computer, for example, with thousands of screens and keyboards in airports and travel agencies). Other networks, including the Internet, are more egalitarian and permit any computer on the network to communicate with any other computer. Many new wireless devices — mobile phones, Palm Pilots, Blackberries, and their ilk — are in this category and expand the reach of the Internet to our very persons.

The Internet isn't really one network — it's a network of networks, all freely exchanging information. The networks range from the big and formal (such as the corporate networks at AT&T, General Motors, and Hewlett-Packard) to the small and informal (such as the one in John's back bedroom, with a couple of old PCs bought at an electronic parts store) and everything in between. College and university networks have long been part of the Internet, and now high schools and elementary schools are joining up. Lately, computers and the Internet have become so popular that more and more households have more than one computer and are creating their own networks at home from which they connect to the Internet.

So What's All the Hoopla?

Everywhere you turn, you can find traces of the Internet. Household products, business cards, radio shows, and movie credits list their Web site address (usually starting with "www" and ending with "dot com") and their e-mail addresses. New people you meet would rather give you an e-mail address than a phone number. Everyone seems to be "going online and getting connected." Are they really talking about this same "network of networks?" Yes, *and* there's more.

The Internet is a new communications technology that is affecting our lives on a scale as significant as the telephone and television. Some people believe that when it comes to disseminating information, the Internet is the most significant invention since the printing press. If you use a telephone, write letters, read a newspaper or magazine, or do business or any kind of research, the Internet can radically alter your worldview.

With networks, size counts for a great deal: The larger a network is, the more stuff it has to offer. Because the Internet is the world's largest interconnected group of computer networks, it has an amazing array of information to offer.

When people talk about the Internet today, they're usually talking about what they can do, what they have found, and whom they have met. Millions of computers connected to the Internet exchange information in a bunch of different ways. These different services are so expansive that we don't have room to give a complete list in this chapter, but here's a quick summary:

- **Electronic mail (e-mail):** This service is certainly the most widely used — you can exchange e-mail with millions of people all over the world. People use e-mail for anything that they might use paper (mail, faxes, special delivery of documents) or the telephone (gossip, recipes, love letters) to communicate — you name it. (We hear that some people even use it for stuff related to work.) Electronic *mailing lists* enable you to join group discussions with people who have similar interests and meet people over the Net. Chapters 10 and 11 have all the details.

- **The World Wide Web:** When people talk these days about surfing the Net, they often mean checking out sites on this (buzzword alert) multimedia, hyperlinked database that spans the globe. In fact, people are talking more about the Web and less about the Net. Are they the same thing? Technically, the answer is "No." But practically speaking, the answer for many people is "Yes." We tell you the truth, the whole truth, and nothing but the truth in Chapter 6.

The Web, unlike earlier Internet services, combines text, pictures, sound, video clips, animation, and even live broadcasts of news, concerts, and wildlife. You can move around with a click of your computer mouse. New Web *sites* (sets of Web pages) are growing faster than you can say "Big Mac with cheese," with new sites appearing every minute. In 1993, when we wrote the first edition of this book, the Internet had 130 Web sites. Today, it has many millions, and statistics indicate that the number is doubling every few months.

The software used to navigate the Web is known as a *browser.* The most popular browsers today are Netscape and Internet Explorer. We tell you all about them in Chapter 6, along with one less popular but worthy alternative.

- **Chat services:** People are talking to people all over the globe about everything under the sun. They enter chat rooms with several other people or one special someone. They're using the chat facilities of America Online, Microsoft, Yahoo, Internet Relay Chat (IRC), or Web-based chat rooms. We tell you how to get chatting in Chapter 15.
- **Instant Messaging (IMing):** With the help of special programs on your computer and on your friend's computer, you can start up a conversation in a heartbeat. Paging programs like Windows Messenger, Yahoo Messenger, and AOL Instant Messenger let you send messages that "pop up" on the recipient's screen. We hear tales of nimble-fingered youth carrying on upwards of 13 IM sessions simultaneously. We tell you about AOL Instant Messenger, ICQ, Windows Messenger, and Yahoo Messenger in Chapter 14.

A Few Real-Life Stories

Seventh-grade students in San Diego use the Internet to exchange letters and stories with kids in Israel. Although it's partly just for fun and to make friends in a foreign country, a sober academic study reported that when kids have a real audience for their stuff, they write better. (Big surprise.)

For many purposes, the Internet is the fastest and most reliable way to move information. In September 1998, when special prosecutor Kenneth Starr delivered his report on the scandal involving President Clinton and Monica Lewinsky to the U.S. House of Representatives, the House quickly put the report online, thus allowing millions of people to read it the day it came out. (We can still debate whether it was a good idea to do that, but the Internet is what made it possible.) And Matt Drudge's *Drudge Report* online gossip sheet broke much of the scandal first.

In the hours and days following the terrorist attacks of September 11, 2001, people gave up on the overloaded phone system (cell phones were particularly useless) and turned to e-mail to find out whether their loved ones and co-workers had survived. The Web provided folks in the U.S. with news coverage from all over the world, thus allowing Americans a glimpse at how the rest of the world saw the situation.

During the 2003 Iraq war, soldiers and civilians kept in touch with friends and relatives by e-mail. One young man in Baghdad kept a widely read weblog (or *blog* — see Chapter 9) that gave people all over the world a view of the run-up to the war.

Medical researchers around the world use the Internet to maintain databases of rapidly changing data. People with medical conditions use the Internet to communicate with each other in support groups and to compare experiences. Forward-thinking physicians make themselves available to their patients via e-mail and encourage their patients to use e-mail instead of the phone for non-emergency questions.

The Internet has more prosaic uses, too. Here are some from our personal experience:

- When we began writing our megabook, *Internet Secrets*, we posted notices on the Internet asking for contributions. We got responses from all over the world. Many of these contributors became our friends. Now we have people to visit all over the world. It could happen to *you.*
- We get mail every day from all over the world from readers of our *For Dummies* books and are often the happy recipients of readers' first-ever e-mail messages.
- The Internet is its own best source of software. Whenever we hear about a new service, it usually takes only a few minutes to find software for our computers (various computers running various versions of Windows and a Macintosh), download it, and start it up. Much of the software available on the Internet is free or inexpensive shareware.
- When Margy wanted to buy a used Subaru, she and her husband found listings of the models they wanted at dealers all over their state. They could even get insurance and registration information about the cars before they went to the dealer, so they knew where and when the cars had been driven, and whether they'd been in major accidents.

The Internet has local and regional parts, too. When John wanted to sell a trusty but tired minivan, a note on the Internet in a local for-sale area found a buyer within two days. Margy's husband sold his used computer within a half-hour of posting a message in the relevant Usenet newsgroup. Carol checks local movie listings and cultural events

Why Is This Medium Different from Any Other Medium?

The Internet is unlike all the other communications media we've ever encountered. People of all ages, colors, creeds, and countries freely share ideas, stories, data, opinions, and products.

Anybody can access it

One great thing about the Internet is that it's probably the most open network in the world. Thousands of computers provide facilities that are available to anyone who has Internet access. Older networks limited what users could do and required specific arrangements for each service, but the Internet connects everyone to everything. Although pay services exist (and more are added every day), most Internet services are free for the taking: that is, after you are online. If you don't already have access to the Internet through your company, your school, your library, or a friend's attic, you probably have to pay for access by using an Internet service provider (ISP). We talk about some ISPs in Chapter 4.

It's politically, socially, and religiously correct

Another great thing about the Internet is that it is what one may call "socially unstratified." That is, one computer is no better than any other, and no person is any better than any other. Who you are on the Internet depends solely on how you present yourself through your keyboard. If what you say makes you sound like an intelligent, interesting person, that's who you are. It doesn't matter how old you are or what you look like or whether you're a student, a business executive, or a construction worker. Physical disabilities don't matter — we correspond with people who are blind or deaf. If they hadn't felt like telling us, we never would have known. People become famous in the Internet community, some favorably and some unfavorably, but they get that way through their own efforts.

Does the Internet really reach every continent?

Some skeptical readers, after reading the claim that the Internet spans every continent, may point out that Antarctica is a continent, even though its population consists largely of penguins, who (as far as we know) are not interested in computer networks. Does the Internet go there? It does. A few machines at the Scott Base on McMurdo Sound in Antarctica are on the Internet, connected by radio link to New Zealand. The base at the South Pole is reported to have a link to the United States, but it doesn't publish its electronic address.

At the time of this writing, the largest, Internet-free landmass in the world is probably Queen Elizabeth Island in the Canadian arctic. We used to say New Guinea, a large jungle island north of Australia, but a reader there sent us e-mail in 1997 telling us about his new Internet provider. ***Note:*** If you are on Queen Elizabeth Island and you're online there, please e-mail us right away!

The Net advantage

Maybe it's obvious to you that Internet technology is changing so quickly that you have barely had time to crack the spine of *The Internet For Dummies*, 8th Edition, and here you are holding the 9th Edition. (We said the same thing about the last couple of editions.) "Could it possibly be all that different?" you ask yourself. Trust us — we've asked ourselves the same thing. The answer, by the way, is a resounding "Yes." It's *that* different again this year. This year, we have to say that the Internet is totally mainstream, and you're falling further behind the curve — and at a faster rate — if you haven't yet gotten started. Increasingly, news gets out on the Internet before it's available any other way, and the cyber-deprived are losing ground.

Here are some of the ways people use the Internet:

- **Getting information:** Many Web sites have information free for the taking. Information ranges from IRS tax forms that you can print out on your computer to help-wanted ads, real estate listings, and recipes. From U.S. Supreme Court decisions and library card catalogs to the text of old books, digitized pictures (many suitable for family audiences), an enormous variety of software, from games to operating systems — you can find virtually anything on the Net. You can find out the weather anywhere in the world, view movie listings, and even see school closings.

  Special tools known as *search engines, directories,* and *indices* help you find information on the Web. Lots of people are trying to create the fastest, smartest search engine and the most complete Web index.

We tell you about Google, the most complete one this year so you at least get the picture. As mentioned in the Introduction to this book, when you see a Web icon in the margin of this book, we describe resources that you can retrieve from the Internet (usually the Web), as described in Chapter 16.

- **Finding people:** If you've lost track of your childhood sweetheart, now's your chance to find him or her anywhere in the country. You can use one of the directory services to search the phone books of the entire United States. We tell you more about this subject in Chapter 7.
- **Finding businesses, products, and services:** New yellow pages directory services enable you to search by the type of company you're looking for. You can indicate the area code or ZIP code to help specify the location. Also, many people are shopping for that hard-to-find, special gift item. A friend told us of her search for a bear pendant that led her to a company in Alaska that had just what she was looking for. John and Margy's dad found exactly the crystal he wanted — in Australia.
- **Research:** Law firms find that information they formerly paid $600 an hour to get from commercial services can be found for free when they go directly to the Internet. Real estate appraisers use demographic data available on the Net, including unemployment statistics, to help assess property values. Genetics researchers and other scientists download up-to-date research results from around the world. Businesses and potential businesses research their competition over the Net.

Where did the Internet come from?

The ancestor of the Internet was the *ARPANET,* a project funded by the Department of Defense (DOD) in 1969, both as an experiment in reliable networking and to link DOD and military research contractors, including the large number of universities doing military-funded research. (*ARPA* stands for Advanced Research Projects Administration, the branch of the DOD in charge of handing out grant money. For enhanced confusion, the agency is now known as *DARPA* — the added *D* is for Defense, in case anyone had doubts about where the money was coming from.) Although the ARPANET started small — connecting three computers in California with one in Utah — it quickly grew to span the continent.

In the early 1980s, the ARPANET grew into the early Internet, a group of interlinked networks connecting many educational and research sites funded by the National Science Foundation, along with the original military sites. By 1990, it was clear that the Internet was here to stay, and DARPA and the NSF bowed out in favor of the commercially run networks that comprise today's Internet. Familiar companies such as AT&T, Sprint, Verizon, and Quest run some of the networks; others belong to specialty companies such as Level3 and Verio. No matter which one you're attached to, they all interconnect, so it's all one giant Internet. For more information, read our Web page located at

`net.gurus.com/history`

- **Education:** Schoolteachers coordinate projects with classrooms all over the globe. College students and their families exchange e-mail to facilitate letter writing and keep down the cost of phone calls. Students do research from their home computers. The latest encyclopedias are online.
- **Buying and selling stuff:** On the Internet, you can buy anything from books to stock in microbreweries. And we hear you can make a mint by cleaning out your closets and selling your old junk on eBay. We talk about the relevant issues later in this chapter and in Chapter 8.
- **Travel:** Cities, towns, states, and countries are using the Web to put up (or *post*) tourist and event information. Travelers find weather information; maps; plane, train, and bus schedules and tickets; and museum hours online.
- **Intranets:** Wouldn't ya know? Businesses have figured out that this Internet stuff is really useful. Companies use e-mail internally and externally to communicate with employees, customers, and other businesses. Many companies use Web pages for company information like corporate benefits, for filing expense reports and time sheets, and for ordering supplies. Stuff you can see from inside a company that folks on the outside can't see is known as an *intranet.* Apparently, e-mail and intranets are reducing the amount of paper circulating in some organizations. We talk about intranets in Chapter 2.
- **Marketing and sales:** Software companies are selling software and providing updates via the Net. (Aside from the large pile of AOL CDs we now use as coasters, most software distribution is migrating to the Internet.) Companies are selling products over the Net. Online bookstores and music stores enable people to browse online, choose titles, and pay for stuff over the Internet.
- **Games and gossip:** Internet-based multiuser games can easily absorb all your waking hours and an alarming number of what would otherwise be your sleeping hours. You can challenge other players who can be anywhere in the world. Many kinds of games are available on the Web, including such traditionally addictive games as bridge, hearts, chess, checkers, and go. In Chapter 20, we tell where to find these games.
- **Love:** People are finding romance on the Net. Singles ads and matchmaking sites vie for users. Contrary to Internet lore, the Net community is no longer just a bunch of socially challenged male nerds under 25.
- **Healing:** Patients and doctors keep up to date with the latest medical findings, share treatment experience, and give one another support around medical problems. We even know of some practitioners who exchange e-mail directly with their patients.

- **Investing:** People do financial research, buy stock, and invest money online. Some online companies trade their own shares. Investors are finding new ventures, and new ventures are finding capital.
- **Organizing events:** Conference and trade-show organizers are finding that the best way to disseminate information, call for papers, and do registration is to do it on the Web. Information can be updated regularly, and paper and shipping costs are dramatically reduced. Registering online saves the cost of on-site registration staff and the hassle of on-site registration lines.
- **Nonprofits:** Churches, synagogues, mosques, and other community organizations put up pages telling Web users about themselves and inviting new people. The online church newsletter *always* comes before Sunday.

Some Thoughts about Safety and Privacy

The Internet is a funny place. Although it seems completely anonymous, it's not. People used to have Internet usernames that bore some resemblance to their true identity — their name or initials or some such combination in conjunction with their university or corporation gave a fairly traceable route to an actual person. Today, with the phenomena of screen names (courtesy of America Online) and multiple e-mail addresses (courtesy of many Internet providers), revealing your identity is definitely optional.

Depending on who you are and what you want to do on the Net, you may, in fact, want different names and different accounts. Here are some legitimate reasons for wanting them:

- You're a professional — a physician, for example — and you want to participate in a mailing list or newsgroup without being asked for your professional opinion.
- You want help with an area of concern that you feel is private, and you don't want your problem known to people close to you who may find out if your name were associated with it.
- You do business on the Internet, and you socialize on the Net. You may want to keep those activities separate.

And a warning to those who may consider abusing the anonymous nature of the Internet: Most Net activities can be traced. If you start to abuse the Net, you'll find you're not so anonymous.

Safety first

The anonymous, faceless nature of the Internet has its downside, too.

In chat rooms and other getting-to-know-you situations, don't use your full name. Never provide your name, address, or phone number to someone you don't know. Never believe anyone who says that he is from "AOL tech support" or some such authority and asks you for your password. No legitimate entity will ever ask you for your password. Be especially careful about disclosing information about kids. Don't fill out profiles in chat rooms that ask for a kid's name, hometown, school, age, address, or phone number because they are invariably used for "targeted marketing" (also known as junk mail).

Although relatively rare, horrible things have happened to a few people who have taken their Internet encounters into real life. Many wonderful things have happened, too. We've met some of our best friends over the Net, and some people have met and subsequently married. We just want to encourage you to use common sense when you set up a meeting with a Net friend. Here are a few tips:

- Talk to the person on the phone before you agree to meet. If you don't like the sound of the person's voice or something makes you feel nervous, don't do it.
- Depending on the context, try to check the person out a little. If you've met in a newsgroup or chat room, ask someone else you know whether they know this person. (Women, ask another woman before meeting a man.)
- Meet in a well-lit, public place. Take a friend or two with you.
- If you're a kid, take a parent with you. Never, ever meet someone from the Net without your parents' explicit consent.

The Net is a wonderful place, and meeting new people and making new friends is one of the big attractions. We just want to make sure that you're being careful.

Protect your privacy

Here in the United States, we've grown up with certain attitudes about freedom and privacy, many of which we take for granted. We tend to feel that who we are, where we go, and what we do is our own business as long as we don't bother anyone else. However, bunches of people are extremely interested in who we are, where we go (on the Net, at least), and, most especially, what we buy.

Some people worry that snoops on the Net will intercept their private e-mail or Web pages. That's fairly unlikely, although if you're worried about it, you can lock them with a secret password. The more serious problem is advertisers who build profiles of the sites you visit and the stuff you buy. Most Web ads are provided through a handful of companies like `doubleclick.com` and `advertising.com`, who can use their ads to tell that the same person (you) is visiting a lot of different Web sites and create a profile. They say they don't, but they don't say they won't.

Throughout this book, we point out when your privacy or security may be in danger, and suggest ways to protect yourself.

Chapter 2

The Internet at Home, at Work, at School, and at Play

In This Chapter

- Using the Internet at home
- The Internet on the job
- Intranets and extranets
- The Internet at school
- Playing on the Internet

We think one reason why you may not already use the Internet is that you haven't had a really good reason to use it. Maybe you tried and gave up, or maybe you couldn't have been bothered. Well, we think that just about everybody has a good reason to be on the Internet today, so in this chapter, we give you a whole pile of useful, fun, interesting, and potentially necessary reasons that may apply to you.

At Home with the Internet

For many people, the Internet has become an essential part of life. Whether it's to keep in touch with folks you care about, get information about news that's critical to you, research medical problems and treatment, find a new job or keep the one you have, the Internet is now an essential part of how the world works. Some people use it all day, every day, while others use it once a day or a couple of times a week. What you use the Internet for is your business — we just want to make sure you know what's out there.

After you get the hang of using the Internet, you'll find yourself thinking, "I wonder if . . ." or "I wonder what . . ." and turning to the Internet for the answers. You can shop for everything from food to footwear and have stuff delivered right to your doorstep. You can watch traffic hotspots on live *webcams* (cameras that broadcast right from an Internet site that you can, in turn, see from your computer). You'll find recipes, maps, health advice, and helpful hints on any subject under the sun (or beyond it, for that matter).

Discover what books and videos are available in your local library, or download music and books that you can transfer to portable players and readers. When it's time to move, you can find a new house, apply for a mortgage, and decorate your new abode with furnishings that you can find right on the Internet. You can find folks to paint, repair, do the windows (the glass kind, not the Microsoft kind), and even deliver cords of firewood.

The Internet can help with your home finances, too. You can get spiffy accounting software right on the Web without having to install it on your own machine. You can buy and sell stocks or download tax forms from the IRS and your state without spending hours on the phone or driving to an office. (The Web address for the IRS is `www.irs.gov`, by the way; we tell you how to get there later. The IRS and some states let you file a short form tax return online.)

Internet audio and video chat let you talk to and see people anywhere in the world for free. Grandparents can get snapshots of their grandchildren and even display them in electronic picture frames. An emerging service called Internet phone lets you plug a phone with a real phone number into your broadband network connection. If you want to make it easy for Grandma to call you from Florida, no matter where you are, your Internet phone can have a Sarasota or Winter Park phone number, so it's a local call for her. (On the Internet, nobody knows you're in North Dakota.)

When you tire of staring at that dumb screen and crave human contact, you can use the Internet to find local hiking clubs, political organizations, volunteer opportunities, houses of worship, or a 12-step program for Internet addiction. If you do choose to leave your wired cave, check the Internet for step-by-step driving instructions (or mass transit maps) so you don't get lost. Whatever you're seeking, the first place to look for it is on the Internet.

The Internet at Work

This year just may be the year you have to find out about the Internet 'cause like it or not, it's part of your job. More and more offices are using the Internet and Internet-like stuff to do everyday office tasks. E-mail has replaced memos; the human resources manual is online; you file your expense reports online; you even book travel, order supplies, send flowers, and gossip — all online.

Finding a job by using the Net

What's that you say? You don't have a job? The Net is an incredible tool for finding one. You can publish your résumé online for prospective employers. You can check out help-wanted Web sites like `www.hotjobs.com`, `www.brassring.com`, and `www.monster.com`. (If you're already employed, be careful about posting your résumé online. If you register on a job site and your employer uses the same one, your résumé may show up exactly where you least desire it.)

Most companies today list an e-mail address or Web site for submitting your résumé. Submitting your résumé online is quicker and cheaper than mailing it with a postage stamp or faxing it. Furthermore, a lot of companies like to make sure that their prospective hires know at least the basics of Internet use before considering them for a job.

Companies find that posting their jobs on the Net is an effective, economical way to recruit talented people. Check out the home pages of companies that interest you, and look for their open positions. Many colleges and universities have career office Web pages, and many professional organizations — from acupuncturists to zoologists — have job sites for their members. All kinds of specialized job sites are available, including ones for government jobs, overseas jobs, and jobs that will pay off your student loans.

You can find out a lot about a company before you go into an interview by reviewing its Web site. You may even find other companies of interest when you think about a company's competitors.

The ins and outs of intranets and extranets

Now that lots of people have cottoned to the idea that this Internet stuff is pretty slick, clever people are adapting all the cool features and putting them to work inside companies, outside companies, and even between companies. You may get the sense that although the names keep changing, everybody's really talking about the same thing. You're right. In this section, we give you some formal definitions so you won't be bamboozled by jargon-slinging cybersnobs, and also so you can sling jargon yourself whenever you want. Our current favorite business-related Internet terms: *intranet* and *extranet.* See whether you can tell the difference.

Intranets and what they're good for

Intranet? Are you sure that that's spelled right? Sure is. Now that everyone knows about the *Internet,* marketroids have invented the *intranet,* which is just the same except different. The idea is simple: Take all that swell technology that has been developed for the Internet during the past 20 years and use it directly inside your company on its own network.

An *intranet* is, specifically, a bunch of services, such as Web pages, that are accessible only within an organization. The World Wide Web works over the Internet with tens of thousands of *Web servers* providing Web pages to the general public. An intranet works over an organization's internal network with Web servers providing Web pages to folks within the organization. An intranet is sort of a private World Wide Web — an Organization Wide Web. (OWW! — another acronym!)

What your organization can do on an intranet is limited only by the imagination of the people in the organization. (We realize that this limitation is more severe in some organizations than in others, but we're optimists.) Here are some examples:

- Nearly all the paper memoranda circulated around a company can be sent more effectively as e-mail messages or as Web pages. This method saves paper and makes the information easier to file and to find, and it keeps everyone up to date.
- Those big, dusty company manuals moldering on the shelf (or perhaps holding up one corner of your desk if the floor is uneven) work much better as Web pages. Catalogs, parts lists, and the like are easy to put on the Web, too. They're easier to search through to find the page you want. Also, the authors can update them as often as necessary so that everyone has instant access to the most current version.
- If several people are working on a project, putting the project information on the Web lets each person look at and update the status of parts of the project, thus enabling everyone to see up-to-date information. That's how the three authors and the editors of this book, who live in three different states (not awake, asleep, and incoherent; they're actually Massachusetts, Vermont, and New York), tracked our progress in updating the book and kept ourselves moving in roughly the same direction — we used a little Web application that John whipped up in an afternoon.
- If your company has a flair for multimedia, now you can have animation, video, and sound right on your desktop. Slightly less dramatic but perhaps more useful are new integrated intranet products that let you put "live" links to Web pages in your e-mail messages. Now you can send around a memo that refers to all types of different material with a link directly to that material. Your readers have to just click the link to see the information you're referencing.
- Filing time cards and expense reports and updating pension and benefits records are now routine intranet tasks. Keeping forms online certainly cuts down on the paperwork shuffle and enables you to change the forms when necessary without having to toss the obsolete ones into the recycling bin.

All in all, we see the technology flowing both ways. As Internet technology, particularly e-mail and Web technology, combines with traditional databases, the ways in which companies manage information are bound to change. Paper memoranda will become about as common as the IBM Selectric, and large metal file cabinets will fill much more slowly.

Extra, extra net, net net

Anything worth doing is worth doing in any number of ways. Start with the Internet; bring it into the company — get an intranet; take the intranet out of the company, and — voilà — you get an *extranet.* Not that this net is *extra,* mind you: We mean *extra* as in "outside," as in *extra*terrestrial.

Here's the idea: Now that people are successfully using Internet technology (browsing, creating Web pages, and using e-mail, for example) *inside* companies, the logical extension is to expand these internal networks to include a company's customers, suppliers, and business partners. After intranets expanded outside the boundaries of an organization to include other entities, someone ingenious created a brand-new buzzword: *extranet.* As is the case with intranets, it's all the same technology — it's just used in a different way.

Extranets can be designed with security in mind and allow only people with legitimate access to use the extranet facilities. The general public is usually not allowed access. When you use a company's extranet, some of what you see will seem just like the Internet to you. The glue that's connecting the Internet site you see to the company or companies that are handling your transactions, however, is really an extranet — the linking of internal systems with the outside.

Here are some of the ways companies are using extranets. Your imagination can no doubt continue where we've left off:

- Newsletters, press releases, product announcements, and any other information that a company would send to customers and suppliers via snail mail (the kind that uses paper and a postage stamp) or fax can be e-mailed and/or put on an extranet Web site.
- Catalogs, brochures, and other reference materials can be placed on the Web to radically reduce printing costs and enable materials to be easily and frequently updated.
- Customers can place and track orders.
- Answers to frequently asked questions can be posted on a Web site to eliminate lots of phone calls.

What's the difference between a company with an extranet and a company with a Web site? Umm, maybe a big consulting bill? Actually, sometimes companies have more than one site — some that are exclusive to a particular customer or set of customers. These special sites are the ones called *extranets.*

The Internet at School

The Internet is certainly finding its way into educational institutions of all levels, although we're not entirely convinced that direct use of the Internet is of great benefit to the youngest of our citizens. (We talk about this more emphatically in Chapter 3.)

An Apple (or PC) for the teacher

Ask teachers, and they'll tell you that most school reforms just add to their burdens and reduce the time and energy that they can devote to classroom teaching. The Internet can save teachers time in researching lesson plans, keeping in touch with colleagues, and dealing with bureaucratic paperwork. Instead of trying to get the Internet in every classroom, we think the goal should be to get every teacher online at home.

A parent's job is never done

Aside from the obvious opportunity to research homework assignments and plagiarize term papers (don't do it, you'll get caught) on the Net, we see the Internet being used to facilitate parent/teacher, teacher/student, student/student, and parent/parent communications. Kids in Japan are in constant contact using wireless, e-mail hand-held devices. Your kids will be demanding one this Christmas or next. The traditional PTA meeting is rapidly being supplemented or replaced by e-mail mailing lists. (See Chapter 13 for more info.) All this raises questions of the "digital divide" as poorer families can be left out. However, subsidizing universal Internet access may save school systems money in the long run.

I'm off to college

If you're in college, you already know how central the Internet has become to your education. If you're planning to enter college soon, reading this book may be your most important preparation. Everything we said about intranets at work applies *mutatis mutandis* to the university. (*Mutatis mutandis* is Latin for "changing what needs to be changed." We don't normally use fancy terms, but you may need it in some course or other.) Most colleges today are run from their intranets. In fact, many schools were using the Internet in this way before the term "intranet" was coined. Course descriptions, professorial and student profiles, class registration, syllabi, homework assignments, grades, arranging job interviews — even some class discussion, at some colleges — are all handled online.

If you're trying to select a college, you can tour a dozen campuses in an evening on the Internet. College Web sites often have an area set aside for student and faculty home pages. Browsing these pages is a great way to explore the personality of each institution and find someone with similar interests with whom you can electronically correspond.

How do you cut a virtual class?

With the power of the Internet, you don't have to be in the classroom to take a course. You can find online e-learning courses on almost any imaginable topic — and a few that are unimaginable. In some cases, the Net *is* the university, but more about this later.

The Internet at Play

If you ask some people, the Internet is nothing *but* play. Nonetheless, the ways in which we can play online are expanding as well.

Meet someone

You can meet people online and just hang out; you can play all kinds of interactive games; you can discuss your favorite sport, hobby, or medical malady (well, it's some people's idea of recreation). You can enter virtual realities and get three-dimensional. You can speak different languages (if you already speak different languages) and meet people from all over the globe.

Meet someone special

Dating on the Internet has really taken off. Introduction services and online personal ads are obvious ways to find that future significant other, but sometimes, as in most areas of romance, a less direct approach is better. However, some unsavory types are also online, so be very careful about meeting people in person whom you only know online. We read you the riot act in Chapter 15.

It's music to my ears

Online exchange of music (MP3) files has exploded, to the chagrin of the recording industry. Their lawsuits shut down the most popular music site, Napster. Other services, like KaZaA, are taking Napster's place.

The recording industry and many recording artists think what's going on is simple theft. The courts have, so far, agreed with them. Other artists and many consumers feel the recording industry has been ripping them off for years and want to break the stranglehold that the industry has on record distribution. Efforts are underway to legitimize online music by charging subscription or pay-per-play fees. You make the ethical choices. We give you the MP3 lowdown in Chapter 16.

What's at the movies?

Of course you can check the show times at your favorite cinema and even buy tickets online. But why leave home? Plenty of free movies are available online. Mostly they are short films that were never able to find a wide audience before. Some sites even let you select the best so you don't have to wade through hours of drivel.

Or you can just surf

Surfing, a term invented years ago by our friend Jean Armour Polly, is the fine art of wandering through the Internet. Pick a topic; search on it; follow its links. Some other idea that you had thought about a long time ago will pop into your head. Search on that. *Bookmark* (or mark as a favorite) a really interesting site that you don't have time to look at just now. You can get back to it mañana. Find someone's newsgroup posting on a topic about which you fancy yourself to be an expert. Tell them where they went wrong. Hours will go by. But hey — at least you're not watching television.

Chapter 3

Kids and the Net

In This Chapter

- Good stuff on the Internet for kids
- Some concerns about the Internet
- Parental guidelines for using the Internet
- Mailing lists and Web sites for kids
- Help for kids (and parents) with problems
- The Internet in schools, and school on the Net

With millions of kids online, a discussion about family Internet use is critical. Obviously, if this isn't your concern, just skip this chapter and go to the next.

Can We Talk?

In earlier editions of this book, we called this chapter "The Internet, Your Kids, and You," but we've wised up and now realize who is really in charge of the family Internet connection: kids just like you. We still feel it would be better if your parents had some say about what you do online, but let's face it — they don't have a clue. So in this chapter, we'll talk to you and throw in some comments for your parents, in case they happen to read this. We'll try not to say anything too embarrassing.

What's in it for you?

Kids are often the first to discover the myriad ways in which the Internet can be exciting. Here are some of the ways in which we think the Internet rocks:

- It provides information about every topic imaginable.
- It's a great way to hang out with your friends and be at home at the same time.

- It provides personal contact with new people and cultures.
- It helps develop and improve reading, writing, research, and language skills.
- It provides support for kids with special needs and for their parents.
- It is an exciting outlet for artistic expression.

But not everything new is wonderful, and not everything wonderful is new. Many of you will spend more of your working life than you'd like in front of a computer. You may want to be doing a lot of other things, such as playing sports, reading a printed book, playing music, cooking, painting, hiking, skating, biking, skiing, or sculpting, just to name a few.

Here are some things you can do online, broken down into four sections: Really cool, so-so, not such a good idea, and truly brain dead.

Really cool ways to use the Net

You can impress your parents by using the Internet for the following:

- **Research homework assignments:** The Internet is an incredible way to expand the walls of a school. The Net can connect you to other schools, libraries, research resources, museums, and other people. You can visit the Louvre (at `www.louvre.fr`, as shown in Figure 3-1) and the Sistine Chapel (`www.vatican.va/museums/patrons`); you can watch spotted newts in their native habitat; you can hear new music and make new friends.

Figure 3-1: The treasures of the ages, direct from Paris.

- **Find out how to evaluate the stuff you read:** When you search for a topic, you may get pages written by the world's greatest authority on that topic, some crackpot pushing a harebrained theory, some college kid's term paper, or some guy on a bulletin board who thinks he's an expert. Some Web sites are maintained by hate groups and push really nasty venom. Becoming able to tell them apart is one of the most valuable skills that you can acquire.
- **Make e-friends in other countries:** School projects such as the Global Schoolhouse connect kids around the world by working collaboratively on all types of projects. The first annual global learning project drew more than 10,000 students from 360 schools in 30 different countries. Since then, annual cyberfairs have brought together over 500,000 students from hundreds of schools in at least 37 countries! You can find out more at the Global Schoolhouse Web site, `www.globalschoolhouse.org`, where you can also subscribe to lots of mailing lists. (We explain how to actually get to these locations in Chapter 6, so you can come back here later and follow up on them.)
- **Practice foreign languages:** You can visit online chat rooms, where you can try out your French or Spanish or Portuguese or Russian or Japanese or even Esperanto.
- **Pay for music you download:** If you are using KaZaA or other file sharing software to download music, consider sending money to the recording artists. One Web site, `www.musiclink.com`, has been set up especially for you to do this.
- **Discover how to make your own Web page:** A Web page can be as serious or as stupid as you like. Put your stories or artwork up for family and friends to admire. You even can start an online business. You can make a home page for a local cause you support. We tell you how to do these things in Chapter 9.

So-so ways to use the Net

Here are some ideas that your parents may consider a waste of time, but hey, we can't be serious all the time. If they give you a hard time, ask if you can inspect their Web time log. (There is no such thing, but they don't know that.)

- **Play games:** Many popular games (both traditional — like chess, bridge, hearts, and go — and video) have options that let you compete against other players on the Internet.
- **IM your friends:** Instant messaging (IM) has become the cool way to get in touch — *instantly*. Wireless options are already happening in many parts of the world.
- **Talk on a videophone:** Software like Yahoo Messenger or PalTalk let you see your friends while you talk to them (not recommended on bad hair days). Chapter 14 talks about free video programs, which you may need after you get your parents to spring for that webcam.

- **Shop:** What can we say? Internet shopping is like the mall, but it's always open and has plenty of free parking. Chapter 8 gets you started.
- **Role-play:** Any number of Internet sites let you pretend to be a character in your favorite science fiction or fantasy book.

Not so good ways to use the Net

Stay away from the following ideas, which will just get you into trouble:

- **Plagiarism:** That's the fancy word for passing off other people's work as your own. Unfortunately, plagiarizing from the Internet is as wrong as plagiarizing from a book and a lot easier for teachers to catch.
- **Cheating:** Using translating software to do your language homework is also no good. (You're gonna get caught, so save yourself the embarrassment.)
- **Revealing too much about yourself:** When chatting on the Net with people you don't know, it's tempting to give out identifying information about yourself or your family, but this is dangerous. Some seemingly innocent questions aren't so innocent, so we go into more detail about this later in this chapter. Even revealing your e-mail address can get you unwanted junk mail.
- **Visiting porn and hate sites:** This is between you and your parents, but find out what rules your parents have made for your online behavior and stick to them.
- **Pretending you are someone else online:** Go ahead and make up a pseudonym so you don't have to use your real name. But, *don't* pretend you're Britney Spears looking for new band members or Joe Millionaire looking for a date.
- **Hanging out in adult chat rooms:** This can get both you and the chat room hosts into big trouble, so don't do it.

Truly brain dead ideas

Here are some ideas that you should never, never consider. We mean it.

- **Meeting online friends in person without telling a parent:** Even adults aren't stupid enough to do this. If you meet someone great online and you want to meet him or her in person, fine. But take precautions! First, tell your parents about it and decide with them how to proceed. Second, never meet someone you met online in a private place: Always meet in a public place, such as a restaurant. Finally, bring someone (preferably your parents) with you.

- **Doing anything illegal — online or off:** The Internet feels totally anonymous, but it's not. If you commit a crime, the police can get the Internet connection records from your Internet service provider (ISP) and find out who was connected via which modem on what day at what time with what numeric Internet (IP) address, and they'll track you down.
- **Breaking into other computers or creating viruses:** The authorities have lost their sense of humor about this. Kids *are* going to jail for this.

The Internet and little kids

We are strong advocates of allowing kids to be kids, and we believe that kids are better teachers than computers are. None of our kids watches commercial TV. Now that you know our predisposition, maybe you can guess what we're going to say next: We are not in favor of sticking a young child in front of a screen. How young is too young? We believe that younger than age seven is too young. We recommend that your younger siblings get as much human attention as possible. At young ages, kids benefit more from playing with trees, balls, clay, crayons, paint, mud, monkey bars, bicycles, other kids, and especially older sibs. Yeah, that means you. We know they can be a pain in the neck, but computers make lousy babysitters, and you won't find much out there for the prereading set anyway. What is out there, they're best off using while sitting in your lap so you can help.

We think that Internet access is more appropriate for somewhat older kids (fourth or fifth grade and older), but your mileage may vary. Even so, we think it's a good idea to limit the amount of time that anyone, especially kids, spends online. We (despite our good looks) have been playing with computers for 30 years (holy cow!), and we know what happens to kids that are allowed to stay glued to their computers for unlimited time — trust us, *it is not good.*

Kids need to be able to communicate with other human beings. Too often kids who have difficulty communicating with other human beings prefer computers. As you may guess, this doesn't really help kids develop their social skills. Instead, problems get worse. Keep a private log of just how much time you spend in front of the screen during one week. Then ask yourself if this is really how you want to spend your life. Find a hobby that doesn't involve a screen. Join a team. Form a band. Do art. Set aside one computer-free day each week. Try to have meals and conversations with actual human beings, face to face.

Surf safe

Make sure you know the safety rules for using the Net. Rule number one is to never reveal exactly who you are. Use only your first name, and don't provide your last name, your address, your phone number, or the name of your school. And never, ever, tell anyone your password. No honest person will ever ask you for it.

Many kids don't have a clue about this. They reveal who they are without even meaning to do so. They may mention the name of their hometown ball team. They may talk about a teacher who they hate at school. They may say what their parents do for a living. They may say which church or synagogue they attend. Such information may be revealed over the course of many messages spread over weeks or months. These seemingly harmless bits of information can help a determined person "triangulate" to home in on a kid. So be very careful about what you say online — in a chat room or instant message or e-mail. Be suspicious of strangers who seem to know a lot about you. Maybe they say they're a friend of your parents who is supposed to pick you up after school or to pick up a package from your house. Never go with a stranger or let him or her into the house without asking a trusted (offline) adult first.

Here are a few more rules:

- **Think about whom you give your e-mail address to.** Many Web sites ask you to register, and many require you to provide a working e-mail address that they verify by sending you a message. Before registering with a Web site, make sure that it's run by a reputable company from which you won't mind getting junk mail.
- **Never agree to talk to someone on the phone or meet someone in person without checking it out with your parents.** Most people you meet online are okay, but a few creepy types out there have made the Internet their hunting ground.
- **Don't assume that people are telling you the truth.** That kid your age and gender who shares your interests and hobbies may actually be a lonely, creepy 40-year-old.
- **If someone is scaring you or making you uncomfortable (especially if the person says not to tell your parents), *tell* your parents.** Ask your parents to talk to your Internet service provider. Remember that you can always turn off the computer.

College and the Net

Although the Internet has had a home in universities for a long time, what's happening with the Web these days is new for everyone. Much of the inspiration and perspiration of the volunteers who are making information available to everyone comes from universities, both students and faculty, who see the incredible potential for learning.

Most campuses provide free or low-cost access to the Internet for their students and staff. Schools that enable you to register early sometimes give you Internet access when you register, even months in advance. If you're going to go anyway, you can get a jump on your Internet education before you even get to campus.

Colleges have found dozens of ways to make the Net useful inside school as well as out. We like what the folks at Thunderbird, The American Graduate School of International Business (`www.t-bird.edu`), did when they created My Thunderbird, which enables both students and professors to share and update profiles. Professors love the opportunity to get to know their students with the pictures and profiles that My Thunderbird provides. Class rosters stay current and the campus stays connected.

Internet technologies such as e-mail, chat, and instant messages are great ways for parents and college kids to stay in touch. They're much cheaper than phoning home and easier than coordinating schedules. Forwarding mail to other family members allows for broader communication. We noticed another surprising benefit: In our experience, families tend to fight less when they're communicating by e-mail. Somehow, when folks have time to think about what they're going to say before they say it, it comes out better.

Going back to school

Your education isn't over when you finish high school or college or (for those of us seriously dedicated to avoiding real life) graduate school. There's always more to learn. Nothing's like learning directly from a first-rate teacher in a classroom, but learning over the Net can be the next best thing to being there, particularly for students who live far from school or have irregular schedules. You can now take everything online from high school equivalency exams to professional continuing education to college and graduate courses leading to degrees. Some courses are strictly online, whereas others use a combination of classroom, lab, and online instruction.

Checking out colleges on the Net

Most colleges and universities have sites on the Web. You can find a directory of online campus tours at `www.campustours.com`, with links to lots more info about the colleges and universities.

After you're a little more adept at using the Net, you can research classes and professors to get a better idea of what appeals to you.

Of paramount concern to parents

You may want to ask your parents to read this sidebar.

High on the list of parents' concerns about the Internet is the question of children's access to inappropriate material, including businesses that try to market and sell directly to children. This concern is legitimate: As time has gone by, both the good stuff and the grody stuff on the Net have increased dramatically. We have no simple answers, but one thing is crystal clear to us: Parents *have* to be involved. Considering the direction of education and edicts from on high, *kids will be involved* with the Internet, as schools hook up at a rapid clip.

Parents who take the time to find out about access issues usually understand that on one hand, the threat is not as great as some would have you believe, and some of the proposed solutions have severe problems of their own. Parents who have thought about the issues on a larger scale are extremely concerned that reactionary sentiment and hyperbole pose a real threat to our freedom of expression and that those reactions are ultimately a great danger to our children. On the other hand, a great deal of garbage lurks online. Parental involvement is essential; we talk about family strategy a little later in this chapter. If you're interested in thrashing out these issues, you can read or subscribe to the CACI (Children Accessing Controversial Information) mailing list by visiting its Web site at `groups.yahoo.com/group/caci-list`.

A few schools like the University of Phoenix (`www.phoenix.edu`) specialize in online education, but schools all over the world now offer online instruction, and if the course is on the Net, it doesn't matter whether the school is across the street or across the ocean. You can find thousands of schools and courses in directories such as `www.petersons.com/distancelearning` and `www.online-colleges-courses-degrees-classes.org`.

Sell, sell, sell!

If you spend a lot of time online, you will soon notice that everyone seems to be trying to sell you something. Kids, particularly those from middle- and upper-income families, are considered the most lucrative target market, and the Net is being viewed as another way to capture this market.

Targeting kids for selling isn't new. Maybe you are old enough to remember Joe Camel of the Camel cigarette campaign that many people claimed was aimed at kids. You may watch Channel One at school, which brings advertising directly to the classroom. If you watch TV, you know how TV programs for kids push their own line of toys and action figures.

You should know that big company marketing departments have already designed kid-friendly, fascinating, captivating software to help them better market to you. Delightful, familiar cartoon characters deftly elicit strategic marketing information directly from the keyboard in your home. You should be aware of this situation and know what to do when someone on the Web is asking for information. You or your parents may want to obtain a copy of the Center for Media Education's report titled *The Web of Deception* by sending $25 to the organization at 1511 K Street NW, Suite #518, Washington, DC, 20005. The Federal Trade Commission has also weighed in on this topic. They are on the Web at `www.ftc.gov`; when you visit this site, click Consumer Protection and then Children's Issues.

The Children's Online Privacy Protection Act (COPPA) limits the information that companies can collect from children under 13 (or at least, children who admit they're under 13) without explicit parental consent, which we think parents should rarely give. We heard of one marketer who said he wanted to use the Net to create a personal relationship with all the kids who use his product. Ugh. We have names for guys who want relationships with kids, and they're not very nice names.

The FTC's Kidz Privacy site (`www.ftc.gov/bcp/conline/edcams/kidzprivacy`) has more useful information for both kids and parents about COPPA and online privacy.

Who's online?

Lots of kids — and grownups — are putting up Web sites about themselves and their families. We think that this is really cool, but we strongly encourage families who use the Net for personal reasons (distinct from businesspeople who use the Net for business purposes) not to use their full or real names. We also advise you never to disclose your address, phone number, Social Security number, or account passwords in online social situations to anyone who asks for this kind of information online or off. This advice applies especially when you receive information requests from people who claim to be in positions of authority, such as instant messages from people claiming that they're from America Online (AOL) tech support. They're not.

People with real authority *never* ask those types of questions.

More than ever, children need to develop critical thinking skills. They have to be able to evaluate what they read and see — especially on the Web.

Regrettably, we have to report that we have seen a great deal of trashy e-mail (*spam*) lately. This situation is likely to get worse until we have effective laws against unsolicited e-mail. In the meantime, one important rule to remember is this: If what an e-mail offers sounds too good to be true, it isn't true, and if an ad for it showed up from someone you don't know, it's probably not true, either.

Consumer's choice

Parents pay for online services, so services that want to remain competitive vie for parental dollars by providing features to help families control Internet access. America Online, for example, enables parents to block access to chat rooms that may not be appropriate for kids and to restrict access to discussion groups and newsgroups based on keywords you choose. Parental blocking is available at no extra cost. AOL and MSN TV (formerly WebTV) enable the master account holder to restrict the material that subaccount holders can view.

Software sentries

More and more products (we count some 50) are appearing on the market to help parents restrict access or monitor usage by some sort of activity report. If you choose to use one of these systems, remember that they're not a substitute for your direct involvement with your child's Internet experience; they all filter based on keywords and fixed lists of systems that the programs' authors believe to have objectionable material. None of them tells you exactly what they block, and your idea of what's appropriate and inappropriate may well not be the same as theirs. Many software sentries seem to have political agendas, blocking sites whose political content doesn't conform to that of the program's authors.

You can try before you buy by downloading evaluation copies of software-blocking packages. (You see how to do that when you find out how to navigate the Web in Chapters 6 and 7.) Visit `www.smartparent.com`, which is a list of current links to dozens and dozens of filtering software sites (click on Safety). They also list Internet service providers (you'll be hearing more about those in the next chapter) who are actively trying to make the Net safe for kids. What's more, SmartParent.com also lists kid-friendly sites.

To parents

Parents, educators, and free-speech advocates alike agree that there's no substitute for parental guidance when it comes to the subject of Internet access. Just as you want your children to read good books and see quality films, you also want them to find the good stuff on the Net. If you take the time to discover the good stuff with your children, you have the opportunity to share the experience and to impart critical values and a sense of discrimination that your children need in all areas of their lives.

The good stuff on the Net vastly outweighs the bad. Plenty of software is available to help parents and educators tap the invaluable resources of the Net without opening Pandora's box. Remember that every child is different and that what may be appropriate for your children may not be appropriate for other kids. You have to find what's right for you.

Establish rules for your family's use of the Net. Outline areas that are off limits. Limit the time spent online, and be explicit about what information kids can give out over the Net.

It takes extra effort from you to establish limits and at the same time give your children the freedom they need to explore. Some families prefer to keep their computers in a family space as opposed to in kids' bedrooms. Wherever they are, check them often; don't let the screen be your babysitter. Don't buy into the hype that just because it's on a computer, it's educational. We're reminded of a cartoon featuring wishful parents reading the newspaper's Help Wanted section and finding that Nintendo players are making $70,000 a year. Everyone knows kids whose lives seem to be lost in front of a screen. Don't let that be your kid.

Kids need explicit rules about talking with and meeting with people they meet on the Net. Never let your kids meet with someone they've met online by themselves. Keep an eye on your phone bill for unusual calls.

Internet Resources for Kids

As you may have guessed, the Internet is replete with resources for kids — and parents, by the way. As we have learned from writing this book nine times in nine years, nothing is as ephemeral as a Net address. To help keep this information as accurate as possible, we're putting our lists of resources on our Web site, both to keep them up-to-date and because they're too long to list here completely. From there, you can get right to the source, and we do our best to keep the sources current.

Visit `net.gurus.com/kids`, which puts you one mouse-click away from the pages described in this section.

Mailing lists for parents and kids

Chapter 13 tells you how to subscribe to mailing lists. Lots of mailing lists for and about kids are listed on our Web page.

Web sites for kids

Okay, we admit it. Web sites can be the coolest thing since sliced bread. Our Web site has links to sites from around the world especially for kids. To get to these sites, you have to know how to use a browser, such as Netscape, Internet Explorer, or Opera. We tell you how in Chapter 6. (But watch out — when your 9-year-old sib finds a Web site that lists 1,000 knock-knock jokes, you'll be hearing them for weeks!)

Help for parents of kids with problems

One of the most heartening experiences available on the Net is the help that total strangers freely offer to one another. The bonds that form from people sharing their experiences, struggles, strengths, and hopes redefine what it means to reach out and touch someone. We encourage everyone who has a concern to look for people who share that concern. Our experience of participating in mailing lists and newsgroups related to our own problems compels us to enthusiastically encourage you to check things out online. You can do so with complete anonymity, if you want. You can watch and learn for a long time, or you can jump into the fray and ask for help.

Remember that everyone who gives advice is not an expert. You have to involve your own practitioners in your process. Many people have found enormous help, however, from people who have gone down similar paths before them. For many of us, it has made all the difference in the world.

Our Web site lists a few of the available online mailing lists and discussion groups at `net.gurus.com/lists`. A mailing list or group that's specific to your needs almost certainly exists regardless of whether we list it, and new groups are created every day. Commercial online services such as America Online and CompuServe have special forums that may interest you as well. Or, visit Google Groups on the Web at `groups.google.com` to read and participate in Usenet newsgroups, an ancient (well, 20-year-old) system of discussion groups.

Notice that some lists are talk lists, which feature free-flowing discussion; some lists have focused discussions; some lists are almost purely academic. The type of discussion is not always obvious from the name. If it looks interesting, subscribe and see what sort of discussion is going on there. It's easy enough to unsubscribe if you don't like it.

The Internet in Schools

As schools hook up to the Net, they are actively debating Internet access for their students. Find out as much as you can and get involved. The more you know, the more you can advocate for appropriate access.

Contractually speaking

Some schools use software to filter Internet access for kids. A variety of filtering systems are available, at a range of costs and installation hassles, that promise to filter out inappropriate and harmful Web sites. Sounds good, but many kids are smart. Smart kids can find ways around rules, and smart kids can find ways around software systems that are designed to "protect" them. Many institutions rely successfully on students' signed contracts that detail explicitly what is appropriate and what is inappropriate system use. Students who violate one of these contracts lose their Internet or computer privileges.

We believe that this approach is a good one. In our experience, kids are quicker, more highly motivated, and have more time to spend breaking into and out of systems than most adults we know, and this method encourages them to do something more productive than electronic lock-picking.

For more information on CIPA, a law intended to mandate filtering software in schools and libraries, see the America Library Association's page about it at `www.ala.org/cipa`.

Real education

Used effectively, the Internet is a terrific educational resource. Used ineffectively, it's a terrific waste of time and money. The difference is research and planning. We were chatting with our local elementary school principal who'd just spent four hours one weekend afternoon searching the Net to help her son, who teaches third grade in a nearby district, develop a unit on Canada — that sounds like a great use of the Internet to us. Lots of educational material is out there. After you get a little familiarity with the Web and the ways to find things online, offer to help your local teachers look for material to bolster their teaching. For teachers, we particularly recommend the Gateway to Educational Materials (`www.thegateway.org`) and the ERIC Clearinghouse on Information & Technology (`www.ericit.org`), both funded by the U.S. Department of Education.

Part II

Internet, Here I Come!

"Hey – here's a company that develops short memorable domain names for new businesses. It's listed at www.CompanyThatDevelopsShort-MemorableDomainNamesForNewBusinesses.com."

In this part . . .

After you're ready to get started, where do you start? Probably the hardest part of using the Internet is getting connected. We help you figure out which kind of Internet service is right for you and help you get connected, with separate instructions for Windows XP/Me/98 and Macs.

Chapter 4

Picking Your Internet Service

In This Chapter

- Choosing a computer for Internet access
- Picking a modem
- Looking at types of accounts
- Considering slow or fast Internet connections
- Deciding where to get an account
- Figuring out what kind of software you need

"Great," you say, "How do I get connected to the Internet?" The answer is "It depends." (You'll be hearing that answer perhaps more often than you'd like.) The Internet isn't one network — it's 100,000 separate networks hooked together, each with its own rules and procedures, and you can get to the Net from any one of them. Readers of previous editions of this book pleaded (they did other things too, but this is a family-oriented book) for step-by-step directions on how to get on, so we make them as step-by-step as we can.

Here are the basic steps:

1. **Figure out what type of computer you have or can use.**
2. **Figure out which types of Internet connections are available where you are.**
3. **Figure out how much you're willing to pay.**
4. **Sign up for your connection.**
5. **Set up your computer to use your new connection, and decide whether you like it.**

You need four things to connect to the Internet:

- A computer (unless you use a "Web appliance," which we talk about in the section, "No way! I even had to borrow this book!")
- A modem (a piece of computer equipment) to hook your computer to the phone line or cable system
- An account with an Internet service provider or online service, to give your modem somewhere to call
- Software to run on your computer

We look at each of these items in turn. The last step — actually configuring your computer to connect up — is described in detail in Chapter 5.

Do You Have a Computer?

Because the Internet is a computer network, the only way to hook up to it is by using a computer. But computers are starting to appear in all sorts of disguises, and they may well already be in your home, whether you know it or not. If you have a computer at work, particularly if it's already set up to handle electronic mail, you may already have an Internet connection there. (See the sidebar, "Are you already on the Internet?".)

No way! I even had to borrow this book!

If you don't have a computer and aren't ready or able to buy one, you still have some options.

A likely place to find Internet access is in your public library. More and more libraries are transforming themselves into local Internet access centers and have found these services to be quite popular. Call ahead to reserve time or find out which hours are less crowded.

Another possibility is a local community college, continuing-education center, or high school, which often have short, inexpensive "Introduction to the Internet" courses. You may ask, "What kind of loser book tells people to go out and take a course?" A course can offer two things you can't possibly get from any book: A live demonstration of what the Internet is like and, more important, someone to talk to who knows the local Internet situation. You can certainly get on the Net without a class (we did, after all); if an inexpensive class is available, though, take it.

Popping up all over are cybercafés. You can surf the Net while sipping your favorite beverage and sharing your cyberexperience. If you want to check out the Internet, cybercafés are a great place to try before you buy. If you decide to go the cybercafé route, check out the section about cybercafé etiquette in Chapter 21.

If you're trying to avoid buying a computer, some *Internet appliances* are available — small computers with built-in programs to get to the Internet. Some, notably MSN TV, use your television for a screen; others have a built-in screen. See the section "Internet appliances" later in this chapter for more information.

Yup! I got this old beige box in the closet

Almost any personal computer made since 1980 is adequate for some type of connection to the Internet. But unless you have a really good friend who is a computer geek and wants to spend a lot of time at your house helping you get online, it isn't worth fooling with that old clunker — unless, of course, you're looking for a reason for the geek to spend a lot of time at your house, but that's your business. If you can possibly afford it, we strongly encourage you to buy a new computer or at least one that's not more than a year old. New computers come with Internet software already installed and are configured for the latest in Web technology. If you already own an older computer, you will spend much more time and energy, and ultimately just as much money, just trying to get the thing to work the way you want. We think that you're best off buying a brand-new computer. New computers are getting cheaper and cheaper, and you can get a downright good one for $500 or less.

Yup! Just got a brand new Thunderstick 2004

Ah, you *do* have a computer. (Or maybe you're thinking about buying one.) Most Internet users connect by having their computer dial in to an Internet service provider, or ISP. When you first turn on your new computer, or when you run one of the Internet programs that come installed, your computer will offer to call an ISP and set up an account right then and there. Don't dial (or let your computer dial) until you've read the rest of this chapter. We have some warnings and some options we think you ought to consider first.

Are you already on the Internet?

If you have access to a computer or a computer terminal, you may already be on the Internet. Here are some ways to check.

If you have an account on an online service, such as CompuServe, America Online (AOL), or Microsoft Network (MSN), you already have a connection to the Internet. All popular online services provide relatively complete Internet connections.

If your company or school has an internal e-mail system or a local area network (LAN), it may also be connected to the Internet directly or indirectly. Ask a local e-mail expert.

A snazzier way to connect, not yet available everywhere, is a *broadband* (high-speed) connection. Your local cable or telephone company brings nifty equipment to your house and connects your computer to a high-speed connection while you sit back and watch. Carol and Margy like this approach best. We tell you why later in the section titled "Faster Connections: The Beauty of Bandwidth." Ask your cable company whether it offers cable modem Internet access or ask your phone company whether it offers something called digital subscriber line (DSL). If either says yes, consider getting broadband.

No, but I can't wait to buy one

People argue at great length about the advantages and disadvantages of various types of computers. We don't do that here. (If you'll buy the beer, though, we'll be happy to argue about it after work.) It's usually safer to talk about politics or religion. The most popular computers are computers running Microsoft Windows XP, 98, or 2000 (usually called *IBM-compatible* or just *PCs*), and Apple Macintoshes. Windows XP and Apple's new iMacs and iBooks are particularly easy to set up. On either Windows or Macintosh computers, you can get the spiffiest type of Internet connection and use the nicest point-and-click programs to get pictures, sounds, and even movies from the Net.

If you have a knowledgeable friend who is willing to help you get on the Internet, consider getting the same type of computer she has. That way, if you have a problem, you'll have someone to ask who'll probably know the answer.

WAP! It's the Web on your phone!

Modern mobile phones have little bitty screens and little bitty keypads, so an industry group called WAP (Wireless Access Protocol) devised a way to show little bitty Web pages on those screens and navigate around them. WAP is quite popular in Japan, where teenage girls use it to get updates on Hello Kitty, but it's not catching on very fast in the U.S. At this point, we'd advise against paying extra for a WAP-ish phone unless you have a specific use in mind and you've tried it out on someone else's phone to see if you can stand using its teeny screen.

Modems, Ho!

A *modem* is the thing that hooks your computer to the phone line or cable system. Unless your computer is at an office or school that is already wired for a direct Internet connection, you need a modem. You need to have the right kind of modem for the type of Internet account you're going to use: a dialup modem for a dialup Internet account, a cable modem for a cable Internet account, or a DSL modem for a high-speed DSL account.

If you choose a DSL or cable Internet account (described in the next chapter), the phone or cable company usually supplies the modem. You're responsible for your own modem if you choose a dialup account.

Dialup modems are the kind of modem you've probably already seen — they've been around for years and connect to normal phone lines. They can dial the phone and connect to the ISP at the other end of the line. Modems come in all sorts of shapes and sizes. Some are separate boxes, known as *external modems,* with cables that plug into the computer and the phone line and a power cord. Others are inside the computer, with just a cable for the phone, and some are tiny credit-card-sized things you slide into the side of your laptop computer. (They still have a cable for the phone — some things never change.) Matching the variety of physical sizes of dialup modems is an equally wide variety of internal features. The speed at which a dialup modem operates (or the rate at which it can stuff computer data into a phone line) is 56,000 bits per second (*bps,* commonly but erroneously called *baud*), usually abbreviated 56K. Most dialup modems can act as fax machines, and some even have more exotic features, such as built-in answering machines.

Most computers sold in the past couple of years come with built-in dialup modems. If you already have a modem, use it — just examine your computer carefully for a phone jack and if you find one, plug a phone wire into it. If you have to buy a dialup modem, get a 56K because anything slower won't be much cheaper. For external modems, be sure to get a cable to connect the modem to your computer, and also be sure that its connectors match the ones on your computer — there may be different types of plugs (serial or Universal Serial Bus [USB]) on the back of a computer.

Note to laptop computer owners: If your computer has credit-card-sized PC Card slots but no built-in modem, get a PC Card modem that fits in a slot so that you don't have to carry around a separate modem when you take your computer on the road.

Who Ya Gonna Call?

Unless you have wrangled a free account somehow, you pay a company to give you your Internet connection. You use your computer and modem (or some other communications device) to call in to the provider's system, and the provider handles the rest of the details of connecting to the Internet.

To connect your computer to the Internet, you have two major choices — or three, if you're lucky:

- **Choice 1: Sign up with an online service, such as America Online or MSN.** Online services are easy to use and they provide information in a way that is more organized than the Internet itself. They usually don't give you the full range of Internet services, however, and you have to use their software. Online services have local dialup phone numbers in all major cities, but don't extend into all rural areas. Some online services offer high-speed accounts in some areas. For a regular dialup account, you need the online service's software and a dialup modem. See the next section for details.
- **Choice 2: Sign up with an Internet service provider (ISP) for a dialup Internet account.** To use an ISP account, you need a dialup program (for dialup accounts only), an e-mail program, and a Web browser program. (We explain all these terms in the next section.) Many ISPs now have zoomy, automated sign-up programs that are just as easy to use as the one America Online uses. See the section "ISPs: The Internet, the whole Internet, and nothing but the Internet" later in this chapter.

- **Choice 3 (If you're lucky): Sign up for high-speed cable or DSL access.** We say "if you're lucky" because cable and DSL access aren't universally available yet. If either is available in your area, however, all you have to do is call your cable company or ISP and arrange for someone to come and install a network card in your computer (and, if you don't already have cable TV wiring in your house, you need a cable connection to your home, or some extra equipment on your phone line, for DSL). Folks in Europe may be able to get an ISDN line from their phone companies, which are almost as good as DSL lines. If you choose any of these high-speed options, you can skip ahead to the section "Faster Connections: The Beauty of Bandwidth."

Big ol' online services

You can choose a big online service, such as America Online (AOL) or MSN (which is owned by Microsoft). Each has its own software package that you run on your computer and that connects you to the service. Each has versions of the packages for Windows, Mac, and even DOS.

Here are some good things about online services:

- They're relatively easy to get connected to and use free software that arrives regularly on CD-ROM in your postal mailbox.
- They claim to have lots of helpful people you can call when you get stuck. (Our firsthand experience doesn't necessarily substantiate these claims. In fact, Carol thinks that AOL Customer Service is an oxymoron.)
- They offer proprietary services and information not available elsewhere on the Net (although much of the material that used to be available solely via these services has now moved to public areas on the Net).
- Many give you a way to limit the material your kids can access.

Here are some bad things about online services:

- Many people complain that the screens are so crowded with advertisements that it's difficult to figure out what's what.
- They limit you to the set of Internet services they choose to offer; if you want something else, you're out of luck. For example, to read your AOL mail, you have to use AOL's mail reader, Netscape 7 Mail (AOL owns Netscape), or AOL's new AOL Communicator; you can't use Pegasus, Eudora, Outlook Express, or other popular e-mail programs.

- Subscribers to some online services seem to get a lot more junk e-mail than subscribers of regular ISPs.
- They make it more difficult, or in some cases impossible, to get to parts of the Net considered controversial. (Some people consider this restriction to be an advantage, of course.)

Figure 4-1 shows a typical screen from AOL using version 8.0 of their software.

ISPs: The Internet, the whole Internet, and nothing but the Internet

An *ISP* (*Internet service provider*: we computer types just love TLAs — three-letter acronyms) is similar to an online service but with the important difference that its primary business is hooking people to the Internet. Because almost all ISPs buy their equipment and software from a handful of manufacturers, the features and services that one ISP offers are much like those of another, with important differences such as price, service, and reliability. Think of it as the difference between a Ford and a Buick, with the differences between your local dealers being at least as important in the purchase decision as the differences between the cars.

Figure 4-1: America Online is on-screen.

When you connect to your ISP, your computer becomes part of the Internet. You type stuff or click in programs running on your computer, and those programs communicate over the Net to do whatever it is they do for you.

You can run several Internet applications at a time, which can be quite handy. You may be reading your electronic mail, for example, and receive a message describing a cool, new site on the World Wide Web. You can switch immediately to your Web browser program (Netscape or Internet Explorer, most likely), look at the page, and then return to the mail program and pick up where you left off. Most e-mail programs highlight *URLs* (Web addresses) and enable you to go straight to your browser by clicking the URL in your e-mail message.

Another advantage of an ISP account is that you're not limited to running programs that your Internet provider gives you. You can download a new Internet application from the Net and begin using it immediately — your ISP just acts as a data conduit between your computer and the rest of the Net.

A few ISPs also provide an older, dying-breed type of access called a *shell account.* (See the sidebar "It's terminal: Using a UNIX shell account" in this chapter.) Shell accounts can be very helpful for computer users with visual disabilities because they display only text, which works well with programs that read screens aloud.

Internet on the run

Everywhere you go, people are carrying laptop computers. Staying connected on the road can be a challenge. One way to get your Internet fix is to plug your modem into the hotel phone and dial your ISP or online service. Check with your ISP to see whether it has local numbers that you can call at your destinations. Many local or regional ISPs belong to organizations like iPass in which all the members provide access to each other's customers, albeit at an extra charge. If you travel internationally, AOL and AT&T Business (at `www.attglobal.net`) are the ISPs in the U.S. with the largest international access networks. Many high-class business hotels provide high-speed Internet access if your computer has a network (Ethernet) port. The connection usually costs about $10 per day.

Most new laptops come with Wi-Fi, wireless radio Ethernet. (If yours didn't, you can get a Wi-Fi adapter card and plug it into one of the slots on the side of the computer.) Wi-Fi "hotspots," where you can get a radio signal and connect to the Net, are remarkably common in coffee shops, hotels, and office buildings. As often as not, you can turn on your PC, pick up someone's Wi-Fi signal, and piggyback your way onto the Net.

If you want to surf while you're in motion, it's possible to equip your laptop with a *cellular modem,* a modem that works as a cellular phone. Cellular modems tend to be expensive and slow and are no substitute for a real Net connection, although they can be handy when you need to get online to send or receive small amounts of information, like a repairman's schedule of places to go.

Internet appliances

If you're not ready to buy a computer, you might consider an *Internet appliance*, a box that just connects to the Internet and does Internet-ish things such as Web browsing and e-mail. In reality, these are small computers with the software already built in. They're usually quite cheap, $100 or so, but you have to use an ISP that supports your particular appliance.

We don't think that Internet appliances are a good investment. For one thing, if the service that supports your appliance goes away, you're left with an expensive paperweight. For another, if you spend a little (well, a few hundred dollars) more to get a real computer, you can do all the Internet stuff an appliance can do, but you can also install new Internet applications from the Net. You can also use computer programs to write letters, balance your checkbook, figure your taxes, and all the other things that people do with computers. The oldest and best-known Internet appliance is WebTV, now called MSN TV, which we discuss in the sidebar "I want my MSN TV!"

It's terminal: Using a UNIX shell account

In the early days of the Internet, before Netscape, before America Online, before the World Wide Web itself (can you remember back that far? — we're talking about 1989), intrepid Internet explorers dealt with the Internet by using UNIX accounts. *UNIX* is an operating system that, in its purest form, requires you to type short, cryptic, and totally unmemorable commands to get anything done. Although UNIX is a powerful system and programmers love it, most mere mortals find it a pain in the neck to use. UNIX accounts are also called *shell* accounts, for the name of the part of UNIX that processes the commands you type.

UNIX accounts used to be widely available, when PCs all ran MS-DOS and the only windows were in the walls of your house. Some ISPs can still give you one, if you ask specifically. You can find out how to use a UNIX shell account by reading this Web page:

```
net.gurus.com/shell
```

MSN: Microsoft's network

When Microsoft introduced Windows 95, it also introduced the Microsoft Network (MSN), a new online service that was going to eat America Online's and CompuServe's lunch. Several years later, AOL still has its lunch (along with those of CompuServe, Prodigy, the Source, and many other dead competitors). MSN has given up its original proprietary design and has become little more than an ISP with special Web pages that you can see only if you're an MSN subscriber. The MSN Explorer program, which you install when you sign up for MSN, includes a Web browser and e-mail program. MSN uses Microsoft's Hotmail e-mail server for its e-mail, so you can't use any non-Microsoft e-mail program to read your mail.

Signing up with MSN is easy if you use Windows because an MSN icon sits right on your desktop. In fact, Microsoft takes pains to offer you lots and lots of opportunities to sign up during the Windows installation process. For more information, take a look at the MSN Web page, at `www.msn.com`.

How Much Does This All Cost?

You can spend a great deal of money on your Internet connection, or you can spend practically none. Here are a few things to look out for.

ISP charges

Pricing schemes vary all over the lot. Most ISPs charge about $20 per month and give you either unlimited hours or a large monthly allotment of 80 to 100 hours. Often, you can get a cheaper $5 rate that only includes three or four hours, with time beyond the included amount charged at $2 per hour or so. Most people prefer a flat rate or at least a large enough allotment that they're unlikely to use it up. Studies have shown that the average Internet use is about 18 hours per month.

If you or your kids become regular online users, you will find that time stands still while you're online and that you use much more online time than you think you do. Even if you think that you will be online for only a few minutes a day, if you don't have a flat-rate plan, you may be surprised when your bill arrives at the end of the month.

High-speed cable and DSL connections appear to cost more, usually $40 to $50 per month, plus installation and the cost of the special modem you need. However, neither cable nor DSL ties up your phone while you are online.

I want my MSN TV!

If you don't have a computer and don't want to buy one, you can connect to the Internet by using your TV. Get MSN TV (formerly called WebTV), a system that includes both hardware and service. The hardware includes a box that you connect to your television set, a remote control, and a keyboard (optional, but indispensable unless you are an extremely patient person); the service consists of an Internet connection for which you pay a monthly fee. The box includes a computer, of course, but don't tell anybody. The computer runs one program, the MSN TV program, and uses your TV as the monitor. MSN TV, which is owned by Microsoft, has had slow sales for several years, but it may be right for you.

For more information about MSN TV, read our Web page about it:

`net.gurus.com/webtv`

Many people who use ordinary modems end up paying for the installation and use of a second phone line. When you add the cost of a second phone line to the cost of your ISP, you may find that DSL or cable is no more expensive. Cable and DSL connections are always available — there's no calling-in process, and they are significantly faster (and, we think, more fun).

Phone charges

If you're not careful, you can end up paying more for the phone call than you do for your Internet service. One of the things you do when you sign up for an ISP is determine the phone number to call. *If at all possible, use an ISP whose number is a free or untimed local call.* If you use a local or regional Internet service provider, that provider will have a short list of phone numbers you can use. Of the national ISPs, AOL and AT&T have their own national networks of dial-in numbers; the rest piggyback on other networks, such as Sprintnet from Sprint and Alternet from MCI. If one national provider has a local number in your area, they probably all do because it's a Sprintnet or Alternet number that works for any of them.

If you can't find an ISP that's a local call for you, your options are limited. If you shop around, you'll probably be able to find long distance service for 4 cents per minute or less. (That's still $2.40 per hour.) Be sure to compare rates for in-state and out-of-state calls because an out-of-state call is usually cheaper even though it's farther away. Beware of toll-free numbers, which almost always levy a stiff hourly surcharge.

Some ISPs give you software that automatically selects a local phone number to dial. Usually it chooses correctly, but we've heard enough horror stories to warn you that you should always verify that the number your computer is calling is, in fact, a local call. Check the front of your phone book or call your phone company's local business office.

Faster Connections: The Beauty of Bandwidth

If you're the type of person who likes to live on the edge, technologically speaking, you're the type of person who wants the fastest Internet connection available so that you can play with all the fancy graphics and download sound and video. Graphics, video, and sound are all bits of information — lots and lots of bits of information — too many for most dialup connections to handle. *Broadband connections* can provide greater *bandwidth,* the amount of data transferred in a specific amount of time, than a connection over a regular phone line. They can be really fast, nominally 1.4 million bits per second, with downloads in practice often exceeding 140,000 bytes per second.

The good news is that high-speed connections are now available and affordable by mere mortals.

After you get used to having a high-speed connection, you will never be able to tolerate an ordinary dialup connection again. It's that good.

You may need a network card

High-speed Internet connections use special modems that the cable or phone company provides. These modems connect to your computer in one of two ways: a network card or a USB port.

Most new computers come with a built-in *network card,* which can also be used for connecting the computer to a local area network, or LAN (that is, a network within a home, school, or office). Network cards (also called *network adapters*, *LAN cards*, or *Ethernet adapters*) have a *RJ-45 connector* that looks like a phone jack's big brother.

New computers usually also come with at least two USB ports, which are used for connecting all kinds of stuff to your computer, from mice to printers. (A USB port looks like a small, narrow, rectangular hole.)

If your cable or DSL modem installer reports that your computer doesn't have the network card or USB port that's needed to connect your high-speed modem, don't panic. If the installer can't provide the needed adapter, contact a local computer store about adding a network card or USB adapter — neither one should cost more than $20.

Cable connections

A *cable Internet account* uses the same cable that brings 250 brain-numbing TV stations into your home. To sign up for an account, you call the cable company to open an account. Unless you decide to install it yourself (which isn't all that hard), a technician comes and installs a network connection doozus (technical term) where your TV cable comes into your house, installs a network card in your computer if it doesn't already have one, brings a special modem (which can look like a laptop computer with a spike hairdo), and hooks them together. Magic.

If you have cable television, the cable is split, and one segment goes to your computer. If you don't have cable television, the cable company may have to install the actual cable before it can wire up your computer. When the technician goes away, however, you have a permanent, high-speed connection to the Internet (as long as you pay your bill, about $40 to $50 a month). It may be cheaper if you also get their TV channels as well. In addition to the high speed and constant access at a fixed price, you aren't tying up a phone line.

Cable access comes in two forms: the older one-way and the newer two-way. With one-way cable, incoming data comes from the Net to your PC at high speed via the cable, but outgoing data still uses a modem and a phone line. With two-way cable, everything goes over the cable. One-way has nearly disappeared, but check with your cable company to find out for sure which kind it offers.

Connecting with DSL

Phone companies have a broadband type of connection, too: *DSL* (digital subscriber line). DSL service is supposed to use your existing phone line and in-house wiring. But DSL often works better if the phone company runs a new wire from outside your building to where you use your computer. (Phone companies call this a *home run.*) For most kinds of DSL to work, you have to live within a couple of miles of your telephone central office, so DSL is unavailable in many rural areas.

DSL is available at different speeds. The higher speeds cost more (surprise, surprise!). The lowest speed (usually 640Kbps) is fast enough for most users.

If DSL service is available in your area, you call either your phone company or an ISP that will arrange for DSL service. Either they ship you the equipment to install yourself, or a phone installer comes with a network connection box (a glorified modem) that you or the installer hook up to your computer. DSL modems connect to a network card (which you may need to add to your computer) or to a USB port (which most new computers already have).

Who's on first?

Your phone company may soon offer video on your DSL, and your cable company may offer local phone service via your cable modem. Confusing, isn't it? DSL was originally supposed to provide *video on demand* (that is, almost any movie or TV show whenever you want it); but when customers demand video, they tend to meet that demand by turning on HBO or running down to the video rental store. DSL has now been reborn as yet another high-speed Internet gateway, but the video capability is still in there.

A hidden cost in getting either cable or DSL Internet access is having to take a day off from work to wait for the installers unless you feel brave enough to install them yourself. Sometimes it takes them two trips to get things working. Try to get the first appointment in the morning. Also, the cable company or phone company is usually also your ISP unless you pay extra, so you don't have a choice of ISPs. In theory, the phone company provides DSL access on equal terms to all ISPs, but in practice, its own ISP somehow always seems to be more equal than the others.

If you're a student

Most colleges and universities provide some type of Internet access for their students: Which type of access varies a great deal. In some cases, it's just a few terminals in a lab somewhere on campus. (If that describes your school, transfer!) Others have high-speed Internet service far superior to what you get from most ISPs, often with direct Internet access in every dorm room.

In all cases, Internet access is inexpensive or free: If you're a student or otherwise affiliated with a college or university, check out what's available on campus before you look elsewhere. In some areas, becoming a student is cheaper than paying for long-distance Internet access.

Some institutions even let alumni use their systems; if you live close to your alma mater, it's worth seeing whether it has some sort of alumni access.

A few lines about Linux

Linux is a free UNIX-style operating system that runs on PCs. Because most servers on the Internet run UNIX, most server software also runs on Linux or can be easily adapted for it by someone with a little programming experience. Although the process of getting Linux installed can be a pain, if you find yourself wanting to put your computer on the Net many hours a day or to test out a set of interrelated Web pages and scripts you have written, Linux is the system to use. By using advanced system-software techniques known since about 1961 (but not yet fully implemented in Windows — even in Windows XP and 2000), Linux protects running programs from each other so that if one program crashes, it almost never takes the system with it. Nobody thinks it at all unusual when Linux systems run continuously for a month or more without having to be restarted.

Although Linux is not as easy to set up as Windows, it's considerably cheaper and much more reliable for use as a server. Check out *Linux For Dummies*, 4th Edition, by Dee-Ann LeBlanc (published by Wiley Publishing, Inc.) for details.

ISDN and other four-letter words

In the early 1980s, AT&T developed what was supposed to be the next generation of telephones, called *ISDN,* alleged to be short for *I Still Don't Know* or *Improvements Subscribers Don't Need.* ISDN uses regular phone wires (which is important because phone companies have about 100 million of them installed) and puts boxes at each end that transmit *digital* data rather than the older *analog* data. In this arrangement, an ISDN line can transmit 128K bits per second, a considerable improvement over the 56K that a regular phone line and modem permits, although far slower than cable or DSL.

Unfortunately, phone companies utterly botched the way they made ISDN available in North America. Installing ISDN is fantastically complicated, so much so that we know full-time telecommunications managers who have been unable to find anyone at their phone company who knows how to install it. Also, ISDN is overpriced: In New York, for example, an ISDN line costs about twice as much as a regular line, and every call you make, even a local call, costs extra. Unless your local ISP arranges the details of an ISDN connection for you and knows the incantations to mutter at the phone company to make the per-call charges go away (phrases such as *multilocation Centrex*), we don't think that ISDN is worth the bother. If you can get DSL, don't even think about getting ISDN. In many parts of Europe, phone companies offer ISDN rather than DSL — if you live there, go for whichever is available in your area.

Picking an ISP

If you have decided to get a cable or DSL account, you don't have many other choices: You sign up with your cable or phone company or one of a handful of ISPs who have deals with them. If you have chosen AOL or MSN, get their sign-up software and install it. But if you decide to sign up for a dialup Internet account, you have to choose an ISP. Your choice is complicated because you have several thousand ISPs from which to choose. If you have access to the Internet through a friend or your library, you can find many on our Web site, at

`net.gurus.com/isp`

A few national ISPs are available, such as Earthlink and AT&T WorldNet. National ISPs have lots of dial-in numbers across the country, which can be handy if you travel, and usually (but sadly, not always) have an extensive support staff to help you. Their price is usually in the range of $20 per month.

You can usually get a better deal from a regional or local ISP. They tend to compete in pricing more than the national ones do and, in many cases, because they stick to one geographic area, they also offer community-oriented online materials. When you're doing your comparison shopping, consider these factors:

- **Price:** Ask about unlimited pricing, or at least pricing for 100 hours, if you plan to use the Net frequently, or lower pricing for a limited number of hours.
- **Access numbers:** Ask what phone numbers your computer can call to connect, and make sure that at least one of them is a local call from your home or office.
- **Support:** Call and talk to members of the support staff before you sign up. We think that good support means support that's available outside of just 9 to 5, not being put on hold for long periods, and, most important, support people who don't think that your questions are stupid and can actually answer them. (You can't take this for granted.)
- **Load:** What is response time like at peak times, and do you get busy signals when you call?
- **Modem speed:** It does you no good to have a fast modem if your provider's modem speed can't match it. Even if your modem and their modem can both run at 56K, if the phone company doesn't provide a clean connection from you to them, you may find you can only connect at 28K.

How to find a local ISP

The most important consideration when choosing an ISP is whether it has a phone number that is a local call from where you are. The cost of the phone call to your ISP is crucial because calls to online systems tend to be long ones. You need an ISP that has a phone number that's a local call for you.

Although a few ISPs have toll-free numbers, their hourly rates have to be high enough to cover the cost of the call. Dialing direct and paying for the call yourself is almost invariably cheaper than calling a toll-free access number; someone has to pay for the call, and that someone is you. Some local providers have local numbers for day-to-day use and a more expensive toll-free number to use while traveling, or belong to a network called iPass that lets you use other ISPs' dial-in numbers when you're out of town.

Here are the best ways we know to find an ISP close to home:

- Check the business pages of your local newspaper for advertisements from local ISPs.
- Ask your public library's research librarian or online services staff.
- Look in your local yellow pages under Internet Services. Use a friend's Internet account or a trial account from an online service to access the World Wide Web. Check our Web page about ISPs (at `net.gurus.com/isp`) for Web sites that list ISPs by state, area code, or country.
- Ask anyone you know in your area who already has access what she's using and whether she likes it.

Signing up

ISPs list two numbers: a voice number and a modem number. We think that it's useful, if you're new at this stuff (some of us are new at it for *years* — don't take it personally) to call and talk to the human beings on the other end of the voice line to get their helpful guidance. Talking to a person enables you to ask the questions you have and, in many cases, goes a long way toward calming the trepidation that often accompanies this step. For an ISP account, talk to your ISP about which software it provides or expects you to have. If you don't get understandable answers or the person you're talking to sounds like he has better things to do than answer customer questions, look for a different ISP.

Most ISPs now have sign-up programs that come on a CD-ROM or preinstalled on your computer. Windows 98 and Me come with sign-up software for AOL and a few national ISPs (choose Start⇨Programs⇨Online Services from the taskbar). Windows XP comes with a New Connection Wizard that can show you a list of ISPs. Some local ISPs provide a CD full of signup software, but if you have Windows XP, even without a CD, the Network Connection Wizard makes setup relatively painless.

Signing up for an account with an ISP generally involves providing your name, address, and telephone number along with billing information, which almost invariably includes a credit card number. Access is often granted immediately, or the service may call you on the phone to verify that you are who you said you were. If you don't use credit cards, call the ISP and find out whether you can pay your account by check.

Fire at the wall

Lots of PCs in big companies are loaded up with Internet software and have network connections with a hookup to the Internet, so if you're so blessed, you can run programs on your computer and hook right up to the Net. Right? Not quite.

If you're in a large organization that has (not altogether unreasonable) concerns about confidential company secrets leaking out by way of the Internet, a *firewall* system placed between the company network and the outside world may limit outside access to the internal network.

All traffic between the organization's internal network and the Internet must go through the firewall. Special programming on the firewall limits which type of connections can be made between the inside and outside and who can make them.

In practice, you can use any Internet service that is available within the company; for outside services, however, you're limited to what can pass through the firewall system. Most standard outside services — such as logging in to remote computers, copying files from one computer to another, and sending and receiving e-mail — should be available, although the procedures, involving something called a *proxy server,* may be somewhat more complicated than what's described in this book.

Often, you have to log on to the firewall system first and from there get to the outside. It's usually impossible for anyone outside the company to get access to systems or services on the inside network (that's what the firewall is for). Except for the most paranoid of organizations, e-mail flows unimpeded in both directions.

Keep in mind that you probably have to get authorization to use the firewall system before you can use *any* outside service other than e-mail.

If you have a cable or DSL connection shared among several computers, you should have a firewall for your own network, too, to keep out nosy bad guys. Fortunately, it's not hard to set up. Windows XP comes with a built-in firewall.

Some phone numbers

Here are the voice phone numbers and Web sites for some of the U.S. national ISPs and online services we have listed in this chapter.

- America Online: 800-827-6364, or www.aol.com
- AT&T WorldNet Service: 800-967-5363, or www.att.net
- AT&T Global (formerly IBM) Network Services: 877-485-1500, or www.att.com/business
- MSN Internet Access: 800-FREE-MSN (the CD with software is free, not the account), or www.msn.com

In Canada, try these ISPs:

- AOL Canada: 888-265-6303, or www.aol.ca
- AT&T WorldNet Service: 888-655-7671, or www.attcanada.ca
- AT&T Global Canada: 800-821-4612, or www.attglobal.net
- Sympatico: 310-SURF in Ontario and Québec, or 800-773-2121 elsewhere in Canada, or www.sympatico.ca

Back to Software

The type of Internet account you have is intimately related to the type of software you need.

- **Online services:** All online services (such as America Online and CompuServe) give you program disks with software that works with their particular systems. Chapter 5 tells you how to get and install the software required to access AOL, the most popular online service, and Chapter 17 tells how to use it.
- **ISP accounts:** If you use an ISP with a dialup account, you need dialup software. You also need programs for the various types of information you want to use over the Internet: an e-mail program for sending and receiving e-mail, a Web browser for looking at Web pages, and other programs. Luckily, almost all computers come with all the programs you need already installed. Chapter 5 tells you how to get and install any programs you need, with sections on Windows and Macs.
- **High-speed accounts:** To connect to an ISDN account, you use the same programs used for other dialup accounts (see Chapter 5). For a DSL account, you use the kind of network software you'd use to connect to a LAN; ask your phone company for help. Cable accounts work with LAN connection software, too, although many cable Internet accounts and some DSL accounts come with their own software.

Chapter 5

Online and On Your Way

In This Chapter

- Getting ready to connect to the Internet
- Dialing into the Internet (like, over the phone)
- Faster options: DSL and cable
- Connecting from a Mac
- AOL's own connection software

Chapter 4 explains the types of accounts that can connect your computer to the Internet. This chapter reveals what you actually have to do to make that connection happen, whether you choose a dialup Internet account, a digital subscriber line (DSL; high-speed phone line) account, a cable Internet account, or America Online.

Your Computer Needs Software to Get Connected

Whichever way you connect to your Internet account, your computer technically becomes part of the Internet. If you connect to an America Online (AOL) or CompuServe account, you're not really on the Internet; instead, you connect to AOL's computers, which in turn connect to the Internet.

If you're fortunate enough to live in an area that provides cable or DSL access to the Internet, and you can afford it, you may be able to skip this chapter altogether. (Apart from the cost of the high-speed modem itself and the installation, which providers waive half the time, the price of DSL or cable compares favorably with a second phone line and dialup access.) Heck, skipping this chapter may be worth the price of a cable modem. DSL and cable providers often come right to your home and do all the setup for you. In some areas, combinations of phone service, cable TV, and Internet access are packaged together to coax you into spending all your dollars with one company. If you think you're likely to take this route, find out what's offered in your area before you slog through the next bunch of pages. If you choose this kind of access and want to know more, we discuss cable and DSL access further below. However, one can often leave all this nasty technical stuff to the nice folks doing the installation and move on to the fun stuff without so much as a grimace.

Getting the programs you need

Many Internet service providers (ISPs) give you a CD full of programs when you sign up for your account, although this is getting less common because most users have Windows PCs or Macs that already have all the software you need to start. The CD usually contains connection software and client programs, a larger selection than what comes with your PC. Be sure to tell your ISP what kind of computer you use (Windows or Mac, and which version), so you get the right CD. (Not all ISPs support Mac OS users and even fewer give a sideways glance to Linux users.) If you use AOL, you have to use either one of the hundreds of AOL CDs you've probably received in the mail and are now using for drink coasters or download the AOL connection program.

To use an Internet or AOL account, you need various programs:

- **A program to get you connected to the account:** The technical term for this type of program is a *TCP/IP stack,* although normal mortal human beings usually call it something like an *Internet connection program.* Versions of Windows since Windows 95 come with one, called Dial-Up Networking. Windows 3.1 users have to get an Internet dialer from somewhere. (See the sidebar, "Are Windows 3.1 users out of luck?") Macintoshes have the basic TCP/IP stuff, called MacTCP, built in as of System 7, and Open Transport for Mac OS 8.x and 9.x. Mac OS X is based on Unix and uses the Unix TCP/IP stack. (See "Connecting for Mac Users" later in this chapter.) Linux comes with a connection program called ppp. If you use AOL, you have to use AOL's own connection program instead.
- **Programs to use various Internet services:** These programs give you access to e-mail, the Web, and other information after you are connected to the Internet. They're known as *client programs* because they're part of a two-part strategy: The client programs that run on your computer get information from the *server programs* that run on your ISP's computer and other Internet host computers. You need an e-mail program to read and send e-mail and a Web browser to surf the Web. Some programs, like Netscape, do both.

If you're starting with a brand new computer (PC or Mac), chances are you have everything you need to get started. If not, your ISP will give you what you need or tell you where to find it — it's their job.

Are Windows 3.1 users out of luck?

Windows 3.1 didn't come with an Internet connection program. Ten (yes, ten!) years ago, the Internet wasn't widely used, and few systems included Internet software. If you use Windows 3.1, we think your best bet is to upgrade to Windows 98, but if you can't, ask your ISP whether it still has a diskette or CD with a 3.1 connection program, e-mail program, and Web browser. AOL has a Windows 3.1 version of its program, too. For more details, check out our Web site about Windows 3.1 and the Internet, at

`net.gurus.com/win31`

Cool programs you can use

Here are some famous Internet client programs available for Windows and Macs:

- **Netscape, Internet Explorer, and Opera:** The two rivals for World's Best Web Browser and a dark horse candidate. (Chapters 6 and 7 tell you how to use them.)
- **RealAudio and Shockwave:** You have to be running Netscape or Internet Explorer to use these and lots of other cool plug-in programs for Netscape and Internet Explorer (see Chapter 6).
- **Eudora, Pegasus, Netscape Mail, and Outlook Express:** Eudora and Pegasus remain our favorite e-mail programs. Netscape Mail and Outlook Express are other good e-mail programs that share the advantage of being free. (Chapters 10 and 11 describe how to use them.) AOL users, take note: The only e-mail programs that work with AOL are Netscape Mail (because AOL owns Netscape) and the similar AOL Communicator. Otherwise, you're stuck with AOL's lousy, built-in e-mail program.
- **Free Agent (for Windows) and Newswatcher MT (for the Mac):** These programs are great for reading Usenet newsgroups, which are online discussions on a wealth of topics. See our Web site for an introduction to newsgroups:

  `net.gurus.com/usenet`
- **mIRC (for Windows) and Ircle (for the Mac):** These programs let you participate in Internet Relay Chat (IRC) for online, real-time, flying purple conversations with lots of people at the same time. See Chapter 15 for some background about online chatting. Read our Web site for the details of using IRC:

  `net.gurus.com/irc`

Where does all this software come from?

Here's where to look for the Internet connection program that connects your computer to the Internet and the e-mail and Web programs you'll want to use:

- **Your operating system may supply them.** All versions of Windows since Windows 95 already have all the software you need to connect to an Internet account, along with e-mail and Web programs. Recent versions of Mac OS have them, too.
- **Your ISP may offer them on a disk.** If your ISP gives you software, use it. That way, when you call for help, your ISP knows what to do (you hope!). Note that the software your ISP gives you may be shareware — which means that if you use it, you're honor-bound to send a donation to the author (and you'll feel really noble when you do it, too).
- **You can get someone to download them from the Internet for you.** A few services, notably AOL and AT&T Global, have special access programs that can be downloaded from the Net if you don't want to wait for a CD. If you have a friend who already has an Internet account, your friend can download the program from the ISP's Web site for you. The problem with this method is that programs have gotten way too large to fit onto diskettes, so your friend needs a CD burner, or you both need a Zip, Jaz, or some other large removable disk drive.

Read the rest of this chapter to find out exactly which programs you may need, depending on which type of computer system you use (Windows or Mac).

The Big Picture

Whether you use a dialup account, DSL account, cable modem, or AOL, your computer needs to be configured to know about the account so it can use it for Internet services like the Web and e-mail.

For cable modem and DSL users, if your setup requires a visit from an installer, he or she can usually set your computer up as well. When your installer leaves, you should be logged onto your account with no need to log off, ready to surf, e-mail and chat, and definitely ready to skip the rest of this chapter. On the other hand, as often as not, they just ship you a box that you plug into your phone line or cable hookup.

Getting hooked up

Here are the general steps for getting your PC on the Internet:

1. **Arrange for an Internet account from an ISP with a local access phone number (for dialup accounts), with DSL phone lines in your area (for DSL), or that provides your town with cable TV (for a cable Internet account).**

   In Chapter 4, we give you ideas about how to choose an ISP. If you plan to use AOL, skip this step.

2. **Connect your computer to your modem or phone line.**

   If you sign up for a dialup Internet account, you just connect your PC's modem to your phone line as if it were another phone extension. With DSL or cable Internet accounts, arrange for an installer to come or follow the instructions that come with your DSL or cable modem.

3. **Get the basic Internet connection software loaded into your computer somehow, either from a disc or over the phone.**

   For dialup accounts, many ISPs mail you a CD full of programs. Recent Windows and Mac machines come with Internet connection software and client programs for e-mail and the Web, so you shouldn't need any additional software, but some ISPs prefer to provide their own programs anyway. For AOL accounts, you can use one of the zillion AOL software CDs you've probably received in the mail.

   If you have a dialup account, read the "Connecting to Dialup Accounts" section later in this chapter about dialup Internet connection software for Windows and Macs. If you choose a high-speed account, see the section "Connecting to DSL and Cable Accounts" later in this chapter.

A home for your programs

Before you begin filling your computer's disk with network software, make a folder in which to put them. You can use this folder for the programs that you download in this chapter in addition to useful little programs that you find on the Net.

- In Windows (95 or later), run My Computer or Windows Explorer, move to the Program Files folder, and choose File⇨New⇨Folder from the menu.
- On a Macintosh, choose File⇨New Folder.

We recommend calling the directory *Temp* (because it's a temporary place to put downloaded files), but you can use any name that you can remember.

4. **Crank up your Internet connection program and fiddle with it until it works.**

   Miracles have been known to happen, and sometimes Internet connection programs work the first time. If yours doesn't, call and ask your ISP to help you. Having only one phone line and having to hang up to call your provider may be difficult and frustrating — another advantage of high-speed access is that it doesn't tie up your regular phone line. We can only sympathize and tell you this part is the *worst* — after your connection is set up, the fun begins.

Sign in, please

Hundreds of millions of people are on the Internet. Because only one of them is you, it would be nice if the rest of them couldn't go snooping through your files and e-mail messages. No matter which type of Internet account you have, you use a security procedure to prove that you are who you say you are.

Your ISP gives each user an account, kind of like a bank account. The account has your user name and a secret password associated with it.

Your *user name* (or *user ID, login, logon name,* or *screen name*) is unique among all the names assigned to your provider's users. It's also your e-mail address, so don't pick a name like *snickerdoodle* unless that's what you want to tell your friends and put on your business cards.

Your password is secret and is the main thing that keeps bad guys from borrowing an account. Don't use a real word or a name. A good way to make up a password is to invent a somewhat memorable phrase and turn each word in the phrase into a single letter or digit. "Computers cost too much money for me" turns into `Cc2m$4m`, for example. *Never tell anyone else your password.* Particularly don't tell people who claim to be from your ISP; they're not.

To connect to a dialup Internet account after you've signed up, you run the connection program that works with your account (later sections of this chapter contain instructions for each version of Windows, for Macs, and for AOL). Before you can use the account, you must sign in, or *log on.* Most DSL and cable Internet accounts are connected all the time, so you don't need to sign in with your user name and password each time. (No more waiting for the modem to dial and connect!) Dialup users can configure Windows and Macs to log in automatically, too.

How to get off the Internet

If you dial in to the Internet (or AOL), you'll eventually want to disconnect (hang up). You don't have to log off, in most cases, but you do need to hang up the phone.

You may have a bunch of programs running while you use the Internet, including your Web browser and your e-mail program. Only one of these programs, however, is the program that connects you to the Internet. That's the one you have to talk to when you're disconnecting from the Internet. In Windows, you disconnect using the Dial-Up Networking or Dial-Up Connection program, which is usually a little icon at the bottom of the screen with two flickering boxes.

Connecting to Dialup Accounts

Internet accounts are easy to use, but they can be tricky to set up. In fact, connecting for the first time can be the most difficult part of your Internet experience. Installing and setting up Internet connection software used to require you to type lots of scary-looking numeric Internet addresses, host names, communications ports — you name it.

But breathe easy — Windows XP comes with the New Connection Wizard, which steps you quickly through the process with only a few questions. If you use an earlier version of Windows, many ISPs give you a good, automated signup program that doesn't ask for arcane technical information.

Make sure that your ISP is helpful and available or choose another ISP. If you can bribe or coerce a friend or relative into helping you, do so. (***Hint:*** Look for someone roughly between the ages of 12 and 16, who can be very knowledgeable, after you get past your humiliation. Chocolate chip cookies always help.)

Because each ISP is just a tad different from the next, we can't go into exact step-by-step directions for everyone. We give the usual steps, help you understand the terms, and coax you through the whole process of setting up your Internet account and connection program. If you find this process totally impossible and have no one you can press into service or just don't like the thought of doing it, don't despair.

Names and numbers

Most new Internet accounts use two cool features that configure your Internet connection for you each time you connect. You used to have to specify a long *IP address* (numeric Internet Protocol address) for your computer, but now ISPs issue your computer an IP address automatically and invisibly when you make the connection. Similarly, you used to have to specify the IP addresses of one or more of your ISP's server computers; now, the connection software takes care of this. Whew!

If you have an older version of Windows, your Internet connection program may uses a bunch of scary-looking technical information to connect to your account. Although in theory you should never need any of this information after your account is set up, we find that having the information on hand is useful, particularly if you have to call your ISP for help. Feel free to write it all down in Table 5-1 (except for your password — just store that one in your head).

Table 5-1 Information about Your Dialup Internet Account

Your Information	*Description*	*Example*
Domain name ______________	The name of your ISP's domain. It's the last part of your Internet address and usually ends with `.net` or `.com` (in the United States, anyway).	`gurus.com`
Phone number ______________	(Dialup only) The number you call to connect to your ISP, exactly as you would dial it by hand, including **1** and the area code, if needed. If you have to dial 9 and pause a few seconds to get an outside line, include **9,** at the beginning. (Each comma tells your modem to pause for two seconds, so stick in extra commas as necessary to get the timing right.) Many modems have speakers so that you can hear them dialing. The noise isuseful when you're trying to figure out whether you have succeeded in getting an outside line when you dial out.	1-340-555-1234
Username ______________	The name on your account with your ISP, also called a *logon name.*	`myoung`
User password ______________	The password for your account. (But don't write it down here!)	`3friedRice`

Make sure that your phone line doesn't have call waiting. If it does, you (or your Internet connection program) have to type ***70** or **1170** at the beginning of your provider's phone number to tell your phone company to turn off call waiting for this phone call; otherwise, an incoming phone call will disturb your Internet connection. Most connection software has this ability built in. Just look for a Call Waiting option or one that use the deactivation number for your phone system.

Connecting for Windows XP users

Windows XP is the latest, greatest version of Windows and replaces all previous versions. It comes with an Internet dialup connection program along with a New Connection Wizard for setting up your computer to use your Internet account. It also comes with Outlook Express for e-mail and Internet Explorer for Web browsing.

Telling Windows about your account

To set up Windows XP to use an existing Internet account, double-click the Connect to the Internet icon on your desktop. If you don't see it, click the Start button and choose All Programs➪Accessories➪Communications➪New Connection Wizard. Click Next on its opening screen to see a window that looks like Figure 5-1.

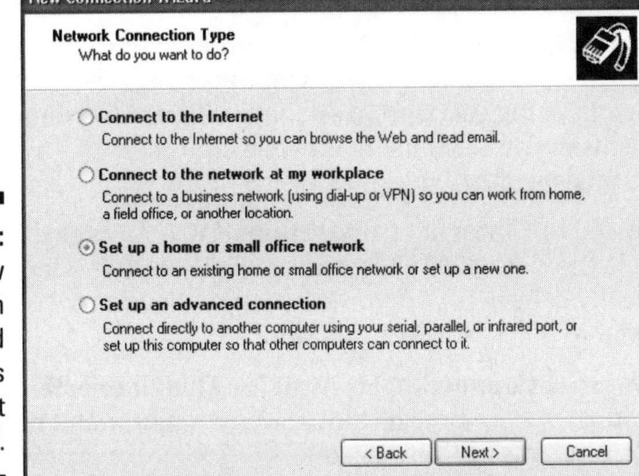

Figure 5-1: The New Connection Wizard helps you get connected.

Click Connect to the Internet and click Next.

If you don't have an Internet account yet, you can click the top button on the screen that appears (Choose from a List of Internet Service Providers) and click Next. Your PC dials the Microsoft Internet Referral Service (a toll-free call in the U.S.) to display a list of ISPs near you. The list is usually pretty short because it includes only big ISPs that have paid Microsoft enough to be included in the service. There may be terrific local ISPs you can use instead. Another problem is that the ISPs listed may not be a local call for you (especially if you live in the boondocks), so you may be in for some big phone bills. If you do choose an ISP from Microsoft's list, you can sign up on the spot — just check with your phone company to make sure that the phone number they give you is really a local call.

Skip Microsoft's referral service and do your own shopping. See Chapter 4 for how to choose an ISP and sign up for an account.

If you already have an Internet account, you can click the middle button (Set Up My Connection Manually) and then click Next. Setting up your account manually isn't as scary as it sounds; it mostly means that you have to type in the ISP's name and phone number and your logon and password yourself. (Wow, makes our fingers hurt just to think about it! Not.) The wizard asks how you connect to the Internet (over a regular, dialup phone line; a DSL or cable Internet connection that requires a password; or a DSL or cable Internet connection that doesn't require a password), your ISP's name, the phone number to dial, your user name, and your password.

The wizard also offers three check boxes that you can select. (They are usually selected for you, but you can click them to remove the check mark.)

- **Use This Account Name and Password When Anyone Connects to the Internet from This Computer:** If your Windows computer is set up for multiple users, choosing this option enables all users to connect with this account. Unless you have users on your computer that you severely distrust, leave this selected.
- **Make This the Default Internet Connection:** If you have several Internet accounts, one is the default (that is, the connection that Windows uses unless you specify otherwise). If you have only one Internet account, like most normal non-geeks, leave this selected, too.
- **Turn on the Internet Connection Firewall for This Connection:** A firewall discourages bad guys from breaking into your computer and reading your files. Definitely leave this option selected!

When you click Next and then Finish, the New Connection Wizard creates a dialup connection for your account, and configures Windows to dial that number automagically whenever you try to browse the Web or send or receive e-mail.

Tweaking your account information

To take a look at your settings, choose Start➪Control Panel➪Network and Internet Settings and then click Set Up or Change Your Internet Connection. You see the Connections tab of the Internet Properties dialog box (shown in Figure 5-2) with your Internet account and other settings.

Figure 5-2: You can use the Internet Properties dialog box to create or change dialup connections.

You can see all your network connections (Internet as well as local area network) by choosing Start➪Control Panel➪Network and Internet Connections ➪Network Connections. (If you use the "Classic" Control Panel, choose Start➪Control Panel➪Network Connections.) The dialup connection that the New Connection Wizard created for you appears in the dialup section. If you need to change your account settings (for example, if your ISP tells you that the access phone number has changed), right-click the icon for your Internet account, choose Properties from the menu that appears, and make your changes.

In the Windows XP Properties dialog box for your Internet account, click the Advanced tab and look for the Internet Connection Firewall section. If it's not already selected, mark the check box to turn on Internet Connection Firewall to protect your computers from hackers.

Signing on and off

To connect to the Internet, run your browser and request a Web page, or run your e-mail program and tell it to check your mail. When Windows sees you requesting information from the Internet, it dials the phone for you. If you see a dialog box asking for your user name and password, type them in and click Connect.

You can tell when you are connected because a two-computer-screen icon appears in the lower-right corner of the screen (just to the left of the digital clock). Double-click this icon to check the speed of your Internet connection or click the Disconnect button on the dialog box that appears to hang up.

Connecting for Windows Me, 2000, and 98 users

Windows 98 comes in two flavors: Original and Second Edition. Windows Me should have been Windows 98 Third Edition because it's not that different. Windows 2000 is the business-oriented version of Windows (based on Windows NT). These versions of Windows come with an Internet connection program called Dial-Up Networking. They also come with automated signup programs for several ISPs (usually AT&T WorldNet and Microsoft Network in the United States, anyway — in other countries, other services appear) and AOL.

Telling Windows about your account

To sign up for an account or to use an existing account with one of these services, click the Start button on the taskbar, choose Programs⇨Online Services, and then choose the service. An MSN signup icon may also appear on your desktop.

If you want to use an account other than the ones with automated signup programs (and the service didn't send you an automated sign-up CD), you can run the Internet Connection Wizard to configure Dial-Up Networking to work with your account. Run the wizard by clicking the Connect to the Internet button on your Windows desktop, if there is one, or by choosing Start⇨Programs⇨Accessories⇨Communications⇨Internet Connection Wizard or Start⇨Programs⇨Internet Explorer⇨Connection Wizard, which is similar to the version that comes with Windows XP but with only three buttons.

If you have no account set up and want Windows to look for an ISP in your area, click the top "new account" button. If you've already arranged for an account, click the middle "transfer my existing Internet account" button whether or not you've set it up on another computer before. If you tried the middle "transfer" button and your ISP is not in the list that Microsoft suggests, which is quite likely if you're using a local ISP, click the bottom "set up manually" or "do nothing" button.

We recommend using the bottom "set up manually" button and typing your ISP information in yourself — it's not hard. All you usually have to know is your ISP's access number (the phone number your computer calls to connect), your user name, and your password. We think you're better off choosing your ISP yourself than turning over the choice to Microsoft.

When you're done, you have an icon for your ISP in your Dial-Up Networking folder. To see it in Windows 98, open the My Computer folder on the desktop and open the Dial-Up Networking folder. In Windows Me, choose Start⇨Settings⇨Dial-Up Networking. In Windows 2000, choose Start⇨Settings⇨Network⇨Dial-Up Connections.

Tweaking your account information

To change the settings for your ISP, right-click its icon in the Dial-Up Networking window and choose Properties from the menu that appears.

You can tell Windows to dial your Internet account automatically when your Web browser or e-mail program needs to connect to the Internet. This setting is in the Internet Properties dialog box (which may appear as the Internet Options dialog box — don't ask us why!). Choose Start⇨Settings⇨Control Panel, double-click the Internet Options icon, and click the Connections tab along the top. Choose the Internet account to use (if you have more than one), and then click Always Dial My Default Connection (as shown in Figure 5-3).

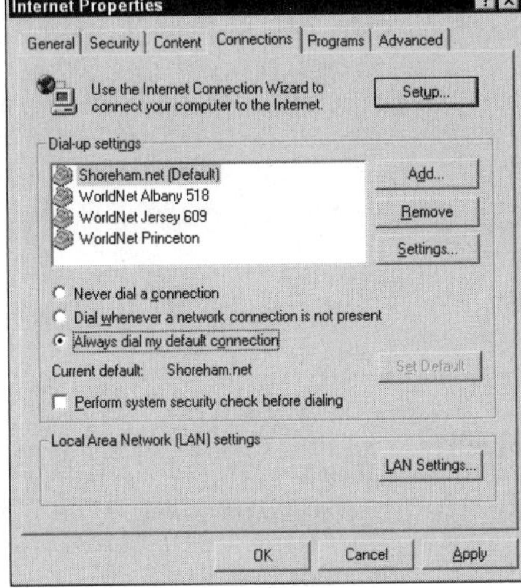

Figure 5-3: Telling Windows to dial your Internet account whenever you start browsing or fetching e-mail.

If you dial your ISP yourself rather than letting Windows dial it when you run your browser or e-mail program, you may want to make the connection icon more convenient. Drag the ISP's icon from the Dial-Up Networking folder to the desktop, and Windows creates a shortcut on your Windows desktop. You can add your Internet connection program to your Start menu: Right-click the Start button and choose Open to display the Start Menu items in a window. Drag your ISP's icon from the Dial-Up Connection window to the Start Menu window. Way cool!

Signing on and off

To call your account, double-click the icon for your ISP, type the user name and password if they don't already appear, and click the Connect button. When you're connected, the Dial-Up Networking two-flickering-boxes icon appears on the Taskbar to the left of the digital clock. To hang up, double-click the icon and click Disconnect.

Connecting for Windows 95 Users

The good news is that Windows 95 comes with Dial-Up Networking. The bad news is that at least three major subversions of Windows 95 exist, and what they call Dial-Up Networking varies a lot.

Except in the earliest version of Windows 95, you get the Internet Setup Wizard, which helps you configure Dial-Up Networking to work with your account. You may be able to run the Wizard by clicking the Start button and choosing Programs⇨Accessories⇨Internet Tools⇨Internet Setup Wizard. (If you don't see the wizard there, look around your Programs menus for it.) If you can start the wizard at all, it works like the Windows 98 wizard, described in the previous section, although perhaps without some of the options. You can also use the automated signup CDs that you can get from many ISPs.

Later versions of Windows 95 came with Microsoft Internet Explorer 4.0, a Web browser, and Microsoft Exchange, an e-mail program we consider rather confusing. If you have Internet Explorer 3.0, you should download a later version. We also recommend that you download a better e-mail program, such as Eudora, Pegasus, or Outlook Express (the latter comes with Internet Explorer). See Chapter 16 to find out how to download and install programs and Chapter 11 for instructions for using Outlook Express, Eudora, and Pegasus.

Connecting for Mac Users

Newer Macs already have all the software you need to connect to the Internet. (Very old Macs — pre-System 8 — need a Mac TCP/IP modem program, such as FreePPP, which your ISP should be able to give you.) The only things you usually need to set are the ISP's phone number, your account name, and your password.

Connecting to DSL and Cable Accounts

DSL and cable Internet accounts — *broadband accounts* — have a lot in common: They're fast, they don't use a regular phone line, they don't use a dialup modem, and they don't use the same Dial-Up Networking program that dialup accounts use. Some broadband accounts have a permanent connection that works a lot like a connection to a local network in an office. Others require you to log on, just like a dialup connection. The good news about both DSL and cable accounts is that the ISP usually provides most of the equipment — like the modem — and often sends an installer to set it up with your computer. The bad news is that you may have to wait weeks (or months) until the installer arrives, and if you're unlucky, your DSL provider may go out of business first. (Two large DSL providers collapsed while we were writing the previous edition of this book; with luck, the shakeout is over by the time you read this.)

Cable and DSL modems

If you have a cable Internet account, you need a cable modem. Your cable company generally provides the modem as part of the service.

DSL modems are for connecting to high-speed DSL phone lines. Don't buy one yourself — you need to make sure that the modem you use is compatible with your DSL line, so smart Internauts get their DSL modems from the ISP that provides their DSL service.

To connect to a DSL or cable account, you use a DSL or a cable modem. These modems connect to your computer in one of three ways:

- **Network adapter:** A *network adapter* (also called a *LAN adapter* or *Ethernet adapter* or *network interface card*) was originally designed for connecting computers together into networks. If you have more than one computer in your home or office, you can use network adapters to connect the computers together into a *local area network* (*LAN*). Most cable and DSL modems connect to a network adapter using a *RJ-45* plug, which looks like a regular phone jack but a little bigger. If your computer doesn't come with a built-in network adapter, you can buy one for about $20. Desktop computers need PCI card network adapters, which you install by turning off the computer, opening the case, finding an empty slot, sliding the card in, screwing it down, and closing up the computer. Laptops often have the LAN adapter built in or use PC Card network adapters, which look like fat credit cards and just slide into a slot on the side of the laptop. Macs have the LAN adapter built in.

- **USB:** Newer computers come with one or more *USB* (Universal Serial Bus, if you care) connectors, and you can get a DSL or cable modem with a USB connector. Older (pre-1998) computers don't have USB connectors.
- **Internally (DSL only):** Some newer DSL modems include the network card within the modem and install right inside your computer. This combination is call a *PCI DSL modem*, and you or your DSL installer has to open up your computer it install it.

Some newer computers come with DSL modems, and you may think that any DSL modem would work with any DSL account. Unfortunately, you'd be wrong. When you sign up for a DSL account, ask your ISP what kind of DSL modem its system needs if it doesn't provide one for you.

Do-it-yourself DSL

Hooking up your DSL modem shouldn't be so tough. One side plugs into the phone line, the other side into your computer. How hard can that be? Well, there are a few little details.

We'll assume you have a DSL modem that connects to a LAN or USB connector. (Installing an internal DSL modem isn't hugely difficult, but opening up your computer's case is more than we have room to explain in this book. (For information on how to do so, see *Upgrading and Fixing PCs For Dummies,* 6th edition, by Andy Rathbone, by Wiley Publishing, Inc.) If you have a LAN connector, you need a crossover LAN cable that should have come with the DSL modem. (Regular noncrossover cables plug into a router or network hub, not directly from a modem to a computer.) If you're using USB, you should have a USB cable with a flat connector on one end and a squarish connector on the other. Turn off and unplug both your computer and the modem from the wall socket, plug in the LAN or USB cable, and then plug everything back in. The modem also connects to the phone line with a regular phone cord. The phone and LAN jacks on the modem are similar, but the LAN connector is the bigger one.

Now skip ahead to the section "After the installer." And be sure to read the sidebar "Avoiding the DSL buzz".

Avoiding the DSL buzz

One of the clever things about DSL is that the DSL connection shares the same phone wires with your phone. You can tell that this is so because on all the phones on the line with DSL, you will hear a loud buzz of Data Hornets swarming up and down your phone line. (Well, not really, but it sounds like it.)

To get rid of the buzz, you need to install a *DSL filter* (which filters out the buzz) between the phone line and all your phones, but of course not between the phone line and your DSL modem. Filters are available from your DSL ISP, but you can probably find them cheaper at stores like RadioShack. The ideal way to install a filter is to run a separate wire from the box where the phone line enters your house to the DSL modem, and to install one DSL filter in that box into which you plug the wire leading to all the phones. But life is rarely ideal, so most of us install a filter for each phone.

For the phone plug where your DSL modem is connected, you'll want a *splitter* filter with a filtered jack into which you plug a phone (the one you use to call tech support when your computer doesn't work) and an unfiltered jack for the DSL modem. For all the other phones, the filter just plugs into the phone jack, and the phone code plugs into the filter. You can also get wall phone filters that fit between the phone and the wall plate that the phone's mounted on, and baseboard phone jacks with filters built in, for that tidy look.

Do-it-yourself cable modems

Connecting a cable modem is not unlike connecting a DSL modem, except that you connect it to your TV cable rather than to your phone line. If a TV is already attached to the cable, unscrew the cable from the TV and throw the TV away because you'll be having much too much fun with your Internet connection to waste time watching TV. (If you're not yet ready to throw away your TV, move it to another cable outlet, or get a cable splitter available at any store that sells cable accessories.) Screw the cable into the cable modem and plug the LAN or USB cable from the modem to the computer just as we described for a DSL modem in the previous section.

After the installer

The installer (which is you, if you installed the modem yourself) configures your computer to communicate with the Internet. Most DSL and cable modems come with a software CD. If you're using a Mac or a version of Windows older than XP, run the software on the CD to install the necessary stuff to set up your connection.

If you're running Windows XP, you can either use the CD or set up the connection using Windows XP's built-in New Connection Wizard. We recommend the wizard because the CD usually has a pile of software that isn't of much use to you. To set up your connection, choose Start⇨All Programs⇨Accessories⇨Communications⇨New Connection Wizard. (They sure don't make it easy to find.) In the Network Connection Type, tell it you want to connect to the Internet, select Set Up My Connection Manually, and then choose either Connect Using a Broadband Connection That Requires a User Name and Password (if your ISP gave you a user name and password), or Connect Using a Broadband Connection That Is Always On. Either way, enter the required information in the boxes and accept the suggested check boxes, particularly the Internet firewall. Then you should be all set.

After your connection is installed, you should be able to start up a Web browser like Internet Explorer and type the name of a Web site into the address box at the top (try our `net.gurus.com`). The Web page should appear momentarily. If you have a connection with a user name, it may ask you whether to connect. Well, yeah, that's the idea.

After you're connected, you can check the status of your connection. In Windows XP, display the Network Connections box by choosing Start⇨Control Panel⇨Network And Internet Connections⇨Network Connections — broadband connections appear in the LAN or High-Speed Internet section. In Windows 98/Me, display the dialog box by choosing Start⇨Settings⇨Control Panel and double-clicking the Network icon. To change the connection's configuration, right-click it and choose Properties from the menu that appears. Macs use the TCP/IP Control Panel in OS 8 and 9. For OS X, choose System Preferences under the Apple menu and click the Network icon. Then select the TCP/IP tab. Your PC communicates with the Internet using the TCP/IP protocol, and you should see it listed on the Properties dialog box for the connection (in Windows XP) or in the Network dialog box (in earlier versions of Windows). Don't fool with these settings unless you are sure you know what you are doing!

Connecting to America Online

AOL, the world's largest online service, provides access to both the Internet and its own proprietary services. AOL has more than 20 million subscribers worldwide. To use AOL, you use software it provides. (Windows and Mac versions are available.) You can also use other software with your AOL account, such as Netscape Navigator and Microsoft Internet Explorer. Like most ISPs, AOL started as a dialup service and has since added DSL and cable connections.

This chapter describes how to get connected to AOL using version 8.0 of the AOL software. Because AOL updates its software and the graphics that appear in its dialog boxes all the time, your screen may not match exactly the figures in this chapter. See Chapter 17 for how to use AOL for e-mail and browsing the Web.

Note: America Online, despite its name, is available outside America. AOL has access numbers in major Canadian cities and throughout the U.K., at no extra charge, as well as versions for several other countries. Although you can also use AOL from other places, you may pay a steep surcharge.

Signing up for America Online

Ready to sign up? No problem! If you have Windows 98 or Me, choose Start➪Programs➪Online Services➪America Online; otherwise, in the unlikely event that you don't already have a stack of AOL disks or CD-ROMs lying around, call 1-800-827-3338 and ask for a trial membership. Specify whether you want the Windows version, the Mac version, the Windows 3.1 version, or the DOS version. The introductory package has instructions and a disk containing the AOL access program. We describe version 8.0, but if your computer has an earlier version, you'll get the general idea. After you have the introductory package, follow the instructions on its cover to install the program and sign up for an account. You need a credit card to sign up.

When you run the AOL program to sign up for an account, you have to tell it which *screen name* (account name) you want to use. Your screen name can be as long as 16 characters and can contain spaces. You can use a combination of capital and small letters, as in FredAndAlice or ChickensRUs. When AOL asks you to enter your screen name, it checks its list of existing names. If someone is already using that name (which is extremely likely, no matter how unusual your name is), you have to invent another one. By now, the 20 million most obvious names have been taken, so get creative. If the screen name you want is already taken, try adding a number to the end to make it unique. For example, if Net Head is taken (and we're sure that it is), maybe you can be NetHead95065.

Your e-mail address will be your AOL screen name with the spaces squeezed out, plus *@aol.com* on the end. Make sure that your screen name looks okay without the spaces!

When the installation program runs, it needs to figure out how you are going to connect to AOL. It checks your computer for modems or LAN connections and asks you which one you want to use. If you plan to dial into AOL, it connects to a toll-free number to find access phone numbers in your area (as shown in Figure 5-4). Choose the ones closest to you (and check with your phone company to confirm that they are a local call for you to avoid huge long-distance bills).

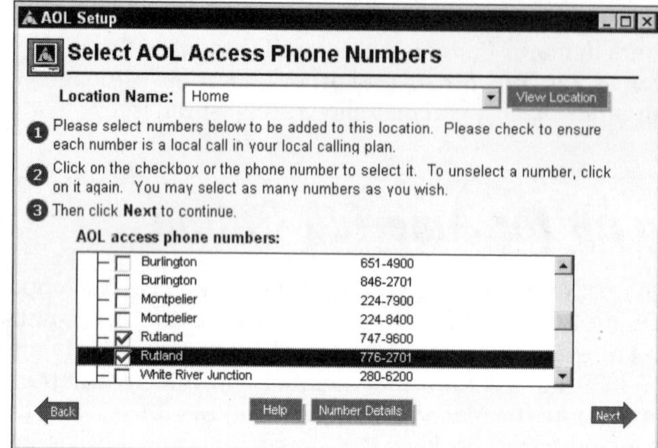

Figure 5-4: America Online finds the closest number to you.

When it finishes, the installation program creates a cute triangular icon named America Online. When you finish, you see the Sign On window in the America Online window. You're ready to boogie!

If you need to change your AOL configuration later (for example, if you get a different modem), click the SETUP button in the AOL Sign On window. To configure AOL to connect using a cable modem, DSL modem, or LAN, click the Expert Setup button in the AOL Setup window. Click Add Location to add a new device, like a cable modem or DSL modem, to the list that appears. If you have trouble installing the AOL software, call AOL at 1-800-827-3338 (in the U.S.).

America is online!

The first time you connect to AOL, set the Select Screen Name box in the Sign On window to either Existing Member (if you already have an AOL account) or New User (to sign up for a new account). Click SIGN ON to connect to AOL and set your computer up for your account.

After AOL knows who you are, you connect your computer to AOL by typing your password in the Enter Password box and clicking SIGN ON. When you are connected, you see the online Welcome window with a list of topics down the left side — click anything that looks interesting.

On the other side of the pond

The ISP situation in the United Kingdom is a little different from the one in the North America. Traditionally, all phone calls in the U.K. have been charged by the minute, even local calls, which can make long online sessions mighty pricey. As a result, there are now three different kinds of ISPs in the U.K.:

- **Traditional:** These ISPs charge a modest monthly fee and provide access via either local numbers or national rate numbers. Unless you are sure you won't spend much time on line, or your ISP provides another service you're using such as Web hosting, these are probably not what you want.
- **Free:** These ISPs charge no monthly fee and support themselves by splitting the per-minute charges with BT (British Telecom). (BT would rather not, but OFTEL, the regulatory agency for the telecom industry in Britain, insists.) If you just want to try out the Net, free ISPs are a good way to start. We don't recommend them for long-term use because the per-minute split is less lucrative than the ISPs hoped, and free ISPs have a disconcerting habit of going out of business on short notice. The tech support also tends to be pretty weak. (It's free — what do you want, your money back?)
- **Flat rate:** These ISPs charge a monthly fee of about £20 but provide an 0800 or other number you can call without per-minute fees. Most users find this the best choice because it makes the bill predictable. The largest flat rate ISPs are AOL (yes, that AOL) and BT. Be warned that even though access is nominally unlimited, if you "camp" on the phone 20 hours a day, your ISP will invoke small print you never noticed and cancel your account.

Depending on where you are and where your ISP is, your phone connection may be anywhere from wonderful to dreadful. If you try one ISP and keep getting slow or unreliable connections, try another.

Now you're connected to AOL. You can click the buttons to read the day's news stories. If e-mail is waiting for you, you can click the You've Got Mail button. For more information about using your AOL account, see Chapter 17.

Don't be surprised if your computer suddenly says, "Welcome!" when you log on to AOL. If you have e-mail, it says, "You've got mail!" Try not to jump right out of your chair when you hear this message.

To disconnect from AOL, choose Sign Off⇨Sign Off from the menu (yes, it's a little redundant). The AOL program hangs up on your connection with the big AOL computer in the sky. Frequently, it insists on downloading some program updates before it quits. Exit the program when you're done.

Sharing Your Internet Connection

We geeks have always had lots of computers at home. John has had a whole computer network at his house for decades. These days, lots of people have more than one computer connected together into a LAN. Because sharing a connection makes the most sense for people with broadband sections, we tell you all about it in Chapter 12, which covers all things broadband.

What's Next?

All recent versions of Windows come with Microsoft Internet Explorer, a reasonably good Web browser. (Chapter 6 explains how to use it.) Windows also comes with an adequate e-mail program called Outlook Express. See Chapter 11 for instructions. You can also use Netscape Navigator, Netscape Mail, Eudora, and other programs — you're not stuck with Microsoft's programs.

Part III
Web Mania

"I'll be right there. Let me just take care of this user. He's about halfway through a 3 hour download."

In this part . . .

No doubt about it, the Web's *the* happenin' place. For many people, the World Wide Web *is* the Internet. We explain what the Web is and how to get around, along with great tips about how to actually find stuff you're looking for among the millions of clamoring Web pages. We also tell you about Web shopping so you can confidently spend your money online, and how to make your own home page so that you can "be on the Web," too.

Chapter 6

Welcome to the Wild, Wonderful, Wacky Web

In This Chapter

- Hyper who?
- Understanding URLs
- Pointing, clicking, browsing, surfing, and other basic skills
- An introduction to Netscape, Mozilla, and Internet Explorer
- Keeping track of your favorite sites
- Filling in Web forms
- Getting plugged in with plug-ins
- Getting rid of pop-ups

People talk about the *Web* today more than they talk about the *Net.* The World Wide Web and the Internet are not the same thing — the World Wide Web (which we call the Web because we're lazy typists) lives "on top of" the Internet. The Internet's network is at the core of the Web, and the Web is like a benevolent parasite that requires the Net for survival.

Okay, enough gross metaphors — so what is it already? The Web is a bunch of "pages" of information connected to each other around the globe. Each page can be a combination of text, pictures, audio clips, video clips, animations, and other stuff. (We're vague about naming the other stuff because they add new types of other stuff every day.) What makes Web pages interesting is that they contain *hyperlinks,* usually called just *links* because the Net already has plenty of hype. Each link points to another Web page, and, when you click a link, your *browser* fetches the page the link connects to. (Stay calm — we talk about browsers in a couple of pages. Your browser is the program that shows you the Web.)

Where did the Web come from?

The World Wide Web was invented in 1989 at the European Particle Physics Lab in Geneva, Switzerland, an unlikely spot for a revolution in computing. The inventor is a British researcher named Tim Berners-Lee, who is now the director of the World Wide Web Consortium (W3C) in Cambridge, Massachusetts, the organization that sets standards and loosely oversees the development of the Web. Tim is terrifically smart and hard working and is the nicest guy you would ever want to meet. (Margy met him through Sunday school — is that wholesome or what?)

Tim invented *HTTP (HyperText Transport Protocol),* the way Web browsers communicate with Web servers; *HTML (HyperText Markup Language),* the language in which Web pages are written; and *URLs (Uniform Resource Locators),* the codes used to identify Web pages and most other information on the Net. He envisioned the Web as a way for everyone to both publish and read information on the Net. Early Web browsers had editors that let you create Web pages almost as easily as you could read them.

For more information about the development of the Web and the work of the World Wide Web Consortium, visit its Web site, at `www.w3.org`. You can also read Tim's book, *Weaving the Web* (HarperSanFrancisco, 1999).

Each page your browser gets for you can have more links that take you to other places. Pages can be linked to other pages anywhere in the world so that after you're on the Web, you can end up looking at pages from Singapore to Calgary, from Sydney to Buenos Aires, all faster than you can say "Bob's your uncle," usually. Give or take network delays, you're only seconds away from any site, anywhere in the world.

This system of interlinked documents is known as *hypertext.* Figure 6-1 shows a Web page (our Web page, in fact.) Each underlined phrase is a link to another Web page. Hypertext, the buzzword that makes the Web go, is one of those simple ideas that turns out to have a much bigger effect than you would think. With a hypertext system, people can create connections among pieces of information that let you go directly to related information. As you draw connections among the pieces of information, you can begin to envision the Web created by the links between the pieces. What's so remarkable about the Web is that it connects pieces of information from all around the *planet,* on different computers and in different databases, all fairly seamlessly (a feat you would be hard pressed to match with a card catalog in a brick-and-mortar library). We sometimes think of the Web as an extremely large but friendly alien centipede made of information.

The other important thing about the Web is that the information in it is searchable. For example, in about ten seconds, you can get a list of Web pages that contain the phrase *domestic poultry,* or your own name, or the name of a book you want to find out about. You can follow links to see each page on the list to find the information you want.

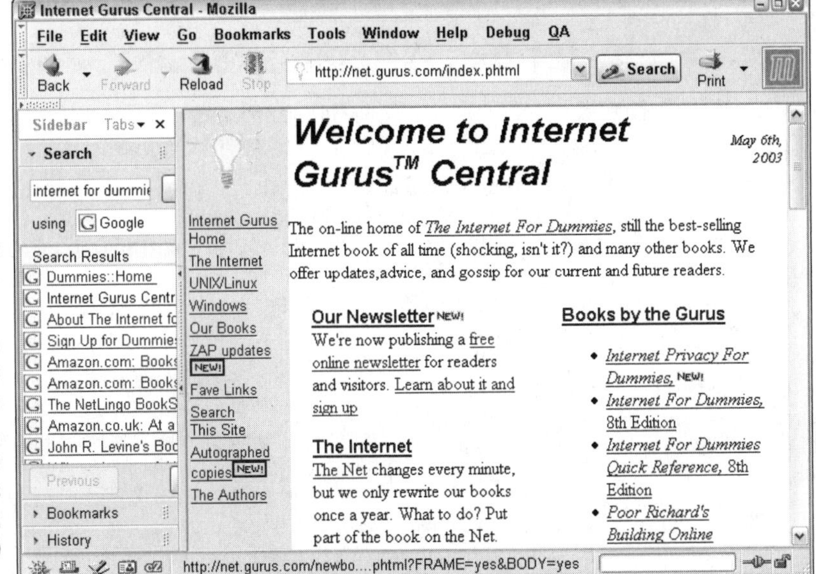

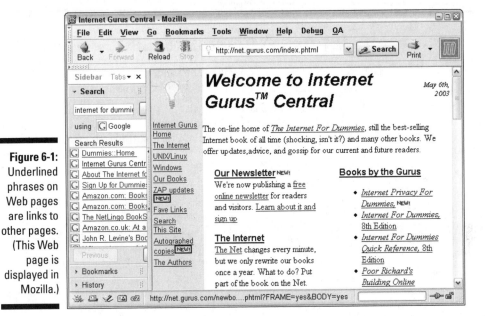

Figure 6-1: Underlined phrases on Web pages are links to other pages. (This Web page is displayed in Mozilla.)

Essentials of hypertext thought

If you can get a handle on the fundamental structure of the Web, you can use it better and think about all the other ways it can be used. *Hypertext* is a way of connecting information in ways that make it easy to find — in theory. Traditional libraries (both the kinds with books and the kinds in computers) organize information in an arbitrary way, such as alphabetical order or the Dewey decimal system. This order reflects nothing about the relationships among different pieces of information; it just reflects the limits of manual indexing. In the world of hypertext, information is organized in relationship to other information. The relationships between different pieces of information are, in fact, often much more valuable than the pieces themselves.

Hypertext can arrange the same set of information in multiple ways at the same time. A book in a conventional library can be on only one shelf at a time; a book about mental health, for example, is shelved under medicine or psychology but not in both places at once. With hypertext, it's no problem to have links to the same document from both medical topics and psychological topics.

Suppose that you're interested in what influenced a particular historical person. Start by looking at her basic biographical information: where and when she was born, the names of her parents, her religion, and other basic stuff like that. Then you can expand on each fact by finding out what else was happening at that time in her part of the world, what was happening in other parts of the world, and what influence her religion may have had on her. You draw a picture by pulling together all these aspects and understanding their connections — a picture that's hard to draw from just lists of names and dates.

Hypertext: A reminiscence

John writes:

The term and concept of hypertext were invented around 1969 by Ted Nelson, a famous computer visionary who has been thinking about the relationship between computers and literature for at least 30 years — starting back when most people would have considered it stupid to think that such a relationship could exist. Twenty years ago, he claimed that people would have computers in their pockets with leatherette cases and racing stripes. (I haven't seen any racing stripes yet, but otherwise he was dead-on.)

Back in 1970, Ted told me that we all would have little computers with inexpensive screens on our desks with superwhizzo graphical hypertext systems. "Naah," I said. "For hypertext, you want a mainframe with gobs of memory and a high-resolution screen." We were both right, of course, because what we have on our desks now are little computers that are faster than 1970s mainframes and that have much more memory and better screens.

Various hypertext projects have come and gone over the years, including one at Brown University (of which Ted was a part) and one at the Stanford Research Institute (which was arguably the most influential project in computing history because it invented screen windows and mice).

Ted's own hypertext system, Project Xanadu, has been in the works for close to 20 years, under a variety of financing and management setups, with many of the same people slogging along and making it work. For a decade, I have been hearing every year that Xanadu, and now a smaller Xanadu Light, which takes advantage of a great deal of existing software, will hit the streets real soon now. Now that the World Wide Web has brought a limited version of hypertext to the masses, Ted and his friends are building a Xanadu system on the Web. Visit `www.xanadu.com` to see what they're up to!

Name That Page

Before you dive in and hit the Web (hmm, that metaphor needs work), you need one more basic concept. Every Web page has a name attached to it so that browsers, and you, can find it. Great figures in the world of software engineering (well, okay, it was Tim) named this name *URL,* or *Uniform Resource Locator.* Every Web page has a URL, a series of characters that begins with `http://` or `www`. (How do you say "URL"? Everyone we know pronounces each letter, *U-R-L* — no one says *earl.*) Now you know enough to go browsing. (For more entirely optional details about URLs, see the sidebar, "Duke of URL.")

Browsing Off

Now that you know all about the Web, you undoubtedly want to check it out for yourself. To do this, you need a *browser,* the software that gets Web pages and displays them on your screen. Fortunately, if you have Windows 95 or later (98, 2000, NT, Me, or XP), any recent Mac, or any computer with Internet access, you probably already have one. Also, one may have come from your Internet service provider (ISP) if you installed their Internet software.

Here are the two and a half most popular browsers:

- **Internet Explorer (IE)** is the browser that Microsoft builds into every version of Windows since Windows 98. In fact, Microsoft insists that it's an integral part of Windows itself. (If it is, how can there be a stand-alone version for the Mac or UNIX? Hmm.) Microsoft now has versions for Windows, the Mac, and a few versions of UNIX. It frequently comes with Outlook Express, Microsoft's e-mail and newsgroup program, which we cover in Chapter 11. AOL's built-in browser is Internet Explorer (strange, because they own Netscape, but that shows the power of Microsoft's clout). The latest version is 6.0, which comes with Windows XP and is available as a free download for Windows 98, Me, and 2000. IE 5.5, which came with Windows Me and 2000, looks a little different but works almost the same.
- **Netscape Navigator 7** comes in several varieties for Windows, Macs, and UNIX. Netscape also comes as part of a suite of programs called Netscape Communicator. (We talk about its mail program in Chapter 11.) Netscape includes a Web page editor, too, in case you want to create your own Web pages. (See Chapter 9 to find out how to create Web pages.) Netscape Navigator and its cousin, Mozilla, are our hands-down favorite browsers. (There — no one can accuse us of hiding our biases!) Every few months, Netscape updates the program a bit: the latest update is 7.02.
- **Mozilla** is the open source browser on which Netscape is based. Mozilla and Netscape are nearly identical except that Netscape removes a few Mozilla features (pop-up blocking, most notably) and adds some AOL-specific stuff (AOL Instant Messenger and the ability to pick up mail from AOL accounts.) Unless you need the AOL stuff, we suggest you use Mozilla. New versions come out often; the latest is 1.4a.

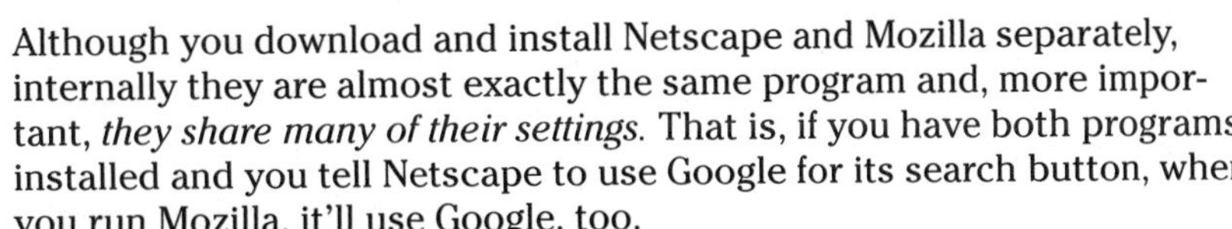

Although you download and install Netscape and Mozilla separately, internally they are almost exactly the same program and, more important, *they share many of their settings.* That is, if you have both programs installed and you tell Netscape to use Google for its search button, when you run Mozilla, it'll use Google, too.

We describe Internet Explorer and Mozilla/Netscape 7 in detail in this book. The quickly growing and feature-packed Opera, another excellent browser, has been relegated to sidebars, but you may want to try it out if you are adventurous (see the sidebar "A night at the Opera" in this chapter). If you don't have a browser, or you want to try a different one, see the section "Getting and Installing a Browser" later in this chapter.

Duke of URL

Part of the plan of the World Wide Web is to link together all the information in the known universe, starting with all the stuff on the Internet and heading up from there. (This statement may be a slight exaggeration, but not by much.)

One key to global domination is to give everything (at least everything that could be a Web resource) a name so that no matter what kind of thing a hypertext link refers to, a Web browser can find it and know what to do with it.

Look at this typical URL, the one for the Web page that was shown in Figure 6-1:

```
http://net.gurus.com/index.phtml
```

The first thing in a URL, the word before the colon, is the *scheme,* which describes the way a browser can get to the resource. Although ten schemes are defined, the most common by far is HTTP, which is the HyperText Transfer Protocol that is the Web's native transfer technique. (Don't confuse HTTP, which is the way pages are sent over the Internet, with HTML, which is the system of formatting codes in Web pages.)

Although the details of the rest of the URL depend on the scheme, most schemes look similar. Following the colon are two slashes (always forward slashes, never backslashes) and the name of the host computer on which the resource lives; in this case, `net.gurus.com` (one of the many names of John's Internet host computer). Then comes another slash and a *path,* which gives the name of the resource on that host; in this case, a file named `index.phtml`.

Web URLs allow a few other optional parts. They can include a *port number,* which specifies, roughly speaking, which of several programs running on that host should handle the request. The port number goes after a colon after the host name, like this:

```
http://net.gurus.com:80/index.
   phtml
```

Because the standard `http` port number is 80, if that's the port you want (it usually is), you can leave it out. Finally, a Web URL can have a *search part* at the end, following a question mark, like this:

```
http://net.gurus.com:80/index.
   phtml?chickens
```

When a URL has a search part, it tells the host computer, uh, what to search for. (You rarely type a search part yourself — they're often constructed for you from fill-in fields on Web pages.)

Three other useful URL schemes are `mailto`, `ftp`, and `file`. A `mailto` URL looks like this:

```
mailto:internet9@gurus.com
```

That is, it's an e-mail address. When you click a `mailto` URL in Netscape, it pops up a window in which you can enter an e-mail message to the address in the URL. In Internet Explorer (IE), clicking a `mailto` URL runs the Outlook Express program or whatever you've designated as your default mail program. (We describe Outlook Express in Chapter 10.) `Mailto` URLs are commonly used for sending comments to the owner of a Web page.

A URL that starts with `ftp` lets you download files from a File Transfer Protocol (FTP) server on the Internet (see Chapter 16 for information about FTP servers). An `ftp` URL looks like this:

```
ftp://ftp.netscape.com/pub/
netscape7/english/7.02/windows/
win32/NSSetup.exe
```

The part after the two slashes is the name of the FTP server (`ftp.netscape.com`, in this case). The rest of the URL is the pathname of the file you want to download.

The `file` URL specifies a file on your computer. It looks like this:

```
file:///C|/www/index.htm
```

On a Windows or DOS computer, this line indicates a Web page stored in the file `C:\www\index.htm` on your own computer. The colon turns into a vertical bar (because colons in URLs mean something else), and the backslashes turn into forward slashes. File URLs are useful mostly for looking at graphics files with `.gif` and `.jpg` filename extensions and for looking at a Web page you just wrote and stuck in a file on your disk.

Surfing with Your Browser

When you start Netscape, you see a screen similar to the one shown in Figure 6-1. The Internet Explorer 6 window looks like the one shown in Figure 6-2. Internet Explorer 5.0 and 5.5 look a little different, but they have almost identical menu choices and toolbar buttons. Which page your browser displays depends on how it's set up. Many ISPs arrange for your browser to display their home page; otherwise, Internet Explorer tends to display a Microsoft page and Netscape usually shows a Netscape page, until you choose a home page of your own.

Figure 6-2: Your typical Web page, viewed in Internet Explorer 6.

A night at the Opera

Opera is a small, fast browser written by a company in Norway. You have two options with Opera: a free version that displays small ads or a version that costs money (only $35) with no ads. For more information, or to download it, see `www.opera.com`.

Opera doesn't have the enormous profusion of baffling features and options that Netscape or Internet Explorer has, which means that it's much smaller and faster than either. If you find that you tire of waiting for your current browser to load, or of downloading yet another patch to fix the Internet Explorer egregious security hole of the week, Opera is definitely worth a look.

Opera isn't totally lacking bells and whistles, of course. As of Version 7, it has mouse gestures, which let you control it by holding down the mouse button and moving the mouse. For example, wiggle the mouse back and forth to tell it to close the current window. It also offers a slideshow mode that can display Web pages with suitable coding (which isn't hard to write) as a sequence of full-screen slides, using full power of a Web browser. Take that, PowerPoint!

At the top of the window are a bunch of buttons and the Location (in Mozilla/Netscape) or Address (in Internet Explorer) line, which contains the URL for the current page. (Netscape Navigator sometimes labels this box Netsite for reasons that doubtless make sense to someone. Microsoft sometimes calls it Shortcut. Go figure.) Remember that URLs are an important part of Web lore because they're the secret codes that name all the pages on the Web. For details, see the sidebar "Duke of URL," elsewhere in this chapter.

The main part of the browser window is taken up by the Web page that you're looking it. After all, that's what the browser is *for* — displaying a Web page! The buttons, bars, and menus around the edge help you find your way around the Web and do things like print and save pages.

Getting around

You need two simple skills (if we can describe something as basic as a single mouse-click as a skill) to get going on the Web. One is to move from page to page on the Web, and the other is to jump directly to a page when you know its URL. (See the section, "Going places," later in this chapter.)

Moving from page to page is easy: Click any link that looks interesting. That's it. Underlined blue text and blue-bordered pictures are links. (Although links may be a color other than blue, depending on the look the Web page designer is going for, they're always underlined unless the page is the victim of a truly awful designer.) Anything that looks like a button is probably a link. You can tell when you're pointing to a link because the mouse pointer changes to a little hand. If you're not sure whether something is a link, click it anyway because if it's not, it doesn't hurt anything. Clicking outside a link selects the text you click, as in most other programs.

Backward, ho!

Web browsers remember the last few pages you visited, so if you click a link and decide that you're not so crazy about the new page, you can easily go back to the preceding one. To go back, click the Back or Previous button on the toolbar (its icon is an arrow pointing to the left, and it's the leftmost button on the toolbar) or press Alt+←.

All over the map

Some picture links are *image maps,* such as the big picture shown in the middle of Figure 6-3. In a regular link, it doesn't matter where you click; on an image map, it does. The image map in this figure is typical and has a bunch of obvious places you click for various types of information. Some image maps are actual maps, whereas others are pictures that contain many different buttons to go different places.

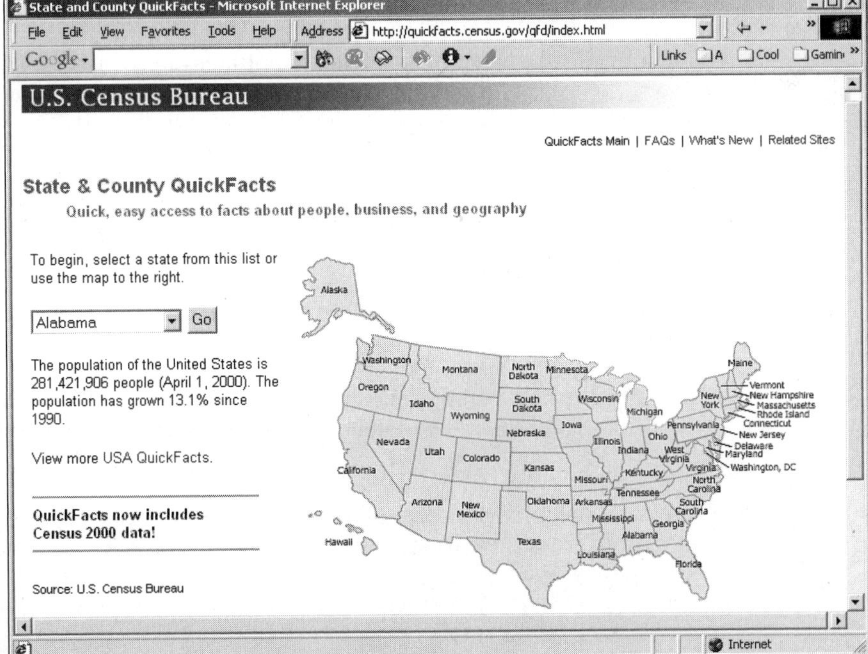

Figure 6-3: Click the part of the image map that you want to choose. (This Web page is displayed by Internet Explorer 5.5.)

As you move the mouse cursor around a Web page, whenever you're pointing at a link, the URL of the place it links to may appear in small type at the bottom of the screen. If the link is an image map, it shows the link followed by a question mark and two numbers that are the X and Y positions of where you are on the map. The numbers don't matter to you (it's up to the Web server to make sense of them); if you see a pair of numbers counting up and down when you move the mouse, however, you know that you're on an image map.

Going places

These days, everyone and his dog has a home page. A *home page* is the main Web page for a person or organization. Chapter 10 shows you how to make one for yourself and your dog (see `members.aol.com/lcg4/pwd.html`). Companies advertise their home pages, and people send e-mail talking about cool sites. When you see a URL you want to check out, here's what you do:

1. **Click in the Location or Address box, near the top of the Mozilla, Netscape, or Internet Explorer window.**
2. **Type the URL in the box. Browsers let you leave off the `http://` part.**

   The URL is something like `http://net.gurus.com` — you can just type **net.gurus.com**. Be sure to erase the URL that appeared before you started typing.
3. **Press Enter.**

If you receive URLs in electronic mail, instant messages, documents, Usenet newsgroup messages, or anywhere else on your computer, you can use the standard cut-and-paste techniques and avoid retyping:

1. **Highlight the URL in whichever program is showing it.**
2. **Press Ctrl+C (⌘+C on the Mac) to copy the info to the Clipboard.**
3. **Click in the Location or Address box to highlight whatever is in it.**
4. **Press Ctrl+V (⌘+V on the Mac) to paste the URL into the box, and then press Enter.**

Most e-mail programs highlight URLs in e-mail messages. All you have to do is click the highlighted link, and your browser pops up and opens the Web page.

You can leave the `http://` off the front of URLs when you type them in the Location or Address box. Your browser can guess that part!

Where to start?

You find out more about how to find things on the Web in Chapter 7; for now, here's a good way to get started: Go to the Yahoo! page. (Yes, the name of the Web page includes an exclamation point — it's very excitable. But we leave it out throughout the book because we find it annoying.) That is, type this URL in the Location or Address box and then press Enter:

```
www.yahoo.com
```

You go to the Yahoo page, in the middle of which are links to a directory of millions of Web pages by topic. Just nose around, clicking links that look interesting, and clicking the Back button on the toolbar when you make a wrong turn. We guarantee that you'll find something interesting.

For updates to the very book you are holding, go to this URL:

```
net.gurus.com
```

Follow the links to the page about our books or about the Internet, and then select the pages for readers of *The Internet For Dummies,* 9th Edition. If we have any late-breaking news about the Internet or updates and corrections to this book, you can find them there. If you find mistakes in this book or have other comments, by the way, please send e-mail to us at `internet9@gurus.com`.

This page looks funny

Sometimes a Web page gets garbled on the way in or you interrupt it (by clicking the Stop button on the toolbar or by pressing the Esc key). You can tell your browser to get the information on the page again: In Mozilla and Netscape, click the Reload button or press Ctrl+R; in Internet Explorer, click the Refresh button or press F5.

Get me outta here

Sooner or later, even the most dedicated Web surfer has to stop to eat or attend to other bodily needs. You leave your browser in the same way that you leave any other program: by choosing File➪Exit (File➪Close for Windows Internet Explorer, we were surprised to notice) or pressing Alt+F4. You can also click the Close (X) button in the upper-right corner of the window. Or, just leave the program running and walk away from your computer.

You can do a few things to speed up your Web browser, which we address later in this chapter. (That's a ploy to keep you reading.)

Getting and Installing a Browser

With luck, a browser is already installed on your computer. (Microsoft's plan is for Internet Explorer to come preinstalled on every computer in the universe, as far as we can tell, and it's working.) All recent browsers are so similar that if you have one, we suggest that you stick with it for now, at least. Without luck, you don't have a browser, or you have a very old one that you ought to upgrade if you want to see all the newer features used in Web pages. If you use a version of Netscape or Internet Explorer older than 6.0, you're missing lots of new features. Fortunately, browser programs are not difficult to get and install, and most are free.

Even if you already have a browser, new versions of Mozilla, Netscape, and Internet Explorer come out every 20 minutes or so, and it's worth knowing how to upgrade because occasionally the new versions fix some bugs so that they're better than the old versions. Microsoft and AOL give away Internet Explorer, Mozilla, and Netscape, so you may as well upgrade to the current version if you have an old version of either. (One can complain about many aspects of Internet Explorer, but not its price, unless you worry about software monopolies, as do we and many others.)

Getting the package

You may get a CD-ROM from your ISP (or with a book or magazine) that includes a copy of Internet Explorer or Netscape. You can also download any of these browsers from the Internet, where there may be newer versions than the one on the CD-ROM. If you have access to any Web browser, try one of these Web sites:

- **TUCOWS:** `www.tucows.com`
- **The Consummate WinSock Applications page:** `cws.internet.com`
- **Netscape home page:** `home.netscape.com/download`
- **Mozilla home page:** `www.mozilla.org/releases` (look for the gray "Try these" box)
- **Microsoft home page (for Internet Explorer):** `www.microsoft.com/windows/ie` for Windows and `www.microsoft.com/mac/ie` for Macs
- **Opera Software (for Opera):** `www.opera.com`

Use your Web browser to go to the page and then follow the instructions for finding and downloading the program. You may also want to consult Chapter 16 for more information about downloading files from the Internet.

If you're upgrading from an older version of your browser to a newer one, you can replace the old version with the new one. The installation program may even be smart enough to remember some of your old settings and bookmarks (favorites).

The first time you run your browser

To run your new browser, click the browser's attractive, new icon. Or choose it from the Start menu.

The first time you run Netscape Navigator, you see a bunch of legal boilerplate stuff describing the license conditions for the program. If you can stand the conditions (many people can), click to indicate your acceptance. Netscape then starts up. It may want to connect to the Netscape Web page so that you can register your copy of Netscape — follow its instructions. The program may also want you to set up separate user profiles if more than one person will be using Netscape (you can accept or decline).

Netscape Navigator also asks you to "activate" the program, which creates a free account for you at the Netscape Web site, including a free e-mail address that ends with `@netscape.net`. Go ahead and follow its directions, or click Cancel to skip it.

Mozilla simply welcomes you to Mozilla and tells you how happy they are that you're helping them test Mozilla. (All that means is that if Mozilla encounters an error, they hope you say yes when it asks if it can send a report back to headquarters.)

The first time you run Internet Explorer, it may run the Internet or New Connection Wizard, which offers to help you get connected to the Internet. If you want Microsoft's advice on selecting an ISP, follow the instructions on-screen. If you already have an Internet connection that works, you have a chance to tell it so.

Upgrade magic

After you install Netscape or Internet Explorer, your software vendor would really, really, REALLY like you not to switch to a competing product. Toward this end, they've both invented more or less automated schemes to upgrade from one version of their software to the next and to help you figure out what needs upgrading in the first place. Mozilla isn't as strident, although they'd just as soon you use the newest version, which should have the fewest bugs.

- **Netscape** has a Smart Update feature. Fire up Netscape, go to `home.netscape.com/download`, click the Smart Update link (you may have to hunt for it on the page: it was near the upper-left corner the last time we looked), and follow the instructions on the page. After the download of the newer version of the program has begun, Netscape opens a small window listing what it's doing with detailed directions on what to click when. Follow them exactly (which can be a little confusing) and it downloads the new programs and installs them, one at a time. Some of the programs are large (new versions of Navigator and Communicator can be more than 20MB), so the downloads may take a while.
- **Mozilla**'s home page can tell which browser you're using. And if it notices it's an old version of Mozilla, it'll nag you to get a new one. There's no update magic: Just download the new version and install it.
- **Internet Explorer** is included in Microsoft Windows' Internet-based update system. In Windows XP, the Automatic Updates system may download Windows updates without any effort on your part (to check whether Automatic Updates is turned on, choose Start⇨Control Panel⇨Performance and Maintenance, click System, and click the Automatic Updates tab). In Windows Me, 2000, and earlier versions, choose Start⇨Windows Update or click the Windows Update icon on the taskbar. Microsoft's programs are even bigger than Netscape's, so the downloads can take a long time.

Windows on the World

If you know how to find your way around the Web, you are ready for some comparatively advanced features so that you can start to feel like a Web pro in no time.

Internet Explorer, Mozilla, and Netscape are known in the trade as *multi-threaded* programs — that is, they can display several pages at once. When we're pointing and clicking from one place to another, we like to open a bunch of windows so that we can see where we've been and go back to a previous page just by switching to another window. You can also arrange windows side by side, which is a good way to, say, compare prices for *The Internet For Dummies,* 9th Edition, at various online bookstores. (The difference may be small, but when you're buying 100 copies for everyone on your Christmas list, those pennies can add up. Oh, you weren't planning to do that? Drat.)

Wild window mania

To display a page in a new Internet Explorer, Mozilla, or Netscape window, click a link with the right mouse button and select Open in New Window from the menu that pops up. To close a window, click the Close (X) button at the top right of the window frame, or press Alt+F4, the standard close-window shortcut. Macs don't have a right mouse button, so hold down the button you use to get contextual menus (the default is the Control key). You close all Mac windows the same way — by clicking the button at the top left of the window. Users with three-button mice can open a link in a new window by clicking the middle button.

You can also create a new window without following a link. Press Ctrl+N or choose File⇨New⇨Navigator Window (in Netscape Navigator), File⇨New Navigator Window (in Netscape and Mozilla), or File⇨New⇨Window (in Internet Explorer). UNIX and Mac users should think "Alt" and "Apple" for "Ctrl" throughout this section.

Tab dancing

Netscape and Mozilla (and Opera for that matter) have *tabs*, which are multiple pages that you can switch among in a window. Figure 6-4 shows a Netscape window with three tabs. Just click any of the tabs near the top of the window to show its page. Click the little star-box thing at the left end of the tab line or press Ctrl+T to make a new empty tab or the X at the right end to get rid of the current tab. Like multiple windows, tabs are multithreaded so you can have one loading in the background while you're reading another, and little rotating arrows in the tab bar show you which ones are loading and which are ready. For most purposes, we find tabs more convenient than windows. You can use both; if you open several windows in Netscape or Mozilla, each window can have several tabs.

Short attention span tips

If you have a slow Internet connection, use at least two browser tabs or windows at the same time. While you're waiting for the next page to arrive in one tab or window, you can read the page that arrived a while ago in the other.

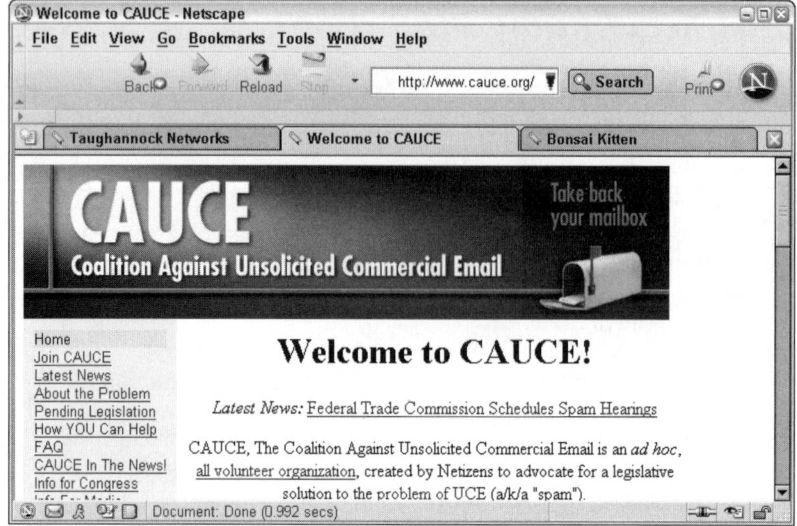

Figure 6-4: A Netscape window with three tabs.

If you ask your browser to begin downloading a big file, it displays, most usefully, a small window in the corner of your screen. Internet Explorer and Netscape display a "thermometer" showing the download progress; Internet Explorer also shows tiny pages flying from one folder to another. Although some people consider watching the thermometer grow or the pages fly enough entertainment (we do when we're tired enough), you can click back to the main browser window and continue surfing.

Doing two or three things at a time in your browser when you have a dialup Net connection is not unlike squeezing blood from a turnip — only so much blood can be squeezed. In this case, the blood is the amount of data your computer can pump through your modem. A single download task can keep your modem close to 100 percent busy, and anything else you do shares the modem with the download process. When you do two things at a time, therefore, each one happens more slowly than it would by itself.

If one task is a big download and the other is perusing Web pages, everything usually works okay because you spend a fair amount of time looking at what the Web browser is displaying; the download can then run while you think. On the other hand, although browsers let you start two download tasks at a time (or a dozen, if you're so inclined), it's no faster to do more than one at a time than one after another, and it can get confusing.

My Favorite Things

The Web really does have cool places to visit. Some you will want to visit over and over again. (We've probably visited the Google Web site thousands of times by now.) All the makers of fine browsers have, fortunately, provided a handy way for you to remember those spots and not have to write down those nasty URLs just to have to type them again later.

Although the name varies, the idea is simple: Your browser lets you mark a Web page and adds its URL to a list. Later, when you want to go back, you just go to your list and pick the page you want. Netscape and Mozilla call these saved Web addresses *bookmarks;* Internet Explorer calls them *favorites.*

You can handle bookmarks in two ways. One way is to think of them as a menu so that you can choose individual bookmarks from the menu bar of your browser. The other is to think of them as a custom-built page of links so that you go to that page and then choose the link you want. Netscape and Mozilla, prime examples of the "Great Expanding Blob" approach to software design, do both. Internet Explorer takes yet another tack: It adds your Web pages to a folder of favorite places to which you may want to return.

Bookmarking with Netscape and Mozilla

Netscape and Mozilla bookmarks lurk under the Bookmarks menu. To bookmark a Web page — that is, to add the address of the page to your bookmarks — choose Bookmarks⇨Bookmark this Page or press Ctrl+D.

After you create some bookmarks, your bookmarks appear as entries on the menu that you see when you click the Bookmarks menu. To go to one of the pages on your bookmark list, just choose its entry from the menu.

If you're like most users, your bookmark menu gets bigger and bigger and crawls down your screen and eventually ends up flopping down on the floor, which is both unattractive and unsanitary. Fortunately, you can smoosh (technical term) your menu into a more tractable form. Choose Bookmarks⇨Manage Bookmarks or press Ctrl+B to display your Bookmarks window (as shown in Figure 6-5).

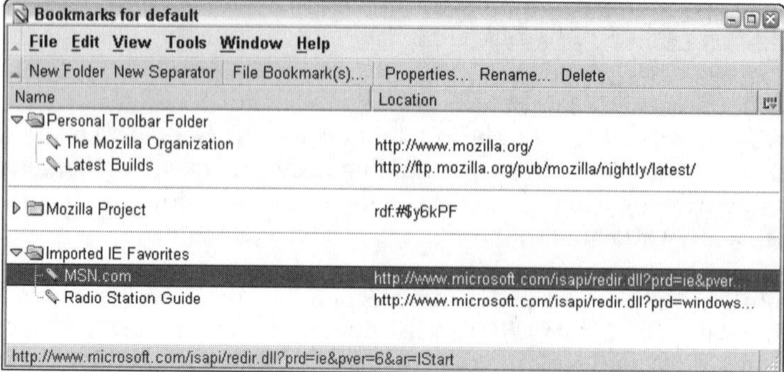

Figure 6-5: The Bookmarks window includes commands for moving, editing, and deleting bookmarks.

Because all these bookmarks are "live," you can go to any of them by clicking them. (You can leave this window open while you move around the Web in other browser windows.) You can also add separator lines and submenus to organize your bookmarks and make the individual menus less unwieldy. Submenus look like folders in the Bookmarks window.

In the Bookmarks window, choose File➪New➪Separator to add a separator line and File➪New➪Folder to add a new submenu. (Netscape asks you to type the name of the submenu before it creates the folder.) You can then drag bookmarks, separators, and folders up and down to where you want them in the Bookmarks window. Drag an item to a folder to put it in that folder's submenu, and double-click a folder to display or hide that submenu. Because any changes you make in the Bookmarks window are reflected immediately on the Bookmarks menu, it's easy to fiddle with the bookmarks until you get something you like. Netscape and Mozilla preload your bookmark window with pages they'd like you to look at, but feel free to delete them if your tastes are different from theirs.

When you're done fooling with your bookmarks, choose File➪Close or press Ctrl+W to close the Bookmarks window.

The Personal toolbar is a row of buttons that usually appears just below the Location box. (If it's not there, choose View➪Show/Hide➪Personal Toolbar to display it.) This row of buttons gives you one-button access to a bunch of Netscape's favorite Web sites. Wouldn't it be nice if your favorite Web sites appeared there instead? No problem! When you organize your bookmarks in the Bookmarks window, stick your top favorite sites in the Personal Toolbar Folder — any sites in this folder automagically appear on the Personal toolbar. You can even add folders with bookmarks in them. Folders appear as folder icons and bookmarks appear as blue ribbons. We love this Netscape/Mozilla feature.

Choosing favorites with Internet Explorer

Internet Explorer uses a system similar to Netscape's, although it calls the saved pages *favorites* rather than bookmarks: You can add the current page to your Favorites folder and then look at and organize your Favorites folder. If you use Windows, this Favorites folder is shared with other programs on your computer. Other programs also can add things to your Favorites folder, so it's a jumble of Web pages, files, and other things. (Luckily, most people use Favorites only for Web pages.)

In Windows 95, 98, and Me, the Favorites folder also usually appears on your Start menu. Choose Start⇨Favorites and then select items from the menu. If the item is a Web page, your browser fires up and (if you're connected to the Internet) displays the Web page. Windows XP doesn't include Favorites on the Start Menu unless you specifically turn it on.

To add the current page to your Favorites folder, choose Favorites⇨Add to Favorites from the menu. The Add Favorite dialog box shown in Figure 6-6 asks whether you want to be able to see the page when you are *offline* (that is, not connected to the Internet) — check this check box if you want to save the page on your computer's disk (we usually don't). Click the Create In button if you want to put the new favorite into a folder, so it appears in a submenu of your Favorites menu.

Figure 6-6: Adding a Web page to your Internet Explorer favorites.

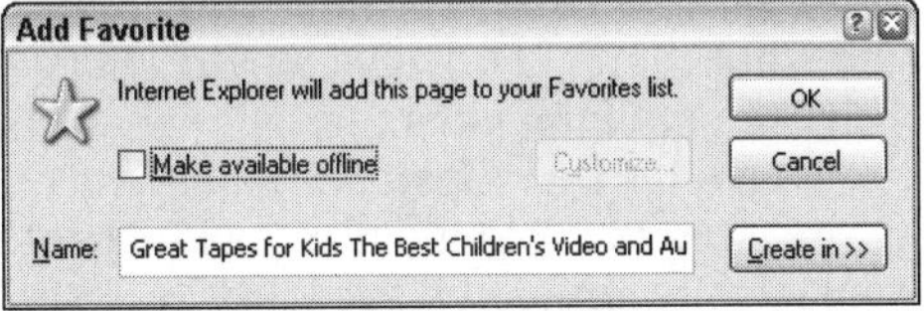

Internet Explorer has a Favorites button on the toolbar that displays your list of Favorites down the left side of your Internet Explorer window — this list is called the *Favorites Explorer Bar* (there's a name for everything!). Click the Favorites button again to make the list go away. You can also press Ctrl+I to display or banish the Favorites Explorer Bar. Then the list of favorites appears — click a favorite to go to it. Another way to go back to a Web site on your favorites list is to choose Favorites from the menu: Your favorites are at the bottom of the menu that appears.

If you want to reorganize your Favorites folder, choose Favorites➪Organize Favorites from the menu. The Organize Favorites window lets you create folders for your favorites, move favorites around, edit them, and delete them. To see what's in a folder, click it. When you're done organizing your favorite items, click the Close button. (In older versions of Internet Explorer, this dialog box looks a little different: In IE 4.0, the Create Folder button is the button with a yellow folder with a little sparkle.) You can also drag around favorites and folders directly on the Favorites bar.

The folders you create in the Organize Favorites window appear on your Favorites menu and the items you put in the folders appear on submenus. To return to a Web page you've added to your Favorites folder, just choose it from the Favorites menu.

In Internet Explorer 5.0 and up, you can make pages available when you're not connected to the Internet. In the Organize Favorites window, click the page and mark the Make Available Offline check box. Internet Explorer immediately fetches the page to your disk and refetches it from time to time when you're connected so that you can view the page when you click it while you're offline.

If you make a lot of pages available offline, you'll find your browser spending a lot of time keeping them up to date. When you no longer need to browse a page offline, deselect the Make Available Offline check box or remove the page from your favorites altogether. We've found the offline pages system to be somewhat unstable in Windows 2000 and Window XP. We would only suggest using offline pages if you are limited to going online only once or a few times a day.

Have you noticed the Links toolbar that usually appears just below or to the right of the Address box? (If it's not there, choose View➪Toolbars➪Links to display it.) We never want to visit any of the sites that appear on this toolbar, but you can put your favorite Web sites there instead! When you organize your favorites, drag your top favorite sites and folders into the Links folder — any sites in the Links folder automagically appear on the Links toolbar. This feature is seriously handy for Web sites you visit often.

Speeding Things Up

Unless you have a high-speed dedicated connection rather than a normal dialup account, you probably spend a great deal of time wishing that the process of getting to stuff on the Web were much faster. (John has a high-speed dedicated connection, and he spends a certain amount of time waiting for the Web, anyway.) Here are a handful of tricks you can use to try to speed things up.

Where do we start?

In Netscape and Mozilla: When Netscape starts up, by default it loads the large and attractive Netscape home page chock full of irresistible offers (at least Netscape's owners at AOL hope they are). Mozilla's has an informative home page, too. After one or two times, beautiful though the page is, you will probably find that you can do without it. You can tell Netscape and Mozilla not to load any Web page, or a different page, when you start the program:

1. **Choose Edit⇨Preferences.**

   You see the Preferences dialog box, as shown in Figure 6-7.

2. **Click Navigator in the Category box down the left side of the window.**

   This category may already be selected, and its settings appear in the Preferences window. The first Navigator setting is called Navigator Starts With (or When Navigator Starts Up, Display) — the Web page that Netscape displays on startup.

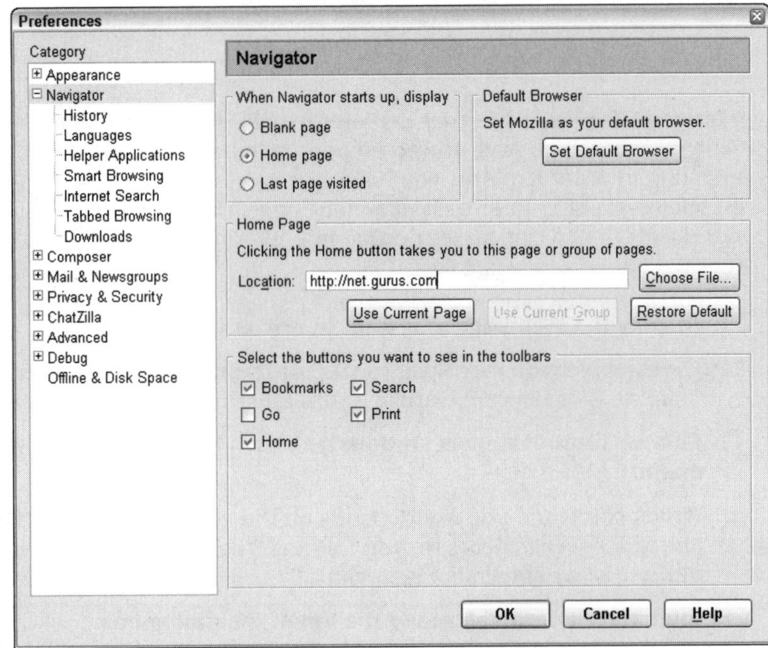

Figure 6-7: Mozilla or Netscape's Preferences window is where you can configure it to start with your favorite Web site.

3. **To start with no Web page, select Blank Page. To choose a page to start with, select Home Page, click in the box below it, and type the URL of a page you would rather see (how about `net.gurus.com`, which is our page?). To make the last page visited your home page, select that option.**

   The home page is (surprise!) the page that Netscape and Mozilla display when you click the Home button on the toolbar. To set the home page to the page you're looking at right now, click Use Current Page. To display a page stored on your own computer, click Browse or Choose File and choose a file.

   You also have the option of starting where you left off last time by selecting Last Page Visited.

4. **Click OK.**

You can set your Netscape and Mozilla home page to your own list of bookmarks — handy! Choose Edit⇨Preferences, click the Navigator category if it's not already selected, click the Browse or Choose File button in the Home Page section, and go to the `Bookmarks.html` file that stores your bookmarks. It's usually in a sub-sub-sub-folder of `C:\Program Files\Netscape` or `C:\Documents and Settings`, but you may need to look around for it using the Windows search feature.

In Internet Explorer: Internet Explorer usually starts by displaying the MSN home page or a Web page stored on your own hard disk, depending on which version of Internet Explorer you have. You can change that start page, or you can tell Internet Explorer to load a blank page. (Loading a home page from your disk is pretty fast, so we do that in preference to blank.) Follow these steps to change your start page:

1. **Display the Web page you want to use as your start page.**

   For example, you may want to start at the Yahoo page, described in Chapter 7, or Internet Gurus Central at `net.gurus.com`.

2. **Choose Tools⇨Internet Options or View⇨Internet Options from the menu.**

   Which command you use depends on the version of Internet Explorer: use whichever appears on your menus! You see the Internet Options dialog box, as shown in Figure 6-8.

3. **Click the General tab along the top of the dialog box.**

   Actually, it's probably already selected, but we say this in case you've been looking around at what's on the other tabs.

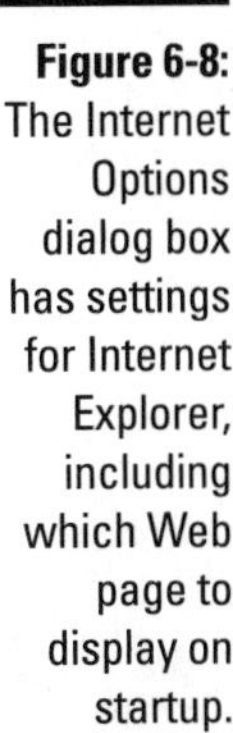

Figure 6-8: The Internet Options dialog box has settings for Internet Explorer, including which Web page to display on startup.

4. **In the Home Page section of the dialog box, click the Use Current button.**

   The URL of the current page appears in the Address box. To start with no page at all, click the Use Blank button.

5. **Click OK.**

Choose a start page that doesn't have many pictures: By starting with a Web page that loads faster or with no start page, you don't have to wait long to start browsing.

Cold, hard cache

When your browser retrieves a page you have asked to see, it stores the page on your disk. If you ask for the same page again five minutes later, the program doesn't have to retrieve the page again — it can reuse the copy it already has. The space your browser uses to store pages is called its *cache* (pronounced *cash* because it's French and gives your cache more *cachet*). The more space you tell your browser to use for its cache, the faster pages appear the second time you look at them.

In Netscape and Mozilla: To set the size of the browser cache, follow these steps:

1. **Choose Edit⇨Preferences from the menu.**

   You see the Preferences dialog box.

2. **Double-click the Advanced category and click the Cache category.**

   You see all the settings that control the cache. The Disk Cache box shows the maximum size of the cache in kilobytes (K): We like to set Disk Cache to 50000K (that is, 50MB). Set it to a higher number if you have a large hard disk with loads of free space — the more space your cache can occupy, the more often you can load a Web page quickly from the cache rather than slowly from the Net.

3. **Click OK.**

In Internet Explorer: To set the size of the Internet Explorer cache, follow these steps:

1. **Choose Tools⇨Internet Options or View⇨Internet Options from the menu.**

   You see the Internet Options dialog box.

2. **Click the General tab if it's not already selected.**

3. **Click the Settings button in the Temporary Internet Files section.**

   You see the Settings dialog box, with information about the cache. (Many versions of Internet Explorer never call it a cache — guess they don't speak French.)

4. **Click the slider on the Amount of disk space to use or Maximum size line and move it to about 10 percent.**

   That is, slide it to one-tenth of the way from the left-hand end. If you have tons of empty disk space, you can slide it rightward to 20 percent. If you're short on space, move it leftward to 1 percent or 2 percent. A box to the right of the slider shows the amount of disk space you've selected.

5. **Click OK twice.**

Some of us hardly ever exit from our browsers, which is probably not a good idea for our long-term mental stability. If you are one of us, however, remember that the pages your browser has cached aren't normally reloaded from the Web (they're taken from your disk) until you reload them. If you want to make sure that you're getting fresh pages, reload pages that you think may have changed since you last visited. Your browser is supposed to check whether a saved page has changed, but because the check sometimes doesn't work perfectly, an occasional Reload or Refresh command for pages that change frequently, such as stock prices or the weather report, is advisable. Click the Reload or Refresh button on your browser's toolbar or press Ctrl+R.

Getting the Big Picture

Browsers have so many buttons, icons, and boxes near the top of the window that not much space is left to display the Web page. Here are some hints on making more space.

In Netscape and Mozilla: You can clear off a little more space in the window by eliminating the Personal Toolbar (the bottommost row of buttons, just above the Web page area), unless you use it for your own personal favorite links. Choose View➪Show/Hide➪Personal Toolbar to remove the check mark to the left of the command. Other commands on the View➪Show/Hide menu let you turn off other rows of buttons. To restore buttons that you just blew away, give the same command again. If you'd rather leave the Personal toolbar in place but have it display your favorite Web sites, see the tip at the end of the "Bookmarking with Netscape and Mozilla" section earlier in this chapter.

In Internet Explorer: You can reclaim screen real estate by removing toolbars. If the Links toolbar appears (usually just below or to the right of the Address box), choose View➪Toolbars➪Links to make it go away. Give the same command again to restore the item you got rid of. You can turn off the other rows of buttons by choosing other options on the View➪Toolbars menu. Alternatively, replace the items on the Links toolbar with your own favorite Web sites: See the tip at the end of the "Choosing favorites with Internet Explorer" section for details.

The latest versions of Netscape, Mozilla, and IE all offer fullscreen mode. You can switch to fullscreen mode by pressing the F11 key: the window borders, menus, and status bar vanish, leaving only the toolbar and the Web page itself. Pressing F11 again returns your browser to normal (if you can call that normal).

IE also has a feature called *rubber toolbars*. They take a little more practice to get used to, but to start, you need to unlock them. First, right-click any blank area of any toolbar and select Unlock or Lock the Toolbars, depending on your version of IE. Next, grab the toolbar you want to move by pointing at the little vertical ridge or row of dots that appears just to the left of the toolbar's name. Finally, drag it around with your mouse. If you take your time, you'll see that all the toolbars can be on the same line as another toolbar. Experiment and you'll find a good arrangement.

Filling in Forms

Back in the Dark Ages of the Web (that is, in 1993), Web pages were just pages to look at. Because that wasn't anywhere near enough fun or complicated enough, Web forms were invented. A *form* is sort of like a paper form, with fields you can fill out and then send in. Figure 6-9 shows a typical form.

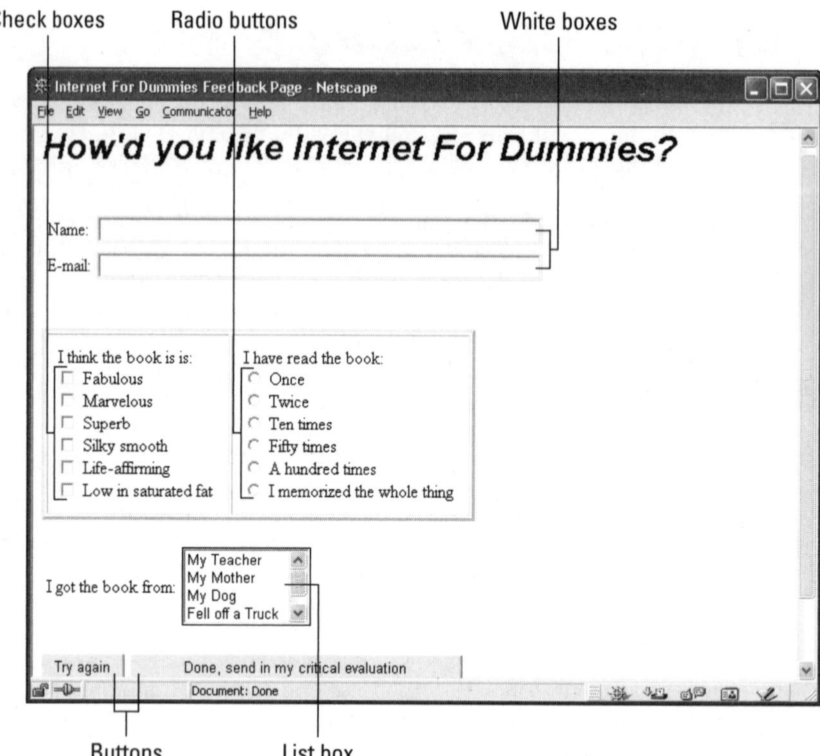

Figure 6-9: Just fill out a few forms.

White boxes in a form are fill-in text boxes in which you type, in this case, your name and e-mail address. Little square boxes are *check boxes,* in which you check whichever ones apply (all of them, we hope, on our sample form). Little round buttons are *radio buttons,* which are similar to check boxes except that you can choose only one of them from each set. In Figure 6-9, you also see a *list box,* in which you can choose one of the possibilities in the box. In most cases, you see more entries than can fit in the box, so you scroll them up and down. Although you can usually choose only one entry, some list boxes let you choose more.

Forms also include buttons. Most forms have two: one that clears the form fields to their initial state and sends nothing, and one, usually known as the *Submit* button, that sends the filled-out form back to the Web server for processing.

After the data is sent from the form back to the Web server, it's entirely up to the server how to interpret it.

Some Web pages have *search items,* which are one-line forms that let you type some text for which to search. Depending on the browser, a Submit button may be displayed to the right of the text area, or you may just press Enter to send the search words to the server. For example, the Google search page at `google.com` has a box into which you type a word or phrase; when you press Enter or click the Google Search button, the search begins. (See the next chapter to find out what happens!)

Lower the Cone of Silence

When you are filling out a form on a Web page, you may need to provide information that you'd prefer not be made public — your credit card number, for example. Not to worry! Modern browsers can *encrypt* the information you send and receive to and from a *secure Web server.* If you use Netscape or Mozilla, you can tell when a page was received encrypted from the Web server by an icon in the lower-right corner of the browser window. If the little lock appears open, the page was not encrypted. If the little lock is locked, encryption is on. Typed-in data in forms in secure pages are almost always sent encrypted as well, making it impossible for anyone to snoop on your secrets as they pass through the Net. Encrypted pages are nice, but in practice, it's unlikely that anyone is snooping on your Web session anyway, encrypted or otherwise. The real security problems are elsewhere (see Chapters 3 and 8).

Netscape, Mozilla, and Internet Explorer have the habit of popping up little boxes to warn you about the dangers of what you are about to do. They display a box when you're about to switch from encrypted to nonencrypted (or back again) transmissions. Most of these warning boxes include a check box you can click to tell the program not to bother you with this type of warning again.

Save Me!

Frequently, you see something on a Web page that's worth saving for later. Sometimes it's a Web page full of interesting information or a picture or some other type of file. Fortunately, saving stuff is easy.

When you save a Web page, you have to decide whether to save only the text that appears or the entire HTML version of the page, with the format codes. (For a glimpse of HTML, see Chapter 9). You can also save the pictures that appear on Web pages.

Choose File⇨Save As to save the current Web page in a file. You see the standard Save As dialog box. (IE 6.0 calls it Save Web Page, but you get the idea.) Specify the name to save the incoming file or use the filename that your browser suggests. Click the Save as Type box to determine how to save the page: Choose Plain Text or Text File to save only the text of the page, with little notes where pictures occur. Choose HTML, HTML Files, or Web Page Complete (in IE) to save the entire HTML file. Then click the Save or OK button.

To save an image you see on a Web page, right-click the image (click the image with your right mouse button). Choose Save Image As or Save Picture As from the menu that appears. When you see the Save As dialog box, move to the folder or directory in which you want to save the graphics file, type a filename in the File name box, and click the Save or OK button.

A note about copyright: Contrary to popular belief, almost all Web pages, along with almost everything else on the Internet, are copyrighted by their authors. If you save a Web page or a picture from a Web page, you don't have permission to use it any way you want. Before you reuse the text or pictures in any way, send an e-mail message to the owner of the site. If an address doesn't appear on the page, write for permission to `webmaster@`*`domain.com`*, replacing *`domain.com`* with the domain name part of the URL of the Web page. For permission to use information on the `net.gurus.com/books.phtml` page, for example, write to `webmaster@gurus.com`.

The Dead-Tree Thing: Printing

For about the first year that Web browsers existed, they all had print commands that didn't work. Eventually the programmers realized that normal people (like you) need to commit Web pages to paper from time to time, so now the print commands all work.

To print a page, click the Print button on the toolbar, press Ctrl+P, or choose File⇨Print. Reformatting the page to print it can take awhile, so patience is a virtue. Fortunately, each browser displays a progress window to let you know how it's doing.

If the page you want to print uses frames (a technique that divides the browser window into subareas that can scroll and update separately), click in the part of the window you want to print before printing. Otherwise, you may get only the outermost frame, which usually just has a title and some buttons.

Pop off, buddy

One of the worst innovations in recent decades is *pop-up* windows that appear on your screen unbidden (by you), when you visit some Web sites. Some pop-ups appear immediately, some are *pop-unders* that are hidden under your main window until you close the main window. The pop-ups you're most likely to see are ads for spy cameras and airline tickets. (No, we're not going to give their names here; they have plenty of publicity already.)

Mozilla and Netscape shocked us all by giving users something they actually want, a way to get rid of pop-ups. On the menu for either, open the Preferences window via Edit➪Preferences, double-click Privacy & Security to expand it if it's not already, and then Popup Windows. Click the box marked Block Unrequested Popup Windows, and your pop-ups should, for the most part, disappear.

Netscape and Mozilla warn you that blocking all pop-ups may make some Web sites stop working, which turns out to be true. In particular, some shopping sites pop up small windows into which you have to type credit card verification information. Netscape and Mozilla thoughtfully include an Allowed Sites button where they've preloaded a list of such sites that you can edit. (As far as we can tell, the sites in their list do in fact use pop-ups for virtuous purposes, not ads.) You also have the option of telling the browser to show a little icon or make a sound when it blocks a pop-up, in case you want to know what you're missing.

What about Internet Explorer? The short answer is now you know why we've been telling you to use Mozilla through the whole chapter. (Or Netscape, or Opera, or nearly any other browser, all of which let you block pop-ups. Microsoft is a wee bit behind the curve here.) If you just have to use IE, visit `www.tucows.com/adkiller95_default.html` for some add-on pop-up blockers you can download and install. AOL users are better off than other IE users: Even though AOL displays Web pages with IE, AOL 8.0 built in a little button right on the bottom of the IE window that lets you block pop-ups.

Keep Your Cookie Crumbs Off My Computer

To enhance your online experience, the makers of Web browsers invented a type of special message that lets a Web site recognize you when you revisit that site. They thoughtfully store this info, called a *cookie,* on your very own machine.

Usually cookies are innocuous and useful. When you're using an airline reservation site, for example, the site uses cookies to keep the flights you're reserving separate from the ones other users may be reserving at the same time. On the other hand, suppose that you use your credit card to purchase something on a Web site and the site uses a cookie to remember your credit card number. Suppose that you provide this information from a computer at work and the next person to visit that site uses the same computer. That person could, possibly, make purchases on your credit card. Oops.

Internet users have various feelings about cookies. Some of us don't care about them, and some of us view them as an unconscionable invasion of privacy. You get to decide for yourself. Contrary to rumor, cookie files cannot get other information from your hard disk, give you a bad haircut, or otherwise mess up your life. They collect only information that the browser tells them about. Internet Explorer, Netscape, and Mozilla let you control whether and when cookies are stored on your computer.

In Internet Explorer 6.0: Use the Tools➪Internet Options command to display the Internet Options dialog box. The cookie controls are on the Privacy tab (shown on the left side of Figure 6-10), so click it. Click the Advanced button to see the Advanced Privacy Settings dialog box. By default, Internet Explorer 6.0 manages cookies rather aggressively, allowing cookies from the server you contacted, but not from *third-party servers* (Web servers other than one that originally stored the cookie on your computer). Third-party servers usually deliver advertisements and those annoying pop-up and pop-under ads. You can elect to manage them yourself by clicking the Override Automatic Cookie Handling check box in the Advanced Privacy Settings dialog. The options are:

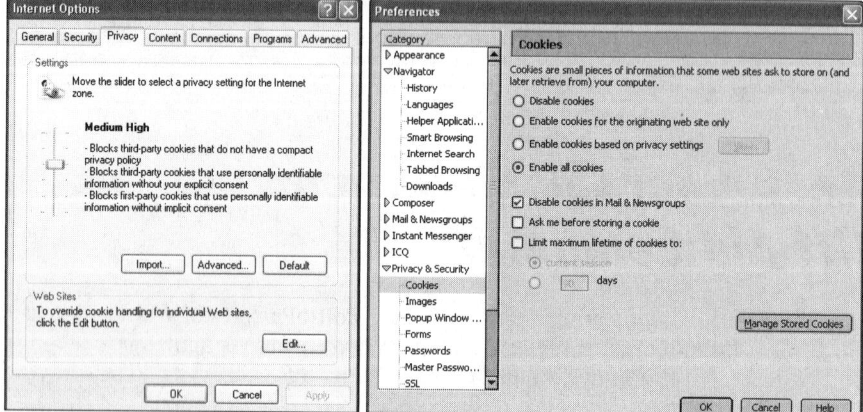

Figure 6-10: Your Web browser, cookies, and you.

- **First-Party Cookies:** These are cookies that come directly from the same server that you are viewing a Web page from. These cookies are typically used to remember you if you signed up as a site member. The convenience is in not having to re-enter your username and password every time. You can choose to Accept, Block, or be prompted to choose, although this option gets tiresome very quickly if you encounter a lot of cookies. Some sites can store three or more cookies *per page.*
- **Third-Party Cookies:** Many Web sites use specialty companies that deliver advertisements to their Web pages for them, and these third-party advertisements usually place cookies on your machine with the aim of gathering marketing data. The options here are the same as the previous set. Third-party cookies are useful only to the advertising companies, so we see no reason ever to accept them.
- **Always Allow Session Cookies:** This option lets all session cookies through, a type of cookie used to track a single instance of your visit to a Web site. These cookies are commonly used by shopping sites such as Amazon.com.

In Internet Explorer 5.0 and 5.5: Use the Tools⇨Internet Options command to display the Internet Options dialog box. The cookie controls are on the Security tab, so click it. Click the Internet Web Content Zone (the colored globe) and then click the Custom Level button to see the Security Settings dialog box. Scroll down the list until you come to the Cookies section. You see two settings:

- **Allow Cookies That Are Stored on Your Computer:** Some cookies are stored on your computer so that if you come back to the Web site tomorrow, the site can remember information about you. ("Welcome back, Tom! Here are your book recommendations for today.") You can turn these off (Disable), turn them on (Enable), or tell IE to ask you before storing each cookie (Prompt).
- **Allow Per-Session Cookies (Not Stored):** Some cookies are stored only until you exit from Internet Explorer. For example, shopping cart systems (Web server programs that let you shop at a Web site and then "check out") may store temporarily information about what items you want to buy. You can choose Disable, Enable, or Prompt.

In Netscape and Mozilla: Choose Edit⇨Preferences and click the Privacy and Security category to display settings that include those for cookies. The options are similar to those in Internet Explorer, as shown in the right side of Figure 6-10:

History? What history?

Most browsers have a somewhat useful feature sometimes called *history.* At the right end of the Location or Address box is a little downward-pointing arrow. When you click it, a list of recently visited URLs drops down. Some of our readers have asked us how to clear out that box, presumably because they meant to type `www.disney.com`, but their fingers slipped, and it came out `www.hot-xxx-babes.com` instead. (It could happen to anyone.) Because some of the requests sounded fairly urgent, here are the occasionally gruesome details about how to do it.

- **Netscape and Mozilla:** Choose Edit⇨Preferences, double-click the Navigator category, click the History subcategory, and click the big Clear Location Bar and, if present, Clear History buttons. Everything should be this easy.
- **Internet Explorer:** Choose View⇨Internet Options or Tools⇨Internet Options, click the General tab, and click the Clear History button. Click Yes when it asks whether you wanted to do that.

- **Disable cookies:** Some sites won't work at all without cookies, including chat sites like Yahoo Groups (`groups.yahoo.com`).
- **Enable cookies for the originating Web site only:** That is, accept first-party cookies but reject third-party. This is the setting we use.
- **Enable cookies based on privacy settings:** Some sites publish privacy policies in a form that the browser can interpret. Too complex for our tastes.
- **Enable all cookies:** Don't worry, be happy!

Additionally, Netscape and Mozilla are willing to warn you whenever they're about to accept a cookie, no matter where it gets sent back. Check the Ask Me before Storing a Cookie option if you want to know.

Getting Plugged In: Singing, Dancing, and Chatting with Your Browser

Web pages with pictures are old hat. Now, Web pages have to have pictures that sing and dance or ticker-style messages that move across the page, or they have to be able to play a good game of chess with you. Every month, new types of information appear on the Web, and browsers have to keep up.

You can extend Netscape and Mozilla's capabilities with *plug-ins* — add-on programs that glue themselves to the browser and add even more features. Internet Explorer can extend itself, too, by using things called *ActiveX* controls, which are another type of add-on program. (ActiveX controls used to be called PCX or OCX controls — as soon as we figure out what they are, they change the name.)

What's a Web browser to do when it encounters new kinds of information on a Web page? Get the plug-in program that handles that kind of information and glue it onto Netscape, Mozilla, or Internet Explorer. *Star Trek* fans can think of plug-ins as parasitic life forms that attach themselves to your browser and enhance its intelligence.

A parade of plug-ins

Here are some useful plug-ins:

- **RealPlayer:** Plays *streaming* sound files while you download them. (Other programs have to wait until the entire file has downloaded before beginning to play.) A free player is available at `www.real.com`, along with more powerful players you have to pay a modest amount for. You may have to browse around to find the free player, but the other players are also a good value (most cost less than $30). Real.com also provides a list of sites that handle RealAudio sound files. Our favorite site is the National Public Radio Web site (`www.npr.org`), where you can hear recent NPR radio stories. Another favorite is the BBC at `www.bbc.co.uk` with news in 43 languages (really) and other BBC programs 24 hours a day.
- **QuickTime:** Plays video files as you download them. Available at `www.apple.com/quicktime/download`.
- **Shockwave:** Plays both audio and video files as well as other types of animations. Available at `www.shockwave.com`.
- **Adobe Acrobat:** Displays Acrobat files formatted exactly the way the author intended. Lots of useful Acrobat files are out there, including many U.S. tax forms (at `www.irs.ustreas.gov`). Available at `www.adobe.com` (or more precisely, at `www.adobe.com/products/acrobat/readstep.html` if you don't mind some extra typing).

How to use plug-ins with your browser

You can find collections of Netscape and Mozilla plug-ins and Internet Explorer ActiveX controls at TUCOWS (`www.tucows.com`), Stroud's Consummate WinSock Applications page (`cws.internet.com`), the Netscape Web site (`home.netscape.com`), and other sources of software on the Web.

After you download a plug-in from the Net, run it (double-click its filename in My Computer or Windows Explorer) to install it. Depending on what the plug-in does, you follow different steps to try it out — usually, you find a file that the plug-in can play and watch (or listen) as the plug-in plays it.

Chapter 7

Needles and Haystacks: Finding Stuff on the Net

In This Chapter

- Basic search strategies
- Finding stuff on the Web
- Built-in searchers
- Finding people on the Web
- Finding stuff by e-mail

"Okay, all this great stuff is out there on the Internet. How do I find it?" That's an excellent question. Thanks for asking that question. Questions like that are what make this country strong and vibrant. We salute you and say, "Keep asking questions!" Next question, please.

Oh, you want an *answer* to your question. Fortunately, quite a bit of (technical term follows) stuff-finding stuff is on the Net. More particularly, indexes and directories of much of the interesting material are available on the Net.

The Internet has different types of indexes and directories for different types of material. Because the indexes tend to be organized, unfortunately, by the type of Internet service that they provide rather than by the nature of the material, you find Web resources in one place, e-mail resources in another place, and so on. You can search in dozens or hundreds of different ways, depending on what you're looking for and how you prefer to search. (John has remarked that his ideal restaurant has only one item on the menu, but it's exactly what he wants. The Internet is about as far from that ideal as you can possibly imagine.)

To provide a smidgen of structure to this discussion, we describe several different sorts of searches:

Index, directory — what's the difference?

When we talk about a *directory,* we mean a listing like an encyclopedia or a library's card catalog. (Well, like the computer system that replaced the card catalog.) It has named categories with entries assigned to categories partly or entirely by human catalogers. You look things up by finding a category that you want and seeing what it contains. In this book, we think of the table of contents as a directory.

An *index,* on the other hand, simply collects all the items, extracts keywords from them (by taking all the words except for *the, and,* and the like), and makes a big list. You search the index by specifying some words that seem likely, and it finds all the entries that contain that word. The index in the back of this book is more like an index.

Each has its advantages and disadvantages. Directories are organized better, but indexes are larger. Directories use consistent terminology, while indexes use whatever terms the underlying Web pages used. Directories contain fewer useless pages, but indexes are updated more often.

Some overlap exists between indexes and directories — Yahoo, the best known Web page directory, also lets you search by keyword, and Google, which is mainly an index, also includes a version of the Open Directory Project (ODP) directory. Many of the indexes divide their entries into general categories that let you limit the search.

- **Topics:** Places, things, ideas, companies — anything you want to find out more about
- **Built-in searches:** Topic searches that a browser does automatically, and why we're not always thrilled about that
- **People:** Actual human beings whom you want to contact or spy on
- **Goods and services:** Stuff to buy or find out about, from mortgages to mouthwash

To find topics, we use the various online indexes and directories, such as Yahoo and Google. To find people, however, we use directories of people, which are (fortunately) different from directories of Web pages. Wondering what we're talking about? Read on for an explanation!

Your Basic Search Strategy

When we're looking for topics on the Net, we always begin with one of the Web guides (indexes and directories) discussed in this section.

You use them all in more or less the same way:

1. **Start your Web browser, such as Netscape, Internet Explorer, or Mozilla.**
2. **Pick a directory or index you like and tell your browser to go to the index or directory's home page.**

   We list the URLs (Web addresses) of the home pages later in this section.

   After you get there, you can choose between two approaches.
3. **a. If a Search box appears, type some likely keywords in the box and click Search.**

   This is the "index" approach: to look for topic areas that match your keywords.

   After a perhaps long delay (the Web is pretty big), an index page is returned with links to pages that match your keywords. The list of links may be way too long to deal with — like 300,000 of them.

   or

   b. If you see a list of links to topic areas, click a topic area of interest.

   In the "directory" approach, you begin at a general topic and get more and more specific. Each page has links to pages that get more and more specific until they link to actual pages that are likely to be of interest.
4. **Adjust and repeat your search until you find something you like.**

   After some clicking around to get the hang of it, you find all sorts of good stuff.

You hear a great deal of talk around the Web about search engines. *Search engines* is a fancy way to say *stuff-finding stuff.* All the directories and indexes we're about to describe are in the broad category called search engines, so don't get upset by some highfalutin' terms.

Search-a-Roo

So much for the theory of searching for stuff on the Net. Now for some practice. (Theory and practice are much farther apart in practice than they are in theory.) We use our favorite search systems for examples: Google, which is mostly an index and then ODP and Yahoo, which are directories.

Google-oogle, our favorite index

Our favorite Web index is Google. It has little robots that spend their time merrily visiting Web pages all over the Net and reporting what they saw. It makes an humongous index of which words occurred in which pages; when you search for something, it picks pages from the index that contain the words you asked for. Google uses a sophisticated ranking system based on how many *other* Web sites refer to each one in the index that more often than not puts the best pages first.

Using Google or any other index is an exercise in remote-control mind reading. You have to guess words that will appear on the pages you're looking for. Sometimes, that's easy — if you're looking for recipes for key lime pie, `key lime pie` is a good set of search words because you know the name of what you're looking for. On the other hand, if you have forgotten that the capital of France is Paris, it's hard to tease a useful page out of an index because you don't know what words to look for. (If you try `France capital`, you find info about investment banking and Fort de France, which is the capital of the French overseas département of Martinique.)

Now that we have you all discouraged, try some Google searches. Direct your browser to `www.google.com`. You see a screen like the one shown in Figure 7-1.

Type some search terms, and Google finds the pages that best match your terms. That's "best match," not "match" — if it can't match all the terms, it finds pages that match as well as possible. Google ignores words that occur too often to be usable as index terms, both the obvious ones such as `and`, `the`, and `of` and terms such as `internet` and `mail`. These rules can sound somewhat discouraging, but in fact it's still not hard to get useful results from Google. You just have to think up good search terms. Try that recipe example, by typing **key lime pie** and clicking the Search button. You get the response shown in Figure 7-2.

The lazy searcher's search page

You may feel a wee bit overwhelmed with all the search directories and indexes we discuss in this chapter. If it makes you feel any better, so do we.

To make a little sense of all this stuff, we made ourselves a search page that connects to all the directories and indexes we use so that we get one-stop searching. You can use it, too. Give it a try at `net.gurus.com/search`.

In the not unlikely event that new search systems are created or some of the existing ones have moved or died, this page gives you our latest greatest list and lets you sign up for mailed updates when we change it.

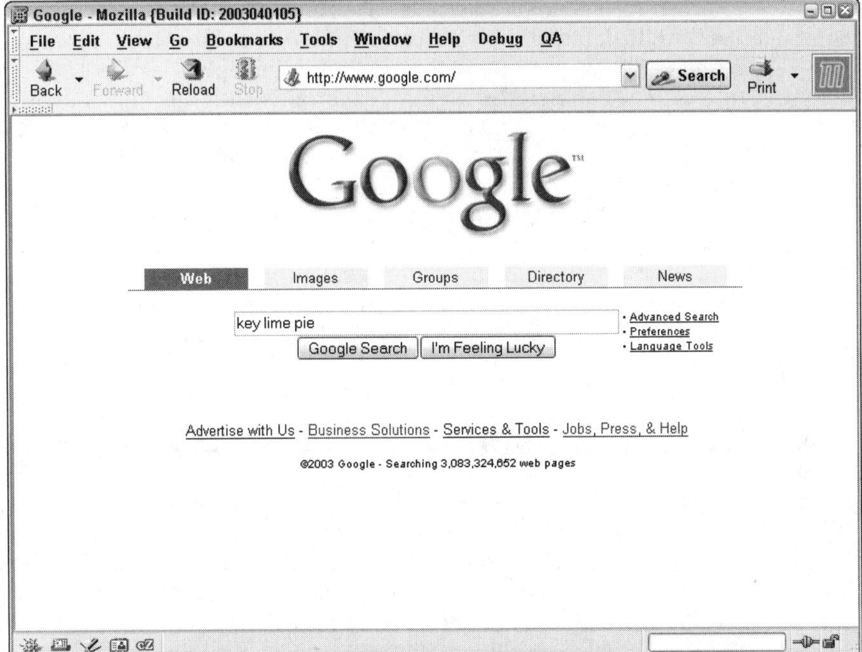

Figure 7-1: Google, ready to roll.

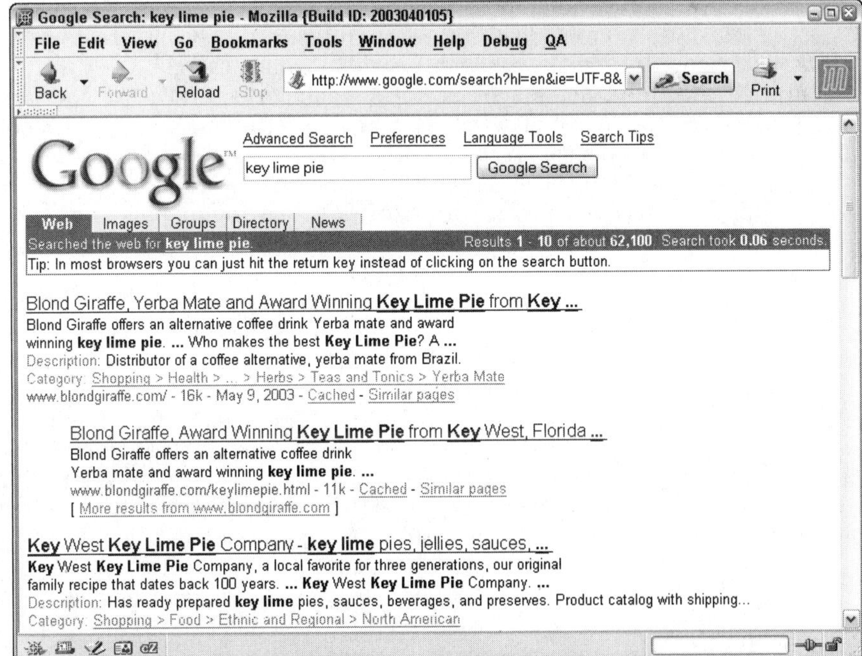

Figure 7-2: Plenty of pages of pie.

Your results will not look exactly like Figure 7-2 because Google will have updated its database since this book went to press. Most of the pages it found do, in fact, have something to do with key lime pie — some have a pretty good recipe. (The list includes a lot of restaurants with Key Lime Pie on the menu and some references to a movie called *Key Lime Pie.* Indexes are pretty dumb; you have to add the intelligence.) Google says it found 62,000 matches (yow!) but it takes pity on you and only will show you about 100 of them, 10 at a time. Although that's still probably more than you wanted to look at, you should at least look at the next couple of screens of matches if the first screen doesn't have what you want. At the bottom of the Google screen are page numbers; click Next to go to the next page. The "I'm Feeling Lucky" button searches and takes you directly to the first link, which works when, well, when you're lucky.

ODP: It's open, it's big, and it's Googleable

Wouldn't it be nice if there were a really big directory with as much stuff as an index? Sure, but who'd ever be able to pay people to build a directory that big? Nobody, but volunteers do it for free. Netscape started the Open Directory Project (ODP), a volunteer effort to create the world's biggest and best Web directory. Propelled by the same community spirit that built Linux and Mozilla, ODP has indeed become a killer Web directory. Because ODP is available for anyone to use for free, dozens of search engines provide ODP along with their own index information.

ODP lives at `www.dmoz.org`, (*dmoz* roughly stands for Directory Mozilla) although it's usually easier to get to it through Google. The directory is a set of categories, subcategories, sub-subcategories, and so on down to an impressive degree of detail. Each category can and usually does contain a bunch of Web pages. You can either start at the top directory level and click your way through the categories, (click the Directory tab on the Google home page to start), or search within the directory to find pages and then look at the categories that include interesting pages.

If you've already done a Google Web search, you can click on the Directory tab near the top of the page, and it shows you only the pages that are in ODP. Because those pages have all been at least glanced at by a person, they're probably of higher quality than the mechanically collected ones in the general Google list. In any Google Web Search results listing, if a given page belongs to a category, you can click on that listing's Category: link to see other pages belonging to the same category. Because we were still hungry and wanted to see more recipes, we clicked one of the category links later in the list in Figure 7-2 to get to the ODP category `Home > Cooking > Baking and Confections > Pies and Pastry` shown in Figure 7-3. You see not only the relevant Web pages, but also links to related categories. There are so many categories in ODP that you often have to click around to find the exact subcategory you want, but when you find it, you generally find some interesting links. (If you don't, see the sidebar "You may already be an expert".)

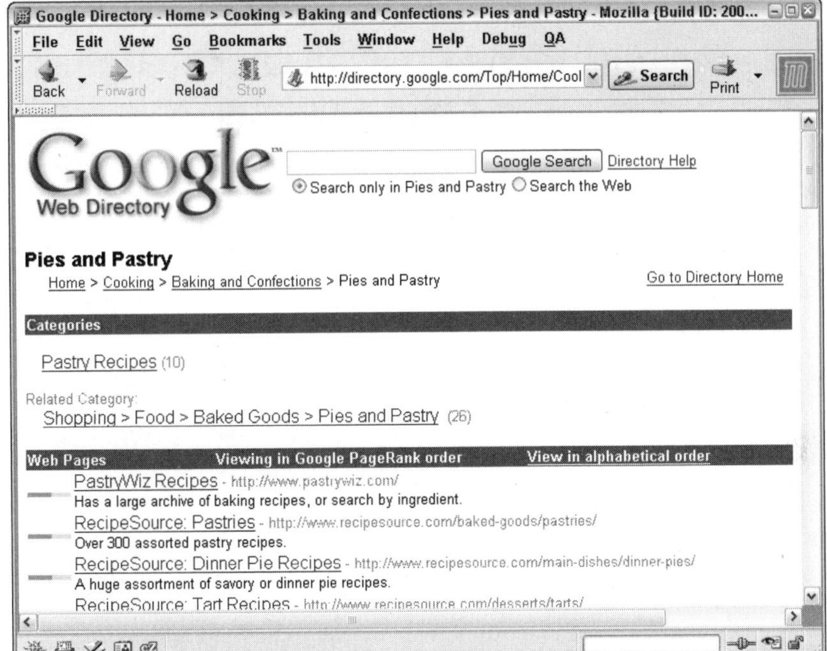

Figure 7-3: Pie ideas from ODP.

Handy index targeting tips

Google makes it easy to refine your search more exactly to target the pages you want to find. After each search, your search terms appear in a box at the top of the page so that you can change them and try again. Here are some tips on how you may want to change your terms:

- Type most search words in lowercase. Type proper names with a single capital letter, such as `Elvis`. Don't type any words in all capital letters.
- If two or more words should appear together, put quotes around them, as in `"Elvis Presley"`. You should do that with the pie search ("key lime pie") because, after all, that is what the pie is called, although in this example, Google is clever enough to realize that it's a common phrase and pretends you typed the quotes anyway.
- Use + and – to indicate words that must either appear or not appear, such as `+Elvis +Costello -Presley` if you're looking for the modern Elvis, not the classic one.

The number one reason your searches don't find anything

Well, it may not be *your* number one reason, but it's *our* number one reason: One of the search words is spelled wrong. Check carefully. John notes that his fingers insist on typing "Interent," which doesn't find much other than Web pages from other people who can't spell. (Thanks to our friend Jean Armour Polly, for reminding us about this problem.)

Even more Google

Although Google looks very simple, it has plenty of other options that can be handy:

- Type in a street address, and Google will offer a link to a map. Type in a person's name and a full or partial address, at least the state abbreviation, and it'll give you addresses and phone numbers. Type in a phone number, and it'll often give you the name and address. (Try 202 456 1414.) The information is all collected from public sources, but if you find this a bit too creepy, look yourself up and if it finds you, it'll include a link to a page where you can have your info removed.
- You can search *Usenet,* the giant collection of Internet newsgroups (online discussion groups). Simply click the Groups tab near the search box. If a topic has been discussed in the past 20 years on Usenet, which most topics have, this technique is the best way to find the messages about that topic. Although Google is only a few years old, its Usenet archive includes contributions from many online pack rats and goes back decades. (John found things there that he wrote in 1981.) For a description of Usenet, see `net.gurus.com/usenet`.
- You can search for images as well as text by clicking the Image tab on any Google search page. Google has no idea what each image is but looks at the surrounding text and the filename of the image and does a remarkably good job of guessing. If you do an image search for "key lime pie," you will indeed see dozens of pictures of tasty pies. A "safe search" feature omits pictures of naked people and the like. If you turn off safe search, you can find some impressively unsafe pictures.
- Google News (click the News tab or start at `news.google.com`) shows a summary of current online news culled automatically from thousands of sources all over the world. ***Warning:*** If you are interested in current events, you can easily waste 12 hours a day following links from here.

- You can limit your search to documents in a specific language. No sense in finding pages in a language you can't read, although Google has a subsystem that can try, with mixed success, to translate pages from some other languages. Click the Language Tools link at the top of the Google window.

Yahoo, ancient king of the directories

Yahoo is one of the oldest directories and still a pretty good one. As with ODP, you can search for entries or click from category to category until you find something you like. We start our Yahoo visit at its home page, at `www.yahoo.com` (at least the page name doesn't use an exclamation point), as shown in Figure 7-4. (As with all Web pages, the exact design may have changed by the time you read this, but Yahoo's layout has remained pretty steady for years.) A whole bunch of categories and subcategories are listed. You can click any of them to see another page that has yet more subcategories and links to actual Web pages. You can click a link to a page if you see one you like or on a sub-subcategory, and so on.

At the top of each Yahoo directory page is the list of categories, subcategories, and so on, separated by colons, that lead to that page. If you want to back up a few levels and look at different subcategories, just click the place on that list to which you want to back up. After a little clicking up and down, it's second nature. Many pages appear in more than one place in the directory because they fall into more than one category. Web pages can have as many links referring to them as they want.

The 404 blues

More often than we want to admit, when you click a link from a search results page, rather than get the promised page, you get a message such as `404 Not Found`. What did you do wrong? Nothing. Web pages come and go and move around with great velocity, and the various Web indexes do a lousy job, frankly, of cleaning out links to old, dead pages that have gone away.

The automated indexes, such as Google and AltaVista, are better in this regard than the manual directories, such as Yahoo. The automated ones have software robots that revisit all the indexed pages every once in a while and note whether they still exist; even so, many lonely months can pass between robot visits, and a great deal can happen to a page in the meantime. Google *caches* (stores) a copy of most pages it visits, so even if the original has gone away, you can click the Cache link at the end of a Google index entry and see a copy of the page as it was when Google last looked at it.

It's just part of life on the online frontier — the high-tech equivalent of riding your horse along the trail in the Old West and noticing that there sure are a lot of bleached-white cattle skulls lying around.

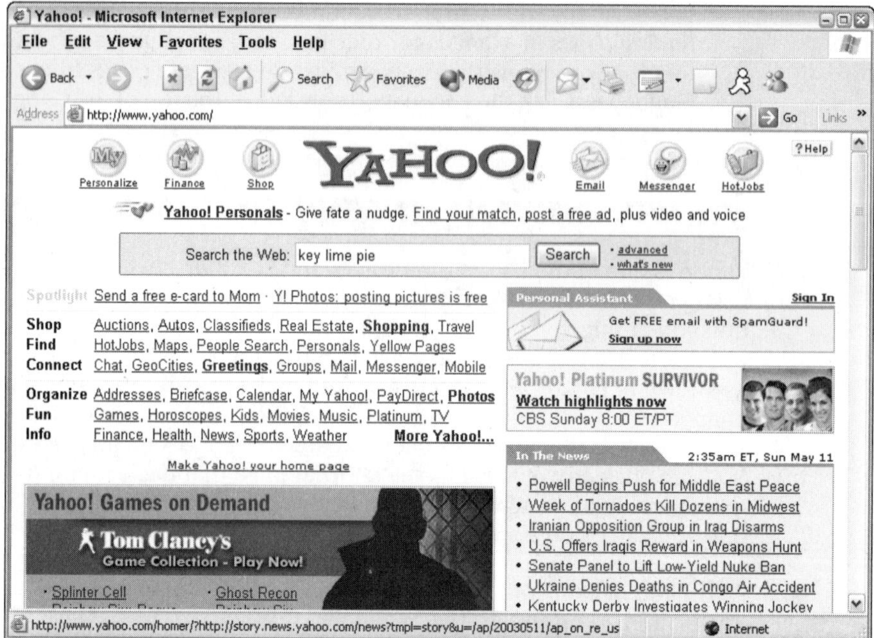

Figure 7-4: Ready to Yahoo.

Although all the categories in the Yahoo list have plenty of subcategories under them, some have many more than others. If you're looking for a business-related page, it helps to know that Yahoo sticks just about everything commercial under the category Business and Economy, as shown in Figure 7-5. If we were looking for Internet Gurus Central, for example (which we think people should look for several times a day, at least), we could click our way to it from the Yahoo home page by clicking Business and Economy, on that page, clicking Shopping and Services, then Books, then Bookstores, then Computers, and then Internet; on that page, you link to pages with lots of Internet books, including ours.

If you know in general but not in detail what you're looking for, clicking up and down through the Yahoo directory pages is a good way to narrow your search and find pages of interest.

Early on, it was easy to get a Web page into Yahoo simply by entering it into their submissions page and waiting a week or so for their editors to look at it. Now that it's so popular, normal submissions take a long, long time before anyone looks at them (months, maybe years), unless you pay them $299 for "express" service. You can draw your own conclusions about the effect on what gets into Yahoo and what doesn't.

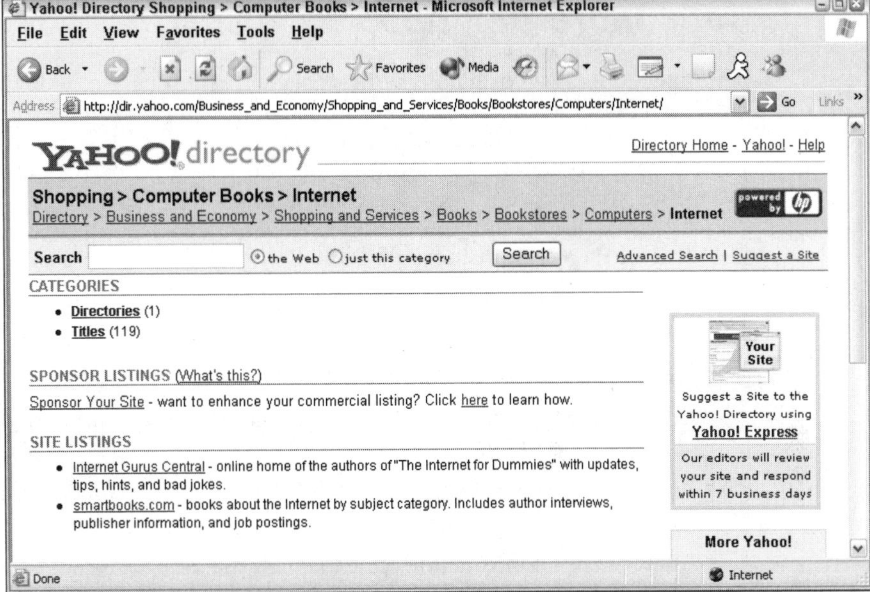

Figure 7-5: A storehouse of commercial information at Yahoo.

Searching through Yahoo

"Click Business And Economy, and then, on that page, click Shopping And Services, then Books, then Bookstores, then Computers, and then Internet? How the heck did they know which categories to click?" you're doubtless asking. We admit it. We cheated — we searched for the page instead.

Yahoo also lets you search its index by keyword, which is the best way to use it if you have some idea of the title of the page you're looking for. Every Yahoo screen has near the top a search box in which you can type words you want to find in the Yahoo entry for pages of interest. For example, we typed **Internet dummies books**, clicked the Search button next to the type-in box, and got a page with one entry for our Web site and one for another online bookstore.

With each entry Yahoo finds, it includes a More sites about link to the page's category if the page is in their directory. Even if the entry isn't quite right, if you click the category, you find other related pages, and some of them may well do the trick.

You can click the Advanced Search link next to the Search button to get to the slightly more advanced Yahoo search page. It lets you limit how far back you want to see pages (three years is the default), and you can tell it to look for either all the words or any of the words you typed.

Tons more at Yahoo

Although Yahoo was originally a directory of resources available on the Web, it's now a *portal,* which means that it has lots of other databases available to encourage you to stick around inside Yahoo. Each has a link you can click just under the box in which you would enter search terms. They add new databases about once a week; some popular ones include

- **Yellow Pages:** A business directory.
- **People Search:** Finds addresses and phone numbers like a white pages directory (see the "Finding People" section).
- **Maps:** Gets a more or less accurate map of a street address you type.
- **Classifieds:** Lets you read and submit ads for automobiles, apartments, computers, and jobs.
- **Personals:** Lets you read and submit ads for dates in all (and we mean *all*) combinations.
- **Chat:** Gets you into online chat through the Web.
- **Email:** Free Web-based, e-mail service.
- **Auctions:** Web-based auctions, not unlike eBay.
- **TV:** Impressively complete TV and cable listings, by area.
- **Travel:** A link to the Travelocity reservation system, as well as a variety of other resources. (See `airline.iecc.com` for our opinions and suggestions about online travel services.)
- **My Yahoo:** A customized starting page just for you with headlines, sports scores, and other news based on your preferences.
- **Today's News, Stock Quotes, and Sports Scores:** News from a variety of wire services, newspapers, and other media.

Yahoo, Google, ODP, and more

Looking in your favorite directory or index is an effective way to search the Web; if you don't find what you want, try following its links to your second and third favorites. If you click "Web Pages" on a Yahoo search page, you see an index that looks not unlike Google, because it *is* Google, along with "sponsor results," which are paid listings. The search business is fiercely competitive, so all the search engines are busy adding new goodies. Poke around on your favorite and second favorite search engine and see what you can find.

Here ends our survey of key lime pies. Just a minute while we run down to the kitchen and have another piece.

You may already be an expert

The Open Directory Project depends on volunteers to manage a category. If you search for something, look at what's in the category, and think "Sheesh, I could do better than that," perhaps it's time to volunteer and do so. The time commitment for a single category is modest — just a few minutes a week to see what's been suggested and edit, add, or reject it.

To volunteer, click the Become an Editor link near the top of any dmoz.org window. There's a small questionnaire that asks who you are, why you're interested, and what entries you would like to add to your category. If you're accepted (most people are), you can start editing in a day or two. There are tutorials and mailing lists for editors, so you don't have to do it all by yourself.

John edits the categories for *compilers,* a kind of software that's a professional interest from his grad school days, as well as the one for Unitarian church camps because he was looking for one camp, saw the category, and thought "Sheesh, I could ... oh, right." Margy edits topics about e-mail mailing lists and restaurants in Vermont.

We're from Your Browser, and We're Here to Help You

In 1998, Netscape and Microsoft both decided to crowbar their way into the search engine market. (Who? Us? Opinionated?) Starting with Netscape 4.06 and Internet Explorer 4.0, both will take you directly to their respective preferred search system if you give them half a chance. These search systems aren't awful, but unless you are the kind of person who turns on the TV and watches whatever is on the first channel you come to, you'll probably find that you prefer to choose your own search engine. Fortunately, enough Web users felt that way that current built-in search features aren't too bad.

Netscape and Mozilla's Smart Browsing

Mozilla and Netscape have two useful built-in search features, the Search button and the sidebar.

To use the Search button, which is to the right of the address box, type in your search words in the address box and click Search. It turns your words into a request to a search engine and displays the result. Netscape comes with the search engine set, not surprisingly, to Netscape search, which at the moment is basically Google with a lot more ads. Fortunately, you can change it. Select

Edit➪Preferences, double-click Navigator to expand it if it's not expanded already, and click Internet Search. There you can select from a list of search engines. Of the ones they offer, Google and dmoz.org (ODP) are the most likely to be useful. (Of the others, Lycos is a search engine that's been around for a long time but is now an also-ran, and Overture is purely paid listings.)

Netscape and Mozilla also have a *sidebar,* an optional pane at the left side of the window that has tabs, providing various features that may be useful. The search tab, shown in Figure 7-6, can be fairly useful because it lets you keep the search results in the sidebar while you visit the pages you found. Press F9 to open the sidebar if it's not already open; then click the Search tab. Pick the search engine you want, type your search words into the box at the top and click search. You get a search summary in the main window and a list of clickable links in the sidebar that stay put as you click them and look at the pages in the main window.

For really dedicated searchers, there's an option in the Edit➪Preferences window for an advanced multisearch-engine search in the sidebar, but we find it more complicated and buggy than it's worth.

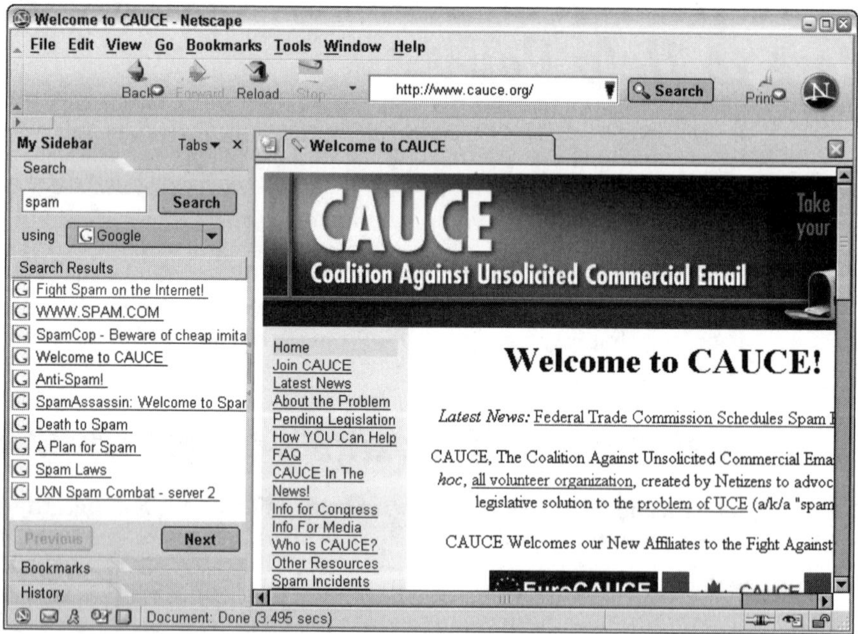

Figure 7-6: Netscape's sidebar helps you search.

Who pays for all this stuff?

You may be wondering who pays for all these wonderful search systems. Advertising supports all except one of them. On every page of most search systems, you see lots and lots of ads. In theory, the advertising pays the costs. In reality, of all the ad-supported systems, only Yahoo is known to have turned a profit. Others raised lots of capital during the dot-com bubble and have been living off it since. Google is privately owned so it doesn't have to publish financial results, but it's reputed to be making a lot of money from the small sponsored links that appear on its result pages.

The exception is the Open Directory Project, which works on the open source model. The vast majority of contributors are unpaid volunteers with a small amount of support for the Web site and coordinators provided by AOL's Netscape subsidiary.

The big Internet "bubble" rapidly deflated in 2000 and 2001 with some engines such as Excite going broke. We expect more of the search systems to run out of money and shut down or merge with others. Visit `net.gurus.com/search` for the latest up- or down-dates.

Microsoft's Autosearch

In Internet Explorer 4.0 or later, if you type keywords into the Address box, Internet Explorer sends them to MSN Search, which uses data from LookSmart, an adequate Web directory, along with a lot of links that look suspiciously like advertisements.

Internet Explorer (IE) also has the Search Bar. If you click the Search button on the toolbar, a Search Bar pane appears to the left of your Explorer window with a small search engine page. In IE 6, the Web search lets you use one or more search engines and combines the results. Click the Customize button to tell it which engines you like. Of the options they offer, Google is the one of choice. While you're at it, you can get rid of the annoying Search Doggie, turn off the useless balloon tips, and otherwise make your browser act more like a tool for you and less like an ad for Microsoft. IE's search box confusingly mixes Web searches with file searches on your own computer; the options called Indexing Service and Files or Folders affect only the way that Windows searches the disk on your own computer, not the Net.

More search magic

Microsoft and Netscape remain in frantic competition for search users, so by the time you read this, there will doubtless be even more search features in each browser. Drop by our Web site at `net.gurus.com/search` to find out what's new.

The Usual Suspects

After you surf around Yahoo, Google, and ODP for a while, you may want to check out the competition.

About.com

`www.about.com`

About is a directory with several hundred semiprofessional "guides" who manage the topic areas. The guides vary from okay to very good, so if you're looking for in-depth information on a topic, it's worth checking About.com to see what the guide has to say.

AltaVista

`www.altavista.com`

AltaVista is a really big index — for many years the biggest, although Google has now blown past it. It doesn't have Google's smarts about putting the most interesting pages first, but for searches for obscure things where you know some keywords, it remains hard to beat.

Bytedog

`www.bytedog.com`

Bytedog assembles the results of searches at other search engines and presents them in a ranked list with cute dog graphics (cuter than Microsoft's, if you ask us). It takes a few extra seconds to respond, but that's because it's filtering out bad links before you have to deal with them. Bytedog is a project of a couple of students at the University of Waterloo, Ontario.

HotBot and Lycos

`www.hotbot.com`
`www.lycos.com`

Lycos started as a largely automated index in a project at Carnegie-Mellon University and has also gone commercial, now mostly accepting paid listings. Although Lycos was one of the earliest Web search systems, at this point, honestly, AltaVista and Google have better indexes, and ODP and Yahoo have better directories. HotBot used to be a directory, too, but now is a gateway to a few other search engines. Both now belong to Telefonica, the dominant Spanish telephone company that planned to use them to make the world's most popular Web portal. (Good luck.)

Looksmart and Zeal

`www.looksmart.com`
`www.zeal.com`

Looksmart is yet another search engine. You can use it directly, but you're more likely to run into it as the engine underlying the search at MSN and other sites that license its content. Listings of commercial sites are all paid, and noncommercial sites are entered through Zeal, which is a peculiar sort-of community directory, except that unlike ODP it only accepts noncommercial entries, and the results are only available to Looksmart's licensees.

Other Web guides

ODP has a directory of several hundred other guides: See `dmoz.org/Computers/Internet/Searching` for links to them.

Finding Companies

The first way to search for companies is to search for the company name as a topic. If you're looking for Great Tapes for Kids, for example, search for `Great Tapes for Kids` in ODP, Google, or any of the other search systems. (That's our experiment in online commerce, as we mention in Chapter 8.) After you do that, a few other places are worth checking for business-related info.

Hoovering in

`www.hoovers.com`

Company home pages vary in informativeness, but they often don't tell you much about the company itself. Hoover's is a business information company that has been publishing paper business directories for quite a while. Now it's on the Net as well. Its Web site offers free company capsules, stock prices, and other company info. If you sign up for its pricey paid service, it offers considerably more. Even the free stuff is quite useful.

Ask EDGAR

`edgar.sec.gov/edgar.shtml` (government)
`www.edgar-online.com` (private)

The U.S. Securities and Exchange Commission (SEC), the people who regulate stock and bond markets, has a system called EDGAR that collects all the financial material that publicly traded companies have to file with the government. Although most of this stuff is dry and financial, if you can read financial statements, you can find all sorts of interesting information, such as Bill Gates's salary.

The government EDGAR site is run directly by the SEC, and the private site, EDGAR Online, is run by an independent company, Cybernet Data Systems, Inc. Although the two sites have pretty much the same information, the private site offers free, limited access and charges a modest price (about $10 per month) for more complete access and automatic e-mail updates when a company you're interested in files EDGAR documents.

The ten-minute challenge

Our friend Doug Hacker claims to be able to find the answer to any factual query on the Net in less than ten minutes. Carol challenged him to find a quote she vaguely knew from the liner notes of a Duke Ellington album, whose title she couldn't remember. He had the complete quote in about an hour but spent less than five minutes himself. How? He found a mailing list about Duke Ellington, subscribed, and asked the question. Several members replied in short order. The more time you spend finding your way around the Net, the more you know where to go for the information you need.

Lots of other business directories

Tons of business information is available on the Net. Here are a few places to begin.

Inc. magazine

```
www.inc.com
www.inc.com/inc500
```

Inc. magazine concentrates on small, fast-growing companies. Each year, its Inc. 500 features the 500 companies it likes the best. Many hot little companies are listed here, with contact information.

Yellow pages

```
www.superpages.com
www.smartpages.com
www.infousa.com
```

Quite a few yellow pages business directories, both national and local, are on the Net. The directories in this list are some of the national ones. Superpages and Smartpages are run by Verizon and SBC respectively, the two largest phone companies in the U.S., but they're all worth a look. InfoUSA even offers credit reports, although we can't vouch for its reliability.

Finding People

Finding people on the Internet is surprisingly easy. It's so easy that, indeed, sometimes it's creepy. Two overlapping categories of people finders are available: those that look for people on the Net with e-mail and Web addresses and those that look for people in real life with phone numbers and street addresses.

In real life

The real-life directories are compiled mostly from telephone directories. If you haven't had a listed phone number in the past few years, you probably aren't in any of these directories.

On the Net

The process of finding e-mail and Web addresses is somewhat hit-and-miss. Because no online equivalent to the official phone book the telephone company produces has ever existed, directories of e-mail addresses are collected from addresses used in Web pages, Usenet messages, mailing lists, and other more or less public places on the Net. Because the different directories use different sources, if you don't find someone in one directory, you can try another. Remember that because the e-mail directories are incomplete, there's no substitute for calling someone up and asking, "What's your e-mail address?"

Googling for people

Type in someone's name and address to Google (for the address, at least the state abbreviation, but more is better), and it'll show you matches from phone book listings.

If you're wondering whether someone has a Web page, use Google or AltaVista to search for just his name. If you're wondering whether you're famous, use Google or AltaVista to search for your own name and see how many people mention you or link to your Web pages. If you get e-mail from someone you don't know, search Google for the e-mail address — it's bound to appear on a Web page somewhere.

Yahoo People Search (Four-eleven)

`www.yahoo.com/search/people`

You can search for addresses and phone numbers and e-mail addresses. If you don't like your own listing, you can add, update, or delete it. This is the system formerly at `www.four11.com`.

InfoUSA white pages

`www.infousa.com`

To access the white pages, click the "Find a Person" on the left side of the window. This site is another white pages directory. After you have found the entry you want, you can ask for a graphical street map of the address.

WhoWhere

www.whowhere.lycos.com

WhoWhere is another e-mail address directory. Although Yahoo usually gives better results, some people are listed in WhoWhere who aren't listed in other places.

Canada 411

www.canada411.com

Canada 411 is a complete Canadian telephone book, sponsored by the major Canadian telephone companies. Aussi disponsible en français, eh? For several years the listings for Alberta and Saskatchewan were missing, leading to concern that the two provinces were too boring to bother with, but they're all there now, proving that they're just as gnarly as everyone else.

Bigfoot

www.bigfoot.com

Bigfoot provides a way to search for people in addition to permanent, free e-mail addresses for life (it promises to forward limited amounts of mail from your Bigfoot address to your Internet account forever for free).

After you're listed in Bigfoot, there is no way whatsoever to remove your listing, even if it's wrong.

Mail, one more time

Mailing lists are another important resource. Most lists (but not all — check before you ask) welcome concrete, politely phrased questions related to the list's topic. See Chapter 11 to find more information about mailing lists, including how to look for lists of particular topics of interest to you.

Getting the Goods

All the commercial directories and indexes now put shopping information somewhere on their home page to help get your credit card closer to the Web faster. Some are even sponsored by VISA. You can find department stores and catalogs from all over offering every conceivable item (and some inconceivable items). We tell you all the do's, don'ts, and how-to's in Chapter 8.

Chapter 8

More Shopping, Less Dropping

In This Chapter

- Why shop online?
- To charge it or not to charge it
- Step-by-step shopping
- Where to find airline tickets, mutual funds, books, clothes, computers, and food online

If you watched the implosion of the dot.com boom, you may have gotten the impression that e-commerce is dead. Surprisingly, much of the hype turns out to be false, and you can still buy all sorts of stuff over the Internet. We have bought lots of things online, from books to pants to plane tickets to stocks and mutual funds to computer parts to musical instruments to, uh, specialized personal products (don't read too much into that), and lived to tell the tale.

Shopping Online: Pros and Cons

Here are some reasons why we shop on the Net:

- Online stores are convenient, open all night, and don't mind if you aren't wearing shoes or if you window-shop for a week before you buy something.
- Prices are often lower online, and you can compare prices at several online establishments in a matter of minutes. Even if you eventually make your purchase in a brick and mortar store, what you find out online can save you money. Shipping and handling is similar to what you'd pay for mail order, and you don't have to drive or park.

- Online stores can sometimes offer a better selection. They usually ship from a central warehouse rather than having to keep stock on the shelf at dozens of branches. If you're looking for something hard to find — for example, a part for that vintage toaster oven you're repairing — the Web can save you weeks of searching.
- Two of the three authors of this book live in small rural towns; a lot of stuff just isn't available locally. (Trumansburg, New York, is a wonderful place, but if you want to buy a book other than the three days a year the library has its book sale, you're out of luck. And Margy couldn't find a harmonium anywhere in the Champlain Valley.)
- Unlike malls, online stores don't have Muzak. (Occasionally Web sites play background music, but we move on to other sites quickly.)

Net shopping's greatest hits

What should you buy online? Here are some good bets:

- **Books and CDs:** Online stores are fiercely competitive, and the prices can be impressively cheap. Browsing is harder, though, and you can't always read the first chapter before you choose. However, you can hear audio clips, which can be fun in its own right.
- **Airplane tickets and other travel arrangements:** You can do better than all but the best travel agents.
- **Computers:** If you know what you want, online is usually cheaper and less hassle than a big computer store.
- **Groceries:** Online food shopping is available only in a few places, and if you must squeeze each melon you buy, it may not be for you. But it is a boon for the mobility-impaired and those of us scarce on free time.
- **Medicine:** With the cost of prescriptions soaring, shopping online for (legal) drugs can save you money. Some people have even found ways to obtain their medications from countries like Canada where prices are much lower. Needless to say, the pharmaceutical industry finds this a bitter pill to swallow and is using every legal method to fight the practice.
- **Stocks and mutual funds:** If you make your own investment decisions, online brokerage is much, much cheaper than a regular broker — $8–$30 per trade rather than as much as $50 for discount or $100 for a full-service broker. Also, online brokers don't get annoyed if you check stock prices 47 times a day.
- **Anything you'd buy from a mail-order catalog:** Most catalog merchants have Web sites, usually with special offers not in the paper catalog. (They'd really like you to order over the Net rather than talk to an expensive human operator at a toll-free number they have to pay for.)

On the other hand, here are some reasons why we don't buy everything on the Net:

- You can't physically look at or try on stuff before you buy it, and in most cases, you have to wait for it to be shipped to you. We haven't had much luck buying shoes online, f'rinstance.
- We like our local stores and prefer to support them when we can.
- You can't flirt with the staff at a Web store or find out about the latest town gossip.

The Credit Card Question

How do you pay for stuff you buy online? Most often with a credit card, the same way you pay for anything else. Isn't it incredibly, awfully dangerous to give out your credit card number online, though? Well, no.

For one thing, most online stores encrypt the message between your computer and the store's server. (An encrypted connection is indicated in your Web browser by a closed lock icon in the bottom-left corner of the window). For another, plucking the occasional credit card number from the gigabytes of traffic that flows every minute on the Net would be close to impossible even without encryption.

When you use plastic at a restaurant, you give your physical card with your physical signature to the wait staff who takes it to the back room, does who knows what with it, and then brings it back. Compared with that, the risk of sending your number to an online store is pretty small. A friend of ours used to run a restaurant and later ran an online store and assures us that there's no comparison: The online store had none of the credit card problems that the restaurant did.

If, after this harangue, you still don't want to send your credit card number over the Net or you're one of the fiscally responsible holdouts who doesn't do plastic, most online stores are happy to have you call in your card number over the phone or send them a check or money order. (Or use PayPal: See the sidebar "E-mail cash to anyone" later in this chapter.)

Credit cards versus debit cards

Credit cards and debit cards look the same and spend the same, but credit cards bill you at the end of the month while debit cards take the money right out of your bank account. In the U.S., consumer protection laws work differently for credit and debit cards, and they're much stronger for credit cards. We recommend that you use a credit card to get the better protection and then pay the bill at the end of the month so you don't owe interest.

Going to the Store

Stores on the Web work in two general ways: with and without virtual *shopping carts.* In stores without carts, you either order one item at a time or fill out a big order form with a check box for everything the store offers. In stores with carts, as you look at the items the store has for sale, you can add items to your cart and then visit the virtual checkout line when you're done, where you provide your payment and delivery information. Until you check out, you can add and remove items from your cart whenever you want, just like in the real world — except that you don't have to put unwanted items back on the shelf.

Simple shopping

For an example of simple shopping, our randomly chosen site happens to sell books written by one of us authors. (Us? Venal? Naah.) Follow the Autographed copies link from our site `net.gurus.com`, and in a few clicks, you'll arrive at the order page shown in Figure 8-1. It shows the selected item and has an order form ready for your details.

In the form, you enter the same stuff you would put on a paper order form. Most forms have a place for typing a credit card number; if you're not comfortable entering it there (refer to the section "The Credit Card Question," earlier in this chapter), leave that blank — the store invariably has a way you can call the number in. Click the Prepare Order button, and you'll see an order review page (as shown in Figure 8-2) where you can check that the details are correct. Click Place Order, and your order is on its way.

You generally get an e-mail message confirming the details of your order and frequently get e-mail updates if any problems or delays occur.

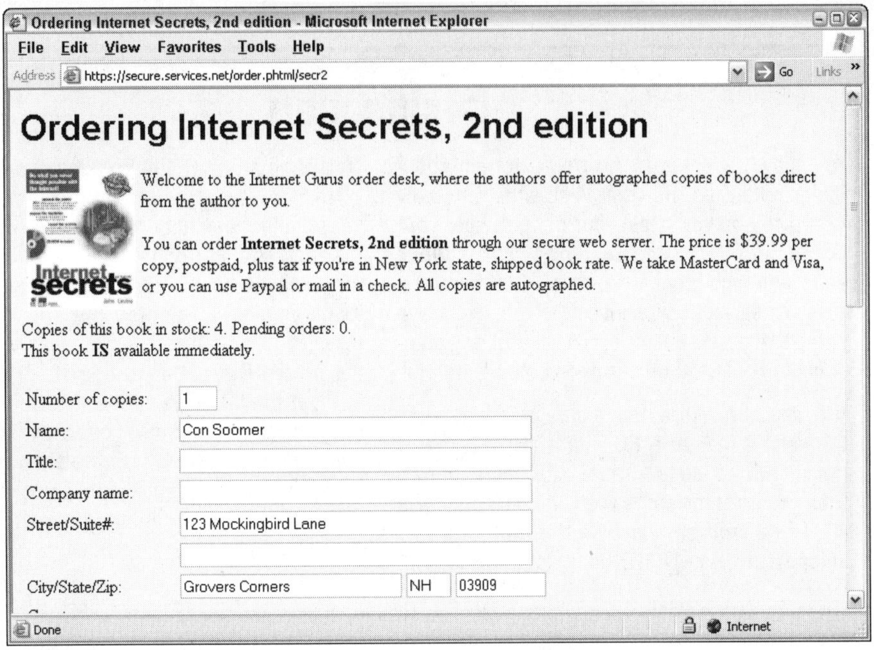

Ordering Internet Secrets, 2nd edition - Microsoft Internet Explorer

File Edit View Favorites Tools Help

Address https://secure.services.net/order.phtml/secr2

Ordering Internet Secrets, 2nd edition

Welcome to the Internet Gurus order desk, where the authors offer autographed copies of books direct from the author to you.

You can order **Internet Secrets, 2nd edition** through our secure web server. The price is $39.99 per copy, postpaid, plus tax if you're in New York state, shipped book rate. We take MasterCard and Visa, or you can use Paypal or mail in a check. All copies are autographed.

Copies of this book in stock: 4. Pending orders: 0.
This book **IS** available immediately.

Number of copies: 1
Name: Con Soomer
Title:
Company name:
Street/Suite#: 123 Mockingbird Lane
City/State/Zip: Grovers Corners NH 03909

Done Internet

Figure 8-1: Welcome to John's secure online store.

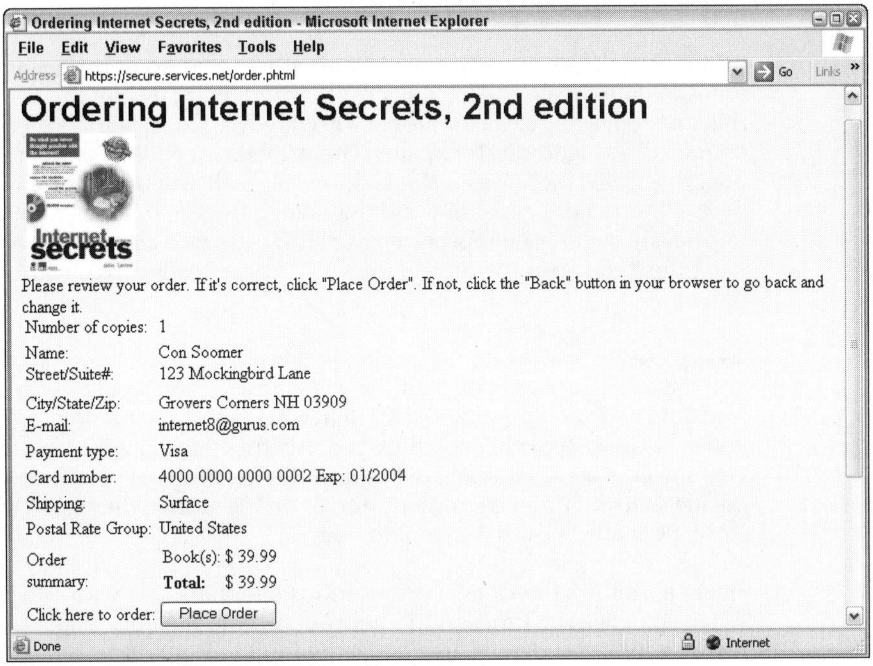

Ordering Internet Secrets, 2nd edition - Microsoft Internet Explorer

File Edit View Favorites Tools Help

Address https://secure.services.net/order.phtml

Ordering Internet Secrets, 2nd edition

Please review your order. If it's correct, click "Place Order". If not, click the "Back" button in your browser to go back and change it.

Number of copies: 1
Name: Con Soomer
Street/Suite#: 123 Mockingbird Lane
City/State/Zip: Grovers Corners NH 03909
E-mail: internet8@gurus.com
Payment type: Visa
Card number: 4000 0000 0000 0002 Exp: 01/2004
Shipping: Surface
Postal Rate Group: United States
Order summary: Book(s): $ 39.99 **Total:** $ 39.99
Click here to order: Place Order

Done Internet

Figure 8-2: Ready to order some quality literature.

Cookie alert

You may have heard horrible stories about things called *cookies* that Web sites reputedly use to spy on you, steal your data, ravage your computer, inject cellulite into your hips while you sleep, and otherwise make your life miserable. After extensive investigation, we have found that most cookies aren't bad; when you're shopping online, they can even be quite helpful.

A *cookie* is no more than a little chunk of text a Web site sends to a PC with a request (not a command) to send the cookie back during future visits to the same Web site. The cookie is stored on your computer in the form of a tiny snippet of text. That's all it is. Mozilla and Netscape store all the cookies in a file called `cookies.txt`, whereas Internet Explorer uses a folder called Cookies with a separate file for each site. For online shopping, cookies let the Web server track your shopping cart of items you have selected but not yet bought, even if you log out and turn off your computer in the interim. Stores can also use cookies to keep track of the last time you visited and what you bought, but they can also keep that data on their own computers, so what's the big deal? (If you really don't want Web sites to store cookies on your computer, you can prevent them; see how in Chapter 6.)

Fancy shopping

Although a simple store works okay for stores that don't have many different items in their catalog or for businesses where you buy one thing at a time, this method is hopeless for stores with large catalogs. Margy runs a little online kids' videotape store called Great Tapes for Kids at `www.greattapes.com`. Originally, there was a single order page with an order form listing every tape in her rapidly expanding catalog. When the Great Tapes order form got hopelessly large, John reprogrammed it to provide a *shopping cart* to help track the items people order. (John will do practically anything to avoid writing.)

As you click your way around a site, you can toss items into your cart, adding and removing them as you want, by clicking a button labeled something like Add Item to Your Shopping Cart. Then, when you have the items you want, you visit the virtual checkout line and buy the items in your cart. Until you visit the checkout, you can always take the items out of your cart if you decide that you don't want them, and at online stores, they don't get shopworn, no matter how often you do that.

Figure 8-3 shows the Great Tapes for Kids shopping cart with two items in it. When you click the Proceed to Checkout button, the next page asks for the rest of your order details, much like the form in Figure 8-1.

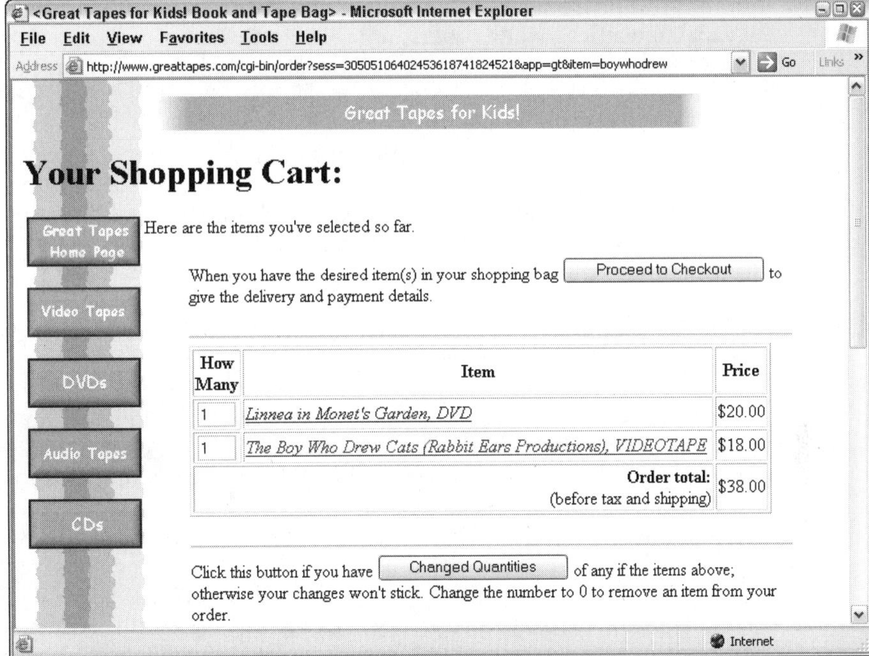

Figure 8-3: Have you finished your holiday shopping?

Up, Up, and Away

We buy lots of airline tickets online. Although the online travel sites aren't as good as the best human travel agents, the sites are now better than so-so agents and vastly better than bad travel agents. Even if you have a good agent, online sites let you look around to see what your options are before you get on the phone. Often airlines themselves offer cheap fares online that aren't available any other way. They know that it costs them much less to let the Web do the work, and they'll pay you (in the form of a hefty discount) to use the Web.

The general theory of airline tickets

Four giant airline computer systems in the United States called Sabre, Galileo, Worldspan, and Amadeus handle nearly all the airline reservations in the country. (They're known as *CRS* for computer reservations systems or *GDS* for Global Distribution System.) Although each airline has a "home" GDS, the systems are all interlinked so that you can, with few exceptions, buy tickets for any airline from any GDS. Some of the low-price, start-up airlines are available via GDS, while others, notably Southwest, don't participate in any of these systems but have their own Web sites where you can check flights and buy tickets.

In theory, all the systems show the same data; in practice, however, they get a little out of sync with each other. If you're looking for seats on a sold-out flight, an airline's home system is most likely to have that last, elusive seat. If you're looking for the lowest fare to somewhere, check all four systems (using different travel Web sites) because a fare that's marked as sold out on one system often mysteriously reappears on another system. Also check Orbitz (see below) which is arranging "direct connect" access to many airlines, bypassing GDS altogether.

Some categories of fares are visible only to travel agents and don't appear on any of the Web sites, particularly if you aren't staying over a weekend, so check with a good agent before buying. On the other hand, many airlines have available some special deals that are *only* on their Web sites and that agents often don't know about. Confused? You should be. We were.

The confusion is even worse if you want to fly internationally. Official fares to most countries are set via a treaty organization called the IATA, so computer systems usually list only IATA fares for international flights. It's easy to find entirely legal "consolidator" tickets sold for considerably less than the official price, however, so an online or offline agent is extremely useful for getting the best price. International airlines also have some impressive online offers, most notably from Cathay Pacific and Lufthansa, which once or twice a year runs online auctions for a plane full of tickets from the United States to Hong Kong and Europe, respectively, with the lowest winning bids often less than half the normal fare.

Here's our distilled wisdom about buying tickets online:

- Check the online systems to see what flights are available and for an idea of the price ranges. Check sites that use different GDS. (Some sites are listed at the end of this section.)
- After you have found a likely airline, check that airline's site to see whether it has any special Web-only deals. If a low-fare airline flies the route, be sure to check that one, too.
- Check prices on flights serving all nearby airports. An extra 45 minutes of driving time can save you hundreds of dollars.
- Check with a travel agent (by phone, e-mail, or the agent's own Web site) to see whether he can beat the online price, and buy your tickets from the agent unless the online deal is better.

- For international tickets, do everything in this list, and check both online and with your agent for consolidator tickets, particularly if you don't qualify for the lowest published fare. For complex international trips such as around-the-world, agents can invariably find routes and prices that the automated systems can't.
- If you bid on airline tickets at a travel auction Web site, make sure that you already know the price at which you can buy the ticket, so you don't bid more.

If you hate flying or would rather take the train, Amtrak and Via Rail Canada offer online reservations (www.amtrak.com and www.viarail.ca). If you are visiting Europe, you can buy your Eurailpass online at www.raileurope.com.

Major airline ticket sites, other than individual airlines, include

- **Expedia:** Microsoft's entry into the travel biz, now a part of the USA Interactive media empire (www.expedia.com).
- **Hotwire:** Multi-airline site offering discounted leftover tickets (www.hotwire.com).
- **Orbitz:** Five big airlines' entry into the travel biz, with most airlines' weekly Web specials (www.orbitz.com).
- **Travelocity:** Sabre's entry into the travel biz (www.travelocity.com). Yahoo Travel and AOL's travel section are both Travelocity underneath.

More about online airlines

Because the online airline situation changes weekly, anything more we printed here would be out of date before you read it. One of the authors of this book is a plane nerd in his spare time; to get his current list of online airline Web sites, Web specials, and online travel agents, visit his Web site, at airline.iecc.com.

Pure Money

If you invest in mutual funds or the stock market (something that's difficult to avoid these days unless you anticipate dying at an early age), you can find a remarkable range of resources online. An enormous amount of stock information is also available, providing Net users with research resources as good as professional analysts had a few years ago.

The most important thing to remember about all the online financial resources is that everyone has an ax to grind and wants to get paid somehow. In most cases, the situation is straightforward; for example, a mutual fund manager wants you to invest with her funds, and a stockbroker wants you to buy and sell stocks with him. Some other sites are less obvious: Some are supported by advertising, and others push other kinds of investments. Just keep a source's interests in mind when you're considering that source's advice.

Mutual funds

Mutual funds are definitely the investment of the Baby Boomer generation. The world now has more mutual funds than it has stocks for the funds to buy. (Kind of makes you wonder, doesn't it?) Most fund managers have at least descriptions of the funds and prospectuses online, and many now provide online access so that you can check your account and move money from one fund to another within a fund group.

Well-known fund groups include

- **Fidelity Investments:** The 500-pound gorilla of mutual funds, specializes in actively managed funds (`www.fidelity.com`)
- **Vanguard Group:** Specializes in low-cost and index funds (`www.vanguard.com`)
- **American Century:** Another broad group of funds (`www.americancentury.com`)

Many of the online brokers listed in the following section also let you buy and sell mutual funds, although it almost always costs less if you deal directly with a fund manager. The Open Directory Project has a long list of funds and fund groups at `http://dmoz.org/Business/Investing/Mutual_Funds`.

Stockbrokers

Most of the well-known, full-service brokerage firms have jumped on the Web, along with a new generation of low-cost online brokers offering remarkably cheap stock trading. A trade that may cost $100 with a full-service firm can cost as little as $8 with a low-cost broker. The main difference is that the cheap firms don't offer investment advice and don't assign you to a specific broker. For people who do their own research and don't want advice from a broker, the low-cost firms work well. For people who do need some advice, the partial- or full-service firms often offer lower-cost trades online, and they let you get a complete view of your account whenever you want. The number of extra services the brokerages offer (such as retirement accounts, dividend reinvestment, and automatic transfers to and from your checking account) varies widely.

Online brokers include

- **Charles Schwab:** One of the oldest discount brokers (www.schwab.com)
- **TD Waterhouse:** A low-cost, limited-advice broker, subsidiary of Toronto-Dominion bank, one of the largest Canadian banks (www.waterhouse.com)
- **Ameritrade:** A very low-cost, no-advice broker (www.ameritrade.com)
- **Smith Barney:** A full-service broker with online access to accounts and research info, subsidiary of Citigroup, one of the largest banks in the world (www.smithbarney.com)

Most fund groups, including the ones in the preceding list, have brokerage departments, which can be a good choice if you want to hold both individual stocks and funds.

Tracking your portfolio

Several services let you track your portfolio online. You enter the number of shares of each fund and stock you own, and at any time they tell you exactly how much they're worth and how much money you lost today. Some of them send by e-mail a daily portfolio report, if you want. These reports are handy if you have mutual funds from more than one group or both funds and stocks. All the tracking services are either supported by advertising or run by a brokerage that hopes to get your trading business.

- **My Yahoo** (my.yahoo.com): You can enter multiple portfolios and customize your screens with related company and general news reports. You can also get lots of company and industry news, including some access to sites that otherwise require paid subscriptions. It's advertiser-supported and very comprehensive and easy to use.
- **Smart Money** (www.smartmoney.com): The online face of *Smart Money* magazine. Track portfolios, read news stories. Although they'd really like you to subscribe to the magazines, the free portfolio tracker isn't bad.
- **MSN MoneyCentral** (http://moneycentral.msn.com): Also has portfolios and lots of information, although we find it a pain to use.

Even More Places to Shop

Here are a few other places to shop that we have visited on the Web. We have even bought stuff from most of them.

Books and such

Although you can't flip through the books in an online bookstore as easily as you can in person (although Amazon.com can come pretty close with a selections of pages from many books online), if you know what you want, you can get good deals.

- **Advanced Book Exchange** (`www.abebooks.com`): ABE offers the combined catalogs of thousands of second-hand booksellers. You'll pay the same as you would in the used bookshop (plus shipping, of course), and you'll save hours of searching. Whether you're looking for a favorite book from your childhood or a rare, first-edition *For Dummies* book, this site is worth visiting.
- **Addall** (`www.addall.com`): Addall is another good used-book site also offering titles from thousands of used book stores as well as a price comparison service for new books.
- **Amazon.com** (`www.amazon.com`): Amazon.com is one of online commerce's great success stories (for the moment), springing up from nothing (if you call several million dollars of seed money nothing) to one of the Net's biggest online stores. Amazon has an enormous catalog of books, music, and a growing variety of other junk, much of which it can get to you in a few days. It also has an "affiliates" program in which other Web sites can refer you to their favorite books for sale at Amazon, creating sort of a virtual virtual bookstore. For an example, see our Web site, at `net.gurus.com`, where we have links to Amazon for every book we have written in case, because of an oversight, you don't already have them all. Amazon sells most books at less than list price. They also have used books, CDs, DVDs, and just about everything else from pogo sticks to underwear.
- **Barnesandnoble.com** (`www.bn.com`): Barnes & Noble is the biggest bookstore chain in the U.S., and its online bookstore is big, complete, and well done. You can even return online purchases at any of its stores. It also has a large selection of music.
- **J&R Music World** (`www.jandr.com`): The online presence of one of New York's largest music stores has a huge selection of music CDs. You can also buy a stereo to listen to your new CDs and a refrigerator to keep appropriate beverages at hand.

- **Reel.com** (www.reel.com): Reel.com sells videotapes and DVDs. For information about movies, reviews, and who's in what movie, see the Internet Movie Database at www.imdb.com.

Clothes

This section points out a few familiar merchants with online stores. Directories such as Open Directory Project (ODP) and Yahoo have hundreds of other stores both familiar and obscure.

- **Lands' End** (www.landsend.com): Most of this catalog is online, and you can order anything you find in any of its individual printed catalogs along with online-only discounted overstocks. It also has plenty of the folksy blather that encourages you to think of the company in terms of a few folks in the cornfields of Wisconsin rather than a corporate mail-order colossus belonging to Sears Roebuck. (It's both, actually.) Moderately cool 3-D virtual models attempt to show what the clothes you're ordering look like on a cyborg with chunky hips just like yours.
- **REI** (www.rei.com): This large sports equipment and outdoorwear co-op is headquartered in Seattle. Members get a small rebate on purchases. The whole catalog is online with occasional online specials and discounts.
- **The Gap** (www.gap.com): Along with the same stuff you'll find in their stores, for those of us who are of unusual vertical or horizontal dimension, it has jeans in sizes the stores don't stock, and the rotating pants are pretty cool.
- **The Real Monica** (therealmonica.com): You can buy purses, totes, and accessories from, well, the real Monica.

Computers

When you're shopping for computer hardware online, be sure that a vendor you're considering offers both a good return policy (in case the computer doesn't work when it arrives) and a long warranty.

- **Dell Computers** (www.dell.com): This site has an extensive catalog with online ordering and custom computer system configurations.
- **IBM** (www.ibm.com): The world's largest computer company has what feels like the world's largest Web site with a great deal of information about both IBM products and more general computing topics. The

online store sells everything from home PCs to printed manuals to midrange business systems. We got as far as putting a $1.1 million AS/400 9406-650 in our cart, but then we chickened out. We did buy a nice manual for the 1965-era 360/67 for our historical collection. (At IBM, nothing seems to go out of print.)

- **Apple Computer** (`store.apple.com`): The Apple site has lots of information about Apple products, and now it has online purchasing of Macintosh systems, too.
- **PC Connection and Mac Connection** (`www.pcconnection.com` and `www.macconnection.com`): For computer hardware, software, and accessories, PC and Mac Connection is one of the oldest and most reliable online sources. And you can get overnight delivery within the continental U.S. even if you order as late as 2 a.m.!

Auctions and used stuff

You can participate in online auctions of everything from computers and computer parts to antiques to vacation packages. Online auctions are like any other kind of auction in at least one respect: If you know what you're looking for and know what it's worth, you can get some great values; if you don't, you can easily overpay for junk. When someone swiped our car phone handset, at eBay we found an exact replacement phone for $31, rather than the $150 the manufacturer charged for just the handset.

An online shopper's checklist

Here are some questions to keep in mind when you're shopping online. An astute shopper will notice that these are the same ones you keep in mind when you're shopping anywhere else.

- Are the descriptions clear enough to know what you're ordering?
- Are the prices competitive, both with other online stores and with mail-order and regular retail?
- Does the store have the products in stock, or does it offer a firm shipping date?
- Does the store have a good reputation?
- Does the store have a clearly written privacy policy that limits what it may do with the data it collects from you?
- Is there a way to ask questions about your order?
- How can you return unsatisfactory goods?

Many auctions, notably eBay (as shown in Figure 8-4), also allow you to list your own stuff for sale, which can be a way to get rid of some of your household clutter a little more discreetly than in a tag sale. A service called *PayPal* (`www.paypal.com`) lets you accept credit card payment from the high bidder via e-mail. (See the sidebar, "E-mail cash to anyone," later in this chapter.)

- **eBay** (`www.ebay.com`): This is the most popular auction site on the Web and sells all sorts of stuff. You can sell stuff, too, by registering as a seller. eBay charges a small commission for auctions, which the seller pays. Searching the auctions at eBay is also a terrific way to find out what something is worth. If you were thinking of selling that rare Beanie Baby, search the completed auctions for the bad news that it's worth slightly less than it was when it was new.
- **Half.com** (`www.half.com`): This division of eBay is more like a consignment shop than an auction. You list used items you want to sell, such as books, CDs, movies, video games, electronic equipment, trading cards, and so on, and you name your price. When a buyer comes along, Half.com collects a 15 percent commission.

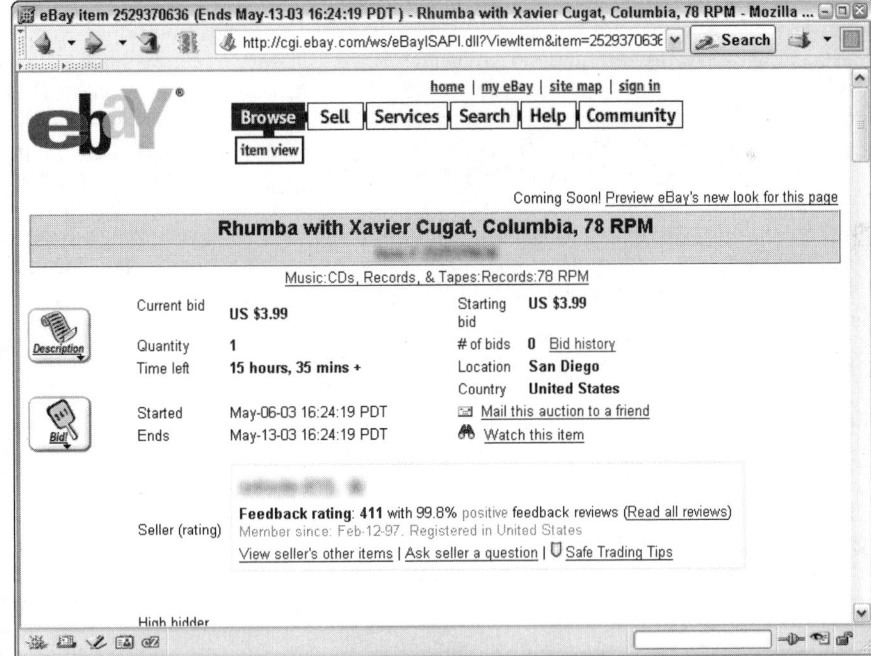

Figure 8-4: To place a bid, scroll down, enter your top price, and click the Review Bid button.

- **Yahoo Auctions** (`auctions.yahoo.com`): eBay was such a big hit that Yahoo decided to hold auctions, too. Yahoo also has an online payment system called PayDirect, similar to PayPal.
- **priceline.com** (`www.priceline.com`): This site sells airline tickets, hotel rooms, new cars, prepaid long distance phone service, and a grab bag of other items. Not really an auction; you specify a price for what you want and they accept or reject it.

E-mail cash to anyone

Credit cards are easy to use — if you're *spending* money. But until recently, it has been all but impossible for individuals to *receive* payments by credit card. Even small businesses found it expensive and time consuming to accept credit card payments. PayPal (`www.paypal.com`) has changed all that.

To send money, you have to have a PayPal account, but they are easy to open. Individual accounts are free, but you can't accept credit card payments. (There's no limit on payments sent from bank accounts.) Premier accounts have no such limit but are charged a small fee on each payment they receive. After you open an account, you can send money to anyone who can receive e-mail. If they don't already have a PayPal account, they will open one when they "cash" your e-mail.

PayPal encourages you to give it your bank account number so it can take money for payments directly without having to pay the credit card companies, and so you can move money you receive into your account. PayPal verifies that it's really your account by making two random deposits of less than a dollar. You then have to tell them the amount of the deposits to complete your registration.

Warning: Some green-eyed monster purporting to be PayPal has been sending out notices claiming to be from PayPal, soliciting your account number and password. PayPal will never, ever ask you for your password or account information in an e-mail message. Help take a "byte" out of crime and forward the fraudulent e-mail to PayPal; go to `www.paypal.com` and click the Security Center link.

PayPal is a boon to individuals who sell at auction sites like eBay (which recently bought PayPal), but it has many other uses, too. PayPal makes it easy to start a small business on the Web; small organizations can use PayPal to collect payments for events like dinners and amateur theater, and it's just about the only way to make payments to individuals in other countries without paying a service charge larger than the amount you're paying. Yahoo started a similar system called Yahoo PayDirect at `paydirect.yahoo.com`. We think both are cool.

Warning: If you are thinking of accepting PayPal for your business, be sure to heed PayPal's warnings regarding shipping only to verified addresses. Be sure to carefully comply with all the fine print to protect yourself against fraud. Don't think you'll do better by setting up a merchant account with one of those well-known credit-card entities. Most first-time sellers find out the hard way that it's they who pay the cost of fraud and even the cost of their customers' innocent errors. PayPal's fraud rate is lower than most credit-card fraud, but it's a case of *merchant beware* — know your customer and take appropriate steps to safeguard your transactions.

Food

To show the range of edibles available online, here are our two favorite online dairies, a coffee roaster, a recipe site, and a grocery delivery service:

- **Cabot Creamery** (`www.cabotcheese.com`): This site sells the best cheese in Vermont. Good bovine sound effects on the Web site, too.
- **Bobolink Dairy** (`www.cowsoutside.com`): A recovering software nerd and his family in rural New Jersey make and sell cheese directly. Their own cheese, which they sell on the Web site, is fabulous — rich, gooey, French-style cheese. You can even order cheese made in Tibet from yak milk. The URL refers to cows out in the pasture rather than tied up in the barn.
- **Gimme Coffee** (`www.gimmecoffee.com`): Highly opinionated coffee from the wilds of upstate New York. Online orders handled through PayPal; follow the Our Locations link to find pictures of the place John goes when in need of literary inspiration, also know as *caffeine.*
- **The Kitchen Link** (`www.kitchenlink.com`): Search their site for the perfect recipe and then shop for the ingredients.
- **Peapod** (`www.peapod.com`): Peapod lets you shop for groceries online and then delivers them to your home. You have to live in an area that their parent grocery chains serve. If you live somewhere else, Netgrocer (`www.netgrocer.com`) delivers nonperishables by rather pricey overnight express.

The Shopping Update

Like everything else on the Net, shopping changes day by day as new businesses appear and old ones change. For the latest updates, see our update pages at `net.gurus.com/shopping`.

Chapter 9

My First Home Page

In This Chapter

- Web page basics
- Up and humming
- Publish or perish

After a while, every Web user thinks about putting up a personal Web page. Although any Web site can consist of many Web pages, the main page of a site is generally known as its *home page*. People have home pages, companies have home pages, and groups of highly talented authors and speakers have home pages. (You can check out Carol's at `www.carolbaroudi.com`, John's at `www.johnlevine.com`, Margy's at `gurus.com/margy`, and Internet Gurus Central at `net.gurus.com`.) If you're ready to have your own home page, you're in the right place.

Although creating a home page is not difficult, it may seem complicated for a new user. But if you can use a word processor like Microsoft Word to type a letter, you can create at least a simple home page. (Indeed, you can use Word or most any other word processor to do so.)

Creating a Web Page

All home pages are Web pages, although not all Web pages are home pages. We tell you how to make a Web page — whether it's a home page is up to you.

Why you don't care (much) about HTML

Just so that you know what *HTML* is, in case someone asks, it stands for *HyperText Markup Language,* and it's the language native to the World Wide Web. Web pages are made up of text and pictures that are stuck together and formatted by using HTML codes. Fortunately, you have waited until now to get started creating a Web page, when clever programs are available that let you create your pages and write the HTML codes for you automatically, so you don't have to write the codes yourself.

If you find you want to write a lot of Web pages, you should eventually master some HTML. Although complex interactive pages require a fair amount of programming, the basics aren't all that complicated. The HTML for **complicated** is `<B>complicated</B>` (that's `<B>` for bold type). In case you decide that you want to be in the Web-page creation business, entire books have been written about how to do it. Stick to recent titles because extensions to HTML are evolving at a furious pace and the books go out of date in less than a year. We recommend *HTML 4 For Dummies,* Fourth Edition (by Ed Tittel and Natanya Pitts, and published by Wiley Publishing, Inc.) for the basics and *Web Design in a Nutshell* (by Jennifer Niederst and published by O'Reilly & Associates) for more advanced information.

The big picture

The basic steps to creating a Web site are pretty simple:

1. **Write some Web pages.**

   One page is plenty to start with. You can use any text editor or word processor, but spiffy Web page authoring programs designed for this purpose are available and many are free, so you may as well use one. Save the pages in files on your computer's disk.

2. **Test your Web pages by using your own browser.**

   Before you make your pages visible to everyone, make sure they look good! Using your Web browser, open the pages (press Ctrl+O and specify the name of the file that contains your page). Ideally, check how they look in recent versions of Internet Explorer, Netscape, and Mozilla, as well as any other browsers your friends may use.

3. **Publish your Web pages on your Internet service provider's (ISP's) system.**

   The rest of the world can't see Web pages in files on your disk. You have to copy them to your ISP's system so that your ISP's *Web server* can offer them to the world. You don't have to use your ISP's Web server, but most Internet accounts come with free Web space, so why not?

Many Web page authoring programs have a Publish, Upload, or Remote Save command on the File menu that sends your creation to your provider's system. If your program doesn't have this command, you can use File Transfer Protocol (FTP), a type of program we discuss in more detail on our Web page at `net.gurus.com/nettcr/ftpsw.html`. In either case, you need to know these details:

- **The name of the computer to which you upload your files:** This isn't always the same as the name of the Web server. At one of our local ISPs, for example, the Web server is `www.lightlink.com`, whereas the FTP upload server is `ftp.lightlink.com`.
- **The user name and password to use for FTP:** Usually this is the same as the name and password you use to connect in the first place and to pick up your e-mail.
- **The name of the folder on the server to which you upload the pages:** At Lightlink, it's `/www/`*`username`*.
- **The filename to use for your home page:** Usually this is `index.html` or `index.htm`. (You can call your Web pages anything you want, but this is the page that people see first.)
- **The URL where your pages will appear:** It's usually `http://www.`*`yourisp`*`.com/~`*`username`* or `http://www.`*`yourisp`*`.com/`*`username`*.

You can usually find this info on your ISP's Web site or, in the worst case, you can call them or e-mail them and ask.

If you don't want to use your ISP's Web server, lots of Web hosting companies will be happy to let you use their servers. Some are even free, if you don't mind their advertisements appearing on your Web pages. The best-known free Web hosting sites are Yahoo's Geocities at `geocities.com` and Lycos's Angelfire at `www.angelfire.lycos.com`.

Picking your pen

The two general approaches to creating Web pages are the geek approach, in which you write all the HTML codes yourself, and the WYSIWYG approach in which a program writes them for you. If you were an HTML geek, you wouldn't be reading this chapter, so we're not going to discuss that approach. The more normal approach is to use one of the WYSIWYG Web-page editors.

WYSIWYG, pronounced *whiz*-ee-wig, stands for *what you see is what you get.* In the case of Web-page editors, it means that as you create your page, instead of seeing seriously unattractive HTML codes, you see roughly what it will look like in a browser. HTML purists point out that WYSIWYG editors churn out less-than-elegant HTML code, but the pages they make generally look fine. If you're planning to create a large, complex Web site, WYSIWYG editors will run out of steam, but for a page or three, they're great. Netscape and Mozilla include Composer, a nice WYSIWYG editor, which is what we use for examples later in this chapter.

You probably already have a Web-page editor — your own word processor. Both Microsoft Word (versions 97 and later) and WordPerfect (versions 8 and later) have capable Web-editing features built right in. Web page authoring tools are usually more convenient, though. If you use Microsoft Excel (a spreadsheet program) or Access (a database program), you can export reports as Web pages, too.

Getting started

A Web page is a file — just like a word-processing document or a spreadsheet. You begin by creating your Web pages directly on your hard disk. You can see how they look by telling your browser to view them from your hard disk. (Browsers are happy to accept file names to display rather than URLs.) Edit and view the pages until you have something you like, and then upload them to your ISP to impress the world.

Here's our step-by-step approach to using Netscape or Mozilla Composer, or Word (97 or later). If you would rather use another program, feel free, although the commands are a little different:

1. **Start up Netscape 7 or Mozilla. If you would rather use your own word processor, skip this step.**

   See Chapter 16 for how to download and install Mozilla or Netscape if you don't have one of them installed already.

2. **Run Netscape/Mozilla Composer or your word processor.**

   To work with Netscape or Mozilla Composer (as shown in Figure 9-1), run Netscape or Mozilla and then choose Window⇨Composer from the menu (or press Ctrl+4). If you want to edit an existing Web page, view it in a Navigator window (if the page is in a file, press Ctrl+O to open it), and then choose File⇨Edit Page (or press Ctrl+E) to open a copy of the page in a Composer window.

   If you started Word, you see your usual word-processing window. If you want to edit an existing page, open it the way you would an ordinary Word file.

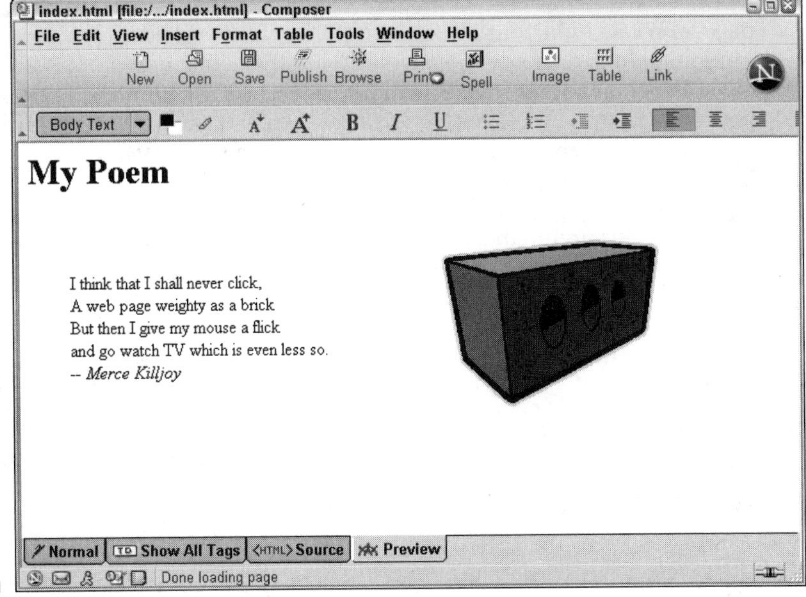

Figure 9-1: Netscape Composer comes with Netscape Navigator.

3. **Create a new Web page or edit the one you opened.**

   Netscape/Mozilla Composer: You're face to face with a big, empty page. Go ahead — make your page the same way you would in a word processor by entering headings and paragraphs of text. Stuck for ideas and where to start? Make a page about your favorite hobby, author, or musician!

   Word: Choose File➪New from the menu bar, click the Web Pages tab in the dialog box that appears, and choose a template (try the Web Page Wizard, a template that talks you through making a Web page).

   When asked for a file name, call the document `index.html` or `index.htm` if it's going to be your home page. These names are the names that most Web servers use.

4. **Save your work.**

   When you've done enough work that you wouldn't want to have to start over from scratch if your computer suddenly crashes, choose File➪Save from the menu bar. In principle, when you're done with your page, you save it, but dismal experience has taught us to save early, save often.

Creating your first Web page is pretty easy. Choosing what you put on your page, however, is harder. What is the page for? Whom do you want to see it? Is it for you and your family and friends and potential friends across the world, or are you advertising your business online? If your page is a personal page, don't include your home address or phone number unless you want random people who see the page potentially calling you up. If it's a business page, by all means include your address and phone number. The content of your first page isn't all that important — we just want you to get the feel of putting it out there. You can always add to it and pretty it up, and you don't have to tell anybody about your site until you're happy with it.

Be extremely careful about putting identifying information about your children on your Web page. We each have kids whom we love dearly, but you won't read anything about them on our home pages. Just knowing your hobbies and your kids' names and where they go to school may be enough for some no-good-nik to pose as a friend of the family and pick them up after school.

Pictures to Go

Most Web pages contain graphics of some sort. Each picture that appears on a Web page is stored in a separate file. To add an image to a Web page, you add an HTML *tag* (command) that includes the name of the file that contains the picture, the size of the picture as it should appear on the screen, a caption for the visually impaired, and positioning information (whether you want the pictures to the left, center, or right, and whether text should flow around it).

Picture formats

Pictures come in dozens of formats. Fortunately, only three picture formats are in common use on the Web: GIF, PNG, and JPEG. Many lengthy . . . er, *free* and *frank* discussions have occurred on the Internet concerning the relative merits of these formats. John, who is an Official Graphics Format Expert, by virtue of having persuaded two otherwise reputable publishers to publish his books on the topic, suggests that photographs work better as JPEG, while clip art, icons, and cartoons are better as PNG or GIF. The GIF format uses a compression technique that is patented by Unisys who occasionally rattles a saber at Web sites that use images produced by unlicensed programs. If in doubt, JPEG files are smaller, download faster, and are patent free. PNG is a superior, new, nonpatented replacement for GIF, with its only disadvantage being that people with old Web browsers (Netscape 3.0 and older, for example) can't easily view PNG files.

If you have a picture in any other format, such as BMP or PCX, you must convert it to GIF, PNG, or JPEG before you can use it on a Web page. Check out the Consummate WinSock Applications page, at `cws.internet.com`, for some suggestions of graphics programs that can do conversions. We like Paint Shop Pro (`www.jasc.com`), a powerful shareware graphics program on Windows, and Graphics Converter on the Mac (`www.lemkesoft.de/en/graphcon/html`).

Where do pictures come from?

That's a good question. You can draw them by using a paint program, scan in photographs, or use that fancy digital camera you got for Christmas. Unless you're a rather good artist or photographer, however, your graphics may not look as nice as you want.

Fortunately, you can find lots of sources of graphical material:

- Plenty of freeware, shareware, and commercial clip art are available on the Net. Yahoo has a long list of clip art sites: Start at `www.yahoo.com` and choose Computers and Internet, and then Graphics, and then Clip Art. The Open Directory Project list is at `www.dmoz.org/Computers/Graphics/Clip_Art`.
- The king of the clip art sites is Clipart.com (`www.clipart.com`, a member of the ArtToday Network). There's a modest annual subscription fee, but they have hundreds of thousands of well-indexed pictures for download.
- If you see an image you want to use on a Web page, write to the page's owner and ask for permission to use it. More likely than not, the owner will let you use the image.
- Lots of regular old software programs totally unrelated to the Internet, such as paint and draw programs, presentation programs, and even word processors, come with clip art collections.
- You can buy CD-ROMs full of clip art, which tends to be of higher quality than the free stuff. These aren't all that expensive, particularly considering how many images fit on one CD-ROM.

Clip art, like any art, is protected by copyright laws. Whether it's already been used on a Web page or whether a copyright notice appears on or near the image doesn't matter. It's all copyrighted. If you use someone else's copyrighted art, you must get permission to do so. Whether your use is educational, personal, or noncommercial is irrelevant. If you fail to secure permission, you run the risk of anything from a crabby phone call from the owner's lawyer to winding up on the losing end of a lawsuit.

Most people are quite reasonable whenever you ask for permission to use something. If an image you want to use doesn't already come with permission to use it, check with the owner before you decide to add it to your own Web page.

Adding a picture to your page

After you've got the graphics file you want to use, you can include it on your Web page, like this:

- **Netscape/Mozilla Composer:** With your cursor at the place in the page where you want the picture to appear, click the Image button on the toolbar. In the Image Location box, type the filename or click Choose File to find the file on your disk. Type a caption in the Alternate Text box. If you want the image to display larger or smaller than its actual size, click the Dimensions tab and set the size. Click the Appearance tab if you want to add space around your picture or change the way it aligns with adjacent text. Then click OK to finish specifying your image. You can also drag the file from a My Computer window into Composer and then right-click and select Image Properties if you want to change its size or appearance.
- **Word:** Choose Insert⇨Picture⇨From File and specify the picture.

Linking to Other Pages

The *hyper* in hypertext is the thing that makes the Web so cool. A *hyperlink* (or just *link*) is the thing on the page that lets you "surf" the Web — go from page to page by just clicking the link. A Web page is hardly a page if it doesn't link somewhere else.

The immense richness of the Web comes from the links that Web page constructors have placed on their own pages. You want to contribute to this richness by including as many links to places you know of that the people who visit your page may also be interested in. Try to avoid including links to places that everyone already knows about and has in their bookmarks. For example, everyone knows were to find Google and Yahoo, so leave them off. If your home page mentions your interest in one of your hobbies, however, such as canoeing or volleyball or birding or your alma mater, include some links to related sites you know of that are interesting.

To make a link on your Web page, follow these instructions:

- **Netscape/Mozilla Composer:** Highlight the text that you want to be a link and click the Link button on the toolbar. In the Link Properties dialog box, type the exact URL into the Link Location box, or click the Choose File button to choose another Web page you've created.
- **Word:** First, select the text that you want to be a link. Then issue the command to make the link. Choose Insert⇨Hyperlink (or press Ctrl+K) and type the exact URL into the Type the File or Web Page Name box, choose the Web page from the list of pages you've visited recently, or click the File or Web Page button to find the page you want.

If you create multiple pages, you can put links among your pages; be sure to upload all the pages to ensure the links still work.

Good Page Design

After you put together a basic Web page, use the tips in this section to avoid some mistakes that novice Websters often make.

Fonts and styles

Don't overformat your text with too many fonts, too many colors, or too much emphasis with **bold**, *italics,* underlining, or some ***combination.*** Experienced designers disparage it as "ransom note" text. Blinking text universally annoys readers.

Background images

Tiled background images can be cool if they're subtle but too often make text utterly illegible. Black text on a solid white background (like the pages of this book) has stood the test of time for thousands of years.

To set your Web page's background color, follow these instructions:

- **Netscape/Mozilla Composer:** Choose Format⇨Page Colors and Background from the menu. Click Use Custom Colors to override the normal colors that the user's browser assigns and then click the colored buttons to set the colors of normal text, link text, and other text. If you have a picture that you'd like to display as the background of the page (tiled — repeating to fill the page), enter its name into the Background Image box or use Choose File to choose it from a menu.

- **Word:** Choose Format⇨Background and choose a color. To tile a picture in the background, choose Format⇨Background⇨Fill Effects.

Big images

Many Web pages are burdened with images that, although beautiful, take a long time to load — so long that many users may give up before the pages are completely loaded. Remember that not everyone has a computer or Internet connection as fast as yours.

Take a few steps to make your Web pages load more quickly. The main step, of course, is to limit the size of the images you use by shrinking them with a graphics editor like Paint Shop Pro. A 20K (20,000 bytes big) image takes twice as long to load as a 10K image, which takes twice as long to load as a 5K image. You can estimate that images load at 1K per second on a 56Kbps dialup connection, so a 5K image loads in about five seconds, which is pretty fast; a 120K image takes two minutes to load, so that image had better be worth the wait.

Consider putting a small image on a page and give visitors an option (via a link) to load the full-size picture. We know that you're proud of your dog, and she deserves a place of honor on your home page, but not everyone visiting your site will wait excitedly for your puppy to download. (We hate it when they do that on the rug.)

In GIF files, images with fewer colors load faster than images with more colors. If you use a graphics editor to reduce a GIF from 256 colors to 32 or even 16 colors, often the appearance hardly changes, but the file shrinks dramatically. Set your graphics program to store the GIF file in *interlaced* format, which lets browsers display a blurry approximation of the image as it's downloading, to offer a hint of what's coming.

In JPEG files, you can adjust the "quality" level to a lower quality, which makes the file smaller. You can set the quality of Web images quite low with little effect on what appears on users' screens.

You can also take advantage of the *cache* that browsers use. The cache keeps copies of previously viewed pages and images. If any image on a page being downloaded is already in the browser's cache, that image isn't loaded again. When you use the same icon in several places on a page or on several pages visited in succession, the browser downloads the icon's file only once and reuses the same image on all the pages. When creating your Web pages, try to use the same icons from one page to the next to give your pages a consistent style and speed up downloading.

Live and learn

If you're looking at other people's Web pages and come across one that's particularly neat, you can look at the source HTML for that page to see how the page was constructed. In Netscape or Mozilla, choose View➪Page Source or press Ctrl+U; in Internet Explorer, choose View➪Source.

Putting Your Page on the Web

After you've made some pages you're happy with (or happy enough with) and you're ready for other people to see them, you have to release your pages to the world. Although nearly every ISP has a user Web server, no two ISPs handle the uploading process in quite the same way.

To upload your files, you need an FTP program. Luckily, well-designed, convenient, and totally groovy Web design programs like Netscape and Mozilla Composer have an FTP program built right in. All of them can store the host name, user name, and password of your Web server the first time you upload a Web page, so you don't have to enter this information over and over. Here's how to use them to upload your Web pages and the graphics files that contain the pictures displayed on the pages:

- **Netscape/Mozilla Composer:** Click the Publish button on the toolbar. To complete the fields on the Settings tab, pick a site name you'll use when you edit these pages in the future, enter the Publishing Address, the FTP address your ISP gave you to upload your pages, and your user name and password. (The HyperText Transport Protocol [HTTP] address is optional.) Most of this information was diligently collected by you in "The big picture" section earlier in this chapter. You may not want to select the Save Password check box to maintain the security of your Web site.

  Next, click the Publish tab and fill out the Page Title (name that you want to appear in the title bar of the browser when your page is displayed) and Filename (file name to use when uploading, usually the same as the filename you use on your own computer, to avoid confusion).

  Click the Publish button to start the upload.

- **Word:** Choose File⇨Save As. Click the Save In box in the upper left corner of the Save As dialog box and choose FTP Locations. To tell Word about the Web server to which you want to upload your Web pages, click Add/Modify FTP Locations. Type the host name of the Web server, your user name (click User), and your password. Click the Add button. When you click OK, you return to the Save As dialog box, and now your Web server's address appears. Click the server and click Open to connect to the Web server — you see the file and folders you have on the server. Click Save to upload your page.

Of course, some Web editing programs don't include FTP programs, so you may be on your own when it comes to uploading your Web pages. Assuming that you have the server details we discussed at the beginning of the chapter, here's what to do:

1. **Run your FTP program.**

   We use WS_FTP (our Web page at `net.gurus.com/nettcr/ftpsw.html` contains instructions), although any FTP program will do. If you have Windows XP, you can use its Web Folders feature, which is described in Chapter 16.

2. **Log on to your provider's upload server, using your own logon and password.**

   You'll have to enter the name of the FTP server, your logon name (usually the same as your account name), and your password (usually the same as the one you use when you connect to your provider).

3. **Change to the directory (folder) where your Web home page belongs.**

   The name is usually something like `/pub/elvis`, `/www/elvis`, or `/pub/elvis/www` (assuming that your username is *elvis*).

4. **Upload your Web page(s).**

   Use ASCII mode, not binary mode, for the Web pages because Web pages are stored as text files. Use binary mode when you're uploading graphics files.

After you finish uploading, if your page on the server is called `mypage.htm`, its URL is something like

```
http:// www.gorgonzola.net/~elvis/mypage.htm
```

Again, URLs vary by provider. Some providers don't follow the convention of putting a tilde (~) in front of your user name.

You should generally call your home page, the one you want people to see first, `index.html`. If someone goes to your Web directory without specifying a filename, such as `www.gorgonzola.net/~elvis`, a universal convention is to display the page named `index.html` or `index.htm`. If you don't have a page by that name, many Web servers construct a page with a directory listing of the files in your Web directory. Although this listing is functional enough because it lets people go to any of your pages with one click, it's ugly. If you make an `index.html` page and it doesn't appear automagically when you type the URL without a file name, ask your ISP whether it uses a different default file name.

Be sure to check out how your page looks after it's on the Web. Inspect it from someone else's computer to make sure that it doesn't accidentally contain any references to graphics files stored on your own computer that you forgot to upload. If you want to be compulsive, check how it looks from various browsers — Netscape/Mozilla, Internet Explorer, Opera, AOL, MSN TV, and Lynx, to name a few.

Blogs, wikis, and other twenty-first century media

After you've created a few Web pages of your own, you'll probably conclude, with the rest of us, that keeping up a Web site one page at a time is (to put it mildly) a pain in the patootie. If you have better things to do than to fiddle with Web page formatting, you can use automated systems that provide standard formatting while you just provide the brilliant, witty, sparkling content.

A *weblog*, usually abrvtd to *blog*, is sort of a public online diary where someone posts more or less regular updates. The best blogs offer cutting edge journalism and commentary, while the worst disprove the old cliché that a million monkeys at a million typewriters would eventually produce the works of Shakespeare. They come and go with such rapidity that it's not worth listing our current favorites here, but if you Google for the word *blog* or *weblog* and some topic words of interest to you, you'll invariably find someone blogging away at it. If you want to start your own blog, keeping in mind our comment about brilliant, witty, sparkling content above, try `blogger.com` (owned by Google but run separately) or `xanga.com` for free blog hosting.

Whereas a blog is basically an exercise in personal vanity publishing, a *wiki* lets a group of people collaborate on a Web site. A wiki can have an unlimited number of authors, all of whom can add and change pages within the wiki's Web site. If this sounds potentially chaotic, it is, but most wikis have ground rules that keep the group moving in more or less the same direction. One of the best wikis is `www.wikipedia.org`, a collaborative encyclopedia which, with over 120,000 entries, is well on its way to including all human knowledge. It's harder to find places to start your own wiki than your own blog, but it's more fun to find a wiki of interest to you, dive in, and start editing your own little corner of it.

Shortly after you upload your pages, you'll probably notice a glaring mistake. (We always do.) To update a page, edit the copy on your own computer and then upload it to your Internet provider, replacing the preceding version of the page. If you change some but not all your pages, you don't have to upload pages that haven't changed.

Be Master of Your Domain

A home page address like

```
www.people.stratford-on-avon-internet.com/~shakespeare/
         PrinceOfDenmark/index.html
```

is just not going to attract as many visitors as

```
www.hamlet.org
```

Getting your own domain name is a lot easier and cheaper than you might think. There are three steps:

1. **Choose a name.**

   You'll want one that's easy to remember and to spell. Pick out a couple of alternate names in case the one you want is taken. Don't use a variation on a popular trademark like Coke or Sony (or Dummies) unless you like dealing with lawyers. Also be sure that it's not already taken; you can check the WHOIS database for .com, .net, and .org at `www.whois.net` or `www.crsnic.net`.

2. **Ask your ISP to "host" your name.**

   That means your ISP breathes some incantations that tell the Internet where to go when someone types in your personal Web address. Many ISPs charge a fee for this service, but a few do it for free. Your ISP may be able to handle the next step, registration, for you, too.

3. **Register your name if your ISP doesn't.**

   Hundreds of registrars compete for business in the popular .com, .net, and .org categories. (We like the registry run by our friends at the Spamcon Foundation where you can support antispam efforts when you register your domain at `www.spamcon.net/domains`.) The going rate is between $10 to $30/year.

Open a Farm Stand on the Information Superhighway

Selling stuff on the Internet used to take hundreds of thousands of dollars worth of software and programming talent. A number of sites now let you create a Web store for very modest fees. We like Amazon.com's zStores, at zstores.amazon.com, which is particularly easy to set up. They even process credit card sales for you, eliminating what was once a horrible pain in the neck. Yahoo provides several ways to sell via their site (auctions, a storefront, and classified ads) — see sell.yahoo.com for information.

If you're not up for creating Web pages and setting up a whole store, you can still sell individual items either on consignment at sites like www.half.com or at auction at sites like www.ebay.com. See Chapter 8 for details.

Shout It Out!

After your page is online, you may want to get people to come and visit. Here are a few ways to publicize your site:

- Visit your favorite Web directories and search engines, such as Google (www.google.com), Yahoo (www.yahoo.com), and AltaVista (www.altavista.com), and submit your URL (the name of your page) to add to their database. These sites all have on their home pages an option for adding a new page. (Sometimes it's a teeny little link near the bottom of the page.) Automated indexes like Google and AltaVista add pages promptly, but manually maintained directories like Yahoo may not accept them at all. Don't pay to have your site included: Every respectable search engine and directory has an option for adding your noncommercial site for free, although it make take a while for your site to show up.

- Visit www.submit-it.com. You can pay Submit It! an annual fee to submit your URL to a bunch of directories, indexes, and search engines.
- Find and visit other similar or related sites and offer to exchange links between your site and theirs.

Getting lots of traffic to your site takes time. If your site offers something different that is of real interest to other folks, it can build a following of its own. Even we *For Dummies* authors have gotten into the action: A few of our homegrown sites that keep growing in popularity are Arnold Reinhold's Math in the Movies page, at www.mathinthemovies.com; Margy's Great Tapes for Kids site, at www.greattapes.com; Margy's Harry Potter Timeline at geocities.com/hptimeline; and John's Airline Information On-Line on the Internet site, at airline.iecc.com. Just imagine what you can come up with!

A few other Web page editors

If you don't like Netscape/Mozilla or Word for Web editing, you have lots of other options. Here are a few possibilities:

- **CoffeeCup Web Page Wizard** (`www.coffeecup.com/software`): This Windows Web editor lets you choose page elements from a list, so you never have to see HTML codes. Your formatting options are limited, but it's a great way to get started. An FTP program is included for uploading your finished pages. This freeware program comes in the same package with the much more complex shareware, CoffeeCup HTML Editor 9.5, although they're separate programs.
- **Microsoft Front Page** (`www.microsoft.com`): FrontPage comes with Microsoft Office. Watch out, though: FrontPage and FrontPage Express have a nasty habit of inserting Microsoft-proprietary codes that only work if your ISP runs a Microsoft Web server.
- **Mac programs:** Mac users can go to `www.apple.com` to get Mac home page templates and links to free HTML editors.

Part IV
E-mail, Chat, and Other Ways to Hang Out Online

The 5th Wave
By Rich Tennant
INSTEAD OF INSTALLING INSTANT MESSAGING TECHNOLOGY, BRAD'S COMPANY INADVERTENTLY INSTALLS INSTANT PESTERING TECHNOLOGY
©RICHTENNANT
Hey! What's up? What're you doin'? What's that you're readin'? Is that your only tie? Why don't you adjust your chair so you don't slump over...?

In this part . . .

You've found out all about the Web, which is very, very slightly like TV because you're mostly looking at stuff that other people created. Now, we turn to the part of the Net that's very, very, slightly like talking on the phone, because you're talking (or typing or waving) to other people. We start with e-mail, just about the oldest, but still the most useful, Net service, both one-to-one and e-mail communities, and then finish with faster-paced modern alternatives, instant messages, and online chat.

Chapter 10

It's in the Mail

In This Chapter

- Finding e-mail addresses
- Sending e-mail
- Receiving e-mail
- Following e-mail etiquette

Electronic mail, or *e-mail,* is without a doubt the most popular Internet service, even though it's one of the oldest and least glitzy. Although e-mail doesn't get as much press as the World Wide Web, more people use it. Every system on the Net supports some sort of mail service, which means that no matter what kind of computer you're using, if it's on the Internet, you can send and receive mail.

Because mail, much more than any other Internet service, is connected to many non-Internet systems, you can exchange mail with lots of people who don't otherwise have access to the Internet, in addition to all the people who *are* on the Net. For example, you can exchange e-mail messages with AOL users and many people with mobile phones, even though they aren't directly connected to the Internet.

What's My Address?

Everyone with e-mail access to the Internet has at least one *e-mail address,* which is the cyberspace equivalent of a postal address or a phone number. When you send an e-mail message, you enter the address or addresses of the recipients so that the computer knows where to send it.

Before you do much mailing, you have to figure out your electronic mail address so that you can give it to people who want to get in touch with you. You also have to figure out some of their addresses so that you can write to them. (If you have no friends or plan to send only anonymous hate mail, you can skip this section.)

Whaddaya mean you don't know your own address?

It happens frequently — usually because a friend uses a private e-mail system that has a gateway to the outside world that provides instructions for how to send messages to the outside but no hint about how outsiders send stuff in. The solution is, fortunately, usually easy: Tell your friend to send you a message. All messages have return addresses, and all except the absolute cruddiest of mail systems put on a usable return address. Don't be surprised if your friend's address has a great deal of strange punctuation. After a message makes it through a few gateways, your friend's address may look something like this:

```
"blurch::John.C.Calhoun"%farp@s
    limemail.com
```

If you type the strange address back in, it usually works, so don't worry about it. Better yet, click Reply so that your e-mail program puts in the address for you, and use your e-mail program's address book to store the address so you'll never have to type it again.

Internet mail addresses have two parts, separated by an @ (the *at* sign). The part before the @ is the *mailbox,* which is (roughly speaking) your personal name, and the part after that is the *domain,* usually the name of your Internet service provider (ISP), such as `aol.com` or `fltg.net`.

The user name part

The mailbox is usually your *user name,* the name your ISP assigns to your account. If you're lucky, you get to choose your user name; in other cases, ISPs standardize user names, and you get what you get. Some user names are just first names, just last names, initials, first name and last initial, first initial and last name, or anything else, including *made-up* names. Over the years, for example, John has had the user names `john`, `johnl`, `jrl`, `jlevine`, `jlevine3` (must have been at least three `jlevine`s there), and even `q0246`; Carol has been `carol`, `carolb`, `cbaroudi`, and `carol377` (the provider threw in a random number); and Margy tries to stick with `margy` but has ended up with `margyl` or `73727,2305` on occasion. A few ISPs assign names such as `usd31516`. Ugh.

For example, you can write to the President of the United States at `president@whitehouse.gov`. The President's mailbox is `president`, and the domain that stores his mailbox is `whitehouse.gov` — reasonable enough.

Back when many fewer e-mail users were around and most users of any particular system knew each other directly, figuring out who had what user name wasn't all that difficult. These days, because that process is becoming much more of a problem, many organizations are creating consistent mailbox names for all users, most often by using the user's first and last names with a dot between them. In this type of scheme, your mailbox name may be something like `elvis.presley@bluesuede.org`, even though your user name is something else. (If your name isn't Elvis Presley, adjust this example suitably. On the other hand, if your name *is* Elvis Presley, please contact us immediately. We know some people who are looking for you.)

Having several names for the same mailbox is no problem, so the new, longer, consistent names are invariably created in addition to — rather than instead of — the traditional short nicknames.

The domain name part

The domain name for ISPs in the United States usually ends with three letters (called the *top-level domain,* or *TLD*) that give you a clue to what kind of place it is. *Commercial* organizations end with `.com`, which includes both providers such as America Online and CompuServe and many companies that aren't public providers but that are commercial entities, such as `aa.com` (AMR Corporation, better known as American Airlines), `greattapes.com` (Margy's online video store), and `taugh.com` (John's hard to pronounce Taughannock Networks). Colleges and universities end with `.edu` (such as `yale.edu`), networking organizations end with `.net`, U.S. government sites end with `.gov`, military sites end with `.mil`, and organizations that don't fall into any of those categories (like nonprofits) end with `.org`. Outside the United States, domains usually end with a country code, such as `.fr` for France or `.zm` for Zambia. See our Web site (at `net.gurus.com/countries`) for a listing of country codes. Small businesses, local governments, and K-12 schools usually end with the two-letter state abbreviation followed by `.us` (such as John's community Web site at `www.trumansburg.ny.us`).

In 1997, an international group proposed adding some extra generic domains like `.firm`, `.arts`, and `.web`. After a lengthy detour through a maze of international intellectual property politics, in 2001 the first new domains appeared, `.biz` and `.info`, done in a clumsy way that practically guaranteed that more often than not `whatever.biz` and `whatever.info` are indistinguishable from `whatever.com`. They've since added `.name`, for personal vanity domains, and a smattering of limited use domains including `.coop`, `.museum`, and `.aero`, for co-ops, museums, and air travel, respectively. None is widely used. We'll put any late breaking updates on the Web at `net.gurus.com/domains`.

Your mailbox usually lives on your ISP's mail server because when you sign up for an Internet account, you almost always get one (or more) mailboxes as part of the deal. But if you don't have an ISP (say, you connect from the public library), all is not lost. Many Web sites provide free mailboxes for you to use — try Hotmail at `www.hotmail.com`, Outblaze at `www.mail.com`, or Yahoo Mail at `mail.yahoo.com`. Yahoo and Hotmail use the Web site's domain name (`yahoo.com` or `hotmail.com`) as the second part of your e-mail address, whereas Outblaze offers a long list of "vanity" domains like `seductive.com` or `doctor.com`.

Putting it all together

Write your e-mail address in Table 10-1 (and fold down the corner of this page, so you can find it again later). Capitalization never matters in domains and rarely matters in mailbox names. To make it easy on your eyes, therefore, most of the domain and mailbox names in this book are shown in lowercase.

Table 10-1 Information Your E-Mail Program Needs to Know

	Description	*Example*
Your e-mail address ________	Your user name followed by an @ and the domain name.	`Internet9@gurus.com`
Your e-mail password ________	The password for your e-mail mailbox (usually the same as the password for your account). Don't write it here! It's a secret!	`dum3my`
Your incoming (POP3 or IMAP) mail server ________	The name of the computer that receives your e-mail messages (get this name from your ISP; skip it if you use Web-based mail, AOL, or MSN.)	`pop.gurus.com`
Is it POP3 or IMAP? ________	Which protocol your mailbox uses, and which your e-mail program needs to use to get your mail. Doesn't apply to Web mail, AOL, or MSN.	
Your outgoing (SMTP) mail server ________	The name of the computer that distributes your outgoing mail to the rest of the Internet (often the same as the POP3 or IMAP server; skip it if you use Web mail, AOL, or MSN).	`smtp.gurus.com`

If you're sending a message to another user in your domain (the same machine or group of machines), you can leave out the domain part altogether when you type the address. If you and a friend both use AOL, for example, you can leave out the `@aol.com` part of the address when you're writing to each other.

If you don't know what your e-mail address is, a good approach is to send yourself a message and use your logon name as the mailbox name. Then examine the return address on the message. Or you can send a message to *Internet For Dummies* Mail Central, at `internet9@gurus.com`, and a friendly robot will send back a message with your address. (While you're at it, tell us whether you like this book because we authors read that mail too and write back when time permits.) If you're planning on testing your e-mail dozens of times and don't care whether we read your message or not, send it to `test@gurus.com`.

My Mail Is Where?

If you're the sort of person who lies awake at night worrying about obscure questions, it may have occurred to you that your computer can receive e-mail only while it's connected to the Internet, so what happens to mail that people send during the 23 hours a day during which you're engaged in real life? (If your computer is permanently connected to the Internet with a DSL, cable Internet, or office connection, this question may never have occurred to you.)

When your mail arrives, the mail doesn't get delivered to your computer automatically. Mail gets delivered instead to an *incoming mail server,* which holds onto the mail until you connect to the net and run your mail program, which then picks up the mail. Two types of incoming mail servers are common: *POP* (also known as *POP3,* for Post Office Protocol version 3) and *IMAP* (Internet Mail Access Protocol). To send mail, your *e-mail program* has to take mail to the post office — your *outgoing mail server* (or *SMTP server,* for Simple Mail Transfer Protocol). It's sort of like having a post office box rather than home delivery — you have to pick it up at the post office and also deliver your outgoing mail there. (Strange but true: Margy and Carol, because they're normal, get their e-mail via a mail server and have their paper "snail" mail delivered to their homes; John, who's abnormal, has his e-mail delivered directly to his home computer but walks to the post office every day, often in the freezing drizzle, to get his regular mail.)

Unless you use your Web browser to read e-mail on a Web-based site, you have to set up your e-mail program with the name of your incoming and outgoing mail servers. (Cable Internet and DSL modem users have to do this, too.) When your e-mail program picks up the mail, it sucks your mail from your ISP's incoming mail server to your PC or Mac at top speed. After you have downloaded your mail to your own computer, if you dial into the Net, you can disconnect, thus freeing up your phone. Then you can read and respond to your mail while you're *offline*. After you're ready to send your responses or new messages, you can reconnect and transmit your outgoing mail to the outgoing mail server, again at top network speed.

Write the names of your incoming (POP3 or IMAP) and outgoing (SMTP) mail servers in Table 10-1. If you don't know what to write, ask your ISP. With luck, your mail program has the server names set automatically, but when (note we don't say if) the setup gets screwed up, you'll be glad you know what to restore the settings to.

AOL has its own mail system, so AOL users don't use a POP, IMAP, or SMTP server. MSN uses Hotmail for its mail system, so it doesn't do POP, IMAP, or SMTP either.

After you send a piece of e-mail, you can't cancel it! Some e-mail programs keep outgoing messages in a *queue* to be sent in batches. But after your messages go to the outgoing mail server, you can't call them back. (Note to AOL users: When you send a message to another AOL address, rather than the Internet, you can cancel the message up until the moment that the recipient opens and read it.)

Too Many E-Mail Programs

It's time for some hand-to-hand combat with your e-mail system. The bad news is that countless e-mail programs exist — programs that read and write electronic-mail messages. (So many of them exist that none of us felt up to the task of counting them.) You've got your freeware, you've got your shareware and your commercial stuff, and stuff probably came with your computer. They all do more or less the same thing because they're all e-mail programs, after all.

Here's a quick rundown of e-mail programs:

- **Windows PC or Mac with an Internet account:** You can use any of a long list of POP or IMAP mail programs. See the next section.
- **America Online (AOL):** You'll be sorry to hear that AOL doesn't have a standard POP or IMAP server, so you can't use standard mail programs to read your AOL mail. Instead, you have to either use the rather limited e-mail capabilities of the AOL software to read and send mail, or you do mail from the AOL Web site at `www.aol.com`. Actually, you have one and a half other possibilities: Now that AOL owns Netscape, you can read and send AOL mail with Netscape. And the Netscape mail program is

way, way better than AOL's built-in mail facility. Or try the new AOL Communicator, which is a spiffed-up version of Netscape mail. After reading this chapter, AOL users can turn to Chapter 17 for detailed instructions.

- **MSN TV (formerly WebTV):** If you use this packaged Web connection, you also get an e-mail service. See our chapter about MSN TV at `net.gurus.com/msntv`.
- **Web-based mail:** Many systems offer free e-mail accounts that you can access through the Web. The best known are Hotmail at `www.hotmail.com`, Outblaze at `www.mail.com`, and Yahoo Mail at `mail.yahoo.com`. You use your Web browser to read and send mail (see Chapter 6 if you need help using a browser).
- **UNIX shell accounts:** You almost certainly can use Pine. If your ISP doesn't have it, demand it. For a description of using Pine, see our Web site at `net.gurus.com/shell/pine.phtml`.

If you're connected in some other way, you probably have a different mail program. For example, you may be using a PC in your company's local area network that runs cc:Mail or Lotus Notes and has a mail-only link to the outside world. We don't describe local area network mail programs here, but don't stop reading. Regardless of which type of mail you're using, the basics of reading, sending, addressing, and filing mail work in pretty much the same way, so it's worth looking through this chapter even if you're not using any of the mail programs we describe here.

Popular E-Mail Programs

After you understand what an e-mail program is supposed to do, it's much easier to figure out how to make a specific e-mail program do what you want. We've picked the three most popular e-mail programs to show you the ropes (AOL users should take a look at Chapter 17):

A contender from down under

Pegasus is a remarkably good and completely free mail program from New Zealand. Widely used outside the U.S. because of good foreign language support, it's one of our favorites here in the U.S. as well. It's fast, reliable, well documented, and you couldn't pay for it if you wanted to. (If you want to support the author, you can buy a downloadable copy of the manual, although the online help is plenty for most people.)

You can get a copy of Pegasus from `www.pmail.com`.

- **Eudora:** This popular e-mail program runs under Windows (all versions) and on the Macintosh and communicates with your mail server. Eudora is popular for two reasons: It's easy to use, and it's cheap. Normally it's "sponsored," which means that it's free but shows ads when you use it. If you like it, you can register your copy for a modest fee; when you do, the ads disappear. Or you can drop back to "free" mode, which has no ads and fewer features. This chapter describes Eudora 5 (which is available for Windows and Macs, the latest version being 5.2).
- **Netscape 7:** The Netscape Web browser we described in Chapter 6 includes a pretty good e-mail program called Netscape Mail. If you use an AOL account, Netscape Mail is the only program (other than the AOL program itself and AOL's new AOL Communicator, which is similar to Netscape Mail) that can send and receive AOL e-mail.
- **Outlook Express:** Windows 98 and later come with versions of Outlook Express, Microsoft's free e-mail program. When you get a copy of the Microsoft Web browser, Internet Explorer, you get Outlook Express too. We describe Outlook Express 6.0, which comes with Windows XP and Internet Explorer 6.0. You can also download it from `www.microsoft.com`. ***Note:*** Despite the similar name, Outlook Express is unrelated to Outlook 97, 98, 2000, or XP, which come with various versions of Microsoft Office.

See Chapter 16 to find out how to get hold of Eudora, Pegasus, Netscape, and other programs from the Net.

To round out our discussion, we also describe a Web-based mail system, Yahoo Mail, which is on the Web at `mail.yahoo.com`. Microsoft's Hotmail (`www.hotmail.com`) is similar. Our instructions for Yahoo Mail have to be a bit vague because, like all Web sites, it could have been completely redesigned twice since the time we wrote this book (even if you get the first copy off the press.)

Setting up Your E-mail Program

Before you can use your e-mail program, you need to tell it where your mailbox is stored (usually on a mail server at your ISP) and where to send outgoing mail (usually to the same or another mail server at your ISP). For Yahoo Mail and other Web-based e-mail servers, you have to create a mailbox for yourself. Follow the instructions in the following sections to get up and running. Later sections describe how to send and receive mail using each program.

Eudora

Download and install Eudora 5 following the instructions in Chapter 16 — you can get it from www.eudora.com or from a software library like TUCOWS (www.tucows.com). When you run the downloaded file to install Eudora, you can choose to install PureVoice, an add-on program that enables you to send voice snippets as well as text. The installation program also asks where you want your mail files: in the User's Application Data folder or in a Custom Data folder. Use the Application Data folder.

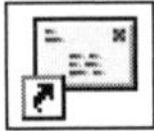

To run Eudora, click its icon on the Windows or Mac desktop or choose it from Window's Start menu (Start⇨Programs, or Start⇨All Programs). The first time you run it, Eudora asks you for information about your e-mail mailbox and mail servers so that it knows how to download the messages from your incoming mailbox and send your outgoing messages. Type in the information from Table 10-1. You can change this information later by giving the Tools⇨Options command. Eudora also asks whether to make her your default e-mail program. Choose Yes.

Most e-mail viruses are designed to work with Outlook Express, so you are relatively safe using Eudora. However, you need to set the following configuration options in Eudora to make sure that no one can trick Eudora into running a malicious program behind your back:

1. **Change your attachments folder.**

   Eudora has a folder in which it stores files that arrive attached to e-mail messages. Change this folder to a different one by choosing Tools⇨Options, scrolling down the Category list at the left and clicking the Attachments category, clicking the large Attachment Directory button, and choosing a folder on your hard disk (how about C:\Downloaded Files?).

2. **Make sure that Allow Executables in HTML Content is not selected.**

   You're still in the Options dialog box that you opened in Step 1, right? Click the Viewing Mail category in the Category list and make sure that the Allow Executables in HTML Content check box is unchecked.

3. **Make sure that Launch a Program from a Message is selected.**

   Still in the Options dialog box, scroll farther down the category list, click the Extra Warnings category, and make sure that the Launch a Program from a Message check box has a check in it.

4. **Click OK in the Options dialog box.**

   Eudora is safe to use — as safe as any e-mail program can be.

After Eudora is up and running, you see its window, which looks like Figure 10-1. The list of your mail folders usually appears at the left (unless someone has moved it), including your In and Out folders.

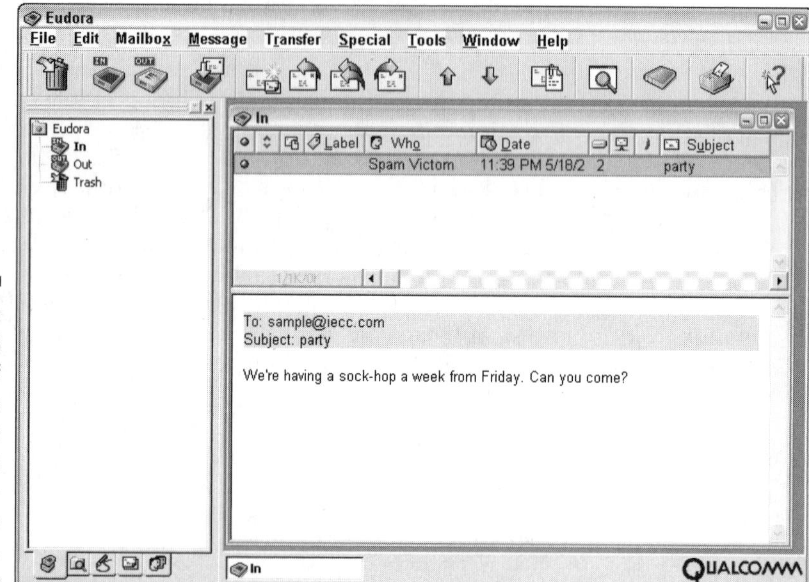

Figure 10-1: Eudora 5 says hello. If you pay the registration fee, the advertisements go away.

Netscape Mail

Netscape 7 comes with a mail program called Netscape Mail. See Chapter 16 for how to download and install the program and Chapter 6 for how to use the Web browser. When you install it, Netscape prompts you to "activate" the program by signing up for a Netscape user name. This process has nothing to do with the Netscape program but gives you a user name for AOL Instant Messenger and an e-mail address at netscape.net. If you use AOL or already have an AOL Instant Messenger user name, type that name for your Netscape user name. If you don't have an AOL Instant Messenger name and don't want one, click Cancel.

Start Netscape by clicking the desktop icon or choosing Start⇨All Programs⇨Netscape⇨Mail. If you're already running Netscape, choose Window⇨Mail & Newsgroups, press Ctrl+2, or click the little envelope icon in the bottom-left corner of the window. The first time you run Netscape Mail, the Account Wizard runs, asking for your name and Netscape user name. Then Netscape Mail opens showing your Netscape.net mailbox (the mail you've received at *username*@netscape.net).

Chances are that you want to read mail from your existing mailbox, right? No problem: Run the Account Wizard again by choosing Edit⇨Mail & News Account Settings and clicking the New Account button. This time, the Account Wizard gives you more choices — click the Next button to move from screen to screen. Choose ISP or Email Provider if you want to use the mailbox that comes with your Internet account, or AOL Account if you use AOL. Type your name, e-mail address, incoming mail server, and outgoing server, copying the information from Table 10-1. When you're done, you see your new account in the Account Settings window, which you can close.

The Netscape Mail window looks like Figure 10-2. A list of your mailboxes ("Mail Folders") appears in the upper left, with My Sidebar (links to other information) below it. To the right are a list of the messages in that mailbox and the text of the selected message. Follow the instructions in the warning at the end of the previous section to prevent Netscape Mail from running JavaScript programs that arrive by e-mail.

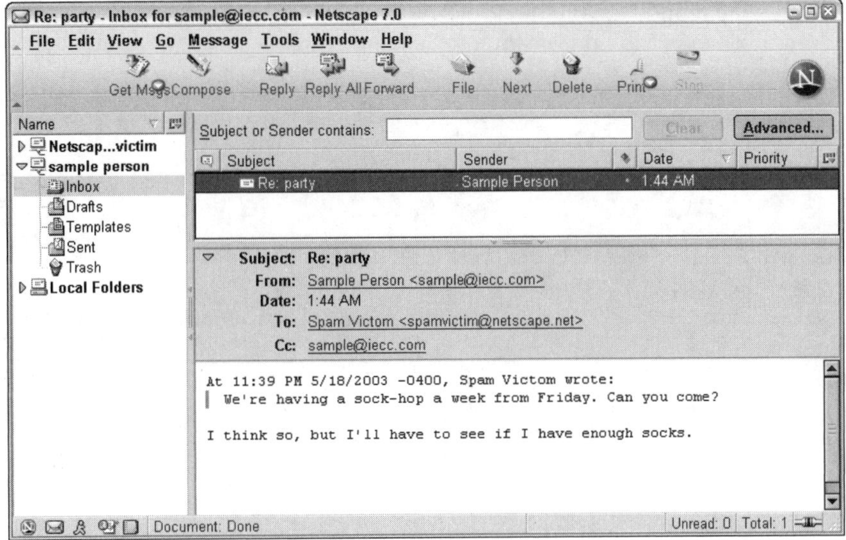

Figure 10-2: Netscape Mail displays your mail folders to the left, messages in the upper right, and the selected message in the lower right.

Outlook Express

If you have Windows, you don't have to install Outlook Express — it's just there. In fact, we don't know of any way to get rid of it. (Microsoft claims that Internet Explorer is an integral part of Windows, and maybe Microsoft is getting ready to make the same claim about Outlook Express.)

To run Outlook Express in Windows XP, choose Start➪E-mail Outlook Express or Start➪All Programs➪Outlook Express. In other versions of Windows, choose Start➪Programs➪Outlook Express or Start➪Programs➪Internet Explorer➪Outlook Express — you're bound to find it in one of those places. Or double-click the Outlook Express icon on your desktop (it's an envelope with blue arrows around it).

The first time you run Outlook Express, the Internet Connection Wizard wakes up and asks some questions: most of the answers you should already have written in Table 10-1. Type in your name, your e-mail address, your incoming (POP or IMAP) mail server, your outgoing (SMTP) mail server, your user name, and your password. Click Next after filling in the information that the Wizard requests, and Finish when the Wizard says that you may leave.

At long last, you see the Outlook Express window, as shown in Figure 10-3.

If you need to add or change your e-mail accounts later, choose Tools➪Accounts from the Outlook Express menu. You can edit an account by clicking it and clicking the Properties button. Add an e-mail account (mailbox) by clicking the Add button.

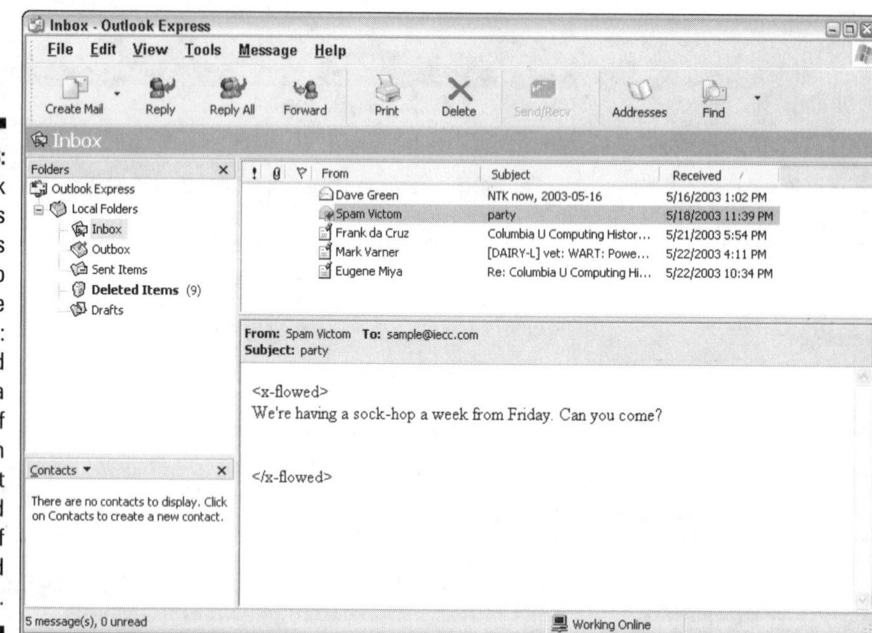

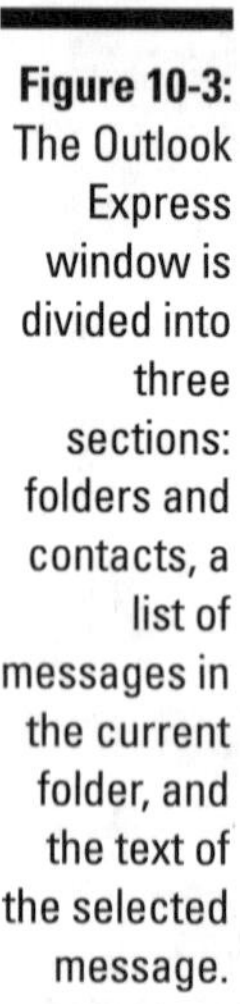
Figure 10-3: The Outlook Express window is divided into three sections: folders and contacts, a list of messages in the current folder, and the text of the selected message.

Outlook Express, because Microsoft has included it with Windows, is slowly taking over the world of e-mail programs. Both for that reason and because it's riddled with security flaws, many viruses specifically target Outlook Express, so if you use Outlook Express, you need to do a few things to protect yourself:

- **Never open an attachment or run a program that someone sends you, even if you know the sender.** Only open an attachment after you check with the sender that he or she actually *meant* to send you the attachment — many viruses spread by people opening infected messages that contain a program that sends infected messages to everybody in your Outlook Express address book without your knowing it. If you get e-mail from someone you don't know, it's best to delete it without ever opening it.
- **Check the Microsoft Web site frequently (like once a week) for security reports.** Go to `windowsupdate.microsoft.com` for the latest security updates, including patches (corrections) for both Outlook Express and Internet Explorer. Be sure to download and install all the security updates in the Critical Updates section.
- **Tell Outlook Express to be careful.** If you don't expect to receive attached files, choose Tools⇨Options, click the Security tab, and select the Do Not Allow Attachments to Be Saved or Opened That Could Potentially Be a Virus check box (maybe Microsoft needs to run its check box names through the grammar checker!). Also select the Warn Me When Other Applications Try to Send Mail as Me check box — this setting may prevent a virus from surreptitiously spreading itself.

Better yet, switch to a safer e-mail program.

Yahoo Mail

Yahoo Mail is our favorite Web-based mail service because of its wide range of features. After you set up a Yahoo ID, you get a mailbox, a Web site at `geocities.com`, and an ID you can use when buying and selling in Yahoo's online stores and auctions. Your Yahoo ID works when using Yahoo Messenger for instant messages, voice conferencing, or video conferencing (see Chapter 14). The exact services (as well as the exact instructions for setting up and using a Yahoo Mail mailbox) vary from week to week as the Yahoo people change their Web site, but we can give you a general idea.

To set up a mailbox, sign up for a Yahoo ID (don't worry, it's free). Go to `www.yahoo.com`, and click the Check Mail link. Alternatively, you can go straight to mail.yahoo.com. You see links for signing in if you already have a Yahoo ID, as well as a Sign Me Up link. Click the Sign Me Up link and fill in the forms with information about yourself. They don't ask anything too nosy. Be sure to click the links to read the terms of service (rules of the game) and privacy policy (what they plan to do with the information you give them).

In Table 10-1, you only need to provide your e-mail address, which is your Yahoo ID followed by @yahoo.com. You don't need to fill in any other information. You're ready!

To get access to your Yahoo Mail mailbox, go to mail.yahoo.com (or click Check Mail at www.yahoo.com) and sign in with your new Yahoo ID and password. You see a Web page with links for sending and reading e-mail (described later in this chapter).

A cool thing about Web-based mailboxes like Yahoo Mail is that you can read and send messages from any computer. Your mailbox is stored on Yahoo's mail servers, and any computer with a Web browser can access it. Of course, no one can read your messages, or send messages as you, without typing your password. In this chapter and the next, when we tell you how to send and receive mail with Yahoo Mail, keep in mind that you don't have to be at your own computer — you can check your mail from a friend's computer or from the computer at the public library. One downside is that reading and sending messages on a Web site tends to be a bit slow unless you have a fast Internet connection because you have to wait for a new Web page to arrive every time you click a new message.

Sending Mail Is Easy

Sending mail is easy enough that we show you a few examples rather than waste time explaining the theory.

Sending mail with Eudora

Here's how to send some mail:

1. **To send a message, click the New Message button on the toolbar in the Eudora window. Or choose Message⇨New Message from the menu. (If you can remember shortcut keys, you can also press Ctrl+N.)**

   Eudora pops up a new message window with spaces in which you type the address, subject, and text of a message.

2. **On the To line, type the recipient's address (`internet9@gurus.com`, for example).**

   For your first e-mail message, you may want to write to us (because we will send you back a message confirming what your e-mail address is) or to yourself (if you know what your e-mail address is).

3. **Press Tab to skip past the From line (which is already filled in with what Eudora thinks is your address) to the Subject line and type a subject.**

   Make the subject line short and specific.

4. **Press Tab two times to skip the Cc and Bcc fields (or type the addresses of people who should get carbon copies and blind carbon copies of your message). Or click in the big blank area at the bottom of the message window.**

   The term *carbon copy* should be familiar to those of you who were born before 1960 and remember the ancient practice of putting sheets of carbon-coated paper between sheets of regular paper to make extra copies when using a typewriter. (Please don't ask us what a typewriter is.) In e-mail, a carbon copy is simply a copy of the message you send. All recipients, on both the To and Cc lines, see who's getting this message. *Blind carbon copies* (Bcc) are copies sent to people without putting their names on the message so that the other recipients can't tell. *You* can figure out why you may send a copy to someone but not want everyone to know that you sent it.

5. **Type your message.**

   If you have set up a *signature* for yourself (as described in the next chapter), it appears at the bottom of the message automagically. Be sure to type your message above your signature.

6. **To send the message, click the Send or Queue button in the upper right corner of the message window (what the button says depends on how Eudora is set up).**

   If the button is marked Send, as soon as you click it, Eudora tries to send the message on the spot. If it's marked Queue, your message is stashed in your outbox, to be sent later.

   The Queue button is useful if you use a dialup connection and your computer isn't connected to the Internet all the time. You can write messages (or respond to mail you've already received) while you're not connected. When you're ready, you can connect to the Internet again and send them all at one time.

7. **If your computer isn't already connected, dial up and get it connected to your provider.**

   You may be able to skip this step. Eudora tries to connect automatically when you send messages (see Step 6).

8. **Switch back to Eudora and choose File⇨Send Queued Messages (Ctrl+T for the lazy) from the menu to transmit all the messages you have queued up.**

Even if you leave your computer connected while you write your mail messages, it's not a bad idea to set Eudora to queue the mail and not send it until you tell it to. (Choose Tools⇨Options from the Eudora menu, click the Sending Mail category, and be sure that Immediate Send isn't checked.) That way, you get a few minutes after you write each message to ponder whether you really want to send it. Even though we have been using e-mail for over 20 years, we still throw away many of the messages we write before we send them.

Eudora can send formatted e-mail, but not everyone can read it. (To people with older e-mail programs, your message may look like it's been through a blender). If you get complaints, you can control whether or not Eudora sends formatted (or *styled*) text): Choose Tools⇨Options from the menu, click Styled Text on the Category list, and choose either Send Plain Text Only or Ask Me Each Time. See the sidebar "To format or not to format" earlier in this chapter.

The same idea, using Netscape Mail

The steps for sending mail from Netscape Mail are almost identical to those for sending mail from Eudora (you're doing the same thing, after all):

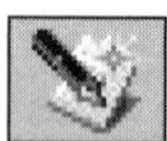

1. **In Netscape Mail, click the Compose button on the toolbar or press Ctrl+M.**

   Yet another window (the Compose window) opens with a blank message.

   If Netscape complains that it doesn't know your e-mail address, click OK. Choose Edit⇨Mail/News Account Settings to fix your e-mail address. Then click the Compose button again.

2. **Fill in the recipient's address (or addresses) in the To box, type the subject, and type the message.**

3. **Click Send to send the message.**

   The message wings its way to your ISP and on to the addressee.

To format or not to format

A few years ago, someone got tired of e-mail's plain, unformatted appearance. After all, now that almost all computers can display boldface, italics, different fonts, and different type sizes, why not use them in e-mail? And formatted e-mail was born.

One problem is that not all e-mail programs can display formatted e-mail. The formatting usually takes one of two forms: MIME (in which the formatted text is sent like an attached file with the message) and HTML (in which Web-page formatting codes are included in the text). If your mail program can't display formatted mail and you receive a formatted message, you see all kinds of gobbledygook mixed in with the text of the message, rendering it unreadable.

Another problem is that any HTML formatted mail can potentially contain viruses, hostile Web pages that take over the screen, and other annoying or dangerous content. Some people turn off HTML mail, both nice mail like yours and the nasty kind, to avoid having to deal with the nasty kind.

If you know that the person to whom you are writing can handle formatted e-mail, go ahead and use it. Boldface, italics, and color can add emphasis and interest to your messages, although they're no substitute for clear, concise writing. If you receive formatted messages from someone, you can send him formatted messages, too. However, if you don't know whether your recipient's mail program can display formatted messages, don't use it. And when sending messages to a mailing list (which we discuss in Chapter 11), be sure not to use formatting — you never know who's on the list and who will be receiving your message.

When you send a message in which you have used formatting (like boldface or italics, using the toolbar buttons in the Composition or Compose window), Netscape may ask you if you really want to send the messages using formatting. See the sidebar "To format or not to format" earlier in this chapter for when to send formatted messages.

Sending mail with Outlook Express

Here's how to send mail, after you run Outlook Express and tell it about your e-mail account:

1. **Start Outlook Express. You don't have to connect to your Internet provider (yet), but it's okay if you're already connected.**

   Click the Outlook Express icon on your desktop or taskbar or choose it from the Start⇨Programs menu.

The Outlook Express window, shown in Figure 10-3, features a list of folders to the left, the contents of the current folder to the upper right, and the text of the current message to the lower right. (When you start the program, no folder or message is selected, so you don't see much.)

2. **Click the Inbox folder.**

   It's listed under Local Folders (that is, folders stored on your own computer) in the folders list.

3. **Click the Create Mail button on the toolbar, press Ctrl+N, or choose Message⇨New Message from the menu.**

   You see a New Message window with boxes to fill in to address the message.

4. **In the To box, type the address to which to send the message and then press Tab.**

   If you want to send the same message to more than one person at a time, press Enter (instead of Tab). You can send this message to as many people as you want by pressing Enter after each address. When you're done including everybody in the To box, press Tab to move on the Cc box.

5. **If you want to send a copy of the message to someone, type that person's address in the Cc box. Then press Tab. In the Subject box, type a succinct summary of the message. Then press Tab again.**

   The cursor should be blinking in the message area, the large empty box where the actual message goes. (If you want to send Bcc copies, choose View⇨All Headers in the New Message window.)

6. **In the large empty box, type the text of the message.**

   When you have typed your message, you can press F7 or choose Tools⇨Spelling to check its spelling.

7. **To send the message, click the Send button (the leftmost button) on the toolbar, press Alt+S (not Ctrl+S, which means Save), or choose File⇨Send Message from the menu.**

   Outlook Express sticks the message in your Outbox folder, waiting to be sent. If you're connected to your Internet provider, Outlook Express may be configured to send the message immediately, and you can skip Steps 8 and 9.

8. **Connect to your Internet provider if you're not already connected.**

   To send the message, you have to climb on the Net.

9. **Click the Send/Recv button on the toolbar, press Ctrl+M, or choose Tools⇨Send And Receive⇨Send All from the menu.**

   Your message is on its way.

If you use formatting commands to choose fonts and colors when you compose your message, some people may have trouble reading the message — specifically, people with older e-mail programs. If you get complaints, choose Format⇨Plain Text in the New Message window when you are composing the message. See the sidebar, "To format or not to format," earlier in this chapter for when to send formatted messages.

Yahoo for Yahoo Mail

Getting started with a Web-based e-mail system like Yahoo Mail is even easier. Go to the Web site (`mail.yahoo.com` or start at `www.yahoo.com` and click the Check Mail link). If you don't already have a mailbox there (or if you want a new one), you can set up one for free.

After you have a Yahoo ID and Yahoo Mail mailbox, follow these steps (more or less — the Yahoo Mail Web site may have changed ten times since we wrote this):

1. **Sign in.**

   Go to `mail.yahoo.com` (or click Check Mail at `www.yahoo.com`) and sign in with your Yahoo ID and password.

2. **Click the Compose link (or any other link about writing and sending a message).**

   You see a Web page that looks like Figure 10-4.

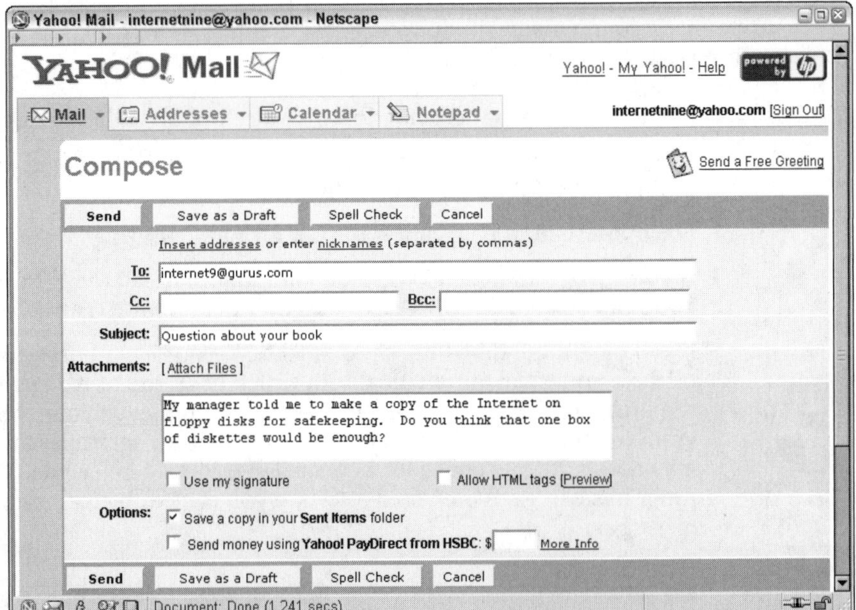

Figure 10-4: Yahoo Mail enables you to read your e-mail on the Web — from any computer on the net.

3. **Type your message.**

   Type the address in the To box and the topic of your message in the Subject box. In the big box, type the text of your message.

4. **Scroll down and click the Send button.**

   That's all it takes!

Mail Coming Your Way

If you begin sending e-mail (and in most cases even if you don't), you begin receiving it. The arrival of e-mail is always exciting, even when you get 200 messages a day. (Exciting in a depressing kind of way, sometimes.)

You can do much of what you do with mail while you're not connected to your account. On the other hand, when you really do want to check your mail, you have to be connected. Eudora can figure out that you're not connected and dial in for you (which, in our experience, doesn't always work).

You can tell your computer to connect to the Internet automagically when you tell your e-mail program to send or fetch your mail. To configure Windows to dial the Internet automatically, see Chapter 5.

Reading mail with an e-mail program

To check your e-mail with Eudora, Netscape, Outlook Express, or almost any other e-mail program, follow these steps:

1. **Make your Internet connection if you're not already connected.**

   You can skip this step if your computer is always connected to the Internet or if it dials automatically whenever you need it to.

2. **Start your e-mail program if it's not already running.**

3. **If your program doesn't retrieve mail automatically, click the Check Mail, Get Msg, or Send/Recv button on the toolbar to retrieve your mail.**

   If you have a full-time Internet connection, your e-mail program may retrieve your mail automatically, in which case you only have to start the program to get your mail. In addition, if you leave your e-mail program running, even hidden at the bottom of your screen as an icon, it may automatically check for new mail every once in a while. Most e-mail programs can even pick up mail while you're reading or sending other messages.

Web mail and regular mail, together at last

Most Internet providers, from AOL on down, provide a Web site from which you can read and send mail, so that their users can check mail on the road or use a Web browser if they like it better than a mail program. Check with your ISP to see if they offer Web mail, how to turn it on if it's not on already, and what the URL is. And in several interesting cases, you can use a regular mail program to read and send mail from Web mail systems.

- **AOL:** Besides the regular AOL mail program (see Chapter 17), you can use AOL's Web mail at `my.aol.com` or the Netscape mail program.
- **Netscape.net (AOL's free Web mail):** Besides the Web mail at `www.netscape.com`, you can use the Netscape mail program.
- **Hotmail and MSN:** Both free Hotmail accounts and paid MSN accounts can use the Web mail at `www.hotmail.com` and Outlook Express.
- **Yahoo Web mail:** If you upgrade to the paid version of Yahoo mail, they offer POP service like an ISP, so you can use any e-mail program to read your messages.

When you use Netscape mail with AOL or Netscape.net, or you use Outlook Express with Hotmail or MSN, rather than downloading mail, you're managing the mail back on the server at headquarters. If you have more than one mail folder, you can use the same folders whether you move messages among folders in the mail program or on the Web.

The program may play a tune, display a message, or show you a cute picture of a mailman delivering a letter when you receive messages. The mail appears in your inbox, usually in a window or folder called In or Inbox, one line per message. If you don't see it, double-click the In or Inbox mailbox in the list of mailboxes that usually appears at the left side of the window.

4. **To see a message, double-click the line or click the line and press Enter.**

   To stop looking at a message, click the Close (X) button in the upper-right corner of the message window (the standard way to get rid of a window), or press Ctrl+W or Ctrl+F4.

Buttons on the e-mail program's toolbar at the top of its window let you dispose of your mail. First, click (once) the message you want to highlight it. Then click the trashcan or delete button on the toolbar to discard the message or the printer icon to print it. You can do lots of other things with messages (like replying, saving, and forwarding), which we discuss in Chapter 11.

Here are some tips for specific e-mail programs:

- **Eudora:** If you need to dial into an Internet account to get your mail, you can tell Eudora to connect to the Internet automagically when you tell it to send or fetch your mail. Choose Tools⇨Options from the menu, scroll the list of icons until you see Internet Dialup, and click it. Select the Have Eudora Connect Using Dial-Up Networking check box. To open your In mailbox, click the In icon on the toolbar.
- **Netscape Mail:** To display your inbox, click your e-mail address or account name in the Mail Folders list, or if it's showing a generic window with a Read Messages link, click that link.
- **Outlook Express:** If you don't see your Inbox, double-click the Local Folders item in the folders list.

Reading Your Yahoo Mail

To read your Yahoo mail, sign in to Yahoo Mail as usual. Then click the Check Mail link to see a list of your incoming messages. Click a message's subject line to see the full text of the message. Is that easy, or what?

Another way to find messages is by clicking the plus box by the Folders link. A list of your mail folders appears, including an Inbox link. The next chapter explains things you can do with mail you receive, like replying to it or deleting it.

A Few Words from the Etiquette Ladies

Sadly, the Great Ladies of Etiquette, such as Emily Post and Amy Vanderbilt, died before the invention of e-mail. Here's what they may have suggested about what to say and, more important, what *not* to say in electronic mail.

E-mail is a funny hybrid, something between a phone call (or voice mail) and a letter. On one hand, it's quick and usually informal; on the other hand, because e-mail is written rather than spoken, you don't see a person's facial expressions or hear her tone of voice.

A few words of advice:

- When you send a message, watch the tone of your language.
- Don't use all capital letters — it looks like you're SHOUTING.
- If someone sends you an incredibly obnoxious and offensive message, as likely as not it's a mistake or a joke gone awry. In particular, be on the lookout for failed sarcasm.

Flame off!

Pointless and excessive outrage in electronic mail is so common that it has a name of its own: *flaming*. Don't flame. It makes you look like a jerk.

When you get a message so offensive that you just *have* to reply, stick it back in your electronic inbox for a while and wait until after lunch. Then, don't flame back. The sender probably didn't realize how the message would look. In about 20 years of using electronic mail, we can testify that we have never, ever, regretted *not* sending an angry message (although we *have* regretted sending a few — ouch).

When you're sending mail, keep in mind that someone reading it will have no idea of what you *intended* to say — just what you *did* say. Subtle sarcasm and irony are almost impossible to use in e-mail and usually come across as annoying or dumb instead. (If you're an extremely superb writer, you can disregard this advice — but don't say that we didn't warn you.)

Another possibility to keep in the back of your mind is that it is technically easy to forge e-mail return addresses. If you get a totally off-the-wall message from someone that seems out of character for that person, somebody else may have forged it as a prank. (No, we're not going to tell you how to forge e-mail. How dumb do you think we are?)

Smile!

Sometimes it helps to put in a :-) (called a *smiley* or *emoticon*), which means, "This is a joke." (Try tilting your head to the left if you don't see why it's a smile.) In some communities, notably CompuServe, `<g>` or `<grin>` serves the same purpose. Here's a typical example:

```
People who don't believe that we are all part of a warm, caring
community who love and support each other are no better than
rabid dogs and should be hunted down and shot. :-)
```

We feel that any joke that needs a smiley probably wasn't worth making, but tastes differ.

For more guidance about online etiquette, see our `net.gurus.com/netiquette` Web page.

How Private Is E-Mail?

Relatively, but not totally. Any recipient of your mail may forward it to other people. Some mail addresses are really mailing lists that redistribute messages to many other people. We've gotten misrouted mail in our `internet8@gurus.com` mailbox with details of our correspondents' lives and anatomy that they probably would rather we forget. (So we did.)

If you send mail from work or to someone at work, your mail is not private. You and your friend may work for companies of the highest integrity whose employees would never dream of reading private e-mail. When push comes to shove, however, and someone is accusing your company of leaking confidential information and the corporate lawyer says, "Examine the e-mail," someone reads all the e-mail. (This situation happened to a friend of ours who was none too pleased to find that all his intimate correspondence with his fiancée had been read.) E-mail you send and receive is stored on your disk, and most companies back up their disks regularly. If anybody really wants to read your mail, it's not hard to do. The usual rule of thumb is not to send anything you wouldn't want to see posted next to the water cooler or perhaps scribbled next to a pay phone.

If you really care about the content of your mail being read by anyone other than your intended recipient, you must encrypt it. The latest e-mail systems are beginning to include encryption features that make the privacy situation somewhat better so that anyone who doesn't know the keyword used to scramble a message can't decode it.

BTW, what does IMHO mean? RTFM!

E-mail users are often lazy typists, and many abbreviations are common. Here are some of the most widely used:

Abbreviation	***What It Means***
AFAIK	As far as I know
BTW	By the way
IANAL	I am not a lawyer, (but...)
IMHO	In my humble opinion
ROTFL	Rolling on the floor laughing
RSN	Real soon now (vaporware)
RTFM	Read the manual — you could have and should have looked it up yourself
TIA	Thanks in advance
TLA	Three-letter acronym
YMMV	Your mileage may vary

Hey, Ms. Postmaster

Every Internet host that can send or receive mail has a special mail address called `postmaster` that is supposed to get a message to the person responsible for that host. If you send mail to someone and get back strange failure messages, you can try sending a message to the postmaster. If `king@bluesuede.org` returns an error from `bluesuede.org`, for example, you may try a polite question to `postmaster@bluesuede.org`. Because the postmaster is usually an overworked volunteer system administrator, it is considered poor form to ask a postmaster for favors much greater than "Does so-and-so have a mailbox on this system?"

The most common tools for encrypted mail are known as S/MIME, PEM (privacy-enhanced mail), and PGP (Pretty Good Privacy). PGP is one of the most widely used encryption programs, both in the United States and abroad. Many experts think it's so strong that even the National Security Agency can't crack it. We don't know about that, but if the NSA wants to read your mail, you have more complicated problems than we can help you solve. S/MIME is an emerging standard encryption system that Netscape and Outlook Express both support.

PGP is available for free on the Net. To find more information about privacy and security issues, including how to get started with PGP and S/MIME, point your Web browser to `net.gurus.com/pgp`.

To Whom Do I Write?

As you probably have figured out, one teensy detail is keeping you from sending e-mail to all your friends: You don't know their addresses. In this chapter, you find out lots of different ways to look for addresses. We save you the trouble of reading the rest of this chapter by starting out with the easiest, most reliable way to find out people's e-mail addresses:

Call them on the phone and ask them.

Pretty low-tech, huh? For some reason, this technique seems to be absolutely the last thing people want to do (see the nearby sidebar, "Top ten reasons not to call someone to get an e-mail address"). Try it first. If you know or can find out the phone number, this method is much easier than any of the others.

Another way to find a person's e-mail address is by using an online directory. Wouldn't it be cool if some online directory listed everybody's e-mail address? Maybe, but the Internet doesn't have one. For one thing, nothing says that somebody's e-mail address has any connection to her name. For another, not everybody wants everybody else to know his e-mail address. Although lots of directories attempt to accumulate e-mail addresses, none of them is complete, most are somewhat out of date, and many work only if people voluntarily list themselves with the service.

Top ten reasons not to call someone to get an e-mail address

- You want to surprise a long-lost friend.
- You want to surprise a long-lost *ex*-friend who owes you a large amount of money and thinks that she has given you the slip.
- You or your friend don't speak English. (Actually happens — many Internauts are outside the United States.)
- You or your friend don't speak at all. (Actually happens — networks offer a uniquely friendly place for most people with handicaps because nobody knows or cares about the handicaps.)
- It's 3 a.m. and you need to send a message right now or else you'll never get to sleep.
- You don't know the phone number, and, because of an unfortunate childhood experience, you have a deathly fear of calling directory assistance.
- The phone takes only quarters; nobody around can break your $100 bill.
- Your company has installed a new phone system, no one has figured out how to use it, and, no matter what you dial, you always end up with Dial-a-Prayer.
- You inadvertently spilled an entire can of soda into the phone and can't wait for it to dry out to make the call.
- You called yesterday, didn't write down the answer, and forgot it. Oops.

This situation reiterates, of course, our point that the best way to find someone's e-mail address is to ask. When that method isn't an option, try one of these "white pages" directories:

- **SuperPages.com** at wp.superpages.com
- **BigFoot** at www.bigfoot.com
- **WhoWhere** at whowhere.lycos.com
- **Yahoo People Search** at people.yahoo.com

Another approach is to go to a search engine like Google (google.com) or AltaVista (altavista.com) and type the person's full name, enclosed in quotes. You'll see a list of pages that include the name — of course, there may be many people with the same name if your friend is called Allen Johnson or Bob Smith. Try searching for your own name and see what you find!

Chapter 11

Putting Your Mail in Its Place

In This Chapter

- Deleting mail
- Responding to mail
- Forwarding and filing mail
- Sending and receiving exotic mail and mail attachments
- Exchanging mail with robots and fax machines
- Dealing with spam

Okay, now you know how to send and receive mail. It's time for some tips and tricks to make you into a real mail aficionado. We describe Eudora 5, Netscape 7 Mail, Outlook Express 6.0, and Yahoo Mail (see Chapter 10 for descriptions of them).

After you see an e-mail message, you can do a bunch of different things with it (much the same as with paper mail). Here are your usual choices:

- Throw it away.
- Reply to it.
- Forward it to other people.
- File it.

You can do any or all these things with each message. If you don't tell your mail program what to do with a message, the message usually stays in your mailbox for later perusal.

Deleting Mail

When you first begin to get e-mail, the feeling is so exciting that it's difficult to imagine just throwing away the message. Eventually, however, you *have* to know how to get rid of messages, or else your computer will run out of room. Start early. Delete often.

Throwing away mail is easy enough that you probably have figured out how to do it already. Display the message, or select it from the list of messages in a folder. Then click the trashcan, big *X*, or other trashy-looking icon on the toolbar, or press Ctrl+D or Del (on the Mac, press ⌘+D or Delete). In Yahoo Mail, click the Inbox or Check Mail link to see a list of your messages. Then click the check box by the message and click the Delete Checked Mail button. When you are looking at a message in Yahoo Mail, you can click the Delete button, too.

You can often delete mail without even reading it. If you subscribe to mailing lists (described in Chapter 13), certain topics may not interest you. After you see the subject line, you may want to delete the message without reading it. If you're the type of person who reads everything Ed McMahon sends to you, you may have problems managing junk e-mail, too. Consider getting professional help.

When you delete a message, most e-mail programs don't throw it away immediately. Instead, they file the message in your Trash mailbox or mail folder, or just mark it as deleted. From time to time (usually whenever you exit the e-mail program), the program empties your trash, truly deleting the messages.

Back to You, Sam: Replying to Mail

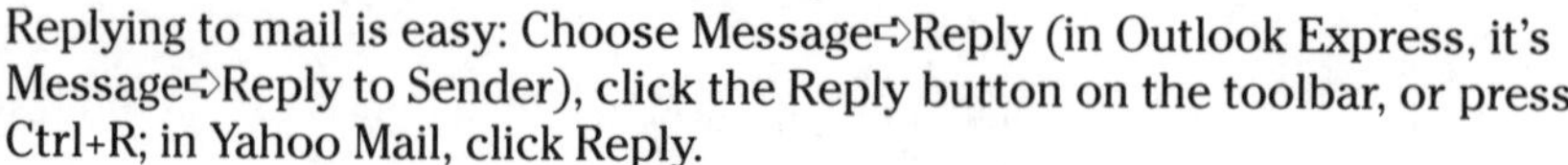

Replying to mail is easy: Choose Message⇨Reply (in Outlook Express, it's Message⇨Reply to Sender), click the Reply button on the toolbar, or press Ctrl+R; in Yahoo Mail, click Reply.

Pay attention to two things in particular:

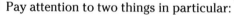

- **To whom does the reply go?** Look carefully at the To line your mail program has filled out for you. Is that who you thought you were addressing? If the reply is addressed to a mailing list, did you really intend to post to that list, or is your message of a more personal nature and may be better addressed to the individual who sent the message? Did you mean to reply to a group? Are all the addresses that you think you're replying to included on the To list? If the To list isn't correct, you can move the cursor to it and edit it as necessary.
- **Do you want to include the content of the message to which you're replying?** Most e-mail programs begin your reply message with the content of the message to which you're replying. In Eudora, if some of the original message was selected when you clicked Reply, only that text appears in the reply. We suggest that you begin by including it and then edit the text to just the relevant material. If you don't give some context

to people who get a great deal of e-mail, your reply makes no sense. If you're answering a question, include the question in the response. You don't have to include the entire text, but give your reader a break. She may have read 50 messages since she sent you mail and may not have a clue what you're talking about unless you remind her.

When you reply to a message, most mail programs fill in the Subject field with the letters *Re:* (short for *regarding*) and the Subject field of the message to which you're replying.

Occasionally you may receive a message that has been sent to a zillion people, with their addresses appearing in dozens of lines in the To section of the message. If you reply to a message like this, look at the To section of your message to make sure not to address your reply to the entire list of recipients.

Keeping Track of Your Friends

After you begin using e-mail, you quickly find that you have enough regular correspondents that keeping track of their e-mail addresses is a pain. Fortunately, every popular e-mail program provides an *address book* in which you can save your friends' addresses so that you can send mail to `Mom`, for example, and have it automatically addressed to `chairman@exec.hq.giantcorp.com`. You can also create address lists so that you can send mail to `family`, for example, and it goes to Mom, Dad, your brother, both sisters, and your dog, all of whom have e-mail addresses.

All address books let you do the same things: save in your address book the address from a message you have just read, use addresses you have saved, and edit your address book.

Eudora's address book

Eudora has a good address book, and adding people to it is easy. If you're reading a message, choose Special⇨Make Address Book Entry (or press Ctrl+K). Eudora suggests using the person's real name as the nickname, which usually works fine. Then click OK.

To use the address book while you're composing a message, you can open the address book by clicking the Address book icon or choosing Tools⇨Address Book (Ctrl+L). In the Address Book window (shown in Figure 11-1), click the nickname to use, and then click the To, Cc, or Bcc button to add the selected address to the message (close the Address Book window when you're done with it by clicking its Close or X button). Or use this shortcut: Type the first few letters of the nickname on the To or Cc line, enough to distinguish the nickname you want from other nicknames, and press Enter. Eudora finishes the nickname for you.

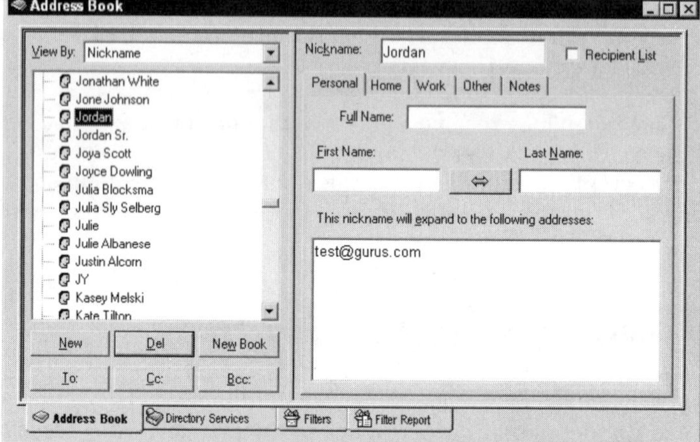

Figure 11-1: Eudora's address book.

To type someone into your address book, click the Address Book button and click the New button to create a new entry called Untitled. This new entry is displayed in the list of nicknames, with no name or address. Change the Nickname to the name you want to use for this person, and enter the full name and e-mail address.

Netscape's address book

To use the address book when you're creating a message in Netscape Mail, click the Address button in the Composition window. Click the address and click the To button before clicking OK. Or type the first few letters of the nickname of someone in your address book until it shows the rest of the name; when you press Tab, Netscape fills it in with the address.

To edit your address book, choose Window⇨Address Book or press Ctrl+5. When the Address Book window appears, it shows two address books, the Personal Address Book where you put your regular entries, and Collected Addresses from all the mail you've sent. Click the name of the address book you want to work with.

You can create an entry for a person by clicking New Card. To edit an entry, select it and click the Properties button on the toolbar. To create a mailing list, click the New List button, which creates an empty list, and then type the addresses you want.

When you're reading a message in Netscape Mail, you can add the sender's address to your address book by right-clicking on the sender's name or address in the From line and choosing Add to Address Book in the menu that pops up. This opens a New Card window in which you can enter the nickname to use and then click OK to add the nickname to the address book.

Outlook Express's address book

The process of copying a correspondent's address into the address book is easy but obscure: Double-click a message from your correspondent to open that message in its own window. Then double-click the person's name in the From line, and click Add to Address Book in the properties window that appears. You can edit the address book entry you're creating if you want, and then click OK. (Another way to do the same thing is to right-click the sender's name on the list of messages in the Outlook Express window, and choose Add Sender to Address Book from the menu that appears.)

To display and edit the Address book, click the Addresses button on the toolbar (you may need to make the Outlook Express window wider to see it — it's near the right end of the toolbar). Click the New button on the Address Book window's toolbar and choose New Contact from the menu that appears.

After you manage to get some entries into your address book, you use them while you're creating a new message by clicking the little book icon to the left of the To or Cc line in the New Message window. In the Select Recipients window that appears, double-click the address book entry or entries you want to use and then click OK. If you don't know someone's e-mail address, choose Edit⇨Find⇨People in the New Message window (or press Ctrl+E) to display the Find People window; you can search in your own address book or in various Internet directories, such as Bigfoot (`www.bigfoot.com`) and Yahoo People Search (`people.yahoo.com`).

Yahoo Mail's address book

When you have logged into Yahoo Mail, click the Address link to display your address book. Click the Add Contact button to add someone. Fill out the form that appears and be sure to enter a *nickname* for the person: This is the name you can type when addressing an e-mail message instead of typing the person's whole e-mail address. Yahoo Mail includes fields for the person's postal address and phone numbers, but you can leave them blank. Then click Save Contact, and assuming you like what you see on the confirmation screen that follows, click Done.

After someone is in your address book, Yahoo Mail provides two ways to address a message: when composing a message, type the person's nickname; when looking at the address book, click the To, Cc, or Bcc box by the person's name and click the Go button next to the Send Email box.

Hot Potatoes: Forwarding Mail

You can forward e-mail to someone else. It's easy. It's cheap. Forwarding is one of the best things about electronic mail and at the same time one of the worst. It's good because you can easily pass along messages to people who need to know about them. It's bad because you (not *you* personally, but, um, people around you — that's it) can just as easily send out floods of messages to recipients who would just as soon not hear *another* press release from the local Ministry of Truth (or another joke that's making the rounds). Think about whether you will enhance someone's quality of life by forwarding a message to him.

What's usually called *forwarding* a message involves wrapping the message in a new message of your own, sort of like sticking Post-It notes all over a copy of it and mailing the copy and Post-Its to someone else.

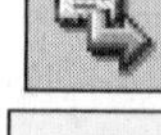

Forwarding mail is almost as easy as replying to it: Select the message and click the Forward button, or choose Message⇨Forward. Pressing Ctrl+L also works in Netscape, while Ctrl+F forwards in Outlook Express. The mail program composes a message containing the text of the message you want to forward; all you have to do is address the message, add a few snappy comments, and send it.

- Eudora and Outlook Express provide the forwarded text in the message part of the window. Each line is preceded by the greater-than sign (>) or a vertical bar. You then get to edit the message and add your own comments. See the nearby sidebar "Fast forward" for tips about pruning forwarded mail.
- Netscape Mail puts the original message at the bottom of your new message, preceded by a line saying (surprise!) "Original Message." Very convenient.
- In Yahoo Mail, clicking Forward sends the original messages as an attachment to your new message. Instead, you can click in the box to the right of the Forward button, set it to Inline Text, and then click Forward.

Fast forward

Whenever you're forwarding mail, it's generally a good idea to get rid of uninteresting parts. All the glop in the message header is frequently included automatically in the forwarded message, and almost none of it is comprehensible, much less interesting, so get rid of it.

The tricky part is editing the text. If the message is short, a screenful or so, you probably should leave it alone:

```
>Is there a lot of demand for
   fruit pizza?
>I checked with our research
   department and found that
   the favorite pizza toppings
   in the 18-34 age group are
   pepperoni, sausage, ham,
   pineapple, olives, peppers,
   mushrooms, hamburger, and
   broccoli. I specifically
   asked about prunes, and they
   found no statistically sig-
   nificant response.
```

If the message is really long and only part of it is relevant, you should, as a courtesy to the reader, cut it down to the interesting part. We can tell you from experience that people pay much more attention to a concise, one-line e-mail message than they do to 12 pages of quoted stuff followed by a two-line question.

Sometimes it makes sense to edit material even more, particularly to emphasize one specific part. When you do so, of course, be sure not to edit to the point where you put words in the original author's mouth or garble the sense of the message, as in the following reply:

```
>I checked with our research
   >department and found that the
   >favorite pizza toppings ...
   >and they found no statisti
   >cally significant response
   >about them.
```

That's an excellent way to make new enemies. Sometimes, it makes sense to paraphrase a little — in that case, put the paraphrased part in square brackets, like this:

```
>[When asked about prunes on
   >pizza, research]found no
   >statistically significant
   >response about them.
```

People disagree about whether paraphrasing to shorten quotes is a good idea. On one hand, if you do it well, it saves everyone time. On the other hand, if you do it badly and someone takes offense, you're in for a week of accusations and apologies that will wipe out whatever time you may have saved. The decision is up to you.

Sometimes, the mail you get may really have been intended for someone else. You probably want to pass it along as is, without sticking the > character at the beginning of every line, and you should leave the sender and reply-to information intact so that if the new recipient of the mail wants to respond, the response goes to the originator of the mail, not to you just because you passed it on. Some mail programs call this feature *remailing* or *bouncing,* the electronic version of scribbling another address on the outside of an envelope and dropping it back in the mailbox.

Eudora calls the process of forwarding *redirecting;* you can redirect mail by choosing Message⇨Redirect from the menu or clicking the Redirect icon on the toolbar. Eudora sticks in a polite by-way-of notice to let the new reader know how the message found her. Because Netscape, Outlook Express, and Yahoo Mail have no redirection, you have to forward messages instead.

Cold Potatoes: Saving Mail

Saving e-mail for later reference is similar to putting potatoes in the fridge for later. (Don't knock it if you haven't tried it — day-old boiled potatoes are yummy with enough butter or sour cream.) Lots of your e-mail is worth saving, just as lots of your paper mail is worth saving. Lots of it *isn't,* of course, but we covered that subject earlier in this chapter.

You can save e-mail in a few different ways:

- Save it in a folder full of messages.
- Save it in a regular text file.
- Print it and put it in a file cabinet with paper mail.

The easiest method usually is to stick messages in a folder (a folder is usually no more than a file full of messages with some sort of separator between each message). E-mail programs usually come with folders called In (or Inbox), Outbox, Sent, and Trash, and perhaps some others. But you can also make your own folders.

People use two general approaches in filing mail: by sender and by topic. Whether you use one or the other or both is mostly a matter of taste. For filing by topic, it's entirely up to you to come up with folder names. The most difficult part is coming up with memorable names. If you're not careful, you end up with four folders with slightly different names, each with a quarter of the messages about a particular topic. Try to come up with names that are obvious, and don't abbreviate. If the topic is accounting, call the folder `Accounting` because if you abbreviate, you will never remember whether it's called `Acctng`, `acct`, or `Acntng`.

You can save all or part of a message by copying it into a text file or word-processing document. Select the text of the message by using your mouse. Press Ctrl+C (⌘+C on a Mac) or choose Edit⇨Copy to copy the text to the Clipboard. Switch to your word processor (or whatever program into which you want to copy the text) and press Ctrl+V (⌘+V on the Mac) or choose Edit⇨Paste to make the message appear where the cursor is.

Filing with Eudora

To file a message in Eudora, click the message and choose Transfer from the menu. The Transfer menu lists all your mailboxes — all the choices you have for where to file your message. Choose the mailbox in which you want to stick your message. Poof — it's there. You can also use your mouse to drag a message from one mailbox to another.

The first time you try to file something, you may notice that you don't have anywhere to file it. Create a new mailbox in which to stick the message by choosing Transfer⇨New. Every time you want to create a new mailbox, choose New. Although you eventually have enough mailboxes to handle most of your mail, for a while it may seem as though you're choosing New all the time. If you need a lot of mailboxes, you can create mailboxes inside folders, to keep your mailboxes organized.

You can see all the messages in a mailbox by choosing Mailbox from the menu. If you want to see all your mailboxes, choose Tools⇨Mailboxes — a mailbox list appears. You can double-click any mailbox in the list to see its contents.

If you want to save the message in a text file, click the message, choose File⇨Save As from the menu, move to the folder in which you want to save the message, type a filename, and click OK.

Filing with Netscape

Netscape Mail lists your mail folders in the Mail Folders, under your e-mail address.

You can save a message in a folder by right-clicking the message, choosing Move Message (or Move To) from the menu that appears, and choosing the folder from the list that appears. Or you can select the message and drag it to a folder on the folder list. To make a new folder, choose File⇨New Folder or File⇨New⇨Folder.

To save a message or several messages in a text file, select the message or messages and choose File⇨Save As⇨File from the menu (or press Ctrl+S). Click in the Save As Type box and choose Plain Text or Text Files from the list that appears. Type a filename and click the Save button.

Filing with Outlook Express

To save a message in Outlook Express, you stick it in a folder. You start out with folders named Inbox, Outbox, Sent Items, Drafts, and Deleted Items. To make a new folder, choose File⇨Folder⇨New from the menu and give the folder a name. (Make one called Personal, just to give it a try.) The new folder appears on the list of folders on the left side of the Outlook Express window. Move messages into a folder by clicking a message header and dragging it over to the folder name or choosing Edit⇨Move To Folder from the menu. You can see the list of message headers for any folder by clicking the folder name. If you have a *lot* of messages to file, you can even create folders within folders, to keep things organized.

You can save the text of a message in a text file by clicking the message and choosing File⇨Save As from the menu, clicking in the Save As Type box and choosing Text Files (*.txt), typing a filename, and clicking the Save button.

Filing with Yahoo Mail

To save a message in a folder, click the Choose Folder box and choose the folder where you want the message. Then click the Move button. To create a new folder, choose New Folder from the list of folders and click Move. Yahoo Mail asks you for a name for the folder.

To see a list of your folders, click the plus button to the left of the Folders link at the left side of the Yahoo Mail Web page. Your folders include Inbox, Sent, Draft, and Bulk Mail (where Yahoo files stuff that looks like spam to them). Click a folder name to see the messages in that folder.

Exotic Mail and Mail Attachments

Sooner or later, just plain, old, everyday e-mail isn't good enough for you. Someone's gonna send you a picture you just have to see, or you're gonna want to send something cool to your new best friend in Paris. To send stuff other than text through the mail, a message uses special file formats. Sometimes, the entire message is in a special format, and sometimes people *attach* things to their plain text mail. The most widely used format for attaching files to messages is called MIME (*m*ultipurpose *I*nternet *m*ail *e*xtensions). All the programs we describe in this chapter can send and receive files attached using MIME, but there are still some older e-mail programs that can't.

You can generally send a file as an e-mail attachment by using your regular mail program to compose a regular message and then giving a command to attach a file to the message. You send the message by using the program's usual commands.

When you receive a file that is attached to an e-mail message, your mail program is responsible for noticing the attached file and doing something intelligent with it. Most of the time, your mail program saves the attached file as a separate file in the folder you specify. After the file has been saved, you can use it just like you use any other file.

Chain letters: Arrrrrgggghhh!

One of the most obnoxious things you can do with e-mail is to pass around chain letters. Because all mail programs have forwarding commands, with only a few keystrokes you can send a chain letter along to hundreds of other people. Don't do it. Chain letters are cute for about two seconds, and then they're just annoying. After 20 years of using e-mail, we've *never* received a chain letter worth passing along. That's **NEVER!** (Please excuse the shouting.) So don't you pass them along either, okay?

A few chain letters just keep coming around and around, despite our best efforts to stamp them out:

- **Make big bucks with a chain letter:** These letters usually contain lots of testimonials from people who are now rolling in dough, and tell you to send $5 to the name at the top of the list, put your name at the bottom, and send the message to a zillion other suckers. Some even say, "This isn't a chain letter" (you're supposedly helping to compile a mailing list or sending reports or something — your 100 percent guaranteed tip-off that it's a chain letter). Don't even think about it. These chain letters are extremely illegal in the U.S. even when they say that they aren't, and, besides, they don't even work. (Why send any money? Why not just add your name and send it on? Heck, why not just replace all the names on the list with yours?) Think of them as gullibility viruses. Send a polite note to the sender's postmaster to encourage her to tell users not to send any more chain letters. If you don't believe that they're illegal, see the Postal Service Web site, at `www.usps.gov/websites/depart/inspect/chainlet.htm`.
- **Big company will send you cash for reading e-mail:** This one has circulated with both Disney and Microsoft as the designated corporation. The message claims that the company is conducting a marketing test and that you can get big bucks or a trip to Disney World for sending the message along. Yeah, right. A variation says that something interesting but unspecified will happen when you forward it; we suppose that's true if having all your friends find out how gullible you are counts as interesting.
- **Hideous virus will wreck your computer:** Occasionally these are true, generally they're not, and when they are true, they tend to be about viruses that have been around since 1992. If you run software that's subject to viruses (Microsoft Outlook Express and Outlook are particularly vulnerable), look at the vendor's Web site and at the sites belonging to antivirus software makers for some more credible reports, downloadable updates, and antivirus advice. Some of the apparent virus warnings are themselves viruses. If a message shows up saying "Install this patch from Microsoft immediately to keep viruses out," it's not a patch, it's a virus.

For example, you can send these types of files as attachments:

- Pictures, in image files
- Word-processing documents
- Sounds, in audio files
- Movies, in video files
- Programs, in executable files
- Compressed files, such as ZIP files

See Chapter 19 for a description of the types of files you may encounter as attachments.

E-mail viruses usually show up as attachments. If you get a message with an unexpected attachment, even from someone you know, **DON'T OPEN IT** until you check with the sender to make sure he or she sent it deliberately. Viruses often suck all the addresses from a victim's address book so the virus can mail itself to the victim's friends. Some kinds of attachments can't carry viruses, notably GIF and JPG images.

Eudora attachments

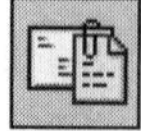

To attach a file to a message with Eudora, compose a message as usual. Then choose Message⇨Attach File from the menu, click the Attach button on the toolbar, or press Ctrl+H. Eudora helps you choose the document you want to attach.

If you drag a file from Windows Explorer, My Computer, or File Manager to Eudora, she attaches the file to the message you're writing. If you're not writing a message, she starts one for you. What service!

When Eudora receives mail with attachments, she automatically saves them to your disk (in a folder you specify in Tools⇨Options, in the Attachments category) and tells you where they are and what they're called.

Netscape attachments

To attach a file to the message you're composing, click the Attach button. Then select the file you want to send. Or just drag the file(s) into the Attachments box in the mail composition window.

For incoming mail, Netscape displays any attachments that it knows how to display itself (Web pages and GIF and JPEG image files). For other types of attachments, it displays a little description of the file, which you can click. Netscape then runs an appropriate display program, if it knows of one, or asks you whether to save the attachment to a file or to configure a display program, which it then runs in order to display it.

Outlook Express attachments

In Outlook Express, you attach a file to a message by choosing Insert➪File Attachment from the menu while you're composing a message or click the paper-clip icon on the toolbar (it may be off the right side of the toolbar — make the Composition window wider to display it). Then select the file to attach. Or just drag the file into the message composition window. Then send the message as usual.

When an incoming message contains an attachment, a paper-clip icon appears in the message on your list of incoming messages and in the message header when you view the message. Click the paper clip to see the filename — double-click, and you may be able to see the attachment.

Microsoft has "solved" some of Outlook Express's chronic security problems by making it refuse to show you many attachments, including a lot of benign ones such as attached text messages and PDF files. You can sort of fix this by choosing Tools➪Options in the main Outlook Express window, clicking the Security tab, and then unchecking the Do Not Allow Attachments to Be Saved or Opened That Could Potentially Be a Virus box. Then Outlook Express will let you open your attachments, although of course when someone *does* send you a virus, Outlook Express will cheerfully open that, too.

Yahoo Mail attachments

To attach stuff with Yahoo Mail, compose a message as usual. Then scroll down to the Attachments box and click the Edit Attachments link. A separate window pops up in which you specify the name of the file you want to attach. Click the Browse button to find the file on your computer (you may need to change the Files of Type box in the File Upload dialog box to All Files to see all your files). Then click the Attach File button and the Done button. Your Web browser copies the file right off your hard disk and sends it to the Yahoo Mail system to include in your message (amazing!). You return to the Yahoo Mail Web page with the file name entered in the Attachments box. Send the message as usual.

When you get a message with attachments, a box appears at the bottom of the message, with the file name and size of the attachment. Click the Download File button to get the file onto your computer.

Hey, Mr. Robot

Not every mail address has an actual person behind it. Some are mailing lists (which we talk about in Chapter 13), and some are *robots,* programs that automatically reply to messages. Mail robots have become popular as a way to query databases and retrieve files because setting up a connection for electronic mail is much easier than setting up one that handles the more standard file transfer. You send a message to the robot (usually referred to as a *mailbot* or *mail server*), it takes some action based on the contents of your message, and then the robot sends back a response. If you send a message to `internet9@gurus.com`, for example, you receive a response telling you your e-mail address. Some companies use mailbots to send back canned responses to requests for information sent to `info@`*`whatever`*`.com`.

Your Own Personal Mail Manager

After you begin sending e-mail, you probably will find that you receive quite a bit of it, particularly if you put yourself on some mailing lists (see Chapter 13). Your incoming mail soon becomes a trickle, and then a stream, and then a torrent, and pretty soon you can't walk past your keyboard without getting soaking wet, metaphorically speaking.

Fortunately, most mail systems provide ways for you to manage the flow and avoid ruining your clothes (enough of this metaphor already). Netscape and Eudora users can create *filters* that can automatically check incoming messages against a list of senders and subjects and file them in appropriate folders. Outlook Express has the Inbox Assistant, which can sort your mail automatically. Most other mail programs have similar filtering features. If you sort mail into separate mailboxes for each mailing list or other category, you can deal with it a lot more efficiently.

For example, you can create filters that tell your mail program, "Any message that comes from the CHICKENS-L mailing list should be automatically filed in the Cluck mail folder." (Figure 11-2 shows this filter in Netscape Mail.) Or you can create filters to highlight messages from particularly interesting friends, or delete certain messages (you know the ones we mean) so you never have to see them.

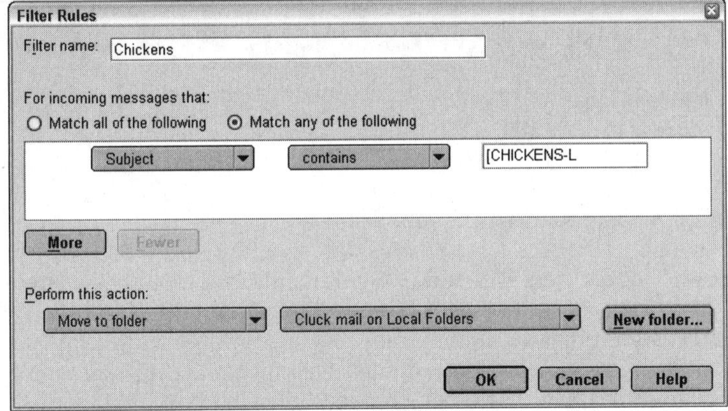

Figure 11-2: Filtering meaty messages.

- **Eudora:** Choose Tools⇨Filters to see the Filters window, which lists filters and lets you create, edit, and delete them. Or right-click on any message in a mailbox window and choose Make Filter to create a filter based on that message's sender or subject.
- **Netscape Mail:** Choose Tools⇨Message Filters from the menu to display the Message Filters window, where you can see, create, edit, and delete filters. Or click the To or From address in a message and choose Create Filter from Message to make a filter for mail sent to or from that address.
- **Outlook Express:** Tell the Inbox Assistant how to sort your mail into folders by choosing Tools⇨Message Rules⇨Mail from the menu.
- **Yahoo Mail:** Click the Mail Options link in the Yahoo Mail Web page, and then click the Filters heading. You can create, edit, or delete your filters.

All this automatic-sorting nonsense may seem like overkill, and if you get only five or ten messages a day, it is. After the mail really gets flowing, however, dealing with it takes much more of your time than it used to. Keep those automated tools in mind — if not for now, then for later.

One-click surfing

Most e-mail programs convert URLs (Web site addresses) in your e-mail messages into links to the actual Web site. You don't have to type these addresses into your browser: All you have to do is click the highlighted link in the e-mail message and — poof — your browser opens and you're at the Web site. If your e-mail program has this feature (all the programs described in this chapter do), URLs in e-mail messages appear underlined and blue.

Spam, Bacon, Spam, Eggs, and Spam

Pink tender morsel,
Glistening with salty gel.
What the hell is it?

— SPAM haiku, found on the Internet

More and more often, it seems, we get unsolicited e-mail from some organization or person we don't know. The word *spam* (not to be confused with SPAM, a meat-related product from Minnesota) on the Internet now means thousands of copies of the same unwanted message, sent to individual e-mail accounts, newsgroups in Usenet, the net's shared bulletin board, and even instant message programs. It's also known as *junk e-mail* or unsolicited bulk e-mail (UBE). The message usually consists of unsavory advertising for get-rich-quick schemes or pornographic offers — something you may not want to see and something you definitely don't want your children to see. The message is *spam,* the practice is *spamming,* and the person sending the spam is a *spammer.*

Spam, unfortunately, is a major problem on the Internet because sleazy business entrepreneurs have decided that it's the ideal way to advertise. We get 100 spams a day (yes, really) and the number continues to increase. Spam doesn't have to be commercial (we've gotten religious and political spam) but it has to be unsolicited; if you asked for it, it's not spam.

Why call it spam?

The meat? Nobody knows. Oh, you mean the unwanted e-mail? It came from the Monty Python skit in which a group of Vikings sing the word *spam* repeatedly in a march tempo, drowning out all other discourse. (Google for "Monty Python spam" and you'll find plenty of sites where you can listen to it.)

Why is it so bad?

You may think that spam, like postal junk mail, is just a nuisance we have to live with. But it's worse than junk mail, in several ways. Spam costs you money. E-mail recipients pay much more than the sender does to deliver a message. Sending e-mail is cheap: A spammer can send thousands of messages an hour from a PC and a dialup connection. After that, it costs you time to download, read (at least the subject line), and dispose of the mail. As of mid-2003, the amount of spam had surpassed the amount of real e-mail, and if spam volume continues to grow at its alarming pace, pretty soon e-mail will prove to be useless because the real e-mail is buried under the junk.

Not only do spam recipients have to bear a cost, but all this volume of e-mail also strains the resources of the e-mail servers and the entire Internet. ISPs have to pass along the added costs to its users. America Online has been reported to estimate that more than half of its incoming e-mail is spam, and many ISPs have told us that as much as $2 of the $20 monthly fee goes to handling and cleaning up after spam.

Spammers advertise stuff you'd never get in postal mail. It's generally fraudulent, dishonest, or pornographic (or all three). Many of the offers are for get-rich-quick schemes. Few honest businesses attempt to advertise by broad- casting on the Internet because of the immense bad publicity it brings — and those that try it once rarely make the same mistake twice.

Many spams include a line that instructs you how to get off their lists, something like "Send us a message with the word REMOVE in it." Why should you have to waste your time to get off the list? But don't bother — spammers' remove lists rarely work. In fact, they can be a method for verifying that your address is real, and they are more likely to send you *more* spam.

What can I do?

The Internet grew from a need for the easy and free flow of information, and everyone using it should strive to keep it that way. Check out these Web sites for information about spam and how to fight it, technically, socially, and legally:

- `spam.abuse.net` (a spam overview)
- `www.cauce.org` (antispam laws)
- `www.abuse.net` (a complaint forwarding service)

We believe that spam is not just a technical problem, and only a combination of technical, social, and legal solutions will work in the long run. In the meantime, every ISP now does at least some spam filtering on incoming mail, and many let you "tune" the filters. Check with your ISP.

I Think I've Got a Virus

Viruses have been around the Internet for a long time. Originally, they lived in program files that people downloaded using a file transfer program or their Web browser. Now, most viruses are spread through files that are sent via e-mail, as attachments to mail messages.

The text of a plain text message can't contain a virus because it's only text, and a virus is a (rather sneaky) program. But attachments can, and sometimes do, contain viruses. For the virus to work (that is, for it to run, infect your computer, and send copies of itself out to other people via e-mail), you need to run it.

In most e-mail programs (including Netscape and Eudora), programs contained in attachments don't run until you click them — so *don't* open programs that come from people you don't know. Don't even open attachments from people you *do* know if you weren't expecting to receive them. Many successful viruses replicate themselves by sending copies of themselves to the first 50 people in your address book; people who know you.

However, if you use Microsoft's Outlook Express 5.0 or later, or Outlook 97 or later, the situation is more dire. Outlook (which comes with Microsoft Office) opens attachments as soon as you view the message. Outlook Express (which comes with Windows) provides a *preview pane* that displays a file and its attachments before you click it at all. Early versions of Outlook Express 5.0 and Outlook 97, 98, and maybe 2000 allowed attached programs to do all kinds of horrible things to your PC. Luckily, Microsoft has changed the default settings on more recent versions of Outlook Express and Outlook.

In Chapter 10, we tell you what we know about ways to make your e-mail program less prone to viruses. Be sure to check your e-mail program's Web site, too, for late-breaking information. Outlook Express users should check Microsoft's `windowsupdate.com` weekly for the latest bug fixes.

Chapter 12

Broadband Mania

In This Chapter

- Sharing your connection
- Listening to music
- Watching movies
- Internet phones that really work

If you have a broadband Internet connection, you'll soon find that it's not just faster than your old dialup connection — it lets you do things that just aren't possible with dialup. Chapter 5 describes how to get online with a broadband connection. This chapter gives you a taste of the new vistas of broadband: connection sharing, streaming audio and video, and Internet phones.

Sharing Your Connection

Some years ago, back when computers were large hulking things found only in glass-walled computer rooms, a wild-eyed visionary friend of ours claimed (to great skepticism) that computers would be everywhere, and so small and cheap that they'd show up as prizes in cereal boxes. We're not sure about the cereal boxes, but it's certainly true that the last time we went to put an old computer in the closet, there wasn't room because of all the other old computers there. Rather than let them rust in the closet, you may as well get some use out of all those computers by connecting them all to the Internet.

With a broadband connection, that turns out to be pretty easy. No more arguing about who's going to use the phone line next! No more pouting from the computer users who didn't get the cable or DSL hookup! Everyone can send e-mail, receive e-mail, chat, and browse the Web at the same time.

First, connect your computers together

If you connect your computers into a network (a *LAN*, for *local area network*) all the computers can share one Internet connection. LANs come in two basic varieties: wired and wireless. In a wired network, a cable runs from each computer to a central box called a *hub*, whereas a wireless network uses radio signals instead of wires, and the central box is called an *access point*. If all your computers are in one room, or you're good at playing home electrician, a wired network's for you; otherwise, wireless is far easier to set up, although the pieces are more expensive. Combos are also possible; John's network uses wires for all the computers in his office and wireless for his wife's computer in her office on the other side of the house. For more details on setting up your LAN, see *Home Networking For Dummies* (by Kathy Ivens, published by Wiley Publishing, Inc.).

Then, connect the LAN to the Net

To share an Internet connection, your cable or DSL modem connects to a *router*, which then connects to the LAN. The router acts as the traffic cop between the Net and all the computers on your LAN. The router can be a separate hardware box, or it can be software running on one of your PCs. The router has two network connections, one to the Internet and one to the rest of the LAN. Router boxes invariably include the hub or access point that you need to connect all your computers to the LAN anyway, and are now so cheap, often under $50, that we recommend them to anyone who wants to share a broadband connection. They have the large advantage over software routers that after you set them up, they stay set up and you don't have to worry about your whole network dying if the PC that runs the routing software crashes, breaks, or otherwise isn't available.

Figure 12-1 shows a typical home network. A cable or DSL connects either to a PC running router software or a hardware router. The PC connects to a network hub (for a wired network) or access point (for wireless), whereas the hardware router has a hub or access point built in. Then the LAN connects to the rest of the computers around the house.

Windows 98 Second Edition, Me, 2000, and XP all come with Internet Connection Sharing (ICS), which is adequate router software. You can also check out WinGate (at `www.wingate.com`) or Sygate (at `www.sygate.com`) for low-cost alternatives that give you a little more information about who's doing what.

To set up Internet connection sharing, be sure that the computer you plan to use is connected both to your cable or DSL modem and to the LAN. If that computer is running Windows Me, choose Start⇨Programs⇨Accessories⇨Communications⇨Home Networking Wizard (you may need to click the little arrows at the bottom of the Communications menu to reveal all the commands). If it's Windows XP, choose Start⇨All Programs⇨Communications⇨New Connection Wizard (the same Wizard you used to set up your Internet connection), and choose Set Up a Home or Small Office Network. The Wizard steps you through the configuration of the *ICS server* (the computer that connects to the Internet) and the *ICS clients* (the rest of the computers).

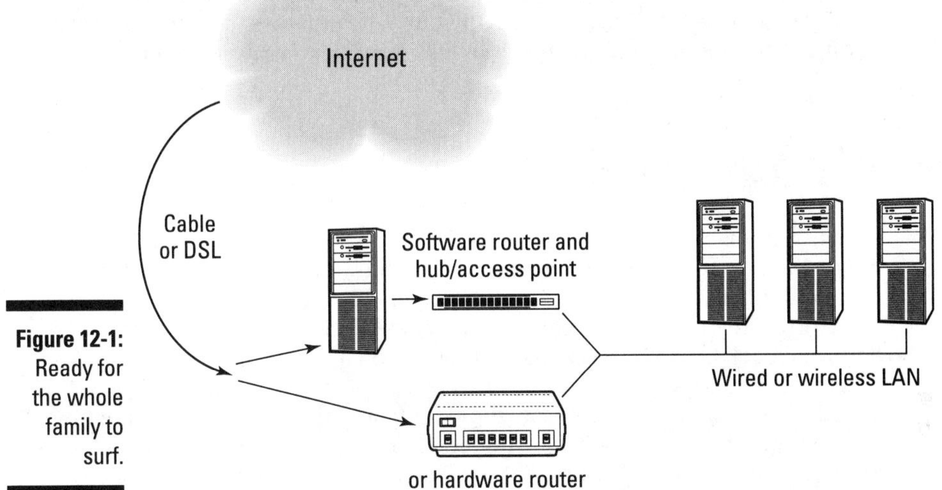

Figure 12-1: Ready for the whole family to surf.

Either way, if you have the kind of connection that requires that you log on (*PPPoE* is the technical term), with luck, your router will log you on automatically when someone on the LAN wants to connect to the Internet. Otherwise, you'll have to use the ICS client program to poke the router and log on. If you have always-on broadband (also known as *DHCP*), the Internet will just be there when you need it.

But be safe!

The good news about shared connections is that all the people in your house can share your network. The bad news is that if you're not careful, unwanted outsiders can share, too. (Putting a new Windows PC on the Net can be sort of like buying a new car, driving it home, and the next morning discovering that a family of raccoons has moved into your trunk.)

All routers, hardware or software, include a filtering component invariably (albeit incorrectly) known as a *firewall.* Be sure the firewall is turned on to keep outsiders out. The normal configuration of your firewall should be adequate for most purposes and will ensure that no matter how sloppily you set up the shared disks and printers on your networks, the sharing stops at the router. Some applications, notably multiuser games, require that you adjust the firewall to let traffic through that would otherwise have been blocked. If you do that, be sure to unadjust the firewall when you're done.

For wireless users, you also have to defend against *wardrivers*, people who drive around with a WiFi laptop and hop on, raccoon style, to any network signal the laptop picks up. Fortunately, WiFi comes with a password scheme called WEP which, although not cryptographically secure, is plenty to discourage wardrivers. When you set up your WiFi network, be sure to pick a distinct network name (known as the *SSID*), turn on WEP, and set a password.

Music Is out There

A dialup connection is just barely fast enough to handle a low-fidelity audio connection or very grainy and jerky video. In theory, you can download video clips and movies, but in practice you can put on your sneakers, walk three miles down the road to the video rental store, pick up a videotape or DVD, and walk back before the download finishes on a dialup connection.

Broadband connections, being a whole lot faster, make multimedia a whole lot more practical. Broadband connections range from about 300,000 bits per second (300K) on the slowest DSL to 10 million (10M) on the most uncongested cable systems. Because full-fidelity CD music is only 44K, that's more than enough speed for high fidelity sound and enough for adequate video.

All [whatever], All the Time!

There are three competing systems for playing online audio and video:

- Real Player, from `www.real.com`
- Apple QuickTime, from `www.apple.com/quicktime`
- Microsoft's Windows Media, from `www.microsoft.com/windows/windowsmedia`

They're all about equally popular, and because they're all available for free, you may as well download and install all three of them. Some sites also offer software of their own, specialized players, or download managers. If they do, they'll let you know and handle the download and installation for you.

You can download music to your computer as files, or you can listen to music that *streams* into your computer as you listen to it. With broadband, streaming is much more fun, like having a radio that can tune in any of a hundred thousand stations all over the world.

Boutique "Internet radio" stations

In the directories below, most stations offer streams at various speeds. Because you have broadband, pick the fastest one for the best sound quality.

Some music directory sites we use include

- www.mp3.com: The largest source of legal MP3 music downloads, most of which cost money.
- www.emusic.com: Another large source of legal MP3 music. Subscriptions allow unlimited downloads for $10 to $15/month.
- www.live365.com: A service that hosts lots of Internet radio. Listen for free with commercials, or for about $5/mo make the commercials go away.
- www.radio-locator.com: A directory of Web sites of over 10,000 radio stations, many of which have Web simulcasts.
- pandia.com/radio: Another directory of radio stations around the world you can listen to online.

We like National Public Radio, so we go to www.npr.org a lot — we like being able to listen to our favorite programs whenever we want to, rather than when they happen to be broadcast.

Lights, Camera, Downloads

Good quality video needs at least 500K bits/second, which is still beyond the limits of many broadband connections. (Even if your local speed is a lot faster, getting all those bits through the network is a challenge.) Most online video sites compromise with so-so quality and small images, which are still enough to watch trailers and short movies. Or you can download movies to watch later, taking advantage of the fact that your computer stays connected all night so it can download while you sleep. The movies we've downloaded are 500K bits for each second of movie, so a two-hour movie will take 2 hours to download if your connection can do 500K, 5 hours to download if it does 200K, and 20 hours to download over a 56K dialup.

Most video sites offer short and low-quality clips for free, with longer and higher quality videos costing money. If you've got the Big Three audio programs installed (we list them earlier in this chapter), you're ready for video, too.

Some movie and video sites we use include

- www.movielink.com: Full length movie rentals via download. The downloads happen automatically in the background, and then you can watch each movie for 24 hours from the time you first start watching it.
- www.ifilm.com: Short movies, movie trailers, TV clips, commercials, music videos, and more, along with lots and lots of movie promos. For $5/month, "plus" service provides more material, higher bandwidth, and fewer ads.

- www.sputnik7.com: Short films ranging from the hilarious to the indescribably strange, music videos, and anime.

See dmoz.org/Computers/Internet/Broadcasting/Video_Shows for lots more sites with broadband videos you can stream or download.

One Ringy-Dingy

When Internet phones first appeared about five years ago, we didn't think much of them. They needed expensive add-on equipment for your computer that was a pain to use, the sound quality was lousy, you could only talk to other people with the same kind of phone software, and the delays made everyone sound like Max He-He-He-Headroom. Times sure have changed! The current generation of Internet phones use regular telephones, the calls sound like real phone calls, your phone has a real phone number, and the price is hard to beat.

The leading Internet phone service is from Vonage (www.vonage.com). When you sign up with them, they ship you a box about half the size of this book with one jack for a cable to your router and another jack for the cord from your phone. Plug everything in, wait about ten seconds for the box to register itself on the network, and then pick up the phone, listen for a dial tone, and make your call. At the time we wrote this, they charge $40/mo for unlimited outgoing calls in the U.S. and Canada, or $26 for unlimited calls to your local area plus 500 minutes/month elsewhere in North America. Incoming calls and calls to 800 numbers are always free, and a long list of features such as caller-ID, call forwarding, and voice mail are included.

The phone has a real phone number that you can select from any of about 150 cities around the U.S. If you live in Texas but you want to make it easy for Mom to call you from back home in New Jersey, you can get a New Jersey phone number. (Actually, you can get as many numbers in as many places as you want, paying $5/mo for each.) If you travel, you can take your Vonage box with you and use it on any broadband Internet connection, with your phone number following your box.

If you want to make really, really, cheap calls (two cents a minute to anyplace in the U.S.), the older variety of PC-based phone service is still around. The best known of them is Net2Phone, www.net2phone.com.

Vonage's service is based on widely available equipment and standards, so we expect that other similar services will appear. For our latest thoughts on Internet phones, visit our Web site at net.gurus.com/phone.

Chapter 13

Online Communities: Let's Get Together

In This Chapter

- What's an online community?
- Ways to get together on the Internet
- Subscribing and unsubscribing to mailing lists
- Other kinds of communities

E-mail is a terrific way to communicate on the Internet, and it's by far the most popular. But other Internet programs let you communicate faster (in real time — that is, right now) or in groups. If you connect a microphone and speakers to your computer, you can even chat over the Internet as if it were a free long-distance phone line. This chapter shows you how to use e-mail mailing lists and Web-based message boards to make friends and influence people.

Look Who's Talking

Yes, the single most popular use for online discussions is to talk about (or participate in) sex, or at least dating, but there's a lot more to it than that. Clubs, churches, and other groups use the Internet to hold meetings. Hobbyists and fans talk about an amazing variety of topics, from knitting to *American Idol* and everything in between. People with medical problems support each other and exchange tips. You get the idea — anything that people might want to talk about is currently under intense discussion somewhere on the Net.

You can talk with groups of people on the Internet in lots of ways:

- E-mail mailing lists, in which you exchange messages via e-mail
- Web-based message boards, where messages appear on a Web page
- Usenet newsgroups, the original Internet discussions groups, which you read with a *newsreading program*

This chapter tells you how to participate in Internet-based discussions using e-mail mailing lists and Web message boards. For a description of Usenet newsgroups and how to read them, see our Web site at `net.gurus.com/usenet`.

For the full story on Internet-based communities, get our book, *Poor Richard's Building Online Communities,* published by Top Floor Publishing.

Mailing Lists: Are You Sure That This Isn't Junk Mail?

An e-mail mailing list is quite different from a snail-mail mailing list. Yes, both distribute messages to the people on the list, but with most e-mail mailing lists, the messages contain discussion among the subscribers rather than junk mail and catalogs.

Here's how an e-mail mailing list works. The list has its own special e-mail address, and anything someone sends to that address is sent to all the people on the list. Because these people in turn often respond to the messages, the result is a running conversation. For example, if the authors of this book hosted a discussion about the use and abuse of chocolate called *chocolate-lovers*, and if the list server program ran at lists.gurus.com, the list of the address would be `chocolate-lovers@lists.gurus.com`. (We do actually run a bunch of lists, but not one about chocolate. Yet.)

Different lists have different styles. Some are relatively formal, hewing closely to the official topic of the list. Others tend to go flying off into outer space, topicwise. You have to read them for a while to be able to tell which list works which way.

Mailing lists fall into three categories:

- **Discussion:** Every subscriber can post a message. These lists lead to freewheeling discussions and can include a certain number of off-topic messages.
- **Moderated:** A moderator reviews each message before it gets distributed. The moderator can stop unrelated, redundant, or clueless postings from wasting everyone's time.
- **Announcement-only:** Only the moderator posts messages. Announcement mailing lists are essentially online newsletters.

Urrp! Computers digest messages!

Some mailing lists are *digested.* No, they're not dripping with digital gastric juices — they're digested more in the sense of *Reader's Digest.* All the messages over a particular period (usually a day or two) are gathered into one big message with a table of contents added at the front. Many people find this method more convenient than getting messages separately because you can easily look at all the messages on the topic at one time.

We prefer to get our messages individually, and to tell our e-mail program to sort our incoming messages into separate folders, one for each mailing list we subscribe to. Eudora, Outlook Express, Netscape Messenger, Netscape Mail, and many other e-mail programs can sort your messages (but AOL's e-mail program can't). See "Your Own Personal Mail Manager" in Chapter 11.

Getting on and off mailing lists

Something or somebody has got to take on the job of keeping track of who is on the mailing list and distributing messages to all the subscribers. This job is *way* too boring for a human being to handle, so programs usually do the job. (A few lists are still run by human beings, and we pity them!) Most lists are run by programs called *list servers* or *mailing list managers.* Popular list server programs include LISTSERV, Majordomo, ListProc, MailMan, and many others, as well as Web-based systems like Yahoo Groups.

Getting on or off most mailing lists is simple: You send a mail message to the list server program. Because a program is reading the message, the message has to be spelled and formatted exactly right. Otherwise, the program just responds with an error message. List servers are computer programs. They're rather simple minded, and you have to speak to them clearly and distinctly, using standardized commands. Web-based mailing lists enable you to get on or off a list by going to the Web site, typing your address (and perhaps your name), and clicking a Subscribe or Join button.

When you send a command to get on or off a list, you don't send a message to the list address, unless you think that the rest of the subscribers would be fascinated by your comings and goings. Instead, you send it to the *list server address* (or *administrative address*), which is the name of the program (for example, LISTSERV or Majordomo) followed by @ and the computer on which the list server runs. For example, we host lists on our lists.gurus.com computer using the Majordomo list server program, so you would send commands to `majordomo@lists.gurus.com`.

Talking to the human being in charge

Someone is in charge of every mailing list: the *list manager*. The list manager is in charge of helping people on and off the list, answering questions about the list, and hosting the discussion. If you have a problem with a list, write a *nice* message to the list manager. Remember, most list managers are volunteers who sometimes eat, sleep, and work regular jobs as well as maintain mailing lists. It can take a day or so to get a response. If it takes longer than you want, be patient. *Don't* send cranky follow-ups — they just cheese off the list manager.

The list manager can do all sorts of things to lists that mere mortals can't do. In particular, the list manager can fix screwed-up names on the list or add a name that for some reason the automatic method doesn't handle. You have to appeal for manual intervention if your mail system doesn't put your correct network mail address on the `From:` line of your messages, as sometimes happens when your local mail system isn't set up quite right or if your address changes.

The list manager's address is usually the same as the list address with the addition of *owner-* at the beginning or *-request* right before the @. For example, the manager of the `chocolate-lovers@gurus.com` list would be `chocolate-lovers-request@gurus.com`.

Getting on lists

To find out how to subscribe to a list, or how to unsubscribe to the list, take a look at the instructions that (with luck) came with whatever information you received about the mailing list. For mailing lists that respond to commands by e-mail, you subscribe by sending mail to the list server address, which is something like `listserv@`*`some.machine.or.other`* or `majordomo@`*`some.machine.or.other`*, where *`some.machine.or.other`* is the name of the particular machine on which the mailing list lives. To join, send a command like this to the list server address:

```
subscribe listname yourname
```

or

```
subscribe listname
```

Refer to the instructions that came with the list — some require your name, whereas others don't work if you include it (so much for consistency). Replace *listname* with the name of the list and *yourname* with your name (not your e-mail address). Type the command as the first line of the message, not the subject line.

Subscribing from the Web

Newer list server programs allow you to subscribe, unsubscribe, and change your subscription settings from the Web. So don't be surprised if the instructions for a mailing list tell you to go to a Web page and fill out a form. Generally you enter your e-mail address in a box on a Web page, click a Send or Subscribe button, and you're on the list. This is often more convenient than sending a command by e-mail.

But before you subscribe, be sure there is some way to get *off* the list, an option that some marketing-oriented outfits neglect to provide.

Suppose that you want to join a LISTSERV list called `DANDRUFF-L` (many mailing list names end with `-L`), which lives at `bluesuede.org`. (This list attracts a lot of flakes.) To join, send to `LISTSERV@bluesuede.org`, the list server address, a message that contains this line:

```
subscribe DANDRUFF-L Ed N. Sholderz
```

You don't have to add a subject line or anything else to this message — it's better not to, so as not to confuse the list server program.

Shortly afterward, you should get back a chatty, machine-generated welcoming message telling you that you have joined the list, along with a description of some commands you can use to fiddle with your mailing-list membership. Usually, this message includes a request to confirm that you received this message and that it was really you who wanted to subscribe. Follow the instructions by replying to this message, or whatever else the instructions say to do. Confirmation helps lists ensure that they aren't mailing into the void, and keeps people from sticking you onto lists without your knowledge. If you don't provide this confirmation, you don't get on the list.

Don't delete the chatty, informative welcome message that tells you about all the commands you can use when you're dealing with the list. For one thing, it tells you how to get *off* the mailing list if it's not to your liking. We have in our mail program a folder called Mailing Lists in which we store the welcome messages from all the mailing lists we join, so we don't have to embarrass ourselves by asking for help unsubscribing later.

After you're subscribed, to send a message to this list, mail to the list address — in this case, `DANDRUFF-L@bluesuede.org`. Be sure to provide a descriptive `Subject:` for the multitudes who will benefit from your pearls of wisdom. Within a matter of minutes, people from all over the world can read your message.

Getting off lists

To get off a list, you again write to the list server address, this time sending this line in the text of the message (not the subject line):

```
signoff listname
```

or

```
unsubscribe listname
```

(Use the actual name of the list.) You don't have to give your name again because after you're off the list, the list software has no more interest in you and forgets that you ever existed.

Some lists are more difficult than others to get on and off. Usually, you ask to get on a list, and you're on the list. In some cases, however, the list isn't open to all comers, and the human list manager screens requests to join the list, in which case you may get some messages from the list manager to discuss your request to join.

Stupid mailing list tricks

Most list servers know some other commands, including commands to hold your mail for a while, send you a daily message that includes all the postings for the day, and see a subscriber list. Refer to the instructions that you received when you subscribed to the list for the exact commands, which vary depending on the list server software. (You did save the welcome message, didn't you?)

Here are some common commands. For each of them, you send a message to the list server address with the command in the text of your message:

- **Temporarily stop mail:** Sometimes, you're going to be away for a week or two, and you don't want to get a bunch of mailing-list mail in the meantime. Because you're planning to come back, though, you don't want to take yourself off all the lists either. For most list servers, send this message:

  ```
  set DANDRUFF-L nomail
  ```

  The list stops sending you messages. To turn the mail back on, send this message:

  ```
  set DANDRUFF-L mail
  ```

- **Get messages as a digest:** If you're getting a large number of messages from a list and would rather get them all at one time as a daily digest, try this message:

  ```
  set DANDRUFF-L digest
  ```

  Although not all lists can be digested, the indigestible ones let you know and don't take offense. If you later want individual messages again:

  ```
  set DANDRUFF-L nodigest
  ```

  or

  ```
  set DANDRUFF-L mail ack
  ```

  For some Majordomo lists, you have to unsubscribe from the list, and subscribe to a list with the same name, but with *–digest* at the end (for example, DANDRUFF-L-DIGEST).

- **Find out who's on a list:** To find out who subscribes to a list, send one of these messages:

  ```
  review DANDRUFF-L
  recipients DANDRUFF-L
  who DANDRUFF-L
  ```

  Some lists can be reviewed only by people on the list and other lists cannot be reviewed at all. Because some lists are enormous, be prepared to get back an enormous message listing thousands of subscribers.

- **Do other things:** Lots of other commands lurk in many list servers, and you can find out what they are by sending this message:

  ```
  help
  ```

  You receive a more or less helpful response that lists other commands.

For more about mailing lists, including lots of list server commands, see our Web site at `lists.gurus.com`.

Sending messages to mailing lists

Okay, you're signed up on a mailing list. Now what? First, wait a week or so to see what sort of messages arrive from the list — that way, you can get an idea of what you should or should not send to it. When you think that you have seen enough to avoid embarrassing yourself, try sending something in. That's easy: You mail a message to the list address, which is the same as the name of the list — `chocolate-lovers@lists.gurus.com` or `dandruff-l@blue suede.org` or whatever. Keep in mind that because hundreds or thousands of people will be reading your pearls of wisdom, you should at least try to spell things correctly. (You may have thought that this advice is obvious, but you would be sadly mistaken.) On popular lists, you may begin to get back responses within a few minutes of sending a message.

Some lists encourage new subscribers to send in a message introducing themselves and saying briefly what their interests are. Others don't. Don't send anything until you have something to say. After you watch the flow of messages on a list for a while, all this stuff becomes obvious.

Some mailing lists have rules about who is allowed to send messages, meaning that just because you're on the list doesn't automatically mean that any messages you send appear on the list. Some lists are *moderated:* Any message you send in gets sent to a human *moderator* who decides what goes to the list and what doesn't. Although this process may sound sort of fascist, moderation can make a list about 50 times more interesting than it would be otherwise because a good moderator can filter out the boring and irrelevant messages and keep the list on track. Indeed, the people who complain the loudest about moderator censorship are usually the ones whose messages most urgently need to be filtered out.

Another rule that sometimes causes trouble is that many lists allow messages to be sent only from people whose addresses appear on the list. It's an excellent rule because it prevents the list from getting overrun with spam. However, this rule becomes a pain if your mailing address changes. Suppose that you get a well-organized new mail administrator and that your official e-mail address changes from `jj@shamu.pol.bluesuede.org` to `John.Jay@bluesuede.org`, although your old address still works. You may find that some lists begin *bouncing* your messages (sending them back to you rather than to the list) because they don't understand that `John.Jay@bluesuede.org`, the name under which you now send messages, is the same as `jj@shamu.pol.bluesuede.org`, the name under which you originally subscribed to the list. Worse, many list servers don't let you take yourself off the list because they don't realize that you are you. To resolve this mess, you have to write to the human list managers of any lists in which this problem arises and ask them to fix the problem by hand.

The fine points of replying to mailing-list messages

Often, you receive an interesting message from a list and want to respond to it. When you send your answer, does it go *just* to the person who sent the original message, or does it go to the *entire list?* It depends on how the list manager set up the list. About half the list managers set things up so that replies automatically go to just the person who sent the original message, on the theory that your response is likely to be of interest only to the original author. The other half set things up so that replies go to the entire list, on the theory that the list is a running public discussion. In messages coming from the list, the mailing-list software automatically sets the Reply-To header line to the address to which replies should be sent.

Fortunately, you're in charge. When you start to create a reply, your mail program should show you the address to which it's replying. If you don't like the address it's using, change the address. Check the To and Cc fields to make sure that you're sending your message where you want. Don't run the risk of sending the message "I agree with you — aren't the rest of these people idiots?" to the whole list if you intend it only for one person.

While you're fixing the recipient's address, you may also want to fix the Subject line. After a few rounds of replies to replies to replies, the topic of discussion often wanders away from the original topic, and it's a good idea to change the subject to better describe what is really under discussion.

How to avoid looking like an idiot

As we say earlier in the chapter, after you subscribe to a list, don't send anything to it until you read it for a week. Trust us — the list has been getting along without your insights since it began, and it can get along without them for one more week.

You can discover what topics people really discuss, the tone of the list, and so on. It also gives you a fair idea about which topics people are tired of. The classic newcomer gaffe is to subscribe to a list and immediately send a message asking a dumb question that isn't really germane to the topic and that was beaten to death three days earlier. Bide your time and don't let this situation happen to you.

The number-two newcomer gaffe is to send a message directly to the list asking to subscribe or unsubscribe. This type of message should go to the list manager or list server program, *not* to the list itself, where all the other subscribers can see that you screwed up.

To summarize: The first message you send, to join a list, should go to the list server address (which starts with `LISTSERV` or `majordomo` or some other list server name), *not* to the list itself. *After* you join the list *and read it for a while*, you can send messages to the list.

Boing!

Computer accounts are created and deleted often enough and mail addresses change often enough that a large list always contains, at any given moment, some addresses that are no longer valid. If you send a message to the list, your message is forwarded to these invalid addresses, and a return message reporting the bad addresses is generated for each of them. Mailing-list managers (both human and computer) normally try to deflect the error messages so that they go to the list owner, who can do something about them, rather than to you. As often as not, however, a persistently dumb mail system sends one of these failure messages directly to you. Just ignore it because you can't do anything about it.

Sometimes you may get an "I'm away on vacation" message or a "click here if you're not a spammer" message in response to list messages you send. Don't respond to those either since vacation and antispam programs shouldn't be responding to list mail at all, but do forward them to the list manager so he or she can suspend their subscriptions until they get their software under control.

Be sure to send plain text messages to mailing lists. Don't send "enriched" formatted messages, attachments, or anything other than text. Many e-mail programs don't handle nontext, and many people don't have the program they would need to open an attachment, anyway. If you have a file you want to distribute on a mailing list, send a message inviting people interested in getting the file to e-mail you privately.

One last thing not to do: If you don't like what another person is posting (for example, some newbie is posting blank messages or "unsubscribe me" messages or is ranting interminably about a topic), don't waste everyone's time by posting a response on the list. The only thing stupider than a stupid posting is a response complaining about it. Instead, e-mail the person *privately* and ask him to stop, or e-mail the list manager and ask that person to intervene.

Discussions on the Web: Posting to Message Boards

Mailing lists are great if you want to receive message by e-mail, but for some people, it's more convenient to read online community messages on the Web. These folks are in luck: *message boards* are Web-based discussion groups that post messages on a Web site. They are also called *discussion boards*, *forums*, or *communities*. Like mailing lists, some message boards are readable only by subscribers, some allow only subscribers to post, and some are moderated (that is, a moderator must approve messages before they appear on the message board). Other messages boards are more like bulletin boards — anyone can post anytime, and there's no continuity to the messages or feeling of community among the people who post.

Many Web sites include message boards. Some Web sites are dedicated to hosting message boards on lots of different topics. Some host messages boards that can also send the messages to you by e-mail, so they are message boards and mailing lists rolled into one.

Great Web-based discussion sites

Here are some of our favorites:

About.com, at www.about.com

About.com hired experts in a wide variety of fields to host sites about each field. For example, the knitting site at `knitting.about.com` is run by a world-class knitter who posts articles and patterns and hosts one or most message boards about knitting. Figure 13-1 shows a discussion of knitting techniques.

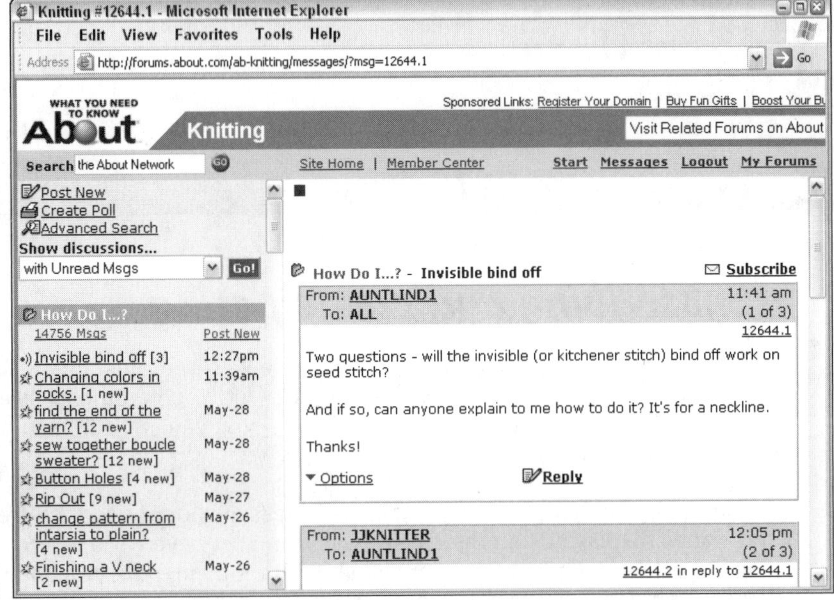

Figure 13-1: About.com hosts sites about many topics, and each includes a message board where you can post questions and comments.

MSN Groups, at groups.msn.com

MSN Groups include message boards, live chat rooms, and other information.

Yahoo Groups, at groups.yahoo.com

Yahoo Groups include message boards and file libraries, and you can read the messages either on the Web site or by e-mail — your choice when you join a group (see Figure 13-2 for a picture of a Yahoo Group). Yahoo Groups also feature calendars for group events and real-time chats right on the Web site. To join, you must first sign up for a fee Yahoo ID, which also gets you a mailbox and free Web space — what a deal! You can also create your own Yahoo Group by clicking links — either a public group for all to join or a private group for your club or family.

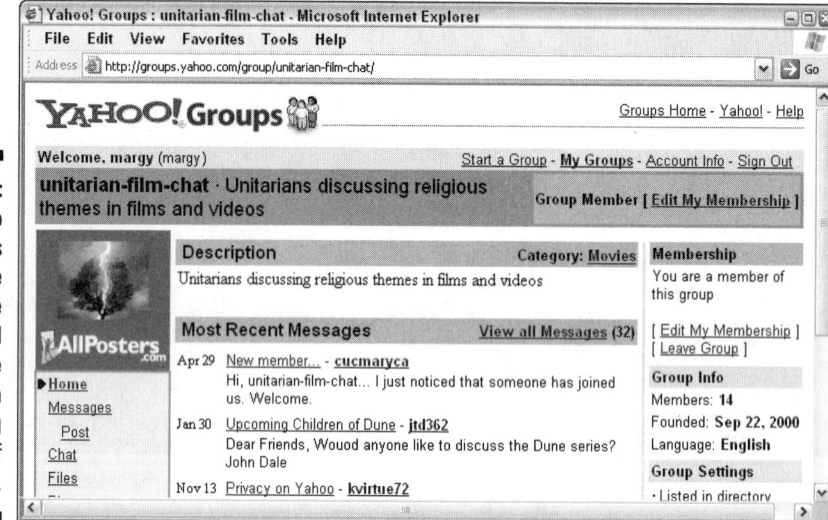

Figure 13-2: Yahoo Groups include message boards and real-time chat on an amazing variety of topics.

Subscribing and participating

To subscribe to a community on one of these Web sites, just follow the instructions on the site. Some community Web sites let you read the messages posted to their lists without actually subscribing — you can click links to display the messages in your Web browser.

You can set up your own mailing lists or message boards, too. It's free because the sites display ads on their Web pages, and may even add ads to the postings on the list. If you have an unusual hobby, job, interest, or ailment, you may want to create a list to discuss it. Or set up a list for a committee or family group to use for online discussions.

Finding Interesting Online Communities

Tens of thousands of communities — in the form of mailing lists, message boards, and hybrids of the two — reside on the Internet, but there's no central directory of them. This is partly because so many lists are intended only for specific groups of people, like members of the Board of Directors of the First Parish Church of Podunk or students in Economics 101 at Tech State.

You can find some communities by searching the Web, as described in Chapter 7, and including the word or phrase *mailing list, community, forum,* or *message board.* Or start at `about.com`, `groups.yahoo.com`, `groups.msn.com`, or `tile.net/lists` and search for your topic.

Chapter 14

Instant Messaging: The Next Best Thing to Being There

In This Chapter

- Setting your computer up with a mike and a webcam
- Sending instant messages with AOL Instant Messenger (even if you don't use AOL)
- Sending instant messages with MSN Messenger or Windows Messenger
- Holding cool voice and video conferences with Yahoo Messenger

Internet e-mail is pretty fast, usually arriving in less than a minute. But sometimes, that's just not fast enough. *Instant message* (*IM*) systems let you pop up a message on someone's screen in a matter of seconds. They also have *buddy lists* that watch to see when one of your buddies comes online so you know the instant you can instantiate an instant message to them. (Excuse us, this gives us a headache. Just a moment while we get some instant coffee. Ahh, that's better.)

The good thing about instant messages is that you can stay in touch with people as fast as talking to them on the phone. The bad thing about them is that they also offer an unparalleled range of ways to annoy people. AOL Instant Messenger, discussed later in this chapter, has about two features to send and receive messages, and about twelve features to reject, denounce, erase, and otherwise deal with unwanted messages. (This may say more about AOL users than the technology, of course.)

Of course, even better than typing messages to another person is talking right out loud. If your computer has a microphone and speakers, you can use IM systems to talk to people over the Net — even groups of people — with no toll charges. If you connect a digital video camera (or *webcam*) to your computer, your friends can even see you as you talk or type. It's not hard to do!

This chapter describes how to use the most popular IM systems: AOL Instant Messenger, Windows or MSN Messenger, and Yahoo Messenger.

Adding Voices and Faces

If you don't want to talk with or see people while you chat — that is, if you don't mind being limited to typing back and forth with your friends — skip this section. If you do, read on.

Say what?

Almost every computer comes with speakers, which are connected to a *sound board* inside the computer. These speakers are what make the various noises that your programs make (like the "You've got mail!" announcement of AOL). Most sound boards also have a jack for a microphone. (Check your computer manual or ask almost any teenager for help with this.) If you don't have a microphone, you can get one that works with almost any computer. A mike should cost less than $20 at your local computer store, RadioShack, or at online computer stores like PC Connection (`www.pcconnection.com`).

To test your mike and speakers on a Windows machine, run the Sound Recorder program and try recording yourself and playing it back. Choose Start⇨All Programs⇨Accessories⇨Entertainment⇨Sound Recorder in Windows XP or Me. Click the red Record button to start recording, and the square Stop button to stop. (Talk, sing, or make other noises in between.) Then click the triangular Play button to hear what you just recorded. Click Record again to add onto the end of your recording. Choose File⇨New to start over and throw away what you recorded. Choose File⇨Save to save it as a WAV (audio) file. (We like to make WAV recordings of our kids saying silly things and e-mail them — the recordings, not the kids — to their grandparents.)

You can adjust the volume of your microphone (for the sound coming into the computer) and your speakers or headphones (for the sound coming out) by choosing Start⇨All Programs⇨Accessories⇨Entertainment⇨Volume Control. If a volume control for your microphone doesn't appear, choose Options⇨Properties, click the Microsoft check box so that a check mark appears, and click OK.

If you want to test how voices from the Net sound on your computer, type the URL `net.gurus.com/ngc.wav` into your browser and see what happens. You may need to click an Open or Open with Default Application button after it downloads. (Yes, that's John's mellifluous voice.)

If you can record yourself and hear the recording when you play it back, you're ready for Internet-based phone calls or chats!

Which instant message system should I use?

Unfortunately, the instant messaging systems don't talk to one another. Because the goal of all these systems is to stay in touch with your friends, use whichever one they use. If you're not sure who your friends are, AOL Instant Messenger is a good bet because it's easy to set up and automatically works with any AOL user because it's the same system that AOL uses internally. We like Yahoo Messenger because it's free, supports text, voice, and video, and allows more than two people to chat. (We've held meetings on Yahoo Messenger with six people on voice, two on video, and everyone typing snide comments at the same time.) If you have Windows XP, you already have Windows Messenger, which comes preinstalled.

If you're really message-mad, you can run more than one system at the same time. While we were writing this chapter, we had Windows Messenger, AOL Instant Messenger, and Yahoo Messenger all running at once. It was an awful lot of blinking and flashing, but it did work.

Other IM programs also exist including ICQ (described in the sidebar "Where did IM come from?") and CUWorld (which used to be CuseeMe, at `www.cuworld.com`).

I see you!

If you want other people to be able to see you during online conversations, consider getting a *webcam*. This is a small digital video camera that can connect to a computer. Webcams come in many sizes and shapes, and prices run from $50 to $500. More expensive webcams send higher-quality images at higher speeds and come with better software. On the other hand, we've had great luck with a $60 webcam for chatting with friends and participating in videoconferences.

Most webcams connect to your computer's USB port, a little rectangular plug on the back of the computer. Older computers don't have USB ports. The better cameras connect to special video capture cards, which you have to open your computer to install.

If you own a digital video camera for taking video of your family and friends, you may be able to connect it to your computer for use as a webcam. Check the manual that came with the camera.

For news and reviews about webcams, see the WebCamWorld site at `www.webcamworld.com`.

AOL Instant Messenger (AIM)

AOL Instant Messenger (*AIM* for short) is one of the simplest chat systems around. All it does is let you type messages back and forth. But it's easier to set up than ICQ and lets you talk directly to AOL users. This section describes AIM version 5.1. If you use AOL, skip forward to Chapter 17 for how to chat in AOL.

Taking AIM

If you're an AOL user, you're already set up for instant messages. If not, you have to install the AIM program. AOL subscribers can also run the AIM program and use their AOL screen name when they're logged onto another kind of Internet account.

AOL, being the hyper-aggressive marketing organization they are, has arranged for AIM to be bundled in with a lot of other packages. In particular, if you have a copy of Netscape, you have AIM already. If you don't have it, visit `www.aim.com` and follow the directions on the Web page to download it. Before you can download the program, you have to choose a screen name, which can be up to 16 letters long (being creative so as not to collide with one of the 31 million names already in use), and a password. You also have to enter your e-mail address. AOL, refreshingly, doesn't want any more personal information. The e-mail address you give has to be real: AOL sends a confirmation message to that address, and you must reply or your screen name is deleted.

Where did IM come from?

ICQ (pronounced *I seek you*) was the original instant messenger and still has many million users, especially outside the U.S. It's available from their Web site at `www.icq.com`. ICQ comes in 18 languages and has about a quadrillion different features and options, but basically, you download and install ICQ and set it up to get an ICQ#, sort of like a phone number, that identifies you. Then you identify some buddies and start sending them instant messages and chatting with them. The ICQ program runs on Windows (all versions starting with 3.1), Macs, Palm Pilots, and, for all we know, certain espresso machines.

AOL bought ICQ several years ago, and we assume that sooner or later they'll integrate it with AIM. For now, however, ICQ and AIM are still separate systems.

Save the downloaded file somewhere on your computer. (C:\Windows\Temp is an okay place if you don't have another folder you use for downloads.) Then run the downloaded program (which is called Install_aim.exe last we looked) to install AIM. Normally, AIM runs in the background whenever you're online. If it's not running, click the AIM icon on your desktop.

The first time you use AIM, you have to enter your AIM or AOL screen name, as in the left part of Figure 14-1. Type your screen name and password and click Sign On. If you want to use AIM every time you're online, check the Save Password and Auto-login boxes before signing on, and AIM will sign you on automatically in the future. After you sign in, you see the AIM window shown in the middle of Figure 14-1. You also see a big window full of news, ads, and links to AOL's Web site — just close it.

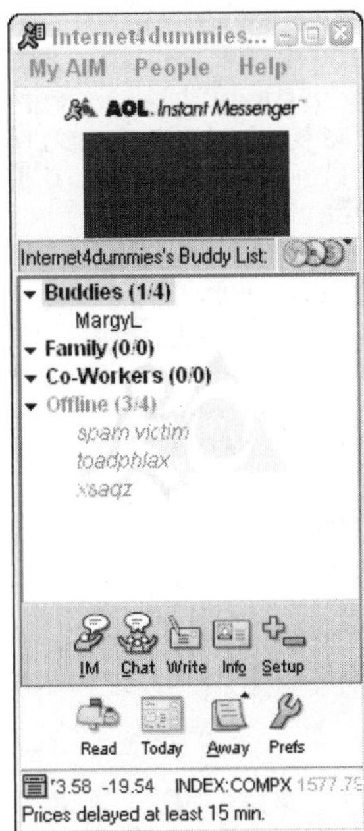

Figure 14-1: Signing on to AIM, the AIM window, and the Buddy List Setup window.

AIM may run the New User Wizard, which offers help getting started. Follow its instructions, or click Cancel to go it alone (you can always return to the wizard by choosing Help⇨New User Wizard from the AIM menu). A stock ticker runs along the bottom of the AIM window for you serious investors. Click the button on its left edge to see news details or customize the ticker.

Getting your buddies organized

First you create your buddy list, and then you can send messages.

When AIM opens, you see your *buddy list*, that is, other AIM users who you like to chat with. The window shows which of your many buddies are currently online (everyone who's not currently listed in the Offline category). What? None of your pals appears? You need to add your friend's AOL or AIM screen names to your buddy list.

In the AIM window, click the Setup or Edit Buddy List button to display the Buddy List Setup window shown on the right side of Figure 14-1. It lists all your groups of buddies. AOL provides three groups: Buddies, Family, and Co-Workers. (You can make other groups, too, using the Add Group button.)

To add a buddy, click the group to which you want to add it, click the Add Buddy button, type the buddy's screen name, and press Enter. If you know the e-mail address but not the screen name, return to the AIM window and choose People➪Find a Buddy Wizard. Doing so starts a wizard that looks for that address and helps you add any screen names that match.

You can drag a buddy from one group to another in the Buddy List Setup window, or get rid of a buddy (at least remove the person from your list, if not your life) by clicking the buddy and then clicking the Delete button.

After you select your buddies, click the Return to Buddy List button, which closes the Buddy List Setup window and returns you to the AIM window. You see your buddy list with offline folks in pale gray and everyone else organized by group.

The AIM window appears tall and narrow, but you can drag its edges around to change its shape — helpful if your friends have long names.

Getting buddy-buddy online

To send a message to someone, double-click the buddy's name to open a message window, type the message, and click the Send button. AIM pops up a window (shown in the left part of Figure 14-2) on the recipient's machine, plays a little song, and you and your buddy can type back and forth. When done, close the message window.

Unless you are a very fast typist or your friend lives in Mongolia, the most effective thing to type is "What's your phone number?" and call the person on the phone — or follow the instructions in the next section.

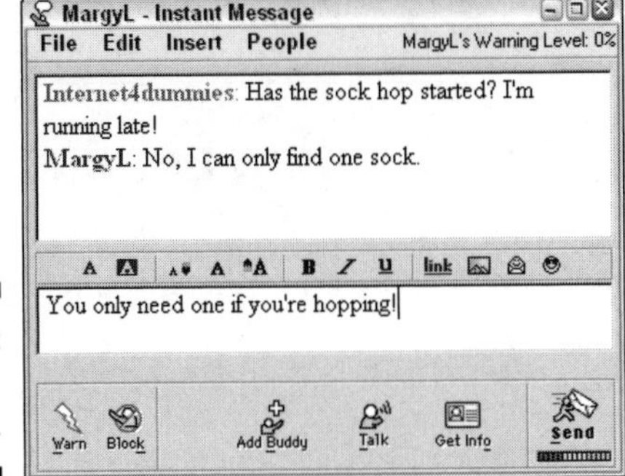

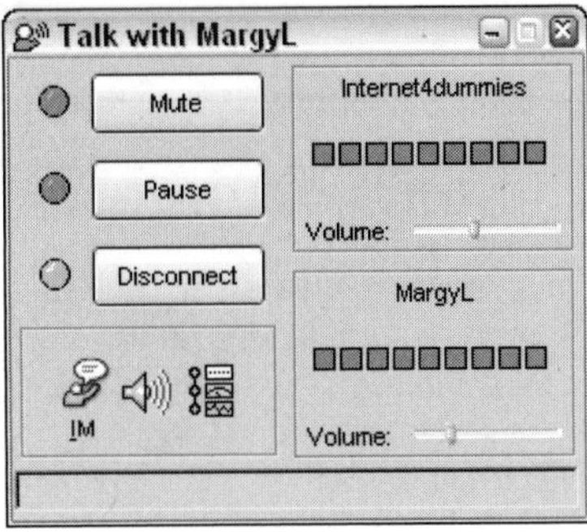

Figure 14-2: Chatting using AIM.

Making noise with AIM

After you establish a conversation using AIM, you can switch to voice (assuming that both parties have computers equipped with microphones and speakers). Click the Talk button and click Connect. Your friend sees a window asking whether he wants to make a direct connection with you. Clicking Accept in that window displays the Talk With window shown in the right part of Figure 14-2. You can use the volume sliders to adjust your volume. Click Disconnect when you are done talking.

Buzz off

AOL evidently has a lot of ill-mannered users, because AIM has a system for warning and blocking users you don't like. When you are chatting with someone and you receive an insulting or annoying message, you can click the Warn button in the lower left corner of the Instant Message window. AIM sends a warning to the sender. With enough warnings (about five), a user is blocked from sending instant messages for a while. If you find a sender to be totally objectionable, click the Block button to refuse all messages from that person.

You can further adjust who is able to send messages to you. In the AIM window, click the Prefs button to display the AOL Instant Messenger Preferences window. Click the Privacy category from the list at the left side. You can limit messages to people on your buddies list, permit specific people, or block specific people. You can also add or delete people from your block list. We recommend choosing Allow Only Users on My Buddy List unless you like being contacted by total strangers at inconvenient moments.

Some obvious rules of messaging conduct

Sending someone an instant message is the online equivalent of walking up to someone on the street and starting a conversation. If it's someone you know, it's one thing; if not, it's usually an intrusion.

Unless you have a compelling reason, don't send instant messages to people you don't know who haven't invited you to do so. Don't say anything that you wouldn't say in an analogous situation on the street.

For some reason, AOL is plagued with childish users who now and then send rude instant messages to strangers or unwilling acquaintances, which is why AIM has its Warn and Block buttons. Not only is it rude to do that, it's silly: AOL has chat rooms full of people eager to converse on all sorts of topics, rude or otherwise.

Most instant message programs allow you to send and receive files. We recommend that unless you specifically plan to use it, turn it off. Unsolicited files from people you don't know are generally spam, viruses, or both. Most virus checkers don't monitor file transfers via an IM program.

The messages that you send with AIM and other chat programs appear to be ephemeral. But it's easy for anyone in the conversation to store the messages. Most IM programs have a "log" feature that saves the series of messages in a text file, which may be embarrassing later.

Finally: If someone tells you to give a series of commands, or download and install a program, don't do it. And never tell anyone any of your passwords.

There is no escape

When you exit from AIM by clicking its Big Red X, the program usually doesn't stop running. Instead, it changes into a tiny icon in your Windows notification area, on the right end of the Windows Taskbar, near the clock. AIM continues to run so that if one of your buddies wants you, it can respond and pop up the incoming message. You can sign off or exit from the program by right-clicking the icon and choose Sign Off or Exit.

Windows Messenger, Alias MSN Messenger

Windows XP comes with the latest instant messaging program, called Windows Messenger. Microsoft must finally have noticed that this was a niche in which they didn't have the dominant program, and so decided to issue everyone a copy of theirs. Windows XP nags you to sign up for a Microsoft .NET Passport, a free account that you use to log on to Windows Messenger, the Hotmail Web site, and other Microsoft Web sites. Now that Microsoft has millions of Windows users signed up for Passports, they sell their Passport service to other Web sites such as eBay, too. We don't see the advantage of Windows Messenger over the other instant message programs: It has far fewer neat features than Yahoo Messenger. It does support voice and video, but only with one person at a time. Microsoft and AOL have been chronically fighting and kissing and making up and fighting again about whether Windows Messenger and AIM can connect, but so far, they don't.

Microsoft has an upgrade to Windows Messenger called MSN Messenger, which you can download and use if you don't have Windows XP or if you want the latest version. Go to `messenger.msn.com` for information and downloads; the program runs on Windows 98/95, NT, 2000, and Macs. Before using the program, you have to sign up for a Microsoft .NET Passport and Hotmail account at `www.hotmail.com`. Old (pre-Windows XP) versions of MSN Messenger can't communicate with Windows Messenger, but new versions can. This chapter describes Windows Messenger version 4.7 and MSN Messenger version 5.1.

Connecting to your Messenger

If you run Windows XP, Windows or MSN Messenger may have been running on your computer for months without you noticing it. Take a look at the right end of the Windows Taskbar, over near the clock, and you may see the Windows/ MSN Messenger icon, probably with a little red X showing that you aren't logged on.

IM by phone

Yahoo Messenger can also communicate with mobile phones that have SMS (short message service) from AT&T Wireless or Cingular. You can also use Yahoo Messenger on Web-enabled phones from AT&T, Cingular, Sprint, and Verizon. You can find out the details at `messenger.yahoo.com`. We've tried the SMS messaging, and it works pretty well, with messages often delivered in a few seconds.

If you use ICQ, you can communicate with dozens of mobile phone systems, but none of them are in the United States. Oh, well. However, SMS providers invariably have e-mail gateways, which means you can exchange e-mail with any SMS user. For example, if your friend has a Cingular phone with phone number 617-936-7584, its address would be `6179367584@mobile.mycingular.com`. You send e-mail to it the same way you send mail to any other address, and your friend can send e-mail back to you.

To get connected, click the Messenger icon to open its window, and then click `Click here to sign in`. If you don't already have a Microsoft .NET Passport, a wizard steps you through the process now. If you already have a Passport, you can just enter the address and password and you're on your way. When you connect, you may see an MSN Today window full of news and ads — just close it.

The Windows or MSN Messenger window (shown in Figure 14-3) lists your buddies just like AIM, except Microsoft calls them *contacts*. Same idea — click Add a Contact to add someone to your list.

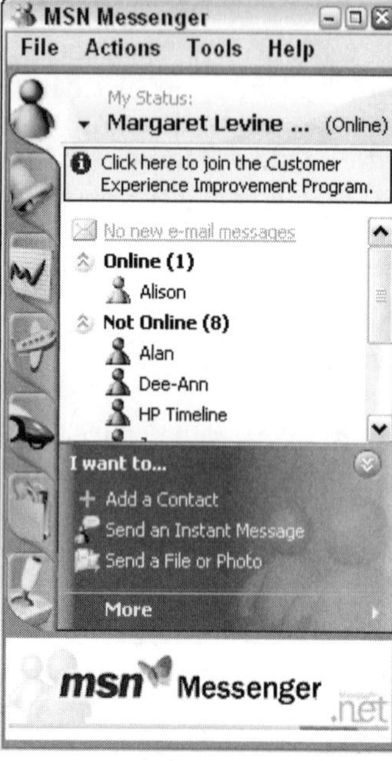

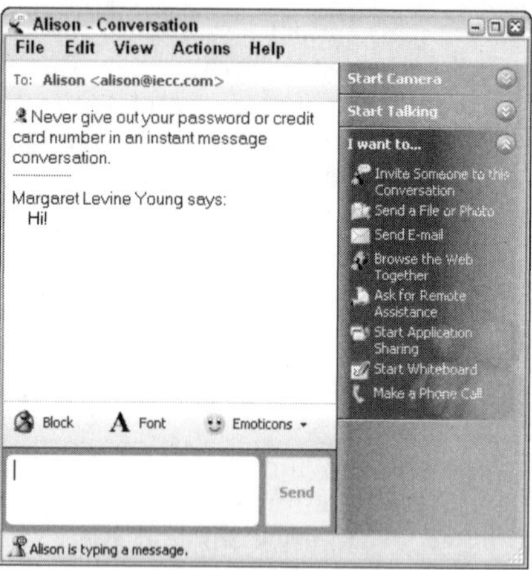

Figure 14-3: Windows and MSN Messenger are different versions of Microsoft's instant message program.

When someone adds you to their contact list, you see a message asking whether this is okay with you, and asking whether you want to add them to your list. Remember that people who have you on their contact list can tell when you are online or offline.

Ready, set, chat

As with AIM, to start an instant message session, just double-click a contact's name and type a message. The Conversation window looks like the right part of Figure 14-3. The list of actions at the right make it easy to use other cool features, including these:

- **Three- (or more) way conversations:** Click Invite Someone to This Conversation in your Conversation window and choose a name from your list of contacts.
- **Send a file:** Click the Send a File or Photo link and then choose the file to send.
- **Give people remote control over your computer:** If you click Start Application Sharing, you give the other people in the conversation the ability to type on your keyboard (virtually, anyway) and move your mouse (the mouse pointer on the screen, that is). Make sure you know your buddies well before trying this!
- **Start Whiteboard:** Click this link to open a window with a shared drawing program, much like Microsoft Paint. Everyone in the conversation can see the whiteboard window and can draw or type on it.
- **Start a voice conversation:** Click the Start Talking button. The Audio and Video Tuning Wizard runs to step you through testing and configuring your microphone and speakers (or headphone). When you've got your system tuned, Messenger pops up a window on the other person's screen, asking whether they'd like to have a voice conversation.
- **Start a videoconference:** Click the Start Camera to begin receiving video from the other person, if they agree to videoconference. Click Stop Camera to end transmission. You can receive video even if you don't have your own webcam.

Yahoo Messenger

Yahoo, the popular Web site, has its own instant message program called Yahoo Messenger. It's our favorite because you can not only type messages and talk using a microphone, but can also see each other if you have a webcam. Better yet, more than three people can join in the conversation. We've held six-person voice and video conference calls using Yahoo Messenger for a total cost of $0.

To get the program, go to `messenger.yahoo.com` and follow the directions to download and install the program. Yahoo Messenger is available in many versions including versions for Windows 95/98/Me/2000/XP, Macs, UNIX, Palm Pilots, and a version that runs as a Java applet in your Web browser on any system that has a Java-enabled browser. It can also exchange messages with mobile phone users; see the sidebar "IM by phone."

When you download the program, it installs automatically. To log on, you create a free Yahoo ID for yourself.

Chapter 15

Groupspeak: Let's Chat

In This Chapter

- Getting involved in online chat
- Understanding chat culture, etiquette, and safety
- Chatting on AOL and on the Web
- Participating in Internet Relay Chat (IRC)

Online chat lets you communicate with other people who are at their computers and connected to the Internet by typing messages back and forth to each other. Chat may seem like just a faster version of e-mail, but it is really a very different experience. Unlike e-mail or even instant messaging (IM; discussed in Chapter 14), chat often takes place among groups of strangers in *chat rooms.* Although kids sometimes use chat to talk to friends from school, one important aspect of chat is the ability to converse with someone new and hopefully interesting, any time you feel like it.

Chat has led to marriages and divorces, to new friendships, and occasionally to ugly incidents that make lurid headlines in the tabloid newspapers. Does chat sound intriguing? We'll tell you how it works and suggest some tips on avoiding trouble.

Look Who's Chatting

Online chat is similar to talking on an old-fashioned party line (or CB radio). In the infancy of the telephone system, people usually shared their phone lines with other families because the cost of stringing telephone lines was expensive. Everyone on the party line could join in any conversation, offering hours of nosy fun for people with nothing better to do.

You begin chatting by entering an electronic *chat room* or *channel.* After you join a room, you can read on-screen what people are saying and then add your own comments just by typing them and clicking Send. Although several people participating in the chat can type at the same time, each person's contribution is presented on-screen in order of its receipt. Whatever people type appears in the general conversation window and is identified by their screen names. On some chats systems, such as AOL, each participant can select a personal type font and color for his or her comments.

If one of the people in a chat room seems like someone you'd like to know better, you can ask to establish a *private room* or *direct connection,* which is a private conversation between you and the other person and not much different from instant messaging. And, of course, you may get such an invitation from someone else. It's not uncommon for someone to be in a chat room and be holding several direct conversations at the same time, though it's considered rude to overdo this, not to mention confusing!

You may also get asked to join a private chat room with several other people. We're not really sure just what goes on in those rooms because we've never been invited.

Who are those guys?

Which groups of people are available when you begin to chat depends on how you're connected to the Internet. If you use America Online, you can chat with other AOL users. MSN Groups (at `groups.msn.com`) and Yahoo Groups (at `groups.yahoo.com`) include a chat room for each group. Many Web-based chat sites provide chat rooms that anyone with access to the Web can use.

An older system called IRC (Internet Relay Chat) is available to anyone with Internet access and is still popular but harder to use — see "Chatting via IRC" at the end of this chapter. Chatting is pretty much the same from system to system, although the participants vary. This chapter gives a sense of the essence of chat no matter where you go to do it. Because AOL is by far the chattiest chat, we use it for our examples.

Each chat room has a name; with luck, the name is an indication of what the chatters there are talking about or what they have in common. Some channels have names such as *lobby,* and the people there are probably just being sociable.

Who am I?

No matter which chat facility you're using, each participant has a *screen name,* or *nickname,* often chosen to be unique, colorful, or clever and used as a mask. Chatters sometimes change their screen names. This anonymity makes a chat room a place where you need to be careful. On the other hand, one of the attractions of chatting is meeting new and interesting people. Many warm and wonderful friendships have evolved from a chance meeting in a chat room.

When you join a group and begin chatting, you see the screen names of the people who are already there and a window in which the current conversation goes flying by. If the group is friendly, somebody may even send you a welcome message.

As in real life, in a room full of strangers you're likely to encounter people you don't like much. Because it's possible to be fairly anonymous on the Internet, some people act boorish, vulgar, or crude. If you're new to chat, sooner or later you'll visit some disgusting places, although you'll find out how to avoid them and find rooms that have useful, friendly, and supportive conversations. Be very careful about letting children chat unsupervised (see Chapter 3). Even in chat rooms that are designed for young people and provide some supervision, there are some unwholesome goings-on from time to time.

Ways to chat

The original chat rooms consisted entirely of people typing messages to each other. Newer chat systems include voice chat, which requires you to have a microphone and speakers on your computer, and even video, which requires a webcam if you want other people to be able to see you. Chapter 14 describes how voice and video work on the Internet.

Your First Chat Room

Your first time in a chat room can seem stupid or daunting or both. Here are some of the things you can do to get through your first encounters:

- Remember that when you enter a chat room, a conversation is probably already in progress. You don't know what went on before you arrived.
- Wait a minute or two to see a page full of exchanges so that you can understand some of the context before you start writing.
- Start by following the comments of a single screen name. Then follow the people that person mentions or who reply to that person. After you can follow one conversation, known in cyberspace as a *thread,* try picking up another. Getting the hang of it takes practice.
- AOL and many Web-based programs can highlight the messages from selected people. This can make things easier to follow.
- You can also indicate people to ignore. Messages from these chatters no longer appear on your screen, although other members' replies to them

do appear. This is usually the best way to deal with obnoxious chatters. You may also be able to get your chat program not to display the many system messages, which announce when people arrive, leave, or are ejected forcefully from the chat room.

- Scroll up to see older messages if you have to, but remember that on most systems, after you have scrolled up, no new messages appear until you scroll back down.

Online etiquette

Chatting etiquette is not that much different from e-mail etiquette, and common sense is your best guide. Here are some additional chatting tips:

- The first rule of chatting is not to hurt anyone. A real person with real feelings is at the other end of the computer chat connection.
- The second rule is to be cautious. You really have no idea who the other people are. Remember, too, that people there may be people hanging out in a chat room quietly collecting information, and you may not notice them because they never say anything. See the next section, "Safety first."
- Read messages for a while to figure out what is happening before sending a message to a chat group. (Reading without saying anything is known as *lurking.* When you finally venture to say something, you're *de-lurking.*) Lurking isn't necessarily a bad thing, but be aware that you may not always have the privacy you think you have.
- Keep your messages short and to the point.
- Don't insult people, don't use foul language, and don't respond to people who do.
- Create a profile with selected information about yourself. Most chat systems have provisions for creating profiles (personal information) that other members can access. Don't give out your last name, phone number, or address. Extra caution is necessary for kids: They should never enter their age, hometown, school, last name, phone number, or address. This is a rule on AOL. Parents should insist on it always.
- Although you don't have to tell everything about yourself in your profile, what you do say should be truthful. The one exception is role-playing chat where everyone is acting out a fantasy character. See the sidebar on MUDs and MOOs.
- If you want to talk to someone in private, send a message saying hi, who you are, and what you want.
- If the tone of conversation in one chat room offends or bores you, try another. As in real life, you'll run into lots of people in chat rooms you *don't* want to meet.

For more information about the history and art of meeting people online, see Philippe Le Roux's essay, "Virtual Intimacy — Tales from Minitel and More" on our Web site at `net.gurus.com/leroux.phtml`. For more netiquette tips, see `net.gurus.com/netiquette`.

Safety first

Here are some guidelines for conducting safe and healthy chats:

- Many people in chat groups lie about their occupation, age, locality, and, yes, even gender. Some think that they're just being cute, some are exploring their own fantasies, and some are really sick.
- Be careful about revealing information that enables someone to find you personally — such as where you live or work, where you go to school, the name of your teacher or team, or your phone number. This information includes your last name, mailing address, and place of worship.
- Never give your password to anyone. No one should ever ask you for it. If someone does, don't respond, but do tell your service provider about the request. (We once received a message saying, "There's been a serious threat to security, and we need your password to help determine the problem." Yeah, right. If you ever get a message like that — any time you're online — it's a fake. If you are on AOL, go to the keyword **Notify AOL** and report the incident.)
- If your chat service offers profiles and a person without a profile wants to chat with you, be extra cautious.
- Kids, never, *ever* meet someone without your parents. Do not give out personal information about yourself or any member of your family, even when you're offered some sort of prize for filling out a form. If you have younger brothers or sisters who are online, make sure they understand these guidelines, too.
- Parents, realize that if your children use chat, others may try to meet them. Review the guidelines in this list with your kids before they log on. Have your kids show you how to log on and try the chat rooms they use for yourself.

If you're a grown-up and choose to meet an online friend in person, use at least the same caution that you would use in meeting someone through a newspaper ad:

- Don't arrange a meeting until you have talked to a person a number of times, including conversations at length by telephone over the course of days or weeks.
- Meet in a well-lit public place with other people around, like a restaurant.

- Bring a friend along if you can. If not, at least let someone know what you're doing and agree to call that person at a certain time (for example, a half-hour) after the planned meeting time.
- Arrange to stay in a hotel if you travel a long distance to meet someone. Don't commit yourself to staying at that person's home. And don't invite the person to stay with you.

Chat abbreviations and smileys

Many chat abbreviations are the same as those used in e-mail, as described in Chapter 11. Because chat is live, however, some are unique. We've also listed some common emoticons (sometimes called *smileys*) — funky combinations of punctuation used to depict the emotional inflection of the sender. If at first you don't see what they are, try tilting your head down to the left. Table 15-1 shows you a short list of chat abbreviations and emoticons.

Getting down in the MUDs

MUDs and MOOs are chat taken to a whole new dimension. You don't just pick a nickname, you take on a whole new identity — a fantasy role you want to play in the MUD.

MUD, which originally stood for Multiple-User Dungeon, was invented to let Internet users play the fantasy role-playing game Dungeons and Dragons. MUDs have evolved from those beginnings, however, into a whole new way for people to interact electronically; so much so that the name *MUD* is usually defined as Multiple-User Dimension or Multiple-User Dialogue.

MOOs are a variant where you not only interact with the other characters there but also can program new rooms and implements. To participate, you use a program called *telnet,* or a special program designed for MUDs.

Some MUDs and MOOs are based on the worlds created in popular films and novels, including *Star Wars, Star Trek,* J.R.R. Tolkien's *The Lord of the Rings,* Douglas Adams's *The Hitchhiker's Guide to the Galaxy,* and especially Anne McCaffrey's *The Dragonriders of Pern.*

Many MUDs are battle oriented with simulated combat and even wars. Your virtual identity can be gruesomely killed online, often repeatedly. Some people find this amusing.

Of the hundreds (thousands?) of MUDs, each has its own personality. Be sure to read about it and find out what software you need to participate before diving in. If the MUD you picked is based on a book or movie, read the book or see the movie. The folks on the MUDs are into the details.

To find a MUD or MOO that's right for you, start at the MUD Connector (`www.mudconnect.com`).

Table 15-1 Chat Shorthand

Abbreviation	*What It Means*
AFK	Away from keyboard
A/S/L	Age/sex/location (response may be 35/f/LA)
BAK	Back at keyboard
BBIAF	Be back in a flash
BBL	Be back later
BRB	Be right back
CYBER	A chat conversation of a prurient nature (short for *cybersex*)
GMTA	Great minds think alike
FTF or F2F	Face to face
IC	In character (playing a role)
IGGIE	To set the Ignore feature, as in "I've iggied SmartMouthSam"
IM	Instant message
J/K	Just kidding
LTNS	Long time no see
LOL	Laughing out loud
M4M	Men seeking other men
NP	No problem
OOC	Out of character (an RL aside during RP)
PM	Private message (same as IM)
RL	Real life (opposite of RP)
ROTFL	Rolling on the floor laughing
RP	Role play (acting out a character)
TOS	Terms of service (the AOL member contract)
TTFN	Ta-ta for now!
WAV	A sound file

(continued)

Table 15-1 *(continued)*

Abbreviation	*What It Means*
WB	Welcome back
WTG	Way to go!
:) or :-)	A smile
;)	A wink
{{{{bob}}}}	A hug for Bob
:(or :-(	Frown
:'(	Crying
0:)	Angel
}:>	Devil
:P	Sticking out tongue
*** or xox	Kisses
<----	Action marker (<----eating pizza, for example)

In addition to the abbreviations in the table, chatters sometimes use simple shorthand abbreviations, as in `If u cn rd ths ur rdy 2 chat.`

Trouble city

Some people act badly online while hiding behind the anonymity that chat provides. You have four good options and one bad option when this situation happens:

- Go to another chat room. Some rooms are just nasty. You don't have to hang around.
- Pay no attention to the troublemaker and just converse with the other folks.

- Make offenders disappear from your screen. On AOL, click the jerk's screen name in the list of people in the chat room, and then click the Ignore Member button.
- Complain to the individual's service provider. This technique is most effective on AOL. See "Calling the AOL cops," later in this chapter.

- If you think someone is in physical danger or children are being exploited, you should report the matter to the police just as you would any other criminal activity.
- (The bad option.) Respond in kind, which just gives the offender the attention he wants and may get *you* kicked off your service. Set a good example or just feel quietly superior.

Let's Chat

Starting to chat on an online service such as AOL is easy because chat service is one of AOL's major attractions. Goodness knows no one goes there for the advertising. In this section, we cover chatting with AOL, Web-based chat, and chatting using IRC. (For how to use AOL in general, see Chapter 17.)

Chatting on AOL

When you chat on AOL, you have a conversation with other AOL users. Only AOL members can participate in the AOL chat rooms. Because AOL can and does eject unruly chatters, its chat rooms are a bit more civilized than many other chat services. The popularity of AOL chat may be why AOL is the largest value-added provider.

You get started chatting in America Online 8.0 or 8.0 PLUS by clicking the Chat icon on the toolbar (or go to the **chat** keyword) to see the AOL People Connection window. Then click the Chat Room Listings icon to display the Find a Chat window shown in Figure 15-1.

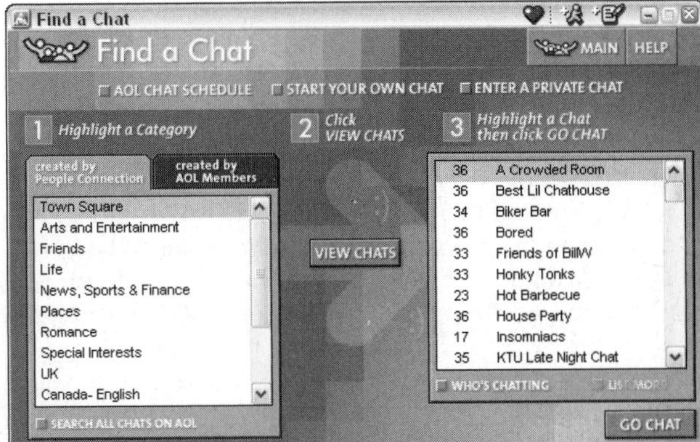

Figure 15-1: What do you want to chat about?

Click a category from the list at the left, click the View Chats button in the middle of the window, and look at the list that appears on the right. Then click a likely looking topic and click the Go Chat button. You see a chat window something like the one in Figure 15-2.

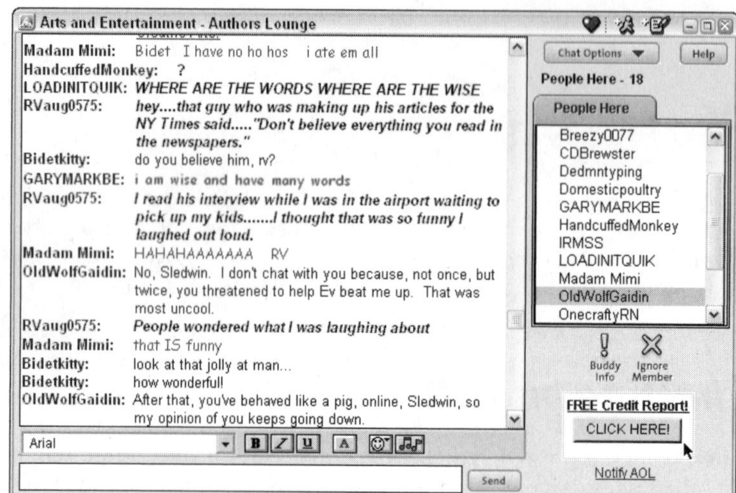

Figure 15-2: Authors are chatting!

In a chat window, the large box on the left shows the ongoing conversation. (We like the way that AOL shows different people's messages in different colors and typefaces to help keep track of who is saying what.) The People Here box shows the AOL screen names of the folks in the chat room.

To send a message, click in the white box at the bottom of the window, type your message, and press Enter or click Send. Your message appears in the conversation box. When you are done chatting, just close the chat window.

Look who's here

If you want to know something about the other occupants of the room, double-click one of their names in the People Here window. A window pops up with the person's profile (if there is one), which may include name, location, marital status, and other information, but which rarely does. This window also enables you to send the person e-mail or an IM message, block e-mail or IM messages from this person, or add the person to your AOL address book or AIM buddy list. (See Chapter 14 for information about IM, AIM, and buddy lists.)

If you do not want to see chat room messages from this person, click the screen name and click the Ignore Member button. This technique is a good way to stop receiving messages from annoying people.

Chat on the go

Americans like to think that all fads originate in California. But there is a teenage phenomenon already wildly popular in Asia that hasn't made it to Hollywood yet. It's a marriage of cell phones and instant messaging that lets kids exchange vapid text messages from anywhere. We hear that one can figure out how to type messages on a cell phone without looking, making it easier to do so sneakily in a boring class. Finding room in the radio bands for this service and related third-generation wireless features has delayed its introduction in the U.S. and Canada, but it's on the way. See the sidebar "IM by phone" at the end of Chapter 14.

"Who am I, and what am I doing here?"

You're identified by your screen name, which, if you do nothing, is the *master screen name,* the one you used when you first signed on to AOL. Many people use, for privacy reasons, a different screen name when they're chatting. AOL lets each account use as many as seven different screen names as long as no other AOL user is already using them. One of the screen names is the master screen name, which can never be changed. If you want to add or change other screen names, you must log on to AOL under the master screen name. After you've established other screen names and passwords, you can log on to AOL by using the alternative name. Each screen name has a separate mailbox. You can use screen names for either different family members or different personalities (for example, your business self and your private self).

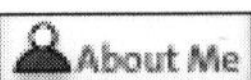

To set your profile, which is the information that other users can see about you when you're chatting, click the About Me or My Directory Listing button under the Settings button on the toolbar. In the About Me window, you can click Create/Edit My Profile to put in information about yourself (it's up to you how accurate this information is).

Stop bothering me!

While you chat on AOL, we find that an instant message pops up about every 30 seconds from someone with a screen name like sexygirl2546787, with whom we are not interested in chatting. (At least, Margy isn't.) In the Settings toolbar menu, click Preferences, and in the Preferences window, click Privacy. Choose Allow Only People on my Buddy List, Block All Others. Click Save and close the Preferences window. There, that's better!

Member-created rooms

In the Find a Chat window (which you display by clicking Chat on the toolbar and then Chat Room Listings), you can create your own chat room. Click the Create a Chat button and then choose to create a Member Chat (open to all) or a Private Chat (only for people whom you invite). Then choose which category you want your room to be in, type a name for your chat room, and click Go Chat. Now all you have to do is wait for people to join you, or you can IM people and invite them to come in.

Private chats

The names of private rooms, unlike public or member rooms, are not revealed. To join one, you have to know its name — that is, someone must invite you to join. When you click the Enter a Private Chat button in the Find a Chat window, you're asked to name the room you want to join. If it doesn't exist, one is created, and you're the sole occupant.

Private rooms enable people to talk more intimately — there's little danger of a stranger popping in. Two (or more) people can agree to create a private room and meet there.

Private rooms have a somewhat sleazy reputation. If you get invited to one, you should be careful about guarding your privacy. Remember that what the other people are saying about themselves may not be true. If you enter a private chat room with someone you don't know, don't be surprised if the talk gets real rude real fast.

Calling the AOL cops

A link in the lower-right corner of the chat window is labeled Notify AOL. If you think that someone is violating the AOL terms of service (TOS) by asking you for your password or credit card number, using abusive language, or otherwise behaving badly, you can and should report that person to AOL. When you click the Notify AOL link, a window pops up to help you gather all the information you want to report: the chat category and room you were in, the offensive chat dialog pasted into a window, and the offender's screen name, for example. You can then send the report to AOL by clicking Send.

Because of this policing and the power of AOL to terminate (permanently) the accounts of people who play without the rules, the AOL chat rooms have a deserved reputation for safety and for being a good place to play. That AOL has so many subscribers who like chat means that you have a good chance of finding a chat room that meets your needs.

Chatting on the Web

Although AOL limits chatting to its paid members, many Web sites enable you to chat with nothing more than your browser. These sites have Java-based chat programs that your browser can download and run automatically. Some other Web chat sites require that you download a plug-in or ActiveX control to add chat capability to your browser. (See Chapter 6 for information on how to use plug-ins.)

Most Web-based chat programs look a lot like AOL's chat screen (refer to Figure 15-2). A large window displays the ongoing conversation, a smaller window displays the screen names of the participants, and a text area is where you type your messages and find a Send button.

Some Web chat sites include

- Yahoo Groups at groups.yahoo.com
- Yahoo Chat at chat.yahoo.com
- MSN Groups at groups.msn.com

Many other Web sites have chats on the specific topic of the site. Search for *Chat* at www.dmoz.org for a variety of chat venues.

Chatting via IRC

IRC (Internet Relay Chat), the classic form of chat, is available from most Internet providers as well as from AOL. To use IRC, you have to install an *IRC client* program on your computer. An IRC client (or just *IRC program*) is another Internet program, like your Web browser or e-mail program, and freeware and shareware programs are available for you to download from the Net. The most popular shareware IRC programs include

- **mIRC** for Windows
- **ircii** for Linux and Unix (freeware)
- **Ircle** for the Macintosh

You can find these IRC programs, along with others, at shareware Web sites, such as TUCOWS (www.tucows.com) or at the IRC Help page (www.irchelp.org).

Chatting on IRC is not so very different from chatting on AOL, but you can use it to chat with people who aren't AOL members. IRC uses networks of servers all over the world, with tens of thousands of people usually chatting at once.

For the full story on IRC, see our Web page about it at net.gurus.com/irc.

Part V
Other Internet Essentials

"Guess who found a Kiss merchandise site on the Web while you were gone?"

In this part . . .

A few topics don't fit anywhere else, but are too important to leave out, so here they are. We describe the essential skill of downloading, getting useful stuff from the Net onto your computer, and then pay a visit to AOL, which isn't exactly part of the Internet, but is close enough, being home to 20 million people living right next door.

Chapter 16

Swiping Files from the Net

In This Chapter

- Using your Web browser to swipe files
- Uploading your Web pages to Web servers
- Sharing files with other Netizens
- Installing software you've swiped from the Net

The Internet is chock-full of computers, and those computers are chock-full of files. What's in those files? Programs, pictures, sounds, movies, documents, spreadsheets, recipes, *Anne of Green Gables* (the entire book and several of the sequels), you name it. Some of the computers are set up so that you can copy some of the files they contain to your own computer, usually for free. In this chapter, we tell you how to find some of those files and how to copy and use them. For a list of the types of files you may want to download and what to do with them after you have them, see Chapter 19. As a free added bonus, we also tell you how to copy files from your own computer to another computer, most often a Web page you've just made to a Web server that makes it available to the rest of the Net.

Downloading means copying files from a computer Up There On The Internet "down" to your computer on or under your desk. *Uploading* is the reverse — copying a file from your computer "up" to a computer on the Internet.

You probably won't be surprised to hear that there are at least three different ways to download and upload files:

- Click a link on a Web page. Web browsers can download files, too. In fact, they do it all time when they download Web pages so you can see them.
- Participate in a file-sharing service.
- Run a file transfer program. *FTP* stands for File Transfer Protocol, an older but still very popular way that computers transfer files across the Internet.

You can also transfer files by attaching them to e-mail messages sent to other e-mail users, which we discuss in Chapter 11.

Downloading Files from the Web

Getting files over the Web is simplicity itself. You probably have been doing it for ages and didn't even know it. Every Web page, every icon or image on a Web page, and every ornate Web background is a file. Every time you click a link or type a URL to go to a Web page, you're getting at least one file. (If it's a page with many graphics, you're getting many files, one per picture. Regardless of how many files it is, your Web browser manages the space it uses for automatically downloaded files so it doesn't fill up your disk.) You've probably already downloaded hundreds of files from the Internet — and you can tell your friends so.

Getting the picture

To download a picture over the Web, first display the picture in your Web browser. When you see a picture you want to save on your hard disk, right-click the picture. From the menu that appears, choose Save Image As or Save Picture As. Tell your browser where to save the picture. That's all it takes!

Graphics files have special filename extensions that identify what graphics format the file is in. When you download a picture, you can change the name of the file but *don't* change the extension. See Chapter 19 for details.

Just because a picture is now stored on your hard disk doesn't mean that you own it. Most pictures on Web pages are copyrighted. Unless a picture comes from a site that specifically offers pictures as reusable *clip art,* you have to get permission to reuse the picture for most purposes or even to upload it to your own noncommercial Web page.

Getting with the program

Downloading a program file over the Web is also easy — you click a link to it, frequently a link that says either *Download* or the name of the program. Your Web browser stops and asks you what to do with the file. If it's a program (in Windows, a file with the extension `.exe`, `.com`, or `.dll`) or a ZIP file, the most reasonable thing for your browser to do is to save it to disk so that you can run it or unzip it later. If it's a ZIP file and you have WinZip (mentioned later in this chapter) installed, you can also tell the browser to run WinZip directly; we find that method less handy than it might seem.

If you're interested in downloading an Internet program, for example, you may go to TUCOWS, The Ultimate Collection of Windows (and Mac) Software, at `www.tucows.com`. After you're at the site, click links to choose the operating system you use, choose a site near you, and choose the type of programs you want to download. TUCOWS displays a list of programs available for downloading. Alternatively, type a program name into the Search box to find programs by that name. When you find the page about the program, you can download its program file; just click the name of the program, the Download Now button, or other appropriate-sounding link. (In Figure 16-1, you click the link for your version of Windows.) After the file is on your computer, skip to the section "It's Not Just a File — It's Software," later in this chapter, to install and run it.

Getting other files

To download other types of files — sound files, video files, whatever — you follow the same steps as for downloading a program. Find a Web page that contains a link to the file you want. Then click the link for the file you want and tell your browser where to store it. (See Chapter 12 for how to play audio and video files.)

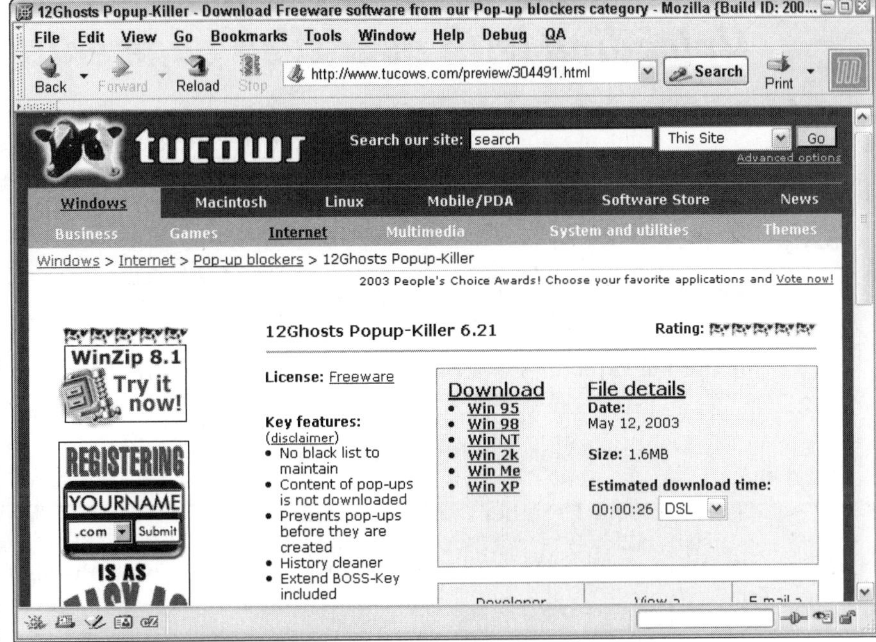

Figure 16-1: Click a button or link in TUCOWS to download the program file.

For music files in MP3 format, try MP3.com (`www.mp3.com`), Audiogalaxy (`www.audiogalaxy.com`), and Lycos Music (`music.lycos.com/downloads`). EMusic (`www.emusic.com`) charges a monthly subscription fee so that artists can get their royalties. Napster (`www.napster.com`), the free music service, had to shut down its original system but may be back online by the time you read this. Also try KaZaA (`www.kazaa.com`), a similar file-sharing service.

If you use Windows XP, you can also use its new Web Folders feature to download files; see "Uploading and Downloading with Web Folders" later in this chapter.

About Face! Up You Go!

Okay, now you know how to retrieve files from other computers — downloading. How about copying the other way — uploading? If you write your own Web pages and want to upload them to your Internet provider's computer, here's how you do it: Upload them to the provider's Web server.

If you use Windows XP, you can use its Web Folders feature to upload files, too.

Uploading with your Web page editor

Good Web editors include a file transfer (FTP) program so that after you've created some awesome Web pages, you can upload them to a Web server. See Chapter 9 for details on how to create and upload Web pages in Netscape Composer or Word.

Uploading with your browser

In Internet Explorer 4.0 or later, you can log on to the Web server as yourself by using an FTP URL, something like this:

```
ftp://yourid@www.yourprovider.com/
```

Use your logon ID rather than *yourid* and the name of your ISP's Web server, which most likely is `www` followed by the ISP's name but may also be something like `ftp.www.fargle.net`. (Ask your ISP if this info isn't in the sign-up packet it gave you.)

The browser asks for your password; use the same one you use when you dial in. If this password works, you see your home Web directory listed on-screen. If you want to upload files to a different directory, click that directory's name so that you see that directory.

After you have the directory you want on-screen, just drag the file to upload from any other program such as Windows Explorer into the browser window. Poof! The file is now uploaded. (It may be a slow poof, depending on how big the file is.)

(Although Netscape was the first browser that offered FTP uploads, current versions of Netscape and Mozilla only do uploads as part of the Composer Web page editor. But uploads in Internet Explorer work just fine.)

Uploading with an FTP program

You can use an FTP program to upload or download files — that's what they are for. Our Web page at `net.gurus.com/ftp` contains instructions.

Uploading and Downloading with Web Folders

Windows XP contains a spiffy new feature called *Web Folders* that lets you use Windows Explorer (the My Computer icon) to transfer files to and from FTP servers. It also works with some Web servers — you guessed it! — but only Web servers that run Microsoft's Web server program.

To use Web Folders to download files from an FTP or Web server, follow these steps in Windows XP:

1. **Choose Start⇨My Network Places.**

   The My Network Places window appears.

2. **In the Network Tasks section of the task pane (the left-hand part of the window), click Add a Network Place.**

   This starts a wizard that helps you create a connection to the FTP or Web server to which you want to download (or upload) files.

3. **Click Next to move to the first screen of the wizard.**

   The wizard asks, "Where do you want to create this network place?"

4. **Indicate where you want to create this network place.**

   You have two options: MSN or somewhere else. (Did we mention that Microsoft owns MSN?) If you have an MSN account and would like to work with a Web site that you maintain there, click MSN Communities. Otherwise, click Choose Another Network Location. Then click Next.

   The wizard asks, "What is the address of this network place?"

5. **Type the URL of the FTP or Web server to which you want to connect. For an FTP server, start the URL with** ftp:// **and for a Web server, use** http://. **Then click Next.**

   For example, to download files from the M.I.T. FAQ library, type

   `ftp://rtfm.mit.edu.`

6. **If you're connecting to a public FTP server, leave the check box selected that indicates that you want to log on anonymously. If you have an account on the server (for example, you're connecting to a Web server on which you maintain a Web site), deselect the check box and type your user name. Click Next.**

7. **Finally, type a name to use for this Web folder.**

   The wizard suggests the name of the server (for example, `rtfm.mit.edu`), but you can change it to whatever you'd like to appear in your My Network Places folder.

8. **Click Next and then click Finish.**

   A new entry appears in the My Network Places folder. Click or double-click it to open a window that displays the files on the server.

FTP and Web servers contain files and folders, just like the disk on your own computer does. Click or double-click a folder to open a window that lists what's inside it. To return to the original folder, click the Back button on the toolbar. (If you connect to the `rtfm.mit.edu` FTP server, open the pub folder and then the faqs folder to see a list of FAQs.)

To copy files to or from the FTP or Web server, open a Windows Explorer window by choosing Start➪My Computer. Drag files from one window to the other.

When you're done downloading or uploading files, close the window that displays the contents of the server.

Sharing among Ourselves

Napster was the most famous peer-to-peer (P2P) file-sharing service. It was not a Web site from which you could download files. Rather, it was a service that allowed Internet users to offer files they had and to transfer the files directly *to each other.* It was a powerful idea, and people have extended it to files way beyond music files.

However, there was a teensy-weensy problem with Napster. Most of the files that people wanted to share were files to which someone else owned the copyright. For example, if you have a Grateful Dead CD, you may own the CD, but you don't own the rights to distribute the songs. The free Napster music-sharing service at `www.napster.com` was shut down because the music recording industry got tired of people downloading songs and *burning* (recording) them onto CDs instead of buying the CDs. (Actually, the evidence that P2P hurts CD sales is shaky at best, and there's some evidence that people buy CDs of stuff they originally discovered via download.)

But peer-to-peer is still considered to be the coming thing on the Internet. Napster is planning to reopen (and may already have done so by the time you read this) as a subscription service: For a flat monthly fee, you'll be able to download and play as many songs as you like. Audiogalaxy (`www.audiogalaxy.com`) also provides a paid service. Other services (for music, software, and other types of files) come and go as they get chased off of Web servers or out of existence.

And file-sharing enthusiasts have another approach. Rather than working off a central site that people use to find the files that they want, each person can download and run a *client* program that connects directly to other people's computers, with requests passed automatically from client to client to client until one offers the desired file. With no central server computer to shut down, stopping file sharing is much harder. That's the theory behind the wildly popular KaZaA (`www.kazaa.com`). Due to an extremely decentralized design and a baffling corporate structure (it is managed in Australia, and headquartered in the remote Pacific tax haven of the Cook Islands), it has so far avoided serious legal challenge.

Gnutella is the open source peer-to-peer system. Visit `www.gnutella.com` or `www.gnutelliums.com` to find out how to download and run the Gnutella client program that enables you to share files directly with other Gnutella users. So far, it's more complicated than using the Web, but it will likely improve. WinMX (`www.winmx.com`) is another peer-to-peer sharing service.

Grokster (`www.grokster.com`) and Morpheus (`www.morpheus.com`) are similar to KaZaA, but both install intrusive pop-ups and *spyware* (software that reports back to the programs' suppliers about the Web sites you visit), so we don't recommend them.

It's Not Just a File — It's Software

Using your Web browser or FTP, you can download freeware and shareware programs and install and use them. You need a few well-chosen software tools, including a program to uncompress compressed files. (Useful little programs like this one are called *utilities* in the jargon.)

Installing downloaded software usually requires three steps:

1. **Using your browser, Web Folders, or FTP, download the file that contains the software.**
2. **If the software isn't in a self-installing file, it's usually in a compressed format, so uncompress it.**
3. **Run the installation program that comes with it, or at least create an icon for the program.**

The first part of this chapter describes how to do Step 1, the downloading part. The rest of this chapter describes Steps 2 and 3: uncompressing and installing. Here goes!

Installing, decompressing, and unzipping

Most downloadable software on the Internet is in a compressed format to save both storage space on the server and transmission time when you download the file. An increasing amount of software is *self-installing* — the file is a program that does the necessary uncompressing and installing. Self-installing Windows files have the extension `.exe`, and nonself-installing compressed files have the extension `.zip`.

To install a self-installing file, just double-click on the file to run it. The file should open itself and walk you through a wizard-style set of windows to collect any needed setup info and then install itself. Figure 16-2 shows a typical self-installer, the one for the Opera Web browser.

If a file is compressed, you need a program to deal with it. Files with the file extension `.zip` identify compressed files (these files are called, amazingly, *ZIP files*). If you use Windows XP, its Compressed Folders feature (which is normally turned on, unless you turned it off) lets you open ZIP files right in Windows Explorer windows. Just click or double-click the ZIP file to see what's inside it.

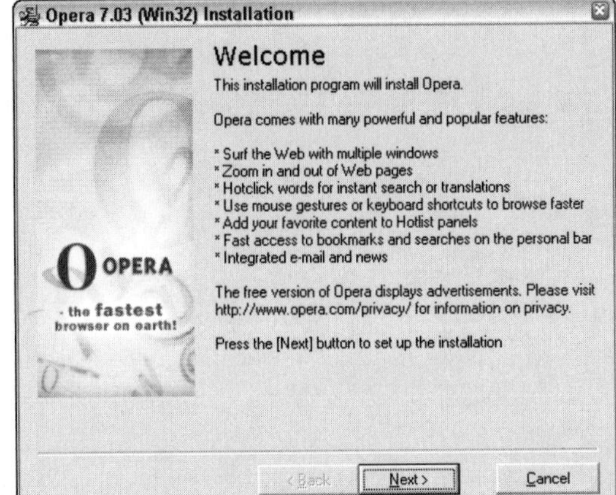

Figure 16-2: Ready to install (the Opera browser, in this case).

If you don't use Windows XP, programs like WinZip (downloadable from `www.winzip.com`) can both unzip and zip things for you. We also like ZipMagic (available from `www.aladdinsys.com/zipmagic/`), which makes ZIP files look like Windows folders. Mac users, see the sidebar "Mac users say StuffIt" in this chapter.

If you use Windows XP or you already have WinZip (which is also available through the mail or from various shareware outlets), skip the next section.

Getting and running WinZip

To get WinZip from the Web, go to `www.winzip.com`, a page full of pictures of outer-space-type blobs. Click Download Evaluation to get to the download page. On that page, click the link for your version of Windows, tell Windows where you want to store the WinZip program, (how about `C:\` or `C:\Windows\Temp`?), and wait for it to download.

To install WinZip:

1. **Run the file you just downloaded.**

   The file is named something like `Winzip90.exe`, depending on the version.

2. **Follow the installation instructions WinZip gives you.**

   Although you have a bunch of options, you can accept the suggested defaults for all of them. We prefer to choose the Classic interface.

Give it a try! Double-click that icon! WinZip looks like Figure 16-3.

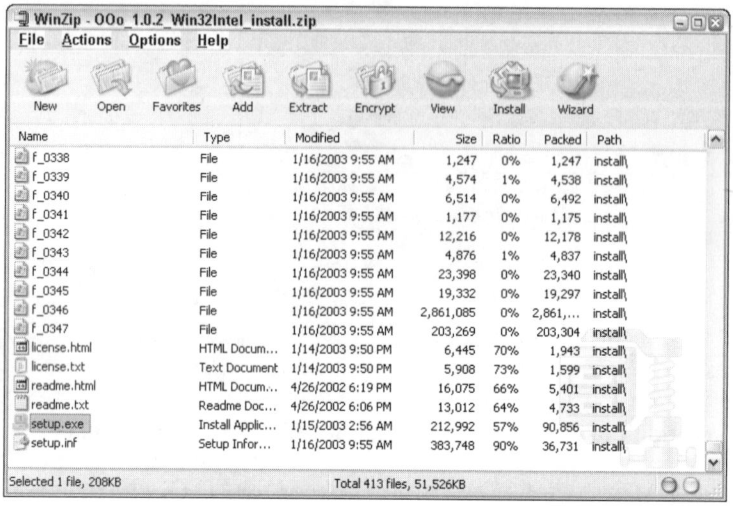

WinZip - OOo_1.0.2_Win32Intel_install.zip

File Actions Options Help

New Open Favorites Add Extract Encrypt View Install Wizard

Name	Type	Modified	Size	Ratio	Packed	Path
f_0338	File	1/16/2003 9:55 AM	1,247	0%	1,247	install\
f_0339	File	1/16/2003 9:55 AM	4,574	1%	4,538	install\
f_0340	File	1/16/2003 9:55 AM	6,514	0%	6,492	install\
f_0341	File	1/16/2003 9:55 AM	1,177	0%	1,175	install\
f_0342	File	1/16/2003 9:55 AM	12,216	0%	12,178	install\
f_0343	File	1/16/2003 9:55 AM	4,876	1%	4,837	install\
f_0344	File	1/16/2003 9:55 AM	23,398	0%	23,340	install\
f_0345	File	1/16/2003 9:55 AM	19,332	0%	19,297	install\
f_0346	File	1/16/2003 9:55 AM	2,861,085	0%	2,861,...	install\
f_0347	File	1/16/2003 9:55 AM	203,269	0%	203,304	install\
license.html	HTML Docum...	1/14/2003 9:50 PM	6,445	70%	1,943	install\
license.txt	Text Document	1/14/2003 9:50 PM	5,908	73%	1,599	install\
readme.html	HTML Docum...	4/26/2002 6:19 PM	16,075	66%	5,401	install\
readme.txt	Readme Doc...	4/26/2002 6:06 PM	13,012	64%	4,733	install\
setup.exe	Install Applic...	1/15/2003 2:56 AM	212,992	57%	90,856	install\
setup.inf	Setup Infor...	1/16/2003 9:55 AM	383,748	90%	36,731	install\

Selected 1 file, 208KB Total 413 files, 51,526KB

Figure 16-3: WinZip is ready to deal with your ZIP files.

To open a ZIP file (which the WinZip folks call an *archive*), click the Open button and choose the directory and filename for the ZIP file. Poof! WinZip displays a list of the files in the archive, with their dates and sizes.

If you want to use a file from a ZIP file, you have to open the ZIP file and *extract* it — that is, you ask WinZip to uncompress it and store it in a new file. To extract a file:

1. **Choose it from the list of files.**

   You can choose a group of files that are listed together by clicking the first one and then Shift+clicking the last one. To select an additional file, Ctrl+click it.

2. **Click the Extract button.**

   A dialog box asks in which directory you want to put the file and whether you want to extract all the files in the archive or just the one you selected.

3. **Select the directory in which to store the unzipped files.**

4. **Click OK.**

   WinZip unzips the file. The ZIP file is unchanged, and now you have the uncompressed file (or files) as well.

Mac users say StuffIt

Mac users can get programs named ZipIt, Unzip, or MindExpander from `www.macorchard.com`. The most popular is a shareware program, by Raymond Lau, known as StuffIt Expander. StuffIt comes in many flavors, including a shareware version and a commercial version from `www.stuffit.com`. StuffIt files of all varieties generally end with the extension `.sit`.

If WinZip can figure out that a ZIP file contains a program to install, it will often offer a Checkout or Install button. Checkout extracts all the files and then makes a menu window where you can easily click on whichever of the extracted files you want to open or run. Install runs a self-installing ZIP file for you.

Although WinZip can do a bunch of other things, too, such as add files to a ZIP file and create your own ZIP file, you don't have to know how to perform these tasks in order to swipe software from the Net, so we skip them. (We bet that you can figure them out just by looking at the buttons on the WinZip toolbar.) WinZip is shareware, so if you use it much, please register it and send Mr. WinZip his fee so he can afford to eat and keep developing new versions.

Now that you know how to unzip software you get from the Internet, you're ready for the next topic: safe software.

Scanning for viruses

We all know that you practice safe software: You check every new program you get to make sure that it doesn't contain any hidden software viruses that may display obnoxious messages or trash your hard disk. If that's true of you, you can skip this section.

For the rest of you, it's a good idea to run a virus-scanning program. You never know what naughty piece of code you may otherwise unwittingly download to your defenseless computer!

It's a good idea to run a virus checker after you have obtained and run any new piece of software. Although the Web and FTP servers on the Internet make every effort to keep their software archives virus free, nobody is perfect. Don't get caught by some prankster's idea of a joke!

If you use WinZip, you can configure it to run your virus checker before you even unzip the ZIP file containing a program. Choose Options⇨Configuration from the menu, click the Program Locations tab, and in the Scan program box, type the pathname of your virus checker program.

Although recent versions of Windows don't come with a virus checker, several commercial ones are available, including the McAfee VirusScan program, which you can download from the McAfee Web site, at `www.mcafee.com`. Another good virus checker is Norton AntiVirus, at `www.symantec.com`. Be sure to update your virus files regularly, like once a week, according to the instructions that come with your virus checker. The program can only check for viruses that it knows about!

Installing the program you unzipped

After you have downloaded a program from the Net and unzipped it (preferably using Checkout), the program is ready to install. To install the program, double-click the name of the setup program in Windows Explorer or My Computer. The setup program probably creates an icon for the program on your desktop. In Windows, it may also add the program to your Start menu.

Some programs don't come with an installation program — you just get the program itself, and after it's unzipped, you need only run the program you extracted from the ZIP file. To make the program easy to run, you need an icon for it. You can create your own icon or menu item for the program. In Windows 95 and later, follow these steps:

1. **Run either My Computer or Windows Explorer and select the program file (the file with the extension `.exe`, or occasionally `.com` or `.msi`).**
2. **Use your right mouse button to drag the filename out on the desktop or into an open folder on the desktop.**

   An icon for the program appears.

Another method is to choose Start⇨Programs or Start⇨All Programs, find the menu choice for the program, hold down the Shift key, drag the menu choice to the desktop, and release the Shift key. Windows copies the menu choice as an icon on the desktop.

To run your new program, you can just click or double-click the icon (depending on how you have Windows configured — try clicking first, and if nothing happens, double-click). Cool!

Configuring the program

Now you can run the program. Hooray!

You may have to tell the program, however, about your Internet address or your computer or who knows what before it can do its job. Refer to the text files, if any, that came with the program or choose Help from the program's menu bar to get more information about how to configure and run your new program. The Web site from which you got the program may have some explanations, too.

Where Is It?

"Downloading programs sounds fine and dandy," you may say, "but what's out there, and where can I find it?" One of the best places to find software is to look at `www.tucows.com`. It has a great collection of FTP sites grouped by platform and category of program. CNET's Download.com site at `www.download.com` also has a huge library of programs.

Also look at Chapter 8, and visit the page of links to our favorite software you can find online, with our current updated list of greatest hits:

```
net.gurus.com/software
```

Chapter 17

AOL: Can Twenty Million Users Really Be Wrong?

In This Chapter

- Introducing America Online
- Using AOL e-mail
- Web surfing with AOL
- Pulling files from FTP servers
- Trying other things

Can twenty million users really be wrong? Sure they can. But if you're brand new to the world of computers as well as to the world of the Internet, you may find using America Online easier than starting off with a traditional Internet service provider (ISP). Also, if you're interested in online chatting, AOL is the world capital of chat. (In his book *Burn Rate,* Michael Wolff claims that AOL's success is primarily due to naughty online chat. He may well be right, although AOL offers plenty of other things to do.)

This chapter tells you how to use e-mail, the World Wide Web, and FTP from AOL. Because chatting is extremely popular all over the Net, it has its own chapter, Chapter 15, which includes a section on chatting with AOL. You probably want to read Chapters 6 through 13 that describe e-mail and the World Wide Web — all the conceptual information there applies to you, too. In this chapter, we give you the specifics for using AOL.

For the full story about AOL, get *AOL For Dummies*, by John and Jenny Kaufeld, published by Wiley Publishing, Inc. The 9th Edition covers AOL 8.0.

Hello, America Online

If you've decided to join the AOL ranks, we tell you how to sign up and then install AOL and connect to it in Chapter 5. After you have AOL running, how do you do all those Internet tricks? We take you on a tour of AOL features using Version 8.0 of the AOL software, which was released in late 2002. Previous versions of the AOL software look similar.

To connect to AOL, you type your *screen name* (what ISPs call your user name) and password, and then click Sign On. When AOL has successfully connected you, you see the America Online window with the Welcome and Buddy List windows inside it, as shown in Figure 17-1. Below the menu are several rows of toolbar buttons, some of which display their own little menus when you click them. On the bottom row of buttons are the Keyword box (with the Go button to its right) and the Search box (with the Search button to its right).

One of the quickest ways to get around in AOL is to "go to" a keyword: You either click in the Keyword box (the wide, white box in the toolbar to the left of the Go button) or press Ctrl+K, and then type one of the AOL keywords. In the rest of this section about AOL, we just say "go to **keyword**." After you've read and closed the Welcome window, you can see a column of buttons down the left side of the AOL window — the *Channel menu*. Click a channel to see information about that topic (for example, click Travel to make airline reservations).

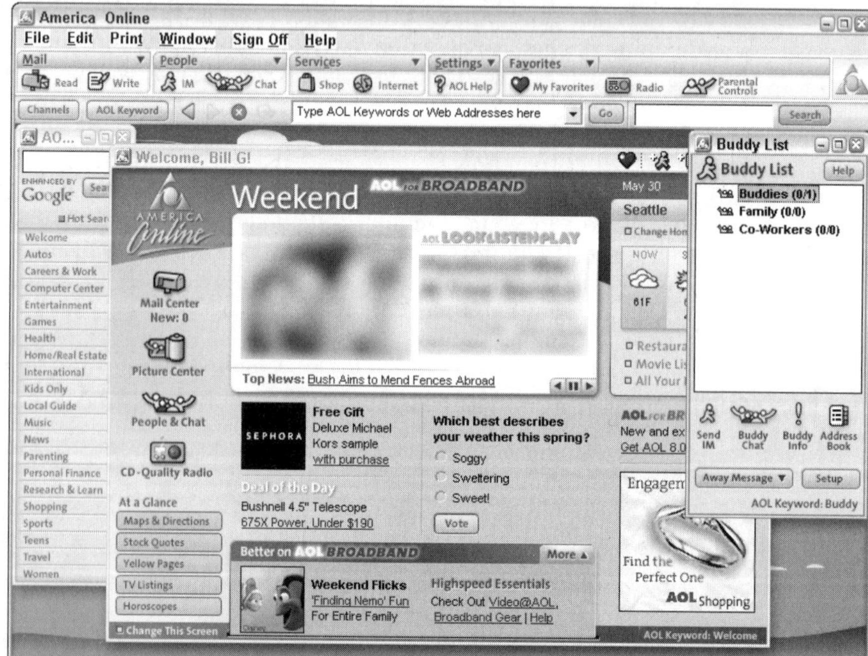

Figure 17-1: AOL welcomes you, and you have mail! Some buddies may want to send you instant messages, too.

As you use AOL, more and more windows appear within the AOL window. We find that from time to time we need to close most of these windows by clicking the Close (X) button in the upper-right corner of the window, while leaving the AOL window open. (Don't close the AOL window until you are ready to sign off.)

Using E-Mail from AOL

The first thing to do is to send mail to all your friends to let them know that you have successfully installed AOL and tell them your e-mail address. You can send messages to other AOL members and to folks on the Internet.

Your Internet mail address is your screen name (omitting any spaces) plus `@aol.com`. Your screen name is the user name you use when you log on. If your screen name is `John Smith`, for example, your e-mail address is `JohnSmith@aol.com`.

"Do I have mail?"

Every time you connect to AOL, it tells you whether you have mail. The Read icon (the leftmost icon on the toolbar) is a little mailbox, and the Welcome window contains a similar mailbox icon with some writing nearby. If the little red flag is up, you have mail, just in case you're from a part of the world where mailboxes don't have little red flags. If your computer has speakers, a voice may also say "You have mail!" — try not to jump right out of your seat when you hear it.

Reading your mail

You probably *do* have mail, in fact, because every new member gets a nice note from the president of AOL and because AOL members tend to get mountains of junk mail, much more than people with other types of accounts. To read your unread mail, follow these steps:

1. **Click any mailbox you can find.**

   It's the Read icon on the toolbar. Alternatively, you can click the Mail icon on the toolbar and choose Read Mail from the menu that appears, or press Ctrl+R. You see the Online Mailbox window with three tabs for New Mail, Old Mail, and Sent Mail.

   On the New Mail tab of the Online Mailbox window, each line on the list describes one incoming mail message with the date it was sent, the sender's e-mail address, and the subject.

2. **To read a message, double-click it or highlight it on the list and then either click Read or press Enter.**

   You see the text of your message in another cute little window.

3. **To reply to the message, click the Reply button. Type the text of your message in the box in the lower part of the window that appears. Then click Send Now (if you're online) or Send Later (if not).**

   You don't have to type an address — AOL uses the address of the person you are replying to.

4. **To forward the message to someone else, click the Forward button. In the Send To box, fill in the e-mail address to which you want to forward the message. You can add a message to go along with the original message, too, by typing it in the large message area box. Then click Send Now or Send Later.**

   If you get annoying or unwanted mail from another AOL member, forward it to TOSspam, a special mailbox at AOL set up to investigate junk e-mail.

5. **To see the next message, click the Next button; to see the preceding message, click the Prev button.**

6. **When you finish with a window, click the Close button, the X button in the upper-right corner of the window.**

It's not always a good idea to respond to messages right away. You may have to get some information or cool off after reading the brainless message some jerk sent you.

Saving a message on your PC

Ninety-nine percent of the time, after you've read and responded to a message, you want to delete it. Just click the Delete button while the message is displayed, or select the message from your list of messages and click the Delete button. If you read a message and don't delete it, AOL moves it to the Old Mail tab in the Online Mailbox window, so it doesn't clutter up your New Mail tab.

If you get a message on AOL that you want to save in a file on your hard disk, display it on-screen as described in the preceding section. Then choose File➪Save from the menu bar or press Ctrl+S. AOL lets you choose the folder and filename in which to save the file on your computer. When you click OK, the e-mail message is saved as a file. Nice and easy! The file is a formatted Web page, so you can open it in your favorite Web browser.

AOL Plus

AOL offers a slightly different version of AOL 8.0 called AOL Plus or AOL 8.0a as a free upgrade intended for broadband users. It makes it easier to get to AOL's broadband content (a sure remedy if your life suffers from too few music videos), a slightly fancier mail program, and other minor improvements. Because it's free, and you can install it along side regular AOL 8.0 and use whichever you prefer, broadband users may as well give it a try. Go to keyword **Upgrade** to download and install it.

Composing a new message

You don't have to reply to other messages — you can begin an exchange of messages, assuming that you know the e-mail address of the person to whom you want to write:

1. **Click the Write button — the second icon from the left on the second row of the toolbar, the picture of a pencil and paper.**

   Alternatively, you can click the Mail icon on the toolbar and choose Write Mail from the menu that appears, or you can press Ctrl+M. You see the Write Mail dialog box, as shown in Figure 17-2.

2. **Type the recipient's address in the Send To box.**

   For AOL members, just type the screen name. For others on the Net, type the entire Internet address.

3. **In the Copy To box, enter the addresses of anyone to whom you want to send a copy.**

   You don't have to send a copy to yourself — AOL keeps copies of mail you have sent.

4. **Type a brief subject line in the Subject box.**

   You have to enter a subject — AOL doesn't let a message leave home without it.

5. **In the box with no name, type the text of your message.**

   If you're sending a message to another AOL user, you can use the buttons above the text box to add underlining, italics, color, and other whizzo formatting to your message. For messages to the Internet, however, be sure your recipient can read formatted mail; if he can't, your correspondent will see ugly formatting codes mixed in with your message.

6. **When you like what you see, click the Send Now or the Send Later button.**

   AOL confirms that the mail is winging on its way.

7. **Click OK.**

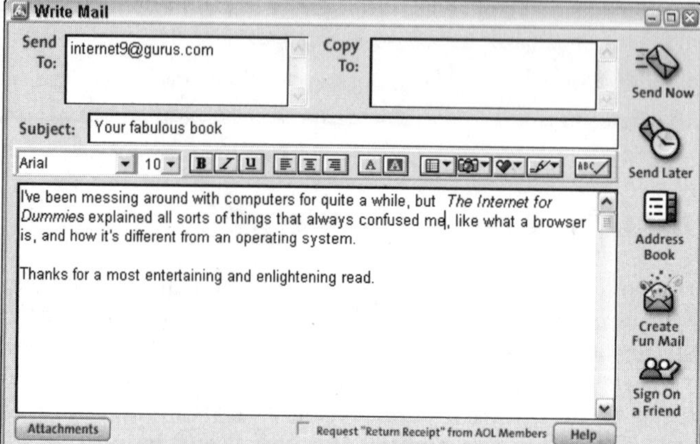

Figure 17-2: Send a message to anyone with an AOL or Internet account.

Attaching a file to your message

If you want to send a file from your computer to someone as an e-mail message, AOL makes this process easy. When you're writing the message, click the Attachments button. You see the Attachments dialog box, which lets you choose any file from your PC. Click Attach, select a file, and click OK.

AOL attaches the file using MIME, a method that most other e-mail programs can deal with. (It's still a good idea to ask first before sending attachments to make sure that the recipient has the necessary program to read the file you want to send.)

Keeping an address book

Because you can't remember, much less type correctly all your online friends' e-mail addresses (well, we can't), AOL provides you with an address book to keep track of them. Along with e-mail addresses, you can keep home and work mailing addresses, phone numbers, birthdays, home pages, and a variety of other information. Addresses can be assigned to built-in categories such as Family, Friends, Co-Workers, or any other categories you create.

Stop the spam!

America Online users get more junk e-mail messages than users of any other online system. Most of the messages are for fraudulent get-rich-quick schemes, porn sites, and offers to advertise *your* product by e-mail to millions of people who are just as fed up with those messages as you are.

As you can imagine, AOL has gotten many complaints about the level of junk mail, especially from users who have to pay by the hour to read it. (Even with flat rates, some people still pay by the minute for phone calls.) The folks at AOL have been fighting the junk e-mailers for some time, including trying to block their messages, and have fought several court battles with the online spammers. Because many junk e-mail messages have forged return addresses, however, it isn't always easy to trace or block them. What's an e-mail reader to do?

Go to the keyword **mail controls**, that's what (or click Mail on the toolbar and choose Mail Controls from the menu that appears). For each screen name on your account, you can block all incoming e-mail, e-mail from sites you select, or only e-mail attachments.

If you use the new AOL Communicator, it has much more sophisticated spam filtering. You can tell it to mark mail that looks spammy and then "train" the filter by telling it when it guesses wrong.

Adding names to your book

To add new entries in your book, click the Mail icon on the toolbar and choose Address Book from the menu that appears. (While you're composing a message, click the Address Book icon.) The Address Book window shows your current address book contents.

Click the Add Contact button to create a new entry and then fill out the first name, last name, and e-mail address of the person to whom you want to write. You can create an entry for a group of people (your church dinner group, for example) by clicking the Add Group button instead. Give the group a name, such as "Dinner Group" or "Marketing Dept.," and then choose people on your contacts list to include in the group. (Groups and categories are different: *Groups* are mailing lists that let you send mail to everyone in the group, and *categories* are just for organizing your address book.)

Using the black book

When you compose a message, you can bring up the address book by clicking its icon in the Write Mail window. In the Address Book window, select the person you want to write to and click the Send To button or just double-click the person's name. To send the person a copy of the message, click Copy To or (for a blind copy) Blind Copy. After you have put addresses in the message, you can remove them by ordinary methods. Close the Address Book window when you don't need it any more.

Netscape and AOL Communicator: The better mail programs

AOL mail uses its own private system rather than the system that all other Internet providers use. This means that you can't use Outlook Express, Eudora, or most other e-mail programs to read and send AOL messages. Until recently, you were stuck with using the rather lame mail program that is built into the AOL software (or the AOL Web interface, which isn't any better). If you wanted to set up mail filters to sort your incoming messages into folders automatically, you were out of luck.

Good news! Now that AOL owns Netscape, current versions (6.1 and later) can work with your AOL mail. Follow the instructions in Chapter 16 to download the program from `home.netscape.com/download`. Chapters 10 and 11 describe how to use Netscape's mail program, including advanced features that the AOL program doesn't have. To tell it about your AOL account, choose Edit➪Mail/News Account Settings from the menu to display the Account Settings dialog box. Click the New Account button and answer the questions: You'll see an option for using your AOL account. When you click OK, your AOL mailbox appears at the bottom of your list of Mail Folders. Click it to read or send mail.

AOL's new AOL Communicator is similar to Netscape mail with a bunch of AOL-isms, notably AOL Instant Messenger and tighter connections to features like Parental Controls. If you don't want to use the full Netscape package, it's a pretty nice mail program. Go to keyword **AOL Communicator** to download and install it.

Both Netscape and AOL Communicator can keep their address books in sync with your address book on AOL. In either, open the address book window by choosing Window➪ Address Book. Then in Netscape, click the Sync button. In AOL Communicator, choose Edit➪AOL Synchronization settings. They'll ask for your screen name and password (Netscape wants your Netscape screen name, but your AOL screen name works just as well) and update the entries to bring your AOL address book and your local address book into sync.

"What if I get an attachment?"

Sometimes when people send you e-mail they send along an attachment — a file from their computer that they attach to the message. If you don't know the person who sent you the message, do not download the attachment, in case it contains a virus or an offensive picture or document.

The name of the attached file is noted at the top of the message as well as its size and estimated time to download. The attachment is not in your computer until you download it from AOL. Click the Download button and choose Download Now or Download Later to download the file and save it on your computer. AOL gives you a chance to choose the folder to save it in. When the download is complete, AOL asks if you want to locate the file. Click Yes to display its filename in a Windows Explorer window where you can double-click the filename to open it.

Don't download files, especially program files, from people you don't know. Even if you do know the sender, never run a program you received by e-mail unless you have confirmed that the sender *meant* to send it to you (that is, that the program isn't a virus that sent itself to you from an unwitting friend's infected PC).

In AOL 6.0 and later, the software gives special treatment to long messages that you receive. Instead of displaying them normally, it turns the text into an attachment, which makes it more confusing to read. If you get a long message (for example, if you subscribe to a mailing list and get its messages as long daily digests), you may receive a message with an attachment containing the text in a compressed format. To read it, download the attachment by clicking the Download button. If the file was *really* big, AOL may have converted it to a ZIP file. AOL will help you download and unzip the message, but after you've done that, it's just a text file, not a mail message, making it painful to reply to it or forward it as a message. To avoid this annoying behavior, read your mail with Netscape or AOL Communicator, both of which handle large messages without trouble. (See the sidebar "Netscape and AOL Communicator: The better mail programs.")

Going Offline

You can work *offline* with AOL — that is, you can disconnect from AOL and read your downloaded e-mail or compose new messages or replies. You may want to work offline to avoid tying up your phone line and give some other family member a chance to use the phone. In fact, when you first run the AOL program, you're not online yet; you can minimize the sign-on window and start composing messages or reading old ones. All the features of AOL that you cannot access because you're not connected are grayed out so that you can't use any features that require you to be online. If you're online and want to go offline without exiting AOL, choose Sign Off⇨Sign Off from the menu bar.

Using AOL to Connect to the Net

Originally (in the early 1990s), AOL provided its own online services — informational pages, chats, and e-mail — without connecting to the Internet at all. When the Internet became popular, AOL began interconnecting to the Net, so that e-mail passes between AOL users and Internet users, and AOL users can see Internet services such as the World Wide Web and Usenet newsgroups.

Mail on the road

AOL users can send and receive mail via the Web without using the AOL software. On any computer with a Web browser such as Netscape, Opera, or Internet Explorer, go to `webmail.aol.com`. On that page, enter your AOL screen name and password, and you'll get a window remarkably similar to the AOL mail program where you can send, receive, and respond to mail.

This is a handy way to keep up with your mail on a computer at the office if you normally use AOL at home, or when you're using a friend's computer, using a Web kiosk at an airport, or using a computer at a cybercafé.

Most people now think of AOL as a convenient way to access the Internet with the side benefit of some AOL-only services like AOL chat rooms. Access to the Internet is intermingled with AOL's content in most AOL windows.

To see a summary of AOL's Internet services in one window, click Internet on the toolbar or go to keyword **internet**. You see the Internet Connection window, with buttons for seeing Web pages or searching the Web.

Web Browsing from AOL

The AOL software includes a built-in Web browser. You can save the addresses of Web pages in your Favorite Places list. You can have a Web browser window open at the same time that other AOL windows are open.

The browser in recent versions of the AOL software is actually Microsoft Internet Explorer (IE), so just about everything we say in other chapters about IE applies to the AOL browser as well. This is strange because AOL owns Netscape, but that shows you how powerful Microsoft is: If AOL doesn't push IE instead of its own Netscape, Microsoft won't include AOL signup software with Windows.

If you have a very old version of the AOL software — version 2.5 or older — the Web browser is awful. Upgrade to a newer version by going to keyword **upgrade** and following the directions on-screen. The good news is that it's easy and that AOL doesn't charge you for the connect time while you're downloading the Web browser program. The bad news is that it takes awhile (as much as an hour or more on some dialup connections) to download the program. If you have a recent AOL coaster, you can install the upgrade from there instead.

Starting the Web browser

To start the AOL Web browser, click in the keyword box (in the bottom row of the toolbar), type the URL of the Web page you want to see (rather than a keyword), and press Enter or click Go. AOL figures out that you typed a URL (probably because it started with *www* or *http://*), opens a World Wide Web window, and starts to display the Web page. For example, to see the Internet Gurus Web site (by the authors of the very book you are holding), type `net.gurus.com` in the box and press Enter.

To use the browser, click any picture that has a blue border or any button or any text that appears underlined. (Chapters 6 and 7 tell you how to find information on the World Wide Web.)

Protecting your kids

In Chapter 3, we talk about the need for parents to be involved with their kids' online experience. Because you're using AOL, you may want to take advantage of its parental controls. If kids use your AOL account, you can create a separate screen name for each kid and control what each kid can do on AOL; go to keyword **parental controls**.

Creating your own Web page

Although it's fun to look at Web pages other people have created, what about making your own? AOL lets you create your own *home page* (a page about you).

Choose People➪Create a Home Page from the toolbar to go to the AOL Hometown Create Your Home Page window. Follow the instructions to create your own home page on the Web. AOL steps you through the creation of a simple, nice-looking page that it stores at the AOL Hometown Web site, at `hometown.aol.com` — the program tells you the exact address of your new page. Read Chapter 9 for help in writing your first home page.

Chatting with AOL and AIM Users

AOL's software includes a chat program that allows you to chat both with other AOL users and with Internet users who are running the AOL Instant Message (AIM) program. AOL Instant Messenger is described in Chapter 14.

The Buddy List Window, which is similar to the AIM window, appears automatically when you sign onto AOL (if it doesn't, choose People⇨Buddy List from the toolbar or go to keyword **buddy view**). As shown on the right side of Figure 17-3, the Buddy List window shows groups as in AIM, like Buddies, Family, and Co-Workers. To add someone to your Buddy List or make other changes, click one of the groups and then click the Setup button. You see the Buddy List Setup window. Click the group to which you want to add the person and click Add Buddy. Type the screen name of each buddy and click Save. When you're done, click Return to Buddy List. You can enter screen names of AOL users and Internet AIM users interchangeably.

The Buddy List window shows your buddies who are online. Double-click the buddy to whom you want to send a message to display a window. Type the message, click Send, and you can type back and forth with the other person, as shown in the middle window of Figure 17-3. Click Close when you're finished.

Incoming messages pop up a window on your screen. Click Respond to accept the message and start a conversation or Close to reject it. After the conversation, click Close to close the window.

AOL evidently has a lot of ill-mannered users because AIM has an elaborate system for warning and blocking users you don't like. Click the Setup button in the Buddy List window and click Preferences. On the Privacy tab of the Buddy List Preferences window, you can permit or block specific users, block all Internet AIM users, or block all users.

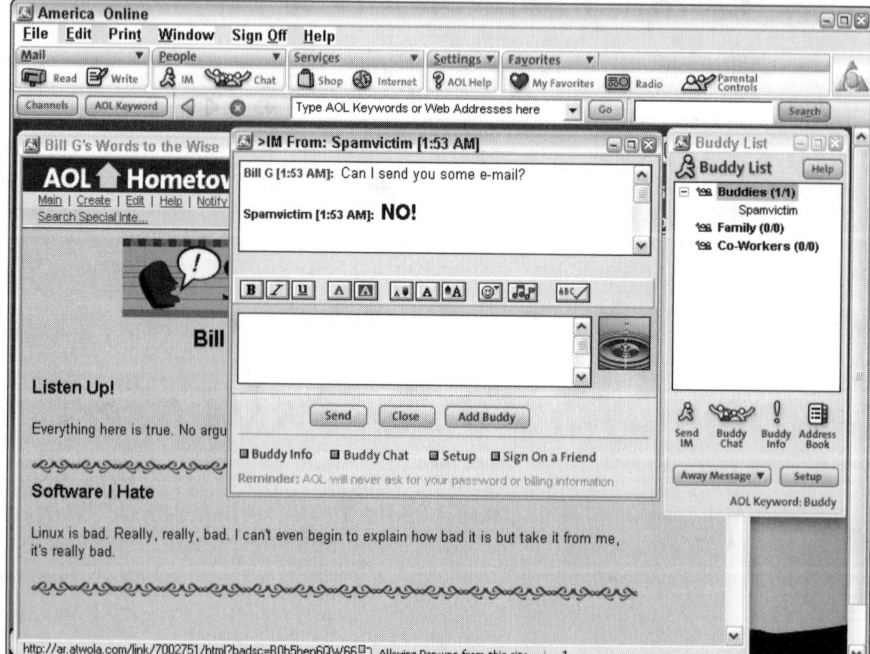

Figure 17-3: Your Buddy List can contain AOL members and anyone who runs AOL Instant Messenger.

Grabbing Files from FTP Servers

AOL lets you download files from FTP servers on the Internet. (See Chapter 16 if you don't know what FTP is.) AOL can do anonymous FTP, in which you connect to an FTP server you don't have an account on, or regular FTP, in which you do have an account. To use the AOL FTP service, you have to know which file you want to download, which FTP server has it, and which folder the file is in. For information about FTP, see `net.gurus.com/ftp`.

Most people now download software via the Web. Links on Web pages may be FTP links — that is, you click a link to start downloading a file.

If you need to use FTP directly, go to keyword **ftp**, click the Anonymous FTP button (anonymous just meaning that you want to FTP from a server that doesn't require individual logons), choose an FTP server from the list that AOL provides, and click Connect. If the FTP server that has the file you want is not listed, click Other Site and type the Internet name of the FTP server. When you have connected to the FTP server of your choice, AOL may display an informational message about it — click OK when you have read it. Then you see a list of the contents of the current directory on the FTP server.

You can open a directory (folder) on the server by double-clicking the directory name. AOL shows little file-folder icons by directory names and little sheet-of-paper icons by filenames. For files, look at the size of each file (in bytes or characters) — the larger the file, the longer it takes to download. When you are done looking in a directory, close its window.

To download a file, choose the file and click Download Now. The Download Manager dialog box appears, asking where to put the file on your computer.

Some FTP servers are extremely busy, and you may not be able to connect. Try again during off hours or try another server. AOL keeps copies of most or all the files on some of the busiest servers to alleviate the traffic jams online.

Using AOL as an Internet Account

It's a tough decision, choosing between a commercial online service, such as America Online, and an Internet account. Although America Online has lots of AOL-only information, it costs a little more than many ISPs, you get a lot more spam, and if you live in the country, AOL may be a long-distance call. What's a cybernaut to do?

Now you don't have to choose — you can have it all. AOL lets you use standard (*Winsock*, in the technical jargon) Internet programs with your AOL account. (If you have a version earlier than AOL 3.0, go to keyword **upgrade**.)

Connecting to AOL via your Internet account

If you already have an Internet account, you can use AOL via the Internet. This technique is handy if no AOL access number is available in your local calling area or your computer is already directly connected to the Net via a fast network at school or work or a cable modem. You connect to your local Internet account and then connect to AOL over that account.

Here's how: Connect to your ISP in the usual way. Then start up the AOL software, but *don't* connect yet. Click the Select Location box and select ISP/LAN Connection. Then connect to AOL. AOL connects via your ISP as just another Internet program, and you can start any other Internet programs you want and click back and forth between AOL and the other programs. When you're finished with AOL, disconnect from AOL and then, if you don't have a permanent connection, disconnect from your ISP.

You pay for both the ISP account and the AOL account, but it can be useful if your ISP provides a faster connection than your local AOL access number or if AOL's closest access number is a long-distance call or if you have a broadband connection and AOL doesn't offer their own broadband service in your area. AOL has a special "bring your own access" price of $14.95 per month if you always connect via an Internet account rather than dialing into AOL.

Getting Internet programs

Lots of freeware and shareware Internet software is available from the World Wide Web. See Chapter 16 for where to look for Internet programs and what to do with them after you've downloaded them. Here are some places to look for Internet software:

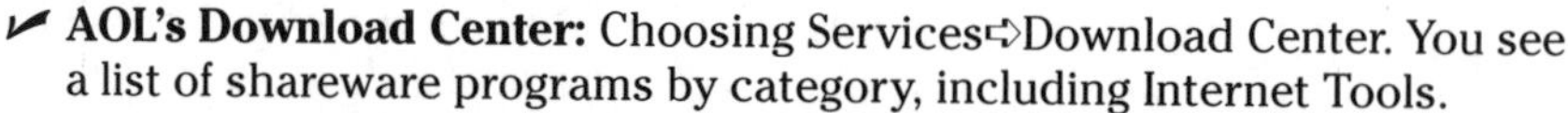

- **AOL's Download Center:** Choosing Services⇨Download Center. You see a list of shareware programs by category, including Internet Tools.

- **TUCOWS (The Ultimate Collection Of Windows Software):** Go to `www.tucows.com` on the Web. When TUCOWS asks where you are, click United States and then Virginia to choose a server. (Regardless of where you are, AOL connects from headquarters in Virginia.) You see an extensive list of Internet programs. Click the type of program you want (Web browsers or newsreaders, for example), and you see names, descriptions, and even reviews of the programs.
- Look in Chapter 16 for other places to get Internet software.

Using Internet programs

Suppose that you want to use Netscape 7 rather than the AOL Web browser. Assuming that you're running AOL Version 8.0 and you have downloaded and installed the Netscape 7 program, here's all you have to do:

1. **Run your Internet program.**

   That's it. That's all you do. To be specific, run AOL and log on to your account. Then run Netscape (or any other Internet program). It works, using your AOL account as its connection to the Internet. The Internet application runs in its own window, even though it's sharing AOL's connection to the world. You can minimize the AOL window if you want to unclutter your screen.

When you finish, exit from your program. Then log off from AOL.

For more information about where to get nifty Winsock programs you may want to use, see Chapter 16.

There's one limitation, though: The only e-mail programs that work with AOL e-mail are Netscape and AOL Communicator. You can't use Outlook Express, Outlook, Eudora, or another other e-mail program because AOL uses a proprietary e-mail system.

Doing Other Things

Because America Online offers tons of information that has nothing to do with the Internet, after you sign up, you may as well check it out. A list of channel buttons runs down the left side of the AOL window, and clicking a button displays a window with more information about that topic. The Chat button on the toolbar takes you to the People Connection window with links to chats of all types. The Kids Only channel button has fun and educational stuff for kids, including games, homework help, and AOL-supervised chat rooms. The Travel channel button lets you make and check your own airline reservations.

It can be hard to *cancel* an AOL account if you decide that you don't want it. You may have to make several phone calls and let your credit card company know that you refuse any additional charges from AOL. One time, one of us cancelled over the phone, sent them a certified letter, and they *still* charged us for months afterward!

Part VI

The Part of Tens

"Awww, cool- a Web Cam! You should point it at something interesting to watch. The fish bowl! The fish bowl!"

In this part . . .

We have lots of interesting odds and ends we want to tell you, so to provide the illusion of organization, we've grouped them into lists. By the strangest coincidence, each list consists of exactly *ten* facts. (*Note to the literal-minded:* You may have to cut off or glue on some fingers to make your version of ten match up with ours. Perhaps it would be easier just to take our word for it.)

Chapter 18

Ten Frequently Asked Questions

In This Chapter

- Answers to some general Internet questions
- Our opinions about computers, Internet service providers, software, and other favorite things

We get lots of questions in our e-mail every day. We've picked some common questions to answer in the hope that the answers can help you.

Now whenever someone asks us one of these questions, we can, rather than answer it, tell them to get a copy of this book and read the chapter. Heh, heh.

If you have more than ten remaining questions after you read this book, surf to our Web site, at `net.gurus.com`, where we tell you where to find hundreds of answers.

"Why Can't You Just Give Me Step-by-Step Instructions?"

We get this question by e-mail all the time: Other *For Dummies* books give detailed, step-by-step instructions, but this book can be frustratingly vague.

Two reasons spring to mind. One is that we don't know what kind of computer you use (Windows XP, Windows 2000, Windows 98, Windows 95, Windows NT, Mac, Linux, or another kind) or what programs you use (America Online, Netscape, Mozilla, Internet Explorer, Outlook Express, Eudora, or other software). We try to give you lots of general background so that you have a good idea about how the Internet works, in addition to specific instructions wherever possible for the most commonly used systems. Our Web site, which we just mentioned, lists books and other Web sites with more specific instructions for many systems and programs.

The other reason is that the programs change continually. Since the last edition of this book, all the programs we describe have been updated. By the time you read this chapter, even newer versions may appear and may work a little differently from the way we describe. We hope you find out enough from reading this book to help you negotiate the inconsistencies you're bound to run into as you discover how to use the Net.

If you're using Windows 98 or Me, you may want to check our *Internet For Windows 98 For Dummies* and *Internet For Windows Me (Millennium Edition) For Dummies* (both published by Wiley Publishing, Inc.), which do have steps for many of the Internet programs that come with Windows. If you use a Mac, get *The Internet For Macs For Dummies,* 3rd Edition, by Charles Seiter. If you want seriously gory details about many Internet programs, get our *Internet Secrets*, 2nd edition (published by Wiley Publishing, Inc.) and *Internet: The Complete Reference*, 2nd Edition (published by Osborne/McGraw-Hill).

"Are the Internet and the World Wide Web the Same Thing?"

Nope. The Internet started out in 1969 and is a network of networks of computers. The World Wide Web, born in 1989, is a system of interconnected Web pages that you can access via the Internet. In recent years, the Web (along with e-mail) has become the most common way of using the Internet, and more and more, Web browsers include traditional Internet technology. For example, you can send and receive e-mail from Netscape and Internet Explorer and join chat rooms from many Web pages. On the other hand, you can find plenty of things other than the Web on the Net, such as instant message systems, multiuser games, and plain old e-mail.

For a fascinating history of the Web, read *Weaving the Web,* by the Web's inventor, Tim Berners-Lee (published by HarperSanFrancisco).

"What's the Difference Between a Browser and a Search Engine?"

A *browser* is the software program that lets your computer show you pages on the World Wide Web. Your browser program runs on your computer. A *search engine* (or directory or index) is a Web site that helps you find pages (on the Web) about specific topics of interest to you. You use your browser to display and use a search engine. Netscape and Internet Explorer are browsers: programs you install on your own computer. Google, AltaVista, Yahoo, Lycos, and a host of other search engines are Web sites that can help you find stuff on the Web. Think of the browser as the telephone and the search engine as the phone book, or maybe the directory assistance operator. See Chapter 6 for more on browsers and Chapter 7 for search engine details.

"Should I Get Cable or DSL?"

DSL and cable Internet accounts are two ways to get fast Internet access for about $45 a month. (In some places, ISDN, a sort of fast phone line, is another option.) If you use the Internet much and hate twiddling your thumbs while Web pages load, you'll probably like one of these faster Internet connections. One nice side effect is that they don't tie up a phone line, so you don't need a second phone line for your computer. Chapters 4 and 5 describe how to sign up for a cable Internet or DSL connection.

"Can I Change My E-Mail Address?"

It depends. (Don't you hate it when we say that?)

On most systems, you can't just change your e-mail address. Your e-mail address is usually your user name assigned by your ISP. Most ISPs let you choose any username you want as long as it's not already taken. If you want to be called SnickerDoodles, that's okay with the ISP, and your e-mail address will be something like `snickerdoodles@furdle.net`.

Later, when it occurs to you that SnickerDoodles will not look real great on your business card, you may want to change your e-mail address. If you're using a small, local ISP, you can probably call up and ask politely, and the company will grumble and change the name. If the ISP doesn't change it, or if you like being SnickerDoodles to your friends, you can usually get a mail alias for a small extra charge.

No law says that each address corresponds to exactly one mailbox, and having several *aliases,* or mail addresses that put all the mail in one mailbox, is a common practice. Although John's true mailbox name is `johnl`, for example, mail addressed to `john`, `johnl`, `jlevine`, and a couple of other misspellings all are aliased to `johnl` so that the mail is delivered automatically. (Because he's the system manager, he can have all the aliases — nicknames — he wants. Because he's a megalomaniac, he's given himself several thousand of them.)

Ask your ISP whether it will give you a mail alias. Most will — it's just a line in a file full of mailing addresses. After the ISP does that, you can set your return address (in Eudora, for example) to the alias so that your address is, as far as anyone can tell, your new alias.

America Online (AOL) is a special case because its users can change their e-mail addresses with wild abandon at a moment's notice. When you sign up for AOL, you choose a screen name, which is your username and e-mail address. Each AOL user can choose as many as six extra screen names, ostensibly for other family members, and can change them at any time. The good news is that AOL users can have any addresses they want (as long as they don't conflict with any of the 25 million AOL addresses already assigned); the bad news is that the rapidly changing addresses make it practically impossible to tell reliably who's sending any particular piece of mail from AOL.

If your ISP can't or won't give you a mail alias, you can check out some third-party e-mail alias services. One is PoBox, which likens itself to a post-office-box service. It gives you, for a modest fee, any addresses you want at `pobox.com`, which it then forwards to your true mail address. Contact PoBox at `www.pobox.com`, or you can send a message to `info@pobox.com`. Zillions of Web sites, including Yahoo Mail, Mail.com, and Hotmail, also offer free, Web-based mail that let you pick your own address. Visit `mail.yahoo.com`, `www.mail.com`, and `www.hotmail.com`.

"How Can I Get a File from My Word Processor into E-Mail?"

It depends. (Oops, we said it again.) Do you want to send the contents in just plain text or do you want to send them in pretty, formatted text? It also depends on to whom you are sending the file and what that person is able to receive.

Everyone can always read plain text and, if that's all you need, the process is easy. Use Copy and Paste commands, either from the Edit menu in your word processor and e-mail programs or by pressing Ctrl+C (⌘+C on the Mac) and Ctrl+V (⌘+V). Select and copy the text of the document in your word processor and then paste it into your e-mail message.

If you and your recipient both use e-mail programs that support formatted text, you can include formatted text in your message. But be sure before you do, or the result will be very different from what you intend — what you think is going to look beautiful will be filled with illegible formatting codes.

If both your e-mail program and that of your recipient can handle attachments and your recipient uses the same word-processing software as you do, you can attach the word-processing file to your e-mail message. (See Chapter 10 for details.)

"Is It Safe to Use My Credit Card on the Net?"

Everyone's idea of what is safe is different. Some people say that using a credit card is a lousy idea — period. Others think that the Internet is full of people trying to steal credit card numbers and in no case should you ever send your card number across the Net.

We think that the risks of online credit card use have been overblown. See Chapter 8, in which we address this topic in detail.

"How Important Is This Internet Stuff?"

Darned important. We're writing this same book for the ninth time in ten years. We're here to tell you that ignoring the Internet is no longer an option. Yeah, you may get away with not knowing about it for a little while longer; however, if you're in school, in business, or looking for a job, like to travel, or stay in touch with friends and relatives, you're doing yourself a big disservice. Catch on now. It's really not that tough.

"What's the Best ISP?"

It dep . . . oh, you know. Do you want the cheapest? The best user support? The fastest?

If all you want is e-mail and access to the World Wide Web, almost any ISP (Internet service provider) will do, although the price ranges vary widely, and how easy it is to get started may be the deciding factor for you. If you have never, ever used a computer in your life and get frustrated easily, we recommend choosing a service that puts a great deal of effort into making your life easier. Look at the ISPs and online services with access numbers that are a local call from where you are. Assuming there's more than one, find out how much help is available from your provider. Talking to someone from an ISP you're considering before you begin, and asking your online friends how they like the services they use, can give you valuable insight into which ISP is best for you. These days, the biggest difference between ISPs isn't technical — it's the level of service. Don't waste time with one that doesn't offer good service.

We generally prefer small local ISPs who have live people in the same town as you and who know the local conditions. (One local ISP we know in a nearby town can tell you based on where in town you live how good your phone line is and how fast a connection you'll be able to get. AOL may be open all night, but they sure can't do that.) If you live in an area that offers cable or DSL access and you intend to use the Internet with any regularity, be sure to check them out. In many cases, they do all the setup for you and cost about the same as dialup if you consider the cost of a second phone line.

For information on how to find an ISP with local numbers near you, look at `net.gurus.com/isp`, where we have links to ISP directories.

"How Can I Make Money on the Net?"

We can't remember exactly how many trillions of dollars of business opportunity the Internet represents according to the people who claim to know about these things. We do see that businesses rely on communication. As a new medium of communication, the doors of the Internet are being flung open for new ways of doing business.

We recommend that, rather than try to figure out how to make money in the Internet business, you spend time getting to know the Net extensively — by checking out mailing lists and message boards in addition to exploring the World Wide Web. The more you see, the more you can think about organic ways in which your business can use the Net. Follow your loves: Find online discussions that excite you. You will meet all kinds of interesting people and get new ideas. We think that what you can find out from the Net can help you find for yourself where your unique opportunities lie.

We have found that the best way to make money on the Net is to write books about it! Then again, we were writing books when dirt was two days old and playing with the Internet for longer than that. If we weren't in the book business, we probably would look at business-to-business commerce, either online services or Net-related "real world" business services, as the most likely candidates.

This should go without saying, but anyone who tells you that you can make big bucks on the Net without working hard and being creative and determined is lying to you. It's no different from the rest of the world.

"What Type of Computer Should I Buy to Use the Internet?"

You can guess what we're going to say, right? "It depends." For many people, the Internet is the first good reason they have for buying a computer. Which type of computer you buy depends on who you are and how you expect to use it.

If you want to buy a computer to use the Internet, buy a new computer or, at worst, one that's no more than a year old. By the time you add whatever you need to add to an old computer, you will probably spend just as much money, invest much more time, and get something not as good, as buying a new one.

If you're purchasing a new computer primarily to surf the Net, you can buy a reasonably fast computer with a monitor for under $800. The World Wide Web is a colorful place; to get the real effect, you have to see it in color. We *don't* recommend any of the deals that give you a rebate in return for signing up with a particular ISP for three years; they're not a very good deal, particularly when you consider that the price you pay for the ISP is fixed even if their list price drops next year.

Pardon our limited vision — we tend to talk about only two categories of computers: Macintoshes and IBM PC clones (although we use UNIX and Linux, too). Which one is for you? Either is okay; they both work. Here's where you have to assess your own abilities and your own resources and those of people around you. Our advice: Buy what your friends have so that you can ask them for help.

When you're talking to other people and asking them what to buy, talk to people who do the same kinds of things you do, not just people who have computers. If you're a chimney sweep, find out what other sweeps use and like and why. Computers are not fair. They're harder to use than they should be. Some people can afford to pay more for a machine than others can. Try to determine which machine you will like using best — you probably can try them out in a computer store. When you evaluate price, don't forget the value of your own time spent finding out how to set up and use a computer and its software programs and your own nature when it comes to mechanical devices. (Not that we always take our own advice. John's been using UNIX systems since the 1970s, so you can guess what he uses to connect to the Net. But it's definitely what he's familiar with.)

Incidentally, if you have some other type of computer, try to track down a local users' group and find out which type of Internet software is available for your machine. More likely than not, someone will have something cheap or free you can use.

"How Can I Erase My Browser's List of the Web Pages I've Been Looking At?"

Gee, why would you want to do that? Aren't you *proud* of the fascinating and intellectual sites you've been visiting? No?

We get this question often, almost always from persons of the male persuasion, frequently with great urgency. So here's how to clear the list of Web sites that appears in your Address or Location bar in lots of different browsers: In Internet Explorer 6.0, choose Tools⇨Internet Options, click the General tab, and click the Clear History button. In the very old Netscape Navigator 4.*x*, choose Edit⇨Preferences, click Navigator on the list of categories, and click the Clear Location Bar button (and while you're at it, click the Clear History button to clear the history list). In Netscape 6 and 7 and Mozilla, choose Edit⇨Preferences, double-click Navigator on the category list, click the History subcategory, and click the Clear Location bar and Clear History buttons. In Opera, choose File⇨Delete private data, and you'll get a box full of things to get rid of. Check the four items in the History area and then click OK. Whew!

"What's Your Favorite Web Page?"

It's `net.gurus.com`, of course. We never said that we aren't vain. (If you visit the site, you can find links to some of our other favorite pages, of course, as well as all sorts of useful Internet information that wouldn't fit into this book.)

Chapter 19

Ten Types of Files and What to Do with Them

In This Chapter

- Document files
- Compressed files
- Graphics files
- Sound files
- Video files
- How to unscramble and otherwise make sense of files

Now that you know how to use the Web and how to download, you probably have already retrieved zillions of files (or maybe three or four). When you look at them with your word processor or text editor, however, you may notice that they seem unintelligible. In this chapter, we describe the various types of files on the Net and how to tell what they are and what to do with them.

How Many Kinds of Files Are There?

Hundreds of kinds, maybe thousands. Fortunately, they fall into five general categories:

- **Text:** Files that contain text, believe it or not, with no formatting codes at all.
- **Executable:** Files you can execute, or run; in other words, programs.
- **Compressed:** Archives, ZIP files, SIT files, and other compressed files.

- **Graphics, audio, and video:** Files that contain pictures and sounds encoded in computer-readable form. Graphics files on Web pages are usually in GIF or JPEG format. Audio files can be in WAV (Windows audio), RAM (RealAudio), MP3 (music), or other formats. Video files contain digitized movies.
- **Data:** Any other type of file. Microsoft Word document files (DOC files) are especially popular.

This chapter describes all five types in more detail.

The name of a file — in particular, its *extension* (the end of the name after the last period) — usually gives you a clue about the type of file it is. Although the person who names the file usually tries to be consistent and follows the conventions for naming files, file naming isn't a sure thing. In the old days of DOS, filenames usually had a three-letter extension at the end, and the period could be used only to separate the extension from the main filename. Because UNIX, Linux, and current versions of Windows allow the period character to be any part of the filename, hard rules about extensions no longer exist. Nevertheless, old habits cling, and computer people still use conventional extensions to help in giving files a name that conveys something about their content. Windows uses the extension to tell what program to use to open a file, so you may sometimes have to rename a file to an extension that will persuade Windows to use the right program.

Macs are different, too

Macintosh files, regardless of what's in them, usually come in two or three chunks, one of which is the data file. Although you don't see the chunks on your own Macintosh, you do see them if you try to upload them to a non-Mac server on the Net. In the Macintosh world, the three files are all pieces of one file and are referred to as *forks* — the data fork, the resource fork, and the information fork. When you upload from a Macintosh what you think is one file, it often appears as three separate files with the extensions DATA, RESC, and INFO appended to the filename. Various schemes exist (described in the section "Packing It In" later in this chapter) to glue the forks back together for transportation over the Net.

The Macintosh operating system uses a hidden, four-letter file type to know what program it should run to read a particular file, but you can tell it about Windows extensions using the File Exchange control panel.

Files attached to e-mail messages don't have to use the right extensions, so it's possible for a file attached to incoming e-mail to have a GIF or JPG extension that looks like a harmless image, but contains something else, like a virus. As we've said in several other places in this book, if you get an attached file you're not expecting, treat it with great skepticism. (If you don't use Windows, though, you can pretty much ignore this warning.)

Just Plain Text

Text files contain readable text without any word-processor-style formatting codes. (What did you expect?) Sometimes, the text is human-readable text, such as the manuscript for this book, which we typed into text files the first time we wrote it. Sometimes, the text is source code for computer programs in languages such as C or Visual Basic for Applications (VBA). Occasionally, the text is data for programs. PostScript printer data is a particular kind of computer program that PostScript printers know how to run and print.

On PCs, text files usually have the file extension .txt (or no extension at all). You can look at these files by using Notepad, WordPad, or any word processor. Mac text files also often have the file type "txt." Read text files on a Macintosh with SimpleText, BBEdit Lite, or any word processor.

We don't have much to say about text files — you know them when you see them. As mentioned in Chapter 16, because the way text is stored varies from one system to another, you should FTP text files in ASCII mode to convert them automatically to your local format. That is, if you're using an FTP program, choose the ASCII rather than Binary (or Image) option when you're downloading files; if you're using a Web browser, never mind. The reason is that, historically, different systems have had trouble agreeing on what character should be used to separate the lines of text. (Why can't we all just get along?) Should the character be a carriage return? A line-feed? A new line? A carriage return followed by a new line? Your browser knows what's best for you.

Many programs use *UNICODE,* a way to store text with non-English characters on a computer. Although ASCII allows only 94 different characters (which is plenty considering that we have only 26 letters in the English alphabet), UNICODE can represent over 65,000 different characters and tries to cover all the writing systems in use in the world today, including Chinese, Japanese, and Korean ideographs.

Formatted text documents are frequently stored in Microsoft Word (DOC) or Rich Text Format (RTF) format; see the section "None of the Above," later in this chapter.

Any Last Requests Before We Execute You?

Executable files are actual programs you can run on a computer. Executable programs are particularly common in archives of stuff for PCs and Macs. Some executable programs are also available on the Net for other kinds of computers, such as various workstations. Any single executable file runs on only a particular type of computer: A Mac executable file is useless on a Windows machine and vice versa.

The most common executable programs are for Windows. These files have file extensions .exe or .com. You run them in the same way as you run any other Windows program: Double-click its filename in My Computer or Windows Explorer.

Some chance always exists that any new PC or Mac program may be infected with a computer virus. (Because of the different ways in which the systems work, UNIX or Linux programs are much less likely to carry viruses.) Stuff from well-run software archives is unlikely to be infected; if you run an unknown program from a sleazy source, however, you deserve whatever you get.

If you receive an executable file that you weren't expecting by e-mail, even if it appears to be from someone you know, *don't run it*. First, check with the person to make sure that he or she actually sent it. The program may be a virus that your unsuspecting friend's computer sent to everyone in your friend's e-mail address book.

Packing It In

Many software packages require bunches of related files. To make it easier to send such a package around, you can glom the files together into a single file known as an *archive*. After you retrieve an archive, you use an *unarchiving program* to extract the original files.

Some files are also *compressed*, which means that they're encoded in a special way that takes up less space but that can be decoded only by the corresponding *uncompressor*. Many files that you receive or download over the Internet are compressed to take less transfer time (fewer bytes equal fewer seconds to wait). In the PC world, archiving and compression usually happen together by using utilities such as WinZip to create *ZIP files.* In the Mac world, the StuffIt program is popular. In the Linux and UNIX world, however, the two procedures — compression and archiving — are usually done separately: The programs *tar* and *cpio* do the archiving, and the programs *compress, bzip* and *gzip* do the compressing.

ZIPping it up

The most widely used compression and archiving program for Windows is the shareware program WinZip. Zipped files (or ZIP files) all end with the extension .zip. Here are programs you can use to create ZIP files that contain one or more files, or get files out of ZIP files:

- Windows Me and XP come with built-in zipping and unzipping — they call ZIP files *compressed folders.*
- Other Windows users can use the excellent shareware WinZip program, mentioned in Chapter 16. It not only handles ZIP files but also knows how to extract the contents of most of the other types of compressed files you run into on the Net. You can download it from `www.winzip.com`. We also like ZipMagic (downloadable from `www.aladdinsys.com/zipmagic`), which makes ZIP files look like folders in Windows Explorer and My Computer.
- Mac users can download a shareware program called ZipIt from `www.maczipit.com`.
- Compatible UNIX/Linux zipping and unzipping programs called *zip* and *unzip* (the authors are creative programmers but not creative namers) are available at `ftp.uu.net` and elsewhere. The Free Software Foundation, which runs the GNU free software project, offers *gzip.* Files that are gzip-ped use the filename extension .gz and can also be decompressed by WinZip.

Many ZIP files you encounter on the Net are *self-extracting,* which means that the ZIP file is packaged with an unzipping program; even if you don't already have an unzipper, you just run the archive, and it extracts its own contents. (PKZIP and WinZip are distributed in this way.) Because self-extracting archives are programs, they have the extension .exe rather than .zip. The prudent will note that just because a program purports to be a self-extracting archive doesn't mean that it really is. We prefer to open them with WinZip and let it tell us what's really inside.

Just StuffIt!

The favorite Macintosh compression and archiving program is a shareware program written by Raymond Lau and known as StuffIt. StuffIt comes in many flavors, including a commercially available version called StuffIt Deluxe. StuffIt files of all varieties generally use the filename extension .sit.

For decompression, you can use the shareware programs UnStuffIt, StuffIt Expander, or DropStuff with Expander Enhancer, widely available for Macs. MindExpander is another unarchiving program that people like. You can download these shareware programs from `www.macorchard.com`.

Other archivers

Dozens of other compressing archivers have come and gone over the years, with names such as Compress, tar, LHARC, ZOO, and ARC. Windows and Mac users can find unarchivers for all of them in shareware repositories like `www.download.com` and `www.shareware.com`. The only other archiver that's widely used is the Japanese LHA because it compresses well and is free.

For the Artistically Inclined

A large and growing fraction of all the bits flying around the Internet is made up of increasingly high-quality digitized pictures. About 99.44 percent of the pictures are purely for fun, games, and worse. We're sure that you're in the 0.56 percent of users who need the pictures for work, so here's a roundup of picture formats.

The most commonly used graphics formats on the Net are GIF, JPEG, and PNG. A nice feature of these file formats is that they do a pretty fair job of compression internally, as if they were prezipped.

I could GIF a . . . .

The most widely used format on the Internet is the CompuServe *GIF* (Graphics Interchange Format). Two versions of GIF exist: *GIF87* and *GIF89.* The differences are small enough that almost every program that can read GIF can read either version equally well. Because GIF is well standardized, you never have problems with files written by one program being unreadable by another. GIF files have the extension .gif. GIF does a good job of storing images with limited numbers of colors and blocks of solid color, such as screen icons and cartoon-style pictures.

Dozens of commercial and shareware programs on PCs and Macs can read and write GIF files. Netscape and Internet Explorer can display them as well; just choose File⇨Open from the menu. The buttons and little pictures on Web pages are usually stored as GIF files, too.

PNG-a-ding

GIF files use a patented compression method, and in 1995, UNISYS began collecting royalties from CompuServe and anyone else it could find who sells software that uses its patented technique. As a result, a group of Net graphics users came up with a patent-free replacement for GIF called PNG (with the extension .png, pronounced *ping*). We expected to see GIF fade away eventually and PNG replace it, but it doesn't seem to be happening, and in the meantime, the GIF patent expired. PNG handles the same kinds of images that GIF does, and most programs that can handle GIF are being updated for PNG.

A few words from the vice squad

We bet that you're wondering whether any free Web sites contain, er, exotic photography, but you're too embarrassed to ask. Well, yes.

In the early days of the Web, the companies and universities that fund most of the free public sites on the Internet were not interested in being accused of being pornographers or in filling up their expensive disks with pictures that had nothing to do with any legitimate work. (At one university archive, when the *Playboy* pictures went away, they were replaced by a note that said that if you could explain why you needed them for your academic research, they would be put back.) But in the late 1990s, a lot of low-budget entrepreneurs realized that the only thing you needed to turn boring pictures into exotic pictures is fewer clothes. A remarkable number of people seem willing to pay to look at that kind of stuff, and online porn boomed.

Now plenty of sites on the Web *do* show you porn if you give them a credit card number to prove you're of age and to pay for it. We're cheap, so we have never looked to see what they offer. They usually have a few screens of free preview pictures that can be pretty raunchy. Don't look at `www.whitehouse.com` or `www.autopr0n.com`.

JPEG: The eyes have it

A few years back, a bunch of digital photography experts got together and decided that a.) It was time to have an official standard format for digitized photographs and b.) None of the existing formats was good enough. They formed the *Joint Photographic Experts Group (JPEG),* and, after extended negotiation, the JPEG format was born. JPEG is designed specifically to store digitized, full-color or black-and-white photographs, not computer-generated cartoons or anything else. As a result, JPEG does a fantastic job of storing photos and a lousy job of storing anything else.

A JPEG version of a photo is about one-fourth the size of its corresponding GIF file. (JPEG files can be *any* size because the format allows a trade-off between size and quality when the file is created.) The main disadvantage of JPEG is that it's considerably slower to decode than GIF; the files are so much smaller, however, that JPEG is worth the time. Most programs that can display GIF files, including Netscape and Internet Explorer, now also handle JPEG. JPEG files usually have filenames with the extension .jpeg or .jpg.

Some people occasionally claim that JPEG pictures don't look anywhere near as good as GIF pictures do. What is true is that if you make a 256-color GIF file from a full-color photograph and then translate that GIF file into a JPEG file, it doesn't look good. So don't do that. For the finest in photographic quality, demand full-color JPEGs.

Let a hundred formats blossom

Many other graphics-file formats are in use, although GIF and JPEG are by far the most popular ones on the Internet. Other formats you run into include

- **PCX:** This DOS format (with extension .pcx) is used by many paint programs — it's also okay for low-resolution photos.
- **TIFF:** This enormously complicated format (with extension .tiff or .tif) has hundreds of options — so many that a TIFF file written by one program often can't be read by another.
- **PICT:** This format (with extension .pict) is common on Macintoshes because the Mac has built-in support for it.
- **BMP:** This Windows bitmap format (with extension .bmp) is not used much on the Net because BMP files tend to be larger than they need to be.

Sound Off!

Audio files — files that contain digitized sound — can be found all over the Web. If you like to listen to National Public Radio news, for example, but can't get around to listening when it's on, you can listen to major news stories from the NPR Web page (at www.npr.org) at any time — totally cool. We also like some of the live concerts and radio stations at broadcast.yahoo.com. Many radio stations now let you listen to the station via their Web sites, too.

You can listen to sounds from the Web in two ways:

- **Download an entire audio file and then play it.** This method has the advantage that you can play the file as many times as you want without downloading it again. Downloading an audio file can take a while, however.
- **Play the audio file *as you download it* so that you don't have to wait for the whole file to arrive before you start hearing it.** This method is called *streaming audio.* Some sites provide streaming audio files that are being created live so you can listen to radio stations and other live reports.

Nonstreaming audio files have extensions such as .wav, .mp3, .au, and .aif. The Windows Media Player, which comes with most versions of Windows, can play WAV files. (Older versions of Windows come with a program called MPLAYER.) You can download sound players from many online software archives (see net.gurus.com/software to find out where to download sound players and plug-ins). The latest Web browsers have built-in sound players, too.

The most popular system for playing streaming audio files is RealAudio, and files in its format have the extension .ra or .ram. To play RealAudio files, you need the RealPlayer plug-in, which you can download from www.real.com or from software archives such as TUCOWS (www.tucows.com). The RealAudio player also handles RealVideo, which has small, blurry moving pictures to go with your sound.

Microsoft decided to create its own streaming audio format and to bundle a player for it with newer versions of Windows. You can play files in Advanced Streaming Format (with extensions .asf or .asx) with the Windows Media Player program.

Another popular streaming format is Apple's QuickTime. QuickTime supports streaming video as well as audio in a variety of formats. The necessary software comes with Macintoshes and is available free for Windows at www.apple.com/quicktime.

Music to My Ears

One of the hottest new activities on the Internet is exchanging music files with your friends in the MP3 file format. MP3 stands for MPEG level 3 (acronyms within acronyms, ya gotta love it) and is simply the soundtrack format used with MPEG movies. Because that format is in the public domain and it does a pretty good job of compressing music down to a reasonable size for downloading, it has been adopted by music lovers on the Net. Many Web sites, such as www.mp3.com, have sprung up devoted to the MP3 format. They are good places to look for the software you need to play MP3 files and even record your own music. One of the most popular is Winamp, which you can download from its rather funky Web site at www.winamp.com.

Napster (at www.napster.com) was the best-known music-exchange service, allowing members to download MP3 music files from each other for free. The system was the first large-scale *peer-to-peer* information exchange (that is, where people exchange files with each other, instead of downloading them from a central library). Eventually, the big record labels sued and shut it down because the free exchange service was in flagrant violation of the music's copyright. The current favorite peer-to-peer system is KaZaA (www.kazaa.com), which has so far resisted legal attacks by having no central index site like Napster did and by being headquartered in an obscure Pacific island sort of near Australia.

For Mac users, Apple has iTunes (www.apple.com/itunes) which lets you buy legal downloaded songs for the fairly reasonable price of 99 cents each.

Naturally, Microsoft has a competing file format called WMA, with the extension .wma. Windows Media Player, which comes with Windows XP, can rip (copy) tracks from music CDs to your computer's hard disk in WMA format.

MP3 on the run

MP3 is so popular that several manufacturers now offer portable MP3 players that store a number of MP3 cuts so you can listen while you jog, travel, or just hang out. It's like a Walkman, but you don't need tapes or CDs. You hook your MP3 player up to your computer whenever you want to download new tunes. The latest players can hold hours of music.

You can find programs called *rippers* that let you transfer music from your CDs to MP3 format so you can transfer selections from CDs to your MP3 player. (Windows Media Player can't rip tracks to MP3, only to its own WMA format.)

More threats and promises

Folks ripping their favorite tunes from CDs and e-mailing them to their 50 closest friends are a hideous threat to the recording industry, not to mention a violation of copyright law. (The previous hideous threats, for those old enough to remember, were cassette tapes and home VCRs, which totally destroyed the music and movie industries. What, they didn't? Hmmm.) The industry's efforts to shut down Web sites that offer ripped songs for free download has been moderately successful, but private e-mail is hard to stop.

The recording industry has come up with a music file format of its own, called SDMI, for the Secure Digital Music Initiative, intended to let you download but not share music. It flopped, partly because it had technical defects quickly analyzed and reported by enterprising college professors and students, and partly because nobody wanted cripple-ware music. As of mid-2003, the recording industry is filing lawsuits against the most visible music sharers. Maybe someday they'll figure out, like Apple did, that if they sold decent music at a reasonable price and let the customers listen to it the way they want to, people will pay for it.

A Trip to the Movies

As networks get faster and disks get bigger, people are starting to store entire digitized movies (still rather short ones, at this point). With faster Internet connections, you can download video clips or watch *streaming video* (video files that start playing on your computer while the rest of the file is still downloading).

The original standard movie format is called *Moving Picture Experts Group (MPEG).* MPEG was designed by a committee down the hall from the JPEG committee and — practically unprecedented in the history of standards efforts — was designed based on earlier work. MPEG files have the extension .mpeg or .mpg.

Microsoft, responding to the challenge of emerging standards that it didn't control, created its own formats. Audio/Visual Interleave (AVI) format is for non-streaming video, with the extension .avi. Advanced Streaming Format (with extensions .asf or .asx) is for streaming both audio and video data.

Web browsers can't play any of these video formats — you need to get a player. You also need a reasonably fast computer to display movies in anything close to real time. Recent versions of Windows come with Windows Media Player, which can play most audio and video formats. If you have a Mac or an older version of Windows, you can download it from www.microsoft.com/windows/windowsmedia. Or you can download RealPlayer for free from www.realnetworks.com/info/freeplayer, as shown in Figure 19-1.

Figure 19-1: The RealPlayer program can play audio and video files as well as tune in to Internet-based radio stations.

A few other movie formats are also popular — notably, Shockwave and Apple QuickTime — and appear on Web pages. You can get Web browser plug-ins that run the movies for you. For Netscape plug-ins, visit home.netscape.com/plugins. For Internet Explorer add-ons, visit www.microsoft.com/msdownload/default.asp. You can also check for other sources at our Web site, at net.gurus.com/software.

If you want to try watching movies online, go to www.bmwfilms.com to see some 10-minute action adventure flicks that, not surprisingly, feature a lot of car chases with BMWs in them.

None of the Above

Some files don't fit any of the descriptions mentioned in this chapter. For example, you occasionally find formatted word-processor files to be used with programs such as WordPerfect (extension .wpd) and Microsoft Word (extension .doc), as well as the industry-standard Rich Text Format (extension .rtf). If you encounter one of these files and don't have the matching word-processor program, you can usually load the file into a text editor, in which you see the text in the file intermingled with nonprinting junk that represents formatting information. In a pinch, you can edit out the junk to recover the text. But before you resort to that method, try loading the file with whatever word processor you have. Most word-processing software can recognize a competitor's format and make a valiant effort to convert the format to something usable so that you aren't tempted to buy the other product.

For the particular case of Microsoft Word, Windows comes with a program called WordPad that can open many Word documents, and Microsoft offers a free Word Viewer that can display and print Word files. See `office.microsoft.com/downloads`.

Another common way to send formatted documents over the Internet is Adobe's Portable Document Format (PDF), with extension .pdf. Unfortunately PDF is a proprietary format, and you must purchase a program from Adobe if you want to *create* PDF files. The program that displays and prints PDF files is free and is included with most new Macs and PCs. It's called Acrobat Reader, and you can download the latest version for PC, Linux, or Mac from `www.adobe.com/products/acrobat`.

Chapter 20

Ten Fun Things You Can Do on the Net

In This Chapter

- Send postage-free cards for all occasions
- Take film-free pictures for family and friends
- Check out on-demand advertisements (and movies)
- Play games
- Take a look at video cams, diaries, and places to visit
- Master a language and find a kid

You can use the Internet in hundreds of ways for work and profit. In this chapter, we focus on fun. When you find new and fun things to do on the Net, let us know. Send e-mail to us at `internet9@gurus.com`, but spare us the illegal, the pornographic, and the get-rich-quick schemes.

Send Greeting Cards

The next time you remember someone's birthday at the last moment, send an online greeting card. Most online cards are free and sometimes arrive within minutes. The cards are just e-mail messages that include cute graphics or animation and a silly tune, with variations available for all occasions. You can even add your own personal greeting.

Here are a few sites you may want to check out:

- Blue Mountain (`www.bluemountain.com`) has a large selection of online greeting cards.
- Virtualinsults (`virtualinsults.com`) offers little digs like "I love you more than broccoli."

- Apple's iCards offer somewhat classier photo cards (go to www.apple.com and click the .Mac tab, and then the iCards button).
- Shockwave (www.shockwave.com) has elaborate animations, but your recipients may have to download the Shockwave plug-in if it's not already on their computers (see Chapter 16).

Online cards are perfect for when you don't care enough to send the very best, can't afford to, can't get to the store or post office, or are too lazy and cheap. After all, it's the thought that counts.

Share Pictures with Your Friends and Family

E-mail attachments (see Chapter 11) are a great way to ship snapshots anywhere in the world for free. You don't even need a digital camera. Many film developing services will digitize your photos and deliver them to you online or on a floppy disk. Other services like Kodak's Ofoto (www.ofoto.com) will develop your pictures and let you organize them into albums on its Web site. You can then give your friends the URL of your album, and they can view the pictures online and order prints of the ones they especially like.

Online photography is even simpler if you do buy a digital camera. They have become more affordable, especially if you consider how much money you save on film and developing costs, and you can choose to print only the pictures you like. Here are some Web sites where you can find out more about digital cameras and still digital photography: www.dcresource.com, www.dpreview.com, and www.megapixel.net.

Watch Short Movies and TV Ads

The Internet has created a new way for makers of short and experimental movies to find an audience. Many sites feature miniflicks that you can watch for free. IFILM (ifilm.com) has a good selection. You can find a long list of movie sites at dmoz.org/Arts/Movies/Filmmaking/Online_Venues. Be aware that the quality of these films varies from dreadful to inspired to the occasionally creepy. If for some reason you miss TV advertising, visit www.advertisementave.com, where you can catch up on all the ads you may have missed. The excellent AdCritic (www.adcritic.com) also features the best current ads and classics, but now requires a paid subscription. Either way, now you can catch those great Super Bowl ads without the tedious football.

These film sites use a variety of video formats — QuickTime, RealNetwork, Windows Media Player, and so on — so expect to download some plug-ins. A fast Internet connection helps a lot. If you're dialing in, particularly at a slow speed, skip videos until you can get higher speed access.

Listen to Current and Classic NPR Programs

Have you ever turned on your radio, found yourself in the middle of a fascinating story, and wished you could have heard the beginning? National Public Radio in the U.S. has many of its past programs available online. If you want to hear the whole program, visit `www.npr.org`. You can also use the site's search feature to browse for stories of interest that you missed completely. Many NPR affiliates and other radio stations have live streaming audio of their programs, so you can listen live to stations all over the country — go to Google and search for the station call letters or the program name.

Play a Game of Checkers

Or chess, hearts, bridge, backgammon, cribbage, or go, or any other board game or card game. The classic games hold up well against the ever-more-bloody electronic games. Now you don't need to round up live friends to play with — you can find willing partners anytime, day or night, at sites like `games.yahoo.com` or `www.zone.msn.com` (Windows users only).

Many bridge aficionados like to think of bridge not as a card game but as a way of life. Some good sites where you can round up a bridge foursome include `www.bridgeclublive.com` and `www.okbridge.com`. Each charges $99/yr after a free trial period. MSN (`zone.msn.com`) also offers bridge.

Watch the World Go By

Webcams are live video cameras that you can access over the Internet. They let you see what is happening right now — wherever that camera is pointing. Watch wildlife, events of the day, a city street, a shopping mall, a highway interchange, Slovakia, or even someone's living room. The views are generally updated every few seconds. Go to `http://www.dmoz.org/Computers/Internet/On_the_Web/Webcams/` or just search on *webcams* at `www.google.com` or `www.yahoo.com`.

Share Your Diary

Posting your private diary on the Internet may seem as bizarre as having a webcam in your bedroom, but many people do it and enjoy getting feedback from other diarists. Check out DiaryLand (www.diaryland.com) to see what it's like. Most of those who post are young. For older folks, it's a window on what kids are thinking about (or not thinking about) these days.

Visit Art Museums around the World

Art museums are a great place to spend a rainy afternoon. Now you can visit museums and galleries all over the world via your browser. Not all museum Web sites have online art works, but many do. Our favorites include the Louvre in Paris (www.louvre.fr), Boston's Museum of Fine Arts (www.mfa.org), The Metropolitan Museum of Art in New York (www.metmuseum.org), and the State Hermitage Museum in Russia (www.hermitagemuseum.org). You'll find a wide selection of others at dmoz.org/Reference/Museums.

Build Your Own World

Virtual worlds are electronic places you can visit on the Web, kind of like 3-D chat rooms. Instead of a screen name, you create a personal action figure, called an *avatar,* that walks, talks, and emotes (but doesn't make a mess on your floor). When you are in one of these worlds, your avatar interacts with the avatars of other people who are logged on in surroundings that range from quite realistic to truly fantastic. In some virtual worlds, you can even build your own places: a room, a house, a park, a city — whatever you can imagine.

Most virtual worlds require you to download a plug-in or special software. Here are some places where you can enter or create a virtual world: www.simcity.com, www.activeworlds.com, www.digitalspace.com/avatars, and www.ccon.org/hotlinks/hotlinks.html.

Tour the Solar System

The last half of the twentieth century will go down in history as the time when humans began to explore outer space. Probes visited several comets and asteroids and every planet but Pluto (www.christinelavin.com/planetx.html). And they sent back amazing pictures: storms on Jupiter, oceans on Europa, mudslides on Mars, and the Earth at night.

Which generation will actually get to play tourist in the solar system remains to be seen, but virtual tours are available now at sites like www.solarviews.com, www.seds.org, and sse.jpl.nasa.gov. Be sure to bookmark the astronomy picture of the day at antwrp.gsfc.nasa.gov/apod/astropix.html. Above all, don't miss NASA's incredible montage of human civilization at antwrp.gsfc.nasa.gov/apod/image/0011/earthlights_dmsp_big.jpg.

Search for Extraterrestrial Life

SETI@home (setiathome.ssl.berkeley.edu) is a scientific experiment that uses Internet-connected home and office computers to search for extraterrestrial intelligence (SETI). The idea is to have thousands of otherwise idle PCs and Macs perform the massive calculations needed to extract the radio signals of other civilizations from intergalactic noise. You can participate by running a free program that downloads and analyzes data collected at the Arecibo radio telescope in Puerto Rico.

If eavesdropping on space aliens seems a bit far out, you may enjoy lending your computer's idle time to solving problems in cryptography and mathematics. Distributed.net (www.distributed.net) is managing several such projects, some of which offer cash prizes to the person who finds the solution.

Adopt a Kid

Do you surf the Web for hours each day? Maybe your life needs more meaning. Adopting a kid is more of a commitment than upgrading to the latest Microsoft operating system, but at least kids grow up eventually. Here are two excellent Web sites that list special children in need of homes: rainbowkids.com and www.capbook.org. It can't hurt to look.

Study Chinese

The Chinese government has an elaborate Web site devoted to teaching Chinese to English speakers at www.speaking-chinese.com. The site offers online courses at every level in both spoken and written Chinese. You can even correspond with an e-teacher in China. One out of every five people on Earth lives in China. A few lessons can go a long way toward demystifying this important part of the world.

Chapter 21

Ten Ways to Avoid Looking Like a Klutz

In This Chapter

- Tips for suave, sophisticated Net usage
- Some bonehead moves not to make
- Some nasty traps to avoid

Gosh, using the Internet is exciting. And gosh, it offers many ways to make a fool of yourself — heaven forbid that you should act like a *clueless newbie.* In this chapter, we round up the usual suspects of unfortunate moves so that you can be the coolest Web surfer on your block. Most of these tips refer to mistakes you can make when sending messages to mailing lists, newsgroups, or other people where people don't know you.

Read Before You Write

The moment you get your new Internet account, you may have an overwhelming urge to begin sending out lots of messages right away. *Don't do it!* Okay, go ahead and send out a few messages to your friends and family to let them know what your e-mail address is, but don't start posting to complete strangers . . . yet.

Read mailing lists, Web pages, and other Net resources for a while before you send anything out. You'll figure out where best to send your messages, which makes it both more likely that you'll contact people who are interested in what you have to say and less likely that you'll annoy people by bothering them with irrelevancies by sending something to an inappropriate place. If you see a *FAQ* (Frequently Asked Questions) section, read it to see whether your question has already been answered.

Netiquette Matters

On the Net, you are what you type. The messages you send are the only way that 99 percent of the people you meet on the Net will know you.

Speling counts

Many Net users feel that because Net messages are short and informal, spelling and grammar don't count. Some even think that strange spelling makes them K00L D00DZ. If you feel that wey, theirs' not much wee can do abowt it. We think that a sloppy, misspelled message is like a big grease stain on your shirt — your friends will know that it's you, but people who don't know you will conclude that you don't know how to dress yourself.

Most mail programs have spell checkers. Eudora checks your spelling after you click the dictionary icon (the ABC one) on the toolbar or choose Edit⇨Check Spelling from the menu. In Netscape, choose Options⇨Check Spelling from the menu. In Outlook Express, you can elect, via the Options menu, to have your outgoing messages checked or choose Tools⇨Spelling to check any message in progress. Spell checkers ensure that your messages consist of 100 percent genuine words, but they can't tell whether they're the words you planned to use, so proofread after you spell check.

DO NOT SEND YOUR ENTIRE MESSAGE IN CAPITAL LETTERS. This technique comes across as shouting and is likely to get you some snappy comments suggesting that you do something about the stuck Shift key on your keyboard. Computer keyboards have handled lowercase letters since about 1970, so avail yourself of this modern technical marvel and aid to literate writing.

Now and then we get mail from someone who says, "i dont use capital letters or punctuation its too much work." Uh-huh.

If you don't have anything to say, don't say it

Avoid trying to sound smart. When you do, the result is usually its opposite. One day on the mailing list TRAVEL-L, someone asked for information about some travel destination. Then came the edifying comment "Sorry, Bud, Can't Help You." Well, duh. We hoped that people who don't know anything could keep their mouths shut, but we were wrong. Each message you post to a list goes to the entire list. Each list member is there on a voluntary basis. Like us, they often have conflicts about mailing-list subscriptions. Does the good content of the list outweigh the noise and inanity? The more inanity, the more sensible subscribers will leave, and the list will deteriorate. If you're going to participate, find a constructive way to do so.

Subscription inscription (and defection)

Signing up for a mailing list is a cool thing. We tell you all about how to do it in Chapter 13. Now maybe this advice is just for people who aren't reading our book, but a classic way to look like a klutz is to send to the list itself a message asking to be added to or taken off a list, where all the people on the list have to read it, but it doesn't actually get the sender subscribed or taken off. Subscribe and unsubscribe requests go to the list server program in a particular format or, in the case of lists that are not automated, to the list owner. Read Chapter 13 carefully please, lest you be the next person impressing every list member with your newbie-tude.

Keep your hands to yourself

Another stupidity we witnessed involved someone subscribing his arch-enemy to an e-mail list against his wishes. Okay, folks. This is not kindergarten. When you start to abuse public lists, they go private. Lists that are un-moderated turn moderated. Moderated lists become "by invitation only." Look around; although some lists thrive on juvenile behavior, it's not the norm, and it's not welcome on most lists.

Read the rules

When you first subscribe to a mailing list, you usually get back a long message about how this particular list operates and how to unsubscribe if you want. Read this message. Save this message. Before you go telling other people on the list how to behave, read the rules again. Some officious newbie, newly subscribed to JAZZ-L, began flaming the list and complaining about the off-topic threads. JAZZ-L encourages this kind of discussion — it says so right in the introduction to the list. Can't say as how she made herself really welcome with that move.

Edit yourself

When you're posting to a mailing list, remember that your audience is the entire world, made up of people of all ethnicities and races speaking different languages and representing different cultures. Work hard to represent yourself and your culture well. Avoid name-calling and disparaging comments about other peoples and places. It's all too easy to be misunderstood. Read several times through whatever you intend to post before you send it. We have seen inadvertent typos change the intended meaning of a message to its complete opposite.

Discretion is the better part

Sooner or later, you see something that cries out for a cheap shot. Sooner or later, someone sends you something you shouldn't have seen, and you want to pass it on. Don't do it. Resist cheap shots and proliferating malice. The Net has plenty of jerks — don't be another one. (See the suggestion later in this chapter about what to do when you're tempted to flame.) Be tolerant of newbies — you were once one yourself.

Keep it private

Okay, someone makes a mistake, such as sending to the entire mailing list a message that says "subscribe" or posting a message that says, "Gee, I don't know!" in response to a request for help with a newsgroup. Yes, it's true; someone made a dumb move. Don't compound it, however, by posting additional messages complaining about it. Either delete the message and forget about it or respond privately by e-mail addressed only to the person, not to the mailing list. The entire mailing list probably doesn't want to hear your advice to the person who blew it.

For example, you can send a private e-mail message saying, "In the future, send subscription and unsubscription messages to `eggplants-request`, not to `eggplants`, okay?" or "This is a list about domestic laying hens, so can you post your message about cats somewhere else?"

Signing off

All mail programs let you have a *signature,* a file that gets added to the end of each mail or news message you send. The signature is supposed to contain something to identify you. Snappy quotes quickly became common, to add that personal touch. Here's John's signature, for example:

```
Regards,
John Levine, johnl@iecc.com, Primary Perpetrator of "The
          Internet for Dummies,"
Information Superhighwayman wanna-be, http://iecc.com/johnl,
          Sewer Commissioner
```

(Yes, he really is the sewer commissioner. Tours! Free samples!) Some people's signatures get way out of hand, going on for 100 lines of "ASCII art," long quotations, extensive disclaimers, and other allegedly interesting stuff. Although this type of signature may seem cute the first time or two, it quickly gets tedious and marks you as a total newbie.

Keep your signature to four lines or fewer. All the experienced Net users do.

Don't get attached

Attachments are a useful way to send files by e-mail. But they work only if the person on the receiving end has a program that can read the files you send. For example, if you send a WordPerfect document to someone who doesn't have a word-processing program, the file is unreadable. Ditto for graphics files, sound files, and other files you may want to send around. Indeed, some older mail systems can't handle attachments at all. Ask *first* before sending an attachment.

Also pay attention to the size of your attached files. A two-page, word-processor file can balloon to multiple megabytes if it contains voice annotations, for example, and your friends may well not appreciate waiting 12 minutes to download a memo with a voiceover saying, "Do you think this is too long?"

Flame Off!

For some reason, it's easy to get VERY, VERY UPSET ABOUT SOMETHING SOMEONE SAYS ON THE NET. (See, it happens even to us.) Sometimes it's something you find on the Web, and sometimes it's personal e-mail. You may be tempted to shoot a message right back telling that person what a doofus he is. Guess what? He will almost certainly shoot back. This type of overstated outrage is so common that it has its own name: *flaming*. Now and then, it's fun if you're certain that the recipient will take it in good humor, but it's always unnecessary. For one thing, e-mail messages always come across as crabbier than the author intended; for another, crabbing back will hardly make the person more reasonable.

A technique we often find helpful is to write the strongest, crabbiest response possible, full of biting wit and skewering each point in turn. Then we throw it away rather than send it. Remember that the fastest way to end an argument is to let the other person have the last word.

Viruses, Spam, Chain Letters, and Other Antisocial Mail

Although we mention these subjects in Chapters 10 and 11, they're worth mentioning here, too: There are a few kinds of messages you should never, ever send. Some are not illegal (at least not in most places), but your mailbox will quickly fill with displeased responses, and your provider will soon cancel your account.

Spreading infected mail

We don't personally know anyone who's intended to pass on a computer virus using e-mail, but we certainly get a ton of infected messages. One surefire way to call negative attention to yourself is to be the one whose computer is used to spread a virus. Unfortunately, being a victim in this case is entirely too easy. Make sure you acquire virus protection software and keep it current — new viruses seem to be cropping up a lot faster these days, and they seem to be getting more and more dangerous.

Often viruses spread as soon as you open infected e-mail or even, with certain mail programs from Redmond, Washington, when a message is previewed on your screen. Never, ever click on an attachment that has the letters vbs, pif, bat, or exe at the end. If you know the sender, know ahead of time what it is he or she is sending and why you want it, you may consider using the file. Otherwise, throw it away and empty your trash.

Outlook and Outlook Express users need to be extra careful because many viruses are designed to take advantage of the address book — opening the Address Book and sending infected mail to everyone in it so that everyone you know (personally and professionally) gets a piece of infected mail from *you.* When you see an unexpected message with a suspicious attachment, delete the file and empty your trash.

Spreading lies

People are growing kittens in bottles! Microsoft will pay you five bucks for each e-mail you send! Well, actually, no, they're not, and no, they won't. Never pass along information that you read on the Internet without checking it out. Search Google for a phrase from the alarming e-mail you received, and you'll usually find ten sites that explain why it's all a hoax.

The chain gang

Sending a chain letter on the Internet is easy: Just click the Forward button, type a few names, and send your letter off. It's a lousy idea. We have never, ever gotten a chain letter that was worth passing along. A bunch of classic chain letters have been circulating around the Net for a decade (for example: the dying child who wants cards, a variety of mythical viruses, the nonexistent modem tax, the overpriced recipe that isn't, and a way not to make money fast). Regardless of where they come from, even if they seem to be for a good cause, please just throw them away.

Some of the online chain letters started as paper letters. We once got a paper version of the Make Money Fast chain letter from, of all places, Guam. We did the same thing with it that we do with computer chain letters — tossed it into the trash.

Spammity spam, horrible spam

One of the least pleasant online innovations in recent years is *spamming,* or sending the same message — usually selling something that was rather dubious in the first place — to as many e-mail addresses or Usenet groups as possible. This practice is annoying, illegal in some places, and against the rules of nearly every Internet service providers (ISP) in the world. Spamming is also ineffective; most ISPs offer e-mail filtering, automatic systems that identify and cancel most Usenet spams within minutes after they occur, and most recipients, including us, presume that anything advertised by spam must be fraudulent. For more information about this topic, see Chapter 11.

Don't Be a Pig

Unbelievable amounts of material are on the Internet: programs, documents, pictures, megabyte after megabyte of swell stuff — all free for the taking. You can download it all. Don't. Go ahead and take whatever you're likely to use, but don't download entire directories full of stuff or leave your computer online for hours at a time "just in case."

Your ISP sets its charges based on the resources a typical user uses. A single user can use a substantial fraction of the provider's Net connection by sucking down files continuously for hours at a time. Providers typically "overcommit" their Net connection by a factor of three or so. That is, if every user tried to transfer data at full speed at the same time, it would require three times as fast a connection as the provider has. Because real users transfer for a while and then read what's on-screen for a while, sharing the connection among all the users works out okay. (The provider is not cheating you by using this method; it's the way they provide access at a reasonable cost. Although you can get guaranteed connection performance if you want it, the price is horrifying.) If users begin using several more connections than the provider budgeted for, prices will go up.

Hang up, already!

This advice applies particularly to providers who offer unlimited connect time per month. Don't leave your computer connected if you're not using it. Most Net software packages have a time-out feature that hangs up if no data is transferred to or from the Net for a specified period. We leave ours set to 15 minutes on our dialup connections; otherwise, other users get a busy signal when they try to connect. (DSL and cable modem uses can ignore this section, of course.)

Cybercafé Etiquette

Cybercafés are new, and our parents never had the opportunity to coach us on the ins and outs. As experienced Internet users, however, we have a few tips to help you ease your way into the scene and not embarrass yourself completely.

No gawking over other people's shoulders

Okay, we understand that you're curious — that's why you're here, to find out about this stuff. Great. Cool. Rent some time, and get some help. Don't stand over other people's shoulders reading their screen. It's rude.

Clean up after yourself

We mean not just the trash around your computer but also the trash you probably left *on* the computer. Many folks don't seem to be aware that most mailer programs keep copies of messages that are sent. If you don't want someone to read your mail, make sure that you find the sent-message folder and delete your mail. Then take the next step and empty the trash. We have found all kinds of interesting goodies we're sure that the sender wouldn't have wanted to share.

Don't order stuff from a public PC

Normally, we think that ordering stuff over the Web or by e-mail is perfectly safe — much safer than handing your credit card to some waiter you've never met! Some shopping sites store information about you, however (including your mailing address and payment info), in a file on your computer. This arrangement works perfectly when you are ordering from your own computer — you don't have to type all that info when you visit the site the next time to place an order. When you order stuff at a cybercafé, however, this personal information may be stored on the cybercafé's computer instead. This means that the next person who comes along to use this computer and go to this site has all your personal data available and may be able to place an order using it. Better not chance it.

Some Web Wisdom

Most ISPs let you put your own private pages up on the World Wide Web. (Chapter 9 helps you get your Web page going.) Again, because what you put on your Web page is all that most people will know about you, this section provides a few suggestions.

Small is beautiful, Part I

Many people who look at your Web page still use dialup modems, which means that big pictures take a long time to load. If your home page contains a full-page picture or animation that takes 12½ minutes to load, you may as well have hung out a Keep Out sign. Keep the pictures small enough that the page loads in a reasonable amount of time. If you have a huge picture that you think is wonderful, put a small "thumbnail" version of it on your home page and make it a link to the full picture for people with the time and interest to look at the big version.

Small is beautiful, Part II

Small pages that fit on a screen or two work better than large pages. Small pages are easier to read, and they load faster. If you have 12 screens full of stuff to put on your Web page, break up your page into 5 or 6 separate pages with links among them. A well-designed set of small pages makes finding stuff easier than does one big page because the links can direct readers to what they want to find.

If we want the White House, we know where to find it

No Web page (or set of Web pages, as we just suggested) is complete without some links to the author's other favorite pages. For some reason, every new user's Web page used to have a link to `www.whitehouse.gov` and maybe to Yahoo, Netscape, and a few other sites that every Net user already knows about. Cool Web sites give you links to interesting pages you *don't* already know about.

Let a hundred viewers blossom

Whenever you create a new Web page, look at it with as many Web browsers as possible. Most people use some version of Netscape or Internet Explorer, but you'd be surprised at how many Web sites work with only one of these. We consider these two a bare minimum and usually try out our pages in Opera as well.

Also keep in mind that some of your visitors may be partially or totally blind, using special software that enlarges parts of the page or reads the text aloud. Be sure your page makes sense for users who just read the text without the pictures.

Don't be dumb

Don't put information on your Web page that you don't want everyone in the world to know. In particular, don't include your home address and phone number. We know at least one person who received an unexpected phone call from someone she met on the Net and wasn't too pleased about it. Why would Net users need this information, anyway? They can send you e-mail!

Glossary

404 Not Found: Error message your Web browser frequently displays when it can't find the page you requested. Caused by mistyping a URL (your fault) or clicking a broken link (not your fault).

ActiveX: A Microsoft standard for computer program building blocks, known as *objects*.

address: Internet users encounter two important types of addresses: e-mail addresses (for sending e-mail to someone; e-mail addresses almost always contain an @) and Web page addresses (more properly called *URLs*).

ADSL: *See* DSL.

AIM: AOL Instant Messenger; a free instant messaging program that non-AOL users can use to chat with each other and with AOL users.

America Online (AOL): A value-added, online service that provides many services in addition to Internet access, including access to popular chat groups. Go to `www.aol.com` for information or read Chapter 17.

applet: A small computer program written in the Java programming language. You can download applets by using a Web browser. Applets must obey special rules that make it difficult for the programs to do damage to your computer.

archive: A single file containing a group of files that have been compressed and glommed together for efficient storage. You have to use a program such as WinZip, PKZIP, tar, or StuffIt to get the original files back out.

attachment: A computer file electronically stapled to an e-mail message and sent along with it.

Baud: The number of electrical symbols per second that a modem sends down a phone line. Often used as a synonym for *bps* (bits per second); although this usage is incorrect, only 43 people on the entire planet know why or care. Named after J. M. E. Baudot, inventor of the teletype.

BCC: Blind carbon copy. BCC addressees get a copy of your e-mail without other recipients knowing about it. *See also* CC.

binary file: A file that contains information other than text. A binary file might contain an archive, a picture, sounds, a spreadsheet, or a word processing document that includes formatting codes in addition to text characters.

BinHex: A file-encoding system popular among Macintosh users.

bit: The smallest unit of measure for computer data. Bits can be *on* or *off* (symbolized by 1 or 0) and are used in various combinations to represent different types of information.

bitmap: Little dots put together in a grid to make a picture.

bookmark: The address of a Web page to which you may want to return. Netscape lets you maintain a list of bookmarks to make it easy to go back to your favorite Web pages.

bounce: To return as undeliverable or redeliver to the appropriate address. If you mail a message to a bad address, it bounces back to your mailbox. If you get e-mail intended for someone else, you can bounce it to her.

bps (bits per second): A measure of how fast data is transmitted. Often used to describe modem speed.

broadband: A fast, permanent connection to the Internet, such as one provided via DSL or a cable modem. *See also* DSL.

browser: A program that lets you read information on the World Wide Web. Some all-singing, all-dancing browsers can do e-mail and other things, too.

byte: A group of eight bits, enough to represent a character. Computer memory and disk space is usually measured in bytes.

cable Internet account: Account that connects your computer to the Internet via your cable TV company.

cable modem: Box that connects your computer to your cable TV company's wiring.

CC: Carbon copy. CC addressees get a copy of your e-mail, and other recipients are informed of it if they bother to read the message header. *See also* BCC.

certificate: Cryptographic data that identifies one computer or person to another.

channel: In IRC, a group of people chatting together. Called "rooms" by value-added providers who use a "channel" to mean a major interest area you can get to easily, like a TV channel.

chat: To talk (or type) live to other network users from any and all parts of the world. To chat on the Internet, you use an instant message program (like AOL Instant Messenger, Yahoo Messenger, or Windows Messenger) or an Internet Relay Chat (IRC) program like mIRC.

client: A computer that uses the services of another computer, or server (such as e-mail, FTP, or the Web). If you dial in to another system, your computer becomes a client of the system you dial in to (unless you're using X Windows — don't ask). *See also* server.

client/server model: A division of labor between computers. Computers that provide a service other computers can use are known as servers. The users are clients. *See also* client, server.

com: When these letters appear as the last part of an address (in `net.gurus.com`, for example), it indicates that the host computer is run by a commercial organization, most often in the United States.

CompuServe (CIS): A value-added, online service that provides many services in addition to Internet access, including forums for many popular business topics. Now owned by AOL.

cookie: A small text file stored on your computer by a Web site you have visited; used to remind that site about you the next time you visit it.

country code: The last part of a geographic address, which indicates in which country the host computer is located, such as `us` for the United States. Country codes are always two letters.

CUWorld: Videoconferencing program, formerly CUSeeMe.

cyber-:A prefix meaning the use of the computers and networks that comprise the Internet, as in *cyberspace* or *cybercop.* Used by itself, it is short for *cybersex*, referring to licentious conversations online.

default: Information that a program uses unless you specify otherwise.

DES (Data Encryption Standard): A U.S. government standard for encrypting unclassified data. Breakable at some expense, although a newer version, triple-DES, is probably safe.

DHCP: Dynamic Host Configuration Protocol; a system that assigns IP addresses for a local area network (LAN) or a broadband system that doesn't require individual logins. *See also* PPPoE.

Dial-up Connection or Dial-Up Networking: The built-in Internet communication program in Windows.

digest: A compilation of the messages that have been posted to a mailing list recently.

domain: Part of the official name of a computer on the Internet — for example, `gurus.com`. Microsoft also calls groups of computers on a LAN controlled by a Windows server a *domain.*

domain name server (DNS): A computer on the Internet that translates between Internet domain names, such as `xuxa.iecc.com`, and numeric IP addresses, such as `208.31.42.42`. Sometimes just called a *name server.*

download: To copy a file from a remote computer "down" to your computer.

DSL (Digital Subscriber Line): A technology that lets you transmit data over phone lines much faster than regular dialup or ISDN, as much as 7 million bps. Nice if you can get it — ask your phone company.

DSL modem: Box that connects your computer to a DSL line.

dummies: People who don't know everything but are smart enough to seek help. Used ironically.

eBay: The original and most successful Web-based auction site, at `www.ebay.com`.

edu: When these letters appear as the last part of an address (in `www.middlebury.edu`, for example), it indicates that the host computer is run by an educational institution, usually a college or university in the United States.

e-commerce: Electronic commerce; mainly buying and selling goods and services over the Internet.

e-mail: Electronic messages sent via the Internet.

emoticon: A combination of punctuation or punctuation and letters intended to communicate emotion on the part of the writer, especially in e-mail, chat, or Instant Messages. Emoticons include smileys (see below) and combinations like <g> for "grin."

Ethernet: The most popular kind of LAN. Comes in several varieties, the most common of which run over cables at 10 or 100 million bits/second.

Eudora: A popular mail-handling program that runs on Windows and Macs. Find it on the Web at `www.eudora.com`.

extranet: An Internet technology used to connect a company with its customers and business partners.

FAQ (Frequently Asked Questions): An article that answers questions that come up often. Many mailing lists and Usenet newsgroups have FAQs that are posted regularly. To read the FAQs for all newsgroups, go to `www.faqs.org`.

Favorites: A list of files or Web pages you plan to use frequently. Internet Explorer lets you maintain a list of your favorite items to make it easy to see them again. Same idea as *bookmarks*.

firewall: A specially programmed computer that connects a local network to the Internet and, for security reasons, lets only certain kinds of messages in and out.

flame: To post angry, inflammatory, or insulting messages. Don't do it!

flame war: Far too much flaming between two or more individuals.

FTP (File Transfer Protocol): A method of transferring files from one computer to the other over the Net.

FTP server: A computer on the Internet that stores files for transmission by FTP.

gateway: A computer that connects one network with another, where the two networks use different protocols.

GIF (Graphics Interchange Format): A patented type of graphics file originally defined by CompuServe and now found all over the Net. Files in this format end in `.gif` and are called *GIF files* or just *GIFs*. Pronounced *jif* unless you prefer to say *gif*.

giga-: Prefix meaning one billion (1,000,000,000).

Google: A search engine used for finding things on the World Wide Web, with extra smarts to look for the most useful pages. Its true name is `www.google.com`.

gov: When these letters appear as the last part of an address (in `cu.nih.gov`, for example), it indicates that the host computer is run by some government body, probably the U.S. federal government.

header: The beginning of an e-mail message containing To and From addresses, subject, date, and other gobbledygook important to the programs that handle your mail.

home page: The entry page, or main page, of a Web site. If you have a home page, it's the main page about you. A home page usually contains links to other Web pages.

host: A computer on the Internet.

hostname: The name of a computer on the Internet (`net.gurus.com`, for example).

HTML (HyperText Markup Language): The language used to write pages for the World Wide Web. This language lets the text include codes that define fonts, layout, embedded graphics, and hypertext links. Don't worry — you don't have to know anything about it to use the World Wide Web. Web pages are stored in files that usually have the extension `.htm` or `.html`.

HTML mail: E-mail messages formatted using HTML codes. Not all e-mail programs can properly display them.

HTTP (HyperText Transfer Protocol): The way in which World Wide Web pages are transferred over the Net. URLs for Web pages start with `http://`, although you almost never have to type it.

HTTPS: A variant of HTTP that encrypts messages for security.

hypertext: A system of writing and displaying text that enables the text to be linked in multiple ways, be available at several levels of detail, and contain links to related documents. The World Wide Web uses both hypertext and hypermedia.

ICANN: The Internet Corporation for Assigned Names and Numbers, at `www.icann.org`. It is responsible for deciding who issues the domain names used on the Internet.

ICQ: "I Seek You;" a popular paging and instant message system that lets users track which of their friends are online and exchange instant messages with them. Owned by AOL but different from AOL Instant Messenger (AIM).

IM: Instant Message; usually used on America Online or by users of AOL Instant Messenger.

IMAP: Internet Message Access Protocol; used for storing and delivering Internet e-mail.

IMAP server: Server that stores your incoming e-mail messages so your e-mail program can display and process them.

incoming mail server: Server that stores your mailbox of e-mail messages until you pick them up and download them to your e-mail program. *See also* POP server, IMAP server.

Internet: All the computers that are connected together into an amazingly huge global network so that they can talk to each other. When you connect your puny little computer to your Internet service provider, your computer becomes part of that network.

Internet Connection Sharing (ICS): Windows feature that allows a computer to share its Internet connection with other computers on a LAN.

Internet Explorer: A Web browser vigorously promoted by Microsoft that comes in Windows, Mac, and (arguably) UNIX flavors.

Internet Relay Chat (IRC): A system that enables Internet folks to talk to each other in real time (rather than after a delay, as with e-mail messages).

intranet: A private version of the Internet that lets people within an organization exchange data by using popular Internet tools, such as browsers.

IP: Internet Protocol; the scheme used to route packets of data through the Net, often used with TCP as TCP/IP. *See also* TCP.

IP address: A four-part number, such as 208.31.42.252, that identifies a host on the Internet.

ISDN (Integrated Services Digital Network): A digital phone service that operates at speeds as high as 128 kilobits per second. Now widely supplanted by DSL. *See also* DSL.

Java: A computer language invented by Sun Microsystems. Because Java programs can run on many different kinds of computers, and most Web browsers can run chunks of Java code called *applets*, Java makes it easier to deliver application programs over the Internet.

JPEG: A type of still-image file found all over the Net. Files in this format end in `.jpg` or `.jpeg` and are called *JPEG* (pronounced *jay*-peg) files. Stands for Joint Photographic Experts Group.

KaZaA: Internet-based file-sharing service often used to swap MP3 files.

Kbyte: 1,024 bytes. Also written *KB* or just plain *K*. Usually used as a measure of a computer's memory or hard disk storage, or as a measure of file size.

kilo-: Prefix meaning one thousand (1,000) or often, with computers, 1,024.

LAN: Local area network; computers in one building connected by cables so they can share files, printers, or an Internet connection.

link: A hypertext connection that can take you to another document or another part of the same document. On the World Wide Web, links appear as text or pictures that are highlighted. To follow a link, you click the highlighted material.

Linux: A version of UNIX; an operating system that runs on a wide variety of computers, including PCs. Many Internet servers run UNIX or Linux.

list server: E-mail mailing list management program; a program that maintains the subscriber list and distributes list postings to those subscribers.

ListProc: Like LISTSERV, a list server program that handles mailing lists.

LISTSERV: A list server program that automatically manages mailing lists, distributing messages posted to the list, adding and deleting members, and so on, which spares the list owner the tedium of having to do it manually. The names of mailing lists maintained by LISTSERV often end with `-L`.

lurk: To read a mailing list or chat group without posting any messages. Someone who lurks is a *lurker.* Lurking is okay and is much better than flaming.

MacBinary: A file-encoding system that's popular among Macintosh users.

mailbombing: Sending someone vast amounts of unwanted e-mail. *Remote mailbombing* is subscribing people to lots of mailing lists against their will so that their e-mail mailboxes fill up with unwanted list postings.

mailbot: A program that automatically sends or answers e-mail.

mailbox: File on your incoming (POP or IMAP) mail server where your e-mail messages are stored until you download them to your e-mail program. Some e-mail programs also call the files in which you store messages *mailboxes.*

mail server: A computer on the Internet that provides mail services.

mailing list: A special type of e-mail address that remails all incoming mail to a list of subscribers to the mailing list. Each mailing list has a specific topic, so you subscribe to the ones that interest you. Often managed using ListProc, LISTSERV, Majordomo, or another list server program.

Majordomo: Like LISTSERV, a list server program that handles mailing lists.

mega-: Prefix meaning one million (1,000,000).

Microsoft Network: *See* MSN.

mil: When these letters appear as the last part of an Internet address or domain name (the zone), it indicates that the host computer is run by some part of the U.S. military.

MIME: Multipurpose Internet Mail Extension; used to send pictures, word-processing files, and other nontext information through e-mail.

mirror: An FTP or Web server that provides copies of the same files as another server. Mirrors spread out the load for more popular FTP and Web sites.

modem: A gizmo that lets your computer talk on the phone or cable TV. Short for *mo*dulator/*dem*odulator.

moderated mailing list: A mailing list run by a moderator.

moderator: The person who looks at the messages posted to a mailing list or newsgroup before releasing them to the public. The moderator can nix messages that are stupid, redundant, off the topic, or offensive.

MP3: Music file format available on the Net.

MPEG: A type of video file found on the Net. Files in this format end in `.mpg` or `.mpeg`. Stands for Moving Picture Experts Group.

MSN: Microsoft Network, Microsoft's Internet provider. They also offer the MSN Explorer, which you can use to browse the Web using your MSN account, and MSN Messenger, Microsoft's instant messaging program.

MSN TV: Formerly WebTV; an online Internet service that includes hardware (an Internet terminal and remote control) you connect to your TV.

MUD (Multi-User Dungeon): Started as a Dungeons and Dragons type of game that many people can play at one time; now, it's an Internet subculture. For information about joining a MUD, consult the Usenet newsgroup `rec.games.mud.announce`.

Napster: Formerly Internet-based, music-sharing service.

net: A network, or (when capitalized) the Internet itself. When these letters appear as the last part of an address (in `www.abuse.net`, for example), it indicates that the host computer is run by a networking organization, frequently an ISP in the United States.

.NET: Microsoft's platform for Web services, which allows applications to communicate and share data over the Internet.

Netscape: A popular Web browser that comes in Windows, Mac, and UNIX flavors (see home.netscape.com).

network: Computers that are connected together. Those in the same or nearby buildings are called *local area networks;* those that are farther away are called *wide area networks;* and when you interconnect networks all over the world, you get the Internet!

newbie: A newcomer to the Internet (variant: clueless newbie). If you have read this book, of course, you're not a clueless newbie anymore!

news server: A computer on the Net that receives Usenet newsgroups and holds them so that you can read them.

newsgroup: A topic area in the Usenet news system. (See the Web page net.gurus.com/usenet for a description of Usenet newsgroups.)

newsreader: A program that lets you read and respond to messages in Usenet newsgroups.

nickname: In IRC, the name by which you identify yourself when you're chatting, synonymous with *screen name* or *handle.*

Opera: A small, fast Web browser from Opera Software in Norway, available at www.opera.com.

org: When these letters appear as the last part of an e-mail address or URL (in www.uua.org, for example), it indicates that the host computer is probably run by a noncommercial organization, usually in the United States.

OS X: Apple's new, UNIX-based operating system for Macintosh computers.

outgoing e-mail server: Server that accepts your outgoing e-mail messages for delivery to the rest of the Internet. *See also* SMTP server.

packet: A chunk of information sent over a network. Each packet contains the address it's going to and the address from which it came.

page: A document, or hunk of information, available by way of the World Wide Web. Each page can contain text, graphics files, sound files, video clips — you name it.

Passport: Microsoft's service in which you store your online identity on their servers for use in identifying yourself to Web sites and e-mail services.

password: A secret code used to keep things private. Be sure to pick one that's hard to guess, preferably two randomly chosen words separated by a number or special character. Never use a single word that is in a dictionary or any proper name.

PayPal: Web-based account from which (or to which) you can make payments by e-mail or from links on Web sites. Owned by eBay.

PDF file: A method for distributing formatted documents over the Net. You need a special reader program called Acrobat. Get it at `www.adobe.com/products/acrobat`.

Pegasus: A popular free e-mail program from New Zealand, available at `www.pmail.com`.

PGP (Phil's Pretty Good Privacy): A program that lets you encrypt and sign your e-mail, written by Phil Zimmerman. Point your Web browser to `net.gurus.com/pgp`.

ping: Sending a short message to which another computer automatically responds. If you can't ping the other computer, you probably can't talk to it any other way, either.

plug-in: A computer program you add to your browser to help it handle a special type of file.

POP (Post Office Protocol): A system by which a mail server on the Net lets you pick up your mail and download it to your PC or Mac. A POP server is the computer from which you pick up your mail. The most recent version is called *POP3.*

POP server: Server that stores your incoming e-mail messages until you download them to your e-mail program.

port number: An identifying number assigned to each program that is chatting on the Net. You hardly ever have to know these numbers — the Internet programs work this stuff out among themselves.

portal: Web site designed to be a starting point for people using the Web.

PPP (Point-to-Point Protocol): The most common way a computer communicates with the Internet over a phone line.

PPPoE: PPP over Ethernet; the way you log into broadband accounts that require an account and password. *See also* DHCP.

protocol: The agreed-on rules that computers rely on to talk among themselves. A set of signals that mean "go ahead," "got it," "didn't get it, please resend," "all done," and so on.

proxy server: Program that translates between a LAN and the Internet.

public key cryptography: A method for sending secret messages whereby you get two keys: a public key you give out freely so that people can send you coded messages and a second, private key that decodes them.

QuickTime: A video and multimedia file format invented by Apple Computer and widely used on the Net. You can download it from `www.apple.com/quicktime`.

RealAudio: A popular streaming audio file format that lets you listen to programs over the Net. You can get a player plug-in at `www.real.com`.

router: A device that connects two or more networks. Can be a separate piece of equipment or software running on a PC.

RTFM (Read The Manual): A suggestion made by people who feel that you have wasted their time by asking a question you could have found the answer to by looking it up in an obvious place.

search engine: A program used to search for things on the Web.

secure server: A Web server that uses encryption to prevent others from reading messages to or from your browser. Web-based shopping sites usually use secure servers so that others cannot intercept your ordering information.

serial port: The place on the back of your computer where you plug in your modem. Also called a *communications port* or *comm port.*

server: A computer that provides a service — such as e-mail, Web data, Usenet, or FTP — to other computers (known as *clients*) on a network. *See also* client.

shareware: Computer programs that are easily available for you to try with the understanding that, if you decide to keep the program, you will send the requested payment to the shareware provider specified in the program. This is an honor system. A great deal of good stuff is available, and people's voluntary compliance makes it viable.

Shockwave: A program for viewing interactive multimedia on the Web. For more information about Shockwave and for a copy of the program's plug-in for your browser, go to `www.shockwave.com`.

skin: Arrangement of buttons, menus, and other items displayed by a program. Some programs (like Opera and Netscape) let you choose among several skins.

SLIP (Serial Line Internet Protocol): An obsolete scheme for connecting to the Internet using a dialup modem. *See also* PPP.

smiley: A combination of special characters that portray emotions, such as :-) or :-(. Although hundreds have been invented, only a few are in active use, and all are silly. Smileys are a type of emoticons, which include letter combinations, like <g> for grin.

S/MIME: Secure Multipurpose Internet Mail Extension; an extension to MIME that includes encryption (to keep mail confidential) and authentication (to prove who sent a message).

SMS (Short Messaging System): A concise format used to send e-mail and instant messages to and from cellular phones.

SMTP (Simple Mail Transfer Protocol): The optimistically named method by which Internet mail is delivered from one computer to another. An SMTP server is the computer that receives incoming e-mail.

SMTP server: Server that accepts your outgoing e-mail messages for delivery to the rest of the Internet.

spam: E-mail sent to thousands of uninterested recipients or Usenet messages posted to many uninterested newsgroups or mailing lists. It's antisocial, ineffective, and often illegal. To fight spam, see `www.cauce.org`.

SSL (Secure Socket Layer): A Web-based technology that lets one computer verify another's identity and allow secure connections; used by secure Web servers.

stationery: Formatted e-mail that you can use when composing messages to send to recipients whose e-mail programs can display HTML or MIME messages.

streaming audio or video: A system for sending sound or video files over the Net that begins playing the file before it finishes downloading, letting you listen or watch with minimal delay. RealAudio (`www.real.com`) is the most popular.

StuffIt: A file-compression program that runs on Macs. StuffIt creates a SIT file that contains compressed versions of one or more files. To restore these files to their former size and shape, you use UnStuffIt.

surfing: Wandering around the World Wide Web and looking for interesting stuff.

T1: A telecommunications standard that carries 24 voice calls or data at 1.544 million bps over a pair of telephone lines.

TCP: Transmission Control Protocol; the system that two computers use to synchronize data. Usually used with IP as TCP/IP to manage connections over the Net. *See also* IP.

TCP/IP: The way networks communicate with each other on the Net. *See also* TCP and IP.

telnet: A program that lets you log in to some other computers on the Net. See `net.gurus.com/telnet`.

terminal: In the olden days, a computer terminal consisted of just a screen and a keyboard. If you have a personal computer and you want to connect to a big computer somewhere, you can run a program that makes it *pretend* to be a brainless terminal — the program is called a *terminal emulator, terminal program,* or *communications program.*

text file: A file that contains only textual characters, with no special formatting, graphical information, sound clips, video, or what-have-you. Because most computers, other than some IBM mainframes, store their text by using a system of codes named *ASCII,* these files are also known as *ASCII text files.*

thread: A message posted to a mailing list or Usenet newsgroup, together with all the follow-up messages, the follow-ups to follow-ups, and so on.

Top-Level Domain (TLD): The last part of an Internet domain or host name. If the TLD is two letters long, it's the country code in which the organization that owns the domain is located. If the TLD is three letters or longer, it's a code indicating the type of organization that runs the domain.

UNIX: A geeky operating system originally developed at Bell Labs. Used on many servers on the Net. Linux is now the most popular version.

upload: To copy your stuff to somebody else's computer.

URL (Uniform Resource Locator): A standardized way of naming network resources, used for linking pages on the World Wide Web.

Usenet: A system of thousands of newsgroups. You read the messages by using a *newsreader.* (See the Web page `net.gurus.com/usenet` for a description of Usenet newsgroups.) *See also* newsreader.

uuencode/uudecode: A method of sending binary files as e-mail. Older and cruddier than MIME.

viewer: A program to show you files that contain stuff other than text.

virus: Self-replicating program, frequently with destructive side effects. Viruses that spread though e-mail messages are also called *worms.*

virus checker: Program that intercepts and destroys viruses as they arrive on your computer.

VoIP: Voice over IP; sending telephone calls via the Net. Go to `net.gurus.com/phone` for more information.

watermark: A message hidden in a music or video file designed to detect and prevent copyright violations.

WAV file: A popular Windows format for sound files (`.wav` files) found on the Net.

Web Folder: Windows XP feature that enables you to use Windows Explorer to see, download from, and upload to an FTP or Web server.

Web page: A document available on the World Wide Web.

Web page editor: Program for editing files in HTML for use as Web pages.

Web server: Program that stores Web pages and responds to requests from Web browsers.

Web site: Collection of Web pages stored on a Web server and belonging to a particular person or organization.

webcam: Digital video camera that attaches to your computer and transmits video over the Internet. The video may appear on a Web page on as part of a chat or conference.

WebTV: *See* MSN TV.

WiFi: The most popular kind of wireless network. Also known as 802.11b, after the number of the standard that defines it.

Winsock: A standard way for Windows programs to work with TCP/IP. You use it if you directly connect your Windows PC to the Internet, with either a permanent connection or a modem using PPP.

wireless network: A network that uses radio rather than cables.

World Wide Web: A hypermedia system that lets you browse through lots of interesting information. The Web will be the central repository of humanity's information in the twenty-first century.

worm: Virus that spreads via e-mail messages.

Yahoo: A Web site (at `www.yahoo.com`) that provides a subject-oriented guide to the World Wide Web and many other kinds of information.

ZIP file: A file with the extension `.zip` that has been compressed using ZipMagic, WinZip, or a compatible program. To get at the files in a ZIP file, you usually need ZipMagic, WinZip, or a compatible program.

zone: A group of domains managed together. Often incorrectly used interchangeably with TLD.

Index

• B •

• C •

• D •

• E •

• F •

• J •

• K •

• O •

• P •

• Q •

• R •

• S •

• T •

• U •

• V •

• W •

• X Y Z •

FOR DUMMIES®

The easy way to get more done and have more fun

PERSONAL FINANCE

0-7645-5231-7

0-7645-2431-3

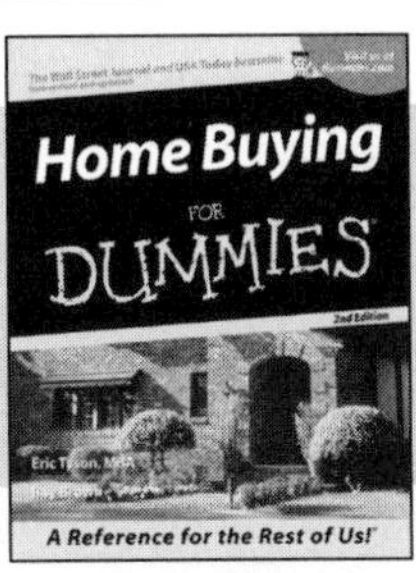

0-7645-5331-3

Also available:

Estate Planning For Dummies (0-7645-5501-4)

401(k)s For Dummies (0-7645-5468-9)

Frugal Living For Dummies (0-7645-5403-4)

Microsoft Money "X" For Dummies (0-7645-1689-2)

Mutual Funds For Dummies (0-7645-5329-1)

Personal Bankruptcy For Dummies (0-7645-5498-0)

Quicken "X" For Dummies (0-7645-1666-3)

Stock Investing For Dummies (0-7645-5411-5)

Taxes For Dummies 2003 (0-7645-5475-1)

BUSINESS & CAREERS

0-7645-5314-3

0-7645-5307-0

0-7645-5471-9

Also available:

Business Plans Kit For Dummies (0-7645-5365-8)

Consulting For Dummies (0-7645-5034-9)

Cool Careers For Dummies (0-7645-5345-3)

Human Resources Kit For Dummies (0-7645-5131-0)

Managing For Dummies (1-5688-4858-7)

QuickBooks All-in-One Desk Reference For Dummies (0-7645-1963-8)

Selling For Dummies (0-7645-5363-1)

Small Business Kit For Dummies (0-7645-5093-4)

Starting an eBay Business For Dummies (0-7645-1547-0)

HEALTH, SPORTS & FITNESS

0-7645-5167-1

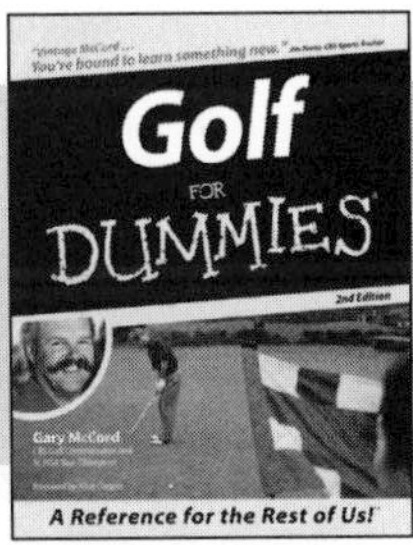

0-7645-5146-9

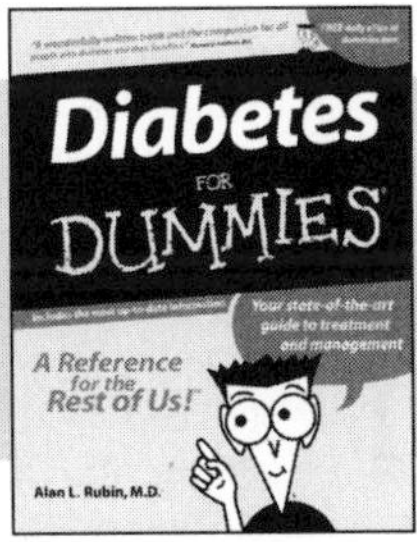

0-7645-5154-X

Also available:

Controlling Cholesterol For Dummies (0-7645-5440-9)

Dieting For Dummies (0-7645-5126-4)

High Blood Pressure For Dummies (0-7645-5424-7)

Martial Arts For Dummies (0-7645-5358-5)

Menopause For Dummies (0-7645-5458-1)

Nutrition For Dummies (0-7645-5180-9)

Power Yoga For Dummies (0-7645-5342-9)

Thyroid For Dummies (0-7645-5385-2)

Weight Training For Dummies (0-7645-5168-X)

Yoga For Dummies (0-7645-5117-5)

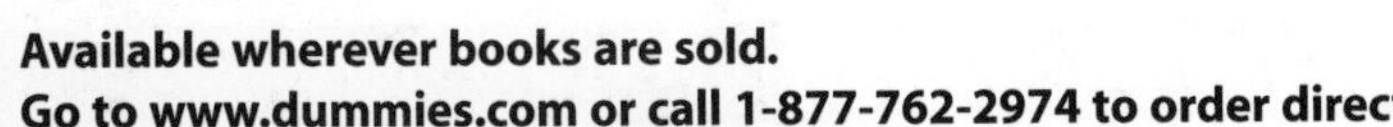

FOR DUMMIES®

A world of resources to help you grow

HOME, GARDEN & HOBBIES

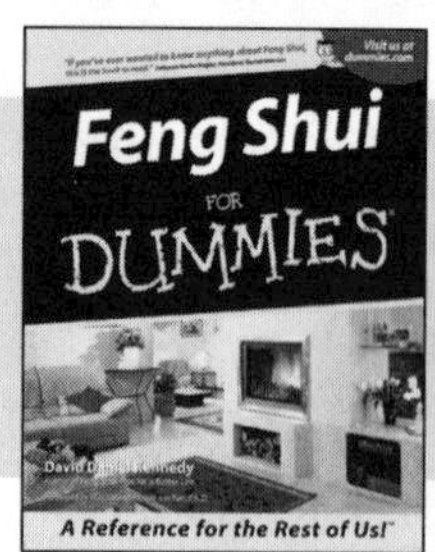

0-7645-5295-3

0-7645-5130-2

0-7645-5106-X

Also available:

Auto Repair For Dummies
(0-7645-5089-6)

Chess For Dummies
(0-7645-5003-9)

Home Maintenance For Dummies
(0-7645-5215-5)

Organizing For Dummies
(0-7645-5300-3)

Piano For Dummies
(0-7645-5105-1)

Poker For Dummies
(0-7645-5232-5)

Quilting For Dummies
(0-7645-5118-3)

Rock Guitar For Dummies
(0-7645-5356-9)

Roses For Dummies
(0-7645-5202-3)

Sewing For Dummies
(0-7645-5137-X)

FOOD & WINE

0-7645-5250-3

0-7645-5390-9

0-7645-5114-0

Also available:

Bartending For Dummies
(0-7645-5051-9)

Chinese Cooking For Dummies
(0-7645-5247-3)

Christmas Cooking For Dummies
(0-7645-5407-7)

Diabetes Cookbook For Dummies
(0-7645-5230-9)

Grilling For Dummies
(0-7645-5076-4)

Low-Fat Cooking For Dummies
(0-7645-5035-7)

Slow Cookers For Dummies
(0-7645-5240-6)

TRAVEL

0-7645-5453-0

0-7645-5438-7

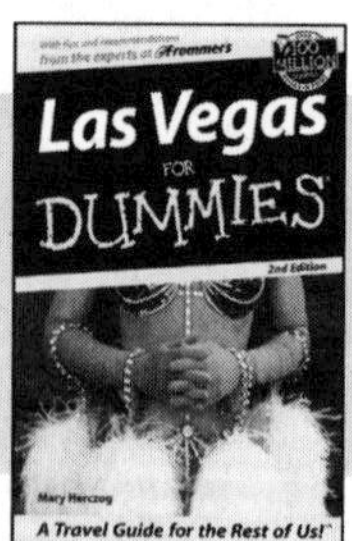

0-7645-5448-4

Also available:

America's National Parks For Dummies
(0-7645-6204-5)

Caribbean For Dummies
(0-7645-5445-X)

Cruise Vacations For Dummies 2003
(0-7645-5459-X)

Europe For Dummies
(0-7645-5456-5)

Ireland For Dummies
(0-7645-6199-5)

France For Dummies
(0-7645-6292-4)

London For Dummies
(0-7645-5416-6)

Mexico's Beach Resorts For Dummies
(0-7645-6262-2)

Paris For Dummies
(0-7645-5494-8)

RV Vacations For Dummies
(0-7645-5443-3)

Walt Disney World & Orlando For Dummies
(0-7645-5444-1)

Available wherever books are sold. Go to www.dummies.com or call 1-877-762-2974 to order direct.

FOR DUMMIES®

Plain-English solutions for everyday challenges

COMPUTER BASICS

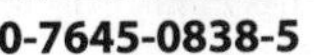

0-7645-1663-9

0-7645-1548-9

Also available:

PCs All-in-One Desk Reference For Dummies (0-7645-0791-5)

Pocket PC For Dummies (0-7645-1640-X)

Treo and Visor For Dummies (0-7645-1673-6)

Troubleshooting Your PC For Dummies (0-7645-1669-8)

Upgrading & Fixing PCs For Dummies (0-7645-1665-5)

Windows XP For Dummies (0-7645-0893-8)

Windows XP For Dummies Quick Reference (0-7645-0897-0)

BUSINESS SOFTWARE

0-7645-0822-9

0-7645-0839-3

0-7645-0819-9

Also available:

Excel Data Analysis For Dummies (0-7645-1661-2)

Excel 2002 All-in-One Desk Reference For Dummies (0-7645-1794-5)

Excel 2002 For Dummies Quick Reference (0-7645-0829-6)

GoldMine "X" For Dummies (0-7645-0845-8)

Microsoft CRM For Dummies (0-7645-1698-1)

Microsoft Project 2002 For Dummies (0-7645-1628-0)

Office XP For Dummies (0-7645-0830-X)

Outlook 2002 For Dummies (0-7645-0828-8)

- **Find listings of even more *For Dummies* titles**
- **Browse online articles**
- **Sign up for Dummies eTips™**
- **Check out *For Dummies* fitness videos and other products**
- **Order from our online bookstore**

Available wherever books are sold. Go to www.dummies.com or call 1-877-762-2974 to order direct.

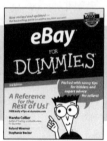

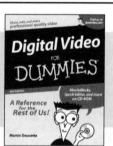

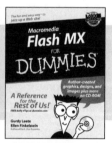

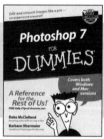

FOR DUMMIES®

We take the mystery out of complicated subjects

WEB DEVELOPMENT

0-7645-1643-4

0-7645-0723-0

0-7645-1630-2

Also available:

ASP.NET For Dummies (0-7645-0866-0)

Building a Web Site For Dummies (0-7645-0720-6)

ColdFusion "MX" For Dummies (0-7645-1672-8)

Creating Web Pages All-in-One Desk Reference For Dummies (0-7645-1542-X)

FrontPage 2002 For Dummies (0-7645-0821-0)

HTML 4 For Dummies Quick Reference (0-7645-0721-4)

Macromedia Studio "MX" All-in-One Desk Reference For Dummies (0-7645-1799-6)

Web Design For Dummies (0-7645-0823-7)

PROGRAMMING & DATABASES

0-7645-0746-X

0-7645-1657-4

0-7645-0818-0

Also available:

Beginning Programming For Dummies (0-7645-0835-0)

Crystal Reports "X" For Dummies (0-7645-1641-8)

Java & XML For Dummies (0-7645-1658-2)

Java 2 For Dummies (0-7645-0765-6)

JavaScript For Dummies (0-7645-0633-1)

Oracle9*i* For Dummies (0-7645-0880-6)

Perl For Dummies (0-7645-0776-1)

PHP and MySQL For Dummies (0-7645-1650-7)

SQL For Dummies (0-7645-0737-0)

VisualBasic .NET For Dummies (0-7645-0867-9)

Visual Studio .NET All-in-One Desk Reference For Dummies (0-7645-1626-4)

LINUX, NETWORKING & CERTIFICATION

0-7645-1545-4

0-7645-0772-9

0-7645-0812-1

Also available:

CCNP All-in-One Certification For Dummies (0-7645-1648-5)

Cisco Networking For Dummies (0-7645-1668-X)

CISSP For Dummies (0-7645-1670-1)

CIW Foundations For Dummies with CD-ROM (0-7645-1635-3)

Firewalls For Dummies (0-7645-0884-9)

Home Networking For Dummies (0-7645-0857-1)

Red Hat Linux All-in-One Desk Reference For Dummies (0-7645-2442-9)

TCP/IP For Dummies (0-7645-1760-0)

UNIX For Dummies (0-7645-0419-3)

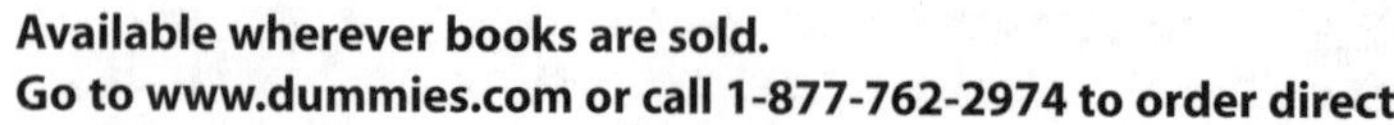

Available wherever books are sold.
Go to www.dummies.com or call 1-877-762-2974 to order direct.